P9-DTZ-639

Resiliency in Native American and Immigrant Families
*By: McCubbin,Thompson,
Thompson, Fromer*

RESILIENCY IN FAMILIES SERIES
Hamilton I. McCubbin, *Series Editor*

Volumes in This Series

Stress, Coping, and Health in Families: Sense of Coherence and Resiliency
Edited by Hamilton I. McCubbin, Elizabeth A. Thompson, Anne I. Thompson, and Julie E. Fromer

Resiliency in Native American and Immigrant Families
Edited by Hamilton I. McCubbin, Elizabeth A. Thompson, Anne I. Thompson, and Julie E. Fromer

Resiliency in African-American Families
Edited by Hamilton I. McCubbin, Elizabeth A. Thompson, Anne I. Thompson, and Jo A. Futrell

Dedication

This book is dedicated to Jean Manchester-Biddick, whose vision for and commitment to the School of Human Ecology led to the establishment of the Center for Excellence in Family Studies at the University of Wisconsin–Madison. She believed that the School had a historical responsibility to address the needs of the families throughout the world, and particularly those in the State of Wisconsin. The knowledge-base developed at the University of Wisconsin–Madison, she believed, could make a difference in people's lives and the well-being of families. The Center for Excellence in Family Studies, which Jean Manchester-Biddick endows, has an important, if not vital, role to play in the sharing of research and the dissemination of knowledge for the well-being of families. Out of her gift emerged the Family Impact and Analysis program designed to build communication and partnership with the legislature, policy makers and State leaders throughout the State to involve the University and its scholars in the formulation and evaluation of social policy. It is fitting that this volume, committed to the well-being and resiliency of ethnic families in America, be dedicated to a leader whose investments in the future of families have and will continue to make a difference.

RESILIENCY IN NATIVE AMERICAN AND IMMIGRANT FAMILIES

EDITORS

HAMILTON I. McCUBBIN

ELIZABETH A. THOMPSON

ANNE I. THOMPSON

JULIE E. FROMER

RESILIENCY IN FAMILIES SERIES

SAGE Publications
International Educational and Professional Publisher
Thousand Oaks   London   New Delhi

Originally published by the Board of Regents of the University of Wisconsin System and th Center for Excellence in Family Studies, 1994, under the title of *Resiliency in Ethnic Minori Families: Native and Immigrant Families.*

For information:

SAGE Publications, Inc.
2455 Teller Road
Thousand Oaks, California 91320
E-mail: order@sagepub.com

SAGE Publications Ltd.
6 Bonhill Street
London EC2A 4PU
United Kingdom

SAGE Publications India Pvt. Ltd.
M-32 Market
Greater Kailash I
New Delhi 110 048 India

Printed in the United States of America

Library of Congress Cataloging-in-Publication Data

Main entry under title:

  Resiliency in Native American and immigrant families / edited by
Hamilton I. McCubbin ... [et al.].
    p. cm. -- (Resiliency in families series ; v. 2)
  Includes bibliographical references.
    ISBN 0-7619-1398-X (cloth : acid-free paper)
    ISBN 0-7619-1399-8 (pbk. : acid-free paper)
    1. Minorities--United States--Family relationships. 2. Resilience (Personality
  trait)--United States. I. McCubbin, Hamilton I.
  II. Series.
    E184.A1 R448 1998
    306.85'086'930973--ddc21
                                    98-9023

This book is printed on acid-free paper.

98 99 00 01 02 03 04 10 9 8 7 6 5 4 3 2 1

ontents

Overview and Theory

Native Americans

a. Native Hawaiians

II b. Latino/Hispanic Americans

Contributors

Manuel Barrera, Jr.
Department of Psychology
Arizona State University
Tempe, AZ

Anna Y. Chan
Department of Human Development
& Family Studies
Cornell University
Ithaca, NY

Laurie Chassin
Department of Psychology
Arizona State University
Tempe, AZ

Jeanne L. Connors
University of Wisconsin Center
System
Madison, WI

Kamana'opono M. Crabbe
Clinical Studies Program
University of Hawai'i
Honolulu, HI

Terry L. Cross
National Indian Child Welfare
Association Inc.
Portland, OR

Rochelle L. Dalla
Department of Family Studies
University of Arizona
Tucson, AZ

Daniel F. Detzner
Family Social Science
University of Minnesota
St. Paul, MN

Anne M. Donnellan
Department of Rehabilitation
Psychology & Special Education
University of Wisconsin–Madison
Madison, WI

Sandra Dyer
Title V Program
Sutton's Bay School
Sutton's Bay, MI

Kelly M. Elver
School of Human Ecology
University of Wisconsin–Madison
Madison, WI

Katherine Fennelly
Department of Agricultural &
Extension Education
The Pennsylvania State University
University Park, PA

Peter A. Frensch
Max Planck Institute for Human
Development in Education
Berlin, Germany

Wendy C. Gamble
Department of Family Studies
University of Arizona
Tucson, AZ

Carina Giusti
Department of Agricultural &
Extension Education
The Pennsylvania State University
University Park, PA

Peter Guarnaccia
Institute for Health, Health Care
Policy & Aging Research
Rutgers University
New Brunswick, NJ

Kwang Chung Kim
Sociology, Anthropology & Social Work
Western Illinois University
Macomb, IL

Shin Kim
Department of Economics
Chicago State University
Chicago, IL

Susan A. Li
Department of Psychology
Arizona State University
Tempe, AZ

Tari A. Malz
Department of Guidance & Counseling
University of Wisconsin–Stout
Menomonie, WI

Anthony J. Marsella
Department of Psychology
University of Hawai'i
Honolulu, HI

Hamilton I. McCubbin
School of Human Ecology
University of Wisconsin–Madison
Madison, WI

Marilyn A. McCubbin
School of Nursing
University of Wisconsin–Madison
Madison, WI

Gale M. Morrison
Counseling/Clinical/School Psychology
    Program
Graduate School of Education
University of California
Santa Barbara, CA

Patricia Mulkeen
Department of Agricultural &
    Extension Education
The Pennsylvania State University
University Park, PA

Paul Y. L. Ngo
Department of Psychology
University of Wisconsin–Stout
Menomonie, WI

Lynn Okagaki
Department of Child Development &
    Family Studies
Purdue University
West Lafayette, IN

Jill Mokihana Oliveira
Clinical Studies Program
University of Hawai'i
Honolulu, HI

Pilar A. Parra
Division of Nutritional Sciences
Cornell University
Ithaca, NY

Carol Milani Plummer
Clinical Studies Program
University of Hawai'i
Honolulu, HI

Jesus Ramirez
Department of Health Behavior &
    Health Education
School of Public Health
University of Michigan
Ann Arbor, MI

Gary D. Sandefur
Department of Sociology
University of Wisconsin–Madison
Madison, WI

Stephanie K. San Miguel
Counseling/Clinical/School Psychology
    Program
Graduate School of Education
University of California
Santa Barbara, CA

Vicky Chiu-Wan Tam
Family Social Science
University of Minnesota
St. Paul, MN

Anne I. Thompson
School of Human Ecology
University of Wisconsin–Madison
Madison, WI

Elizabeth A. Thompson
School of Human Ecology
University of Wisconsin–Madison
Madison, WI

Maura I. Toro-Morn
Department of Sociology &
    Anthropology
Illinois State University
Normal, IL

Julia C. Torquati
Department of Family & Consumer
    Sciences
University of Nebraska
Lincoln, NE

Haunani-Kay Trask
Center for Hawaiian Studies
University of Hawai'i
Honolulu, HI

Benjamin Walter
Lucas County District Board of
    Health
Toledo, OH

Kathleen M. Washienko
Northwest AIDS Education and
    Training Center
Seattle, WA

Teresa Weissglass
Health Start Implementation
    Program
Santa Barbara School Districts
Santa Barbara, CA

Elaine Wethington
Department of Human Development
    & Family Studies
Cornell University
Ithaca, NY

Marc A. Zimmerman
Department of Health Behavior &
    Health Education
School of Public Health
University of Michigan
Ann Arbor, MI

Series Preface

Families at Their Best

The scholarly work of Aaron Antonovsky on *salutogenesis* brings our current emphasis in Resiliency in Families into sharper focus by underscoring the importance of the *sense of coherence* as a vital dispositional world view that expresses the individual's and the family's shared dynamic feeling of confidence that the world is comprehensible, manageable, and meaningful. The construct of sense of coherence fits within the broader rubric of *resiliency*, the positive behavioral patterns and functional competence individuals and families demonstrate under stressful or adverse circumstances.

It was more than coincidence that the Center for Excellence in Family Studies at the University of Wisconsin–Madison would launch its initial lecture and publication series, Resiliency in Families, by inviting Professor Antonovsky to present and discuss his current work and efforts with colleagues who have studied and examined his theories, propositions, and hypotheses. At the core of salutogenesis and the sense of coherence is the fundamental belief that individuals and families have dispositional qualities that serve to promote their health and well-being. The search for knowledge about these central concepts, incorporating a cross-cultural perspective, will shed light on why some families manage life events with relative ease and recover from adversity with renewed strength, harmony, and purpose. The invitational conference laid the foundation for the special publication entitled *Stress, Coping, and Health in Families: Sense of Coherence and Resiliency,* the first publication in the Resiliency in Families Series.

The Center for Excellence in Family Studies, approved and established by the Board of Regents of the University of Wisconsin System, has also created for itself a research focus and agenda that would best be stated in this inaugural publication. The theme of Resiliency in Families places the creation, integration, application, and dissemination of knowledge about the *power of families* of all forms, structures, ethnic groups, and cultures to recover from adversity as the highest priority in the Center's agenda. In its efforts to advance research on resiliency in families, the Center will draw from and foster the advancement of research that:

- searches for family resources (e.g., financial well-being, management skills) that will buffer the family from the disabling effects of stressors, promote the family's recovery in the face of adversity, and promote adaptation.

- searches for family member strengths and capabilities (e.g., the sense of coherence, personality) that will buffer the family from the disabling effects of stressors, promote the family's recovery in the face of adversity, and promote adaptation.

- searches for established patterns of family functioning (e.g., family traditions and routines) that will buffer the family from the disabling effects of stressors, promote the family's recovery in the face of adversity, and promote adaptation.

- searches for new and instituted patterns of functioning (e.g., effective utilization of health care and mental health services) that families create to facilitate the family's recovery from adversity and that promote adaptation.

- searches for family dispositional traits and competencies (e.g., the sense of coherence, hardiness) that families develop over time that will buffer the family from the disabling effects of stressors, promote the family's recovery in the face of adversity, and promote adaptation.

- searches for family processes of appraisal (e.g., schema, paradigms) that will buffer the family from the disabling effects of stressors, promote the family's recovery in the face of adversity, and promote adaptation.

- searches for family patterns of unproductive coping and adaptations (e.g., avoidance, denial), which have the short-term value of promoting adaptation but which, if adopted as an established pattern, have adverse maladaptive outcomes.

- searches for family patterns of productive coping and adaptations (e.g., problem-solving behavior, social support), which have both short- and long-term positive adaptive outcomes.

- searches for family-oriented intervention programs and public policies that have the value of promoting the resistance resources in families under stress and fostering the resiliency in families faced with crises and adversity.

- searches for dysfunctional patterns in families that increase the family's vulnerability to stressors and that curtail the family's recovery from adversity.

Out of the ten strategic agendas of resiliency in families research, only one focuses upon the study of dysfunctional families. Consistent with the salutogenic framework, research on the resiliency in families underscores the importance of understanding the natural resistance resources in families and the capabilities and patterns of functioning that families call upon to manage the ebb and flow of life and all its hardships. From this salutogenic and resiliency orientation, the well-being of families can be best understood by studying the natural capabilities of families to endure, survive, and even thrive in the face of crises. While helpful, the theories and methodologies flowing from the study of dysfunctional families may limit and skew our search for the productive responses and capabilities of families. The resiliency in families may have the greatest potential of coming to light through theories and research that focus on why families succeed and endure in spite of adversities and crises. With this perspective in mind, this publication is offered to continue our search for knowledge about families at their best.

HAMILTON I. MCCUBBIN
Editor, Resiliency in Families Series

Preface

Resiliency in Native American and Immigrant Families is the first volume in a unique two-volume collection devoted to issues facing racial and ethnic minority families. In a field dominated by deficiency and deviance models for minority families, these chapters are the product of an innovative conference held on the University of Wisconsin–Madison campus, which focused on the strengths and resources of minority families. In focusing on the issue of resiliency, the positive behavioral patterns and functional competence individuals and families demonstrate under stressful or adverse circumstances, particular attention was given to the role that culture and ethnicity play in the families' development of coping strategies and meaning given to stressful life events.

This book is divided into three parts:

Part I. *Overview and Theory* addresses theoretical issues and issues related to multiple ethnic groups. The introductory chapter provides an overview of theoretical developments on the Resiliency Model of Family Stress, Adjustment and Adaptation as applied to racial and ethnic minority families. The authors of this part apply a resiliency framework to explorations of educational outcomes for students of different racial and ethnic backgrounds, and marital stability among interracial couples.

Part II. *Native Americans* focuses on issues of resiliency in a range of life situations facing families of Native American descent. In this publication we have adopted the definition of Native American as proposed to the Office of Information and Regulatory Affairs (OIRA) in July of 1994.

> A person having origins in any of the indigenous peoples who inhabited and exercised sovereignty in any of the lands which now comprise the United States, which person maintains cultural identification through political affiliation or community recognition. This group includes, for example, American Indians, Alaskan Natives, and Native Hawaiians.

This part is divided into two sections: Native Hawaiians and Native American Indians. The authors of the first chapters address issues of stress, coping, and cultural survival as experienced by Native Hawaiians. Although Native Hawaiians are recognized as indigenous peoples, this population is seldom included in academic studies of Native Americans. These chapters explore the relationship of cultural, political, and situational factors to the resilient adaptation of Native Hawaiian families. Likewise, the chapters in the second section examine this relationship for Native American Indian families. The authors offer an interpretation of Native American world views, which sheds light on the tension between Native and Anglo perspectives on family, social service delivery, and the perpetuation of cultural values.

Part III. *Immigrant Americans* investigates the resilient factors specific to racial and ethnic immigrant families. This part is also divided into two sections: Asian Americans and Latino/ Hispanic Americans. The first section focuses on several issues of resiliency in Asian American families. The authors of these chapters explore intergenerational social support and transmission of cultural identity, as well as the affect of cultural beliefs and values on attitudes toward work roles and educational attainment. The second section explores various subjects related to resiliency in Latino/Hispanic families. The authors apply a resiliency perspective to discussions of caregiving and coping with hardship and discrimination, as well as the availability of community and social support to Latino/Hispanic families.

Throughout the book, some diacritical marks in Native Hawaiian, Filipino, and Native American languages could not be reproduced because of printing limitations. The editors apologize for those unavoidable omissions.

This publication attempts to make a contribution to the social science literature on racial and ethnic minority families. By adopting a resiliency model for research, we can begin to identify and appreciate the strengths and capabilities of these families, and the knowledge gained through this perspective may result in ethnically and culturally sensitive family services and treatment programs.

HAMILTON I. MCCUBBIN
ELIZABETH A. THOMPSON
ANNE I. THOMPSON
JULIE E. FROMER
Editors

Acknowledgments

Families of color and their ability to endure, thrive, and survive in the face of adversity is the focus of this publication. This theme is special in the annals of family research because of its emphasis on why families succeed when, for all practical purposes, they might fail or falter. The development of this special volume also involved the talents of unique and special people. Jo Futrell is new to the team of editors, and her contributions were not only noted and valued, but they made a substantial difference in the quality of the volume. Wade Masshardt continues to bring the computer to life as a tool for writing, presenting, editing, and publishing. His talents are reflected throughout and admired.

As in the past, the success of a team is shaped by the quality of a supporting cast of individuals whose continuous efforts on our behalf gave us minutes and seconds to devote to research, writing, and editing. We are deeply grateful for the contributions of Christine Davenport, and George Fisher, Diane Sosa, and Gloria McCord. We have come to appreciate the challenges of publishing and printing fine work; we have come to know and appreciate the special talents of Hjalmer (Jim) Harried of Extension duplicating. These publications, which bring together the work of scholars from throughout the United States, emerged out of special efforts of the University of Wisconsin Foundation to bridge the University with alumni and friends who are committed to the continuous development of our fine University. We are grateful for the support and the efforts of leaders within the Foundation, namely, Andrew Wilcox, Timothy Reilley, Marion Brown, Martha Taylor, John Feldt, and Nancy Gibson.

This initial publication emphasizing the importance of resiliency in ethnic families is a result of a unique collaborative effort between the Center for Excellence in Family Studies, the University of Wisconsin System's Cooperative Extension Service, and the Institute on Race and Ethnicity. Dean Ayse Somersan and Dr. Ellen Fitzsimmons of the Cooperative Extension Service, and Director Winston Van Horne and Associate Director Thomas Tonnesen of the Institute on Race and Ethnicity shared with us a vision that we could improve our understanding of strengths and capabilities of ethnic families in America. We were grateful for the opportunity to pursue this important collaborative venture.

Finally, we thank all of the contributors to this volume and to the conference Resiliency in Racial and Ethnic Minority Families. Through the sharing of their work we can take another step forward in fulfilling our mission to publish works devoted to understanding families at their best.

I. Overview and Theory

Chapter 1

Resiliency in Ethnic Families

A Conceptual Model for Predicting Family Adjustment and Adaptation[1]

Hamilton I. McCubbin, Marilyn A. McCubbin, Anne I. Thompson, and Elizabeth A. Thompson

The family has always been implicitly and explicitly recognized as a critical social unit mediating cultural beliefs and traditions from one generation to another. This includes the mediation of beliefs and practices regarding the management of stressful life events. There is, however, a dearth of research and inductive theory-building linking cultural and ethnic factors to the ways in which ethnic families respond to and cope with catastrophes and life's traumas, despite the recognition that effective coping involves an awareness of the strong, often covert, influence of culture in shaping family reactions and responses to stress. Ethnicity and culture affect behavioral interactions, the types and expressions of a behavioral or psychological disorder, service utilization and treatment outcome (Kumbabe, Nishida, & Hepworth, 1985; Miranda & Kitano, 1976; Sue & Morishima, 1982; Cheung & Snowden, 1990). In fact, in working with ethnic families under stress cultural and ethnic sensitivity alone is no longer adequate; professionals must also be ethnically and culturally competent, that is, be able to recognize, respect, and engage ethnic diversity in a way that leads to mutually desirable outcomes. This expectation for cultural competence is directly related to the ever-growing percentage of ethnic minorities in the United States, particularly the increase in the number of persons of Southeast Asian, Filipino, and Hispanic origin, the increased risk minority status places on child development, and the emerging emphasis on, if not renaissance of, cultural and ethnic identity (see Agbayani-Siewert, 1994; Trask, 1995).

Experience informs us that families from different ethnic backgrounds faced with the same stressful situation can respond in dramatically different ways; one Native Hawaiian family rallies its members to deal constructively with the demands it faces, whereas another family is immobilized by the situation, exacerbates the situation by increasing family conflicts, and begins to unravel as demands are placed on it. One Native American Indian family relies totally upon its family members to cope while another seeks help from friends in the community. One Asian American family views community programs as a source of help while another sees such programs as a threat to the family's integrity. How can these differences in ethnic family responses, adaptation, coping and appraisal be understood and predicted? The Resiliency Model of Family Stress, Adjustment, and Adaptation (M.A. McCubbin & H.I. McCubbin, 1993) discussed in this chapter provides a framework to assist in determining whether or not a family falters or is resilient in the face of adversity. This chapter describes the Resiliency Model and its application in understanding the responses, processes, and components of ethnic families or families of color in the face of traumatic life events that threaten the stability and well-being of the family unit. By drawing from research, particularly those studies conducted on Native American (Hawaiian and Indian) and Filipino families, this chapter also examines the validity and usefulness of the Resiliency Model as a guide to assessing critical elements of family functioning, the knowledge of which can be useful in designing family-based prevention or treatment programs to assist them.

The Resiliency Model of Family Stress, Adjustment, and Adaptation is based on the landmark work of Reuben Hill (1949, 1958) and his emphasis on the A(stressor), B(resources), C(definition of the stressor), and X(crisis) factors that mediate families from deteriorating into a crisis situation. The Double ABCX Model (H.I. McCubbin & Patterson, 1981, 1983a, 1983b) followed with its focus on the factors, particularly coping and social support, that facilitate family adaptation to a crisis situation. The FAAR (Family Adjustment and Adaptation Response) Model evolved as part of the Double ABCX with an emphasis on the processes of balancing demands and resources (H.I. McCubbin & Patterson, 1983a; Lavee, H.I. McCubbin, & Patterson, 1987). Subsequently, the Typology Model of Family Adjustment and Adaptation (M.A. McCubbin & H.I. McCubbin, 1987,

1989) was introduced to emphasize the importance of the family's established patterns of functioning, referred to as Typologies, as buffers against family dysfunction and as targets for change as the family adapts to a crisis. These earlier theory-building efforts focused on introducing *post-crisis* factors such as coping that facilitated family recovery (Double ABCX Model), the balancing processes involved in family recovery and how the family responds to crises (the FAAR Model), and the need to understand the importance of the family's established patterns of functioning (Typologies) and the family's appraisal processes involving family values, beliefs, and expectations (Typology Model). The Resiliency Model, the most current extension of these earlier models, emphasizes the family's relational processes of *adaptation* and the family's *appraisal processes involving ethnicity and culture* that facilitate the family's ability to institute new patterns of functioning and achieve harmony while promoting the well-being and development of its members (M.A. McCubbin & H.I. McCubbin, 1993; Kosciulek, M.A. McCubbin, & H.I. McCubbin, 1993). Recognizing that family stress frameworks emerged largely out of the study of Caucasian families, and particularly middle-class families, the recent emphasis on families of color and of low-income family units has played a vital role in the development of the Resiliency Model of Family Stress, Adjustment, and Adaptation (H.I. McCubbin & M.A. McCubbin, 1988; M.A. McCubbin & H.I. McCubbin, 1993; H.I. McCubbin, Thompson, Thompson, & M.A. McCubbin, 1994). As will be discussed, the Resiliency Model of Family Stress, Adjustment, and Adaptation brings to center stage the importance of ethnicity and culture as critical elements in family adaptation and particularly in the appraisal and relational processes families use to manage change and adaptation. The Resiliency Model is characterized as having two discernible phases: Adjustment and Adaptation.

The Adjustment Phase in Ethnic Families

The family adjustment phase of the Resiliency Model, outlined in Figure 1, may be described as a series of interacting components that shape the family process and outcomes. Outcomes vary along a continuum from the more positive *bonadjustment*—in which established patterns of functioning are maintained—to the other extreme of *maladjustment*—a family crisis that demands changes in the established patterns of functioning while managing the stressful situation.

In the face of a stressor a successful or unsuccessful family adjustment is determined by many interacting components.

> *The stressor (A) and its severity* interacts with the family's *vulnerability (V)*, which is shaped by the "pileup" of family stresses, transitions, and strains occurring in the same period as the stressor. Family vulnerability (V) interacts with the family's typology, which is the *established patterns of functioning (T)*. Family routines such as meals together or problem-solving together as a unit are family patterns. These components, in turn, interact with the family's *resistance resources (B)*. Quality communication between husband and wife and a family's willingness to be supportive of each other are examples of resistance resources. This, in turn, interacts with the family's *appraisal (C) of the stressor* (i.e., the family's shared definition of the problem as being minor, a setback, or a catastrophe). The family appraisal interacts with the family's *problem-solving and coping strategies (PSC)*, such as adopting an affirming communication style, seeking help from the medical community, and taking advantage of the advice made available by friends.

Although these components interact with one another to shape the level of adjustment in the family, it nevertheless would be instructive to examine each separately and describe its relative importance in shaping the family's resiliency, its ability to bounce back and recover with minimal, if any, changes in family functioning.

The Stressor (A) and Its Severity. A *stressor* is a demand placed on the family that produces, or has the potential of producing, changes in the family system. This change, or threat of change, may affect all areas of family life—the marital relationship, the parent-child relationship, the sibling relationship, the family-system boundaries (who is in or out of the family unit), the family's goals, the family's established patterns of functioning, and the family's values. The severity of the stressor is determined by the degree to which the stressor threatens the stability of the family unit, disrupts the functioning of the family unit, or places significant demands on and depletion of the family's resources and capabilities (see M.A. McCubbin, 1986, 1990).

Family Vulnerability (V)—Pileup and Family Life Cycle Changes. Vulnerability is the fragile interpersonal and organizational condition of the family system. This condition, ranging from "high" to "low," is determined by (1) the accumulation, or *pileup*, of demands on or within the family unit, such as financial debts, poor

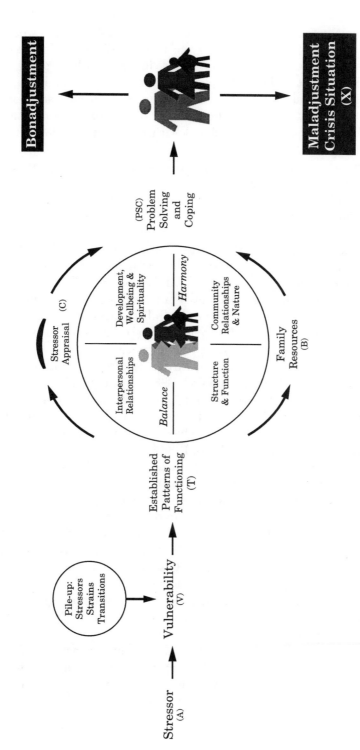

Figure 1

Adjustment Phase of the Resiliency Model of Family Stress, Adjustment and Adaptation and the Relational Processes of Balance and Harmony

health status of relatives, and changes in a parent's work role or work environment, and (2) the trials and tribulations associated with the family's particular life-cycle stage with all of its demands and changes. For example, relocating a family or losing a job is likely to cause more problems for families at the adolescent or launching stage of the family life cycle because of the accumulation of life changes or strains associated with raising an adolescent and the depletion of family interpersonal, social, and economic resources at this stage (Olson et al., 1983; H.I. McCubbin, Thompson, Pirner, & M.A. McCubbin, 1988).

Family Typology of Established Patterns of Functioning (T). A family's typology is defined by a set of attributes that explain how the family system operates or behaves. The family type is the predictable and discernible pattern of family functioning. Recent investigations indicate how important it is to understand the wide range of family types and established patterns. In the face of normative transitions, resilient families (those with established patterns of family bonding and flexibility) are better able to manage hardships and promote other family strengths of hardiness, coherence, and predictability, as well as marital and family satisfaction (H.I. McCubbin, Thompson, Pirner, & M.A. McCubbin, 1988; H.I. McCubbin & M.A. McCubbin, 1988). For example, in the face of a severe chronic illness situation, balanced families (those with established, but not extreme, patterns of cohesiveness and adaptability) appear to have more positive health outcomes for the chronically ill child (M.A. McCubbin, 1986, 1988).

Family Resistance Resources (B)—Capabilities and Strengths. The family's resistance resources have been described as a family's abilities and capabilities to address and manage the stressor and its demands by preventing the situation from creating a crisis or disruption in the family's established patterns of functioning (Burr, 1973; Hansen & Johnson, 1979; M.A. McCubbin & H.I. McCubbin, 1989). The goal of adjustment is to manage the stressor without introducing major or lasting changes in the family's established patterns of functioning. Resources or family strengths then become part of the family's capability for resisting a crisis and promoting family resiliency leading to a successful adjustment. The critical family resources are economic stability, cohesiveness, flexibility, hardiness, shared spiritual beliefs, open communication, traditions, celebrations, routines, and organization (Curran, 1983; Olson et al., 1983; H.I. McCubbin et al., 1988).

Family Appraisal of the Stressor (C). The family's appraisal of the stressor is the family's definition of the seriousness of a stressor and its related hardships. The family's appraisal of a stressor may range from interpreting it as being uncontrollable and forecasting the family's disintegration to viewing it as "no big thing" and as a challenge to be met with growth-producing outcomes (Howard, 1974; H.I. McCubbin & Patterson, 1983b; M.A. McCubbin, 1988).

Family Problem Solving and Coping (PSC). The problem-solving and coping component in the Resiliency Model indicates the family's management of stress through the use of problem-solving and coping skills. Problem solving refers to the family's ability to organize a stressor into manageable components, to identify alternative courses of action to deal with each component, to initiate steps to resolve the discrete issues, as well as the interpersonal issues, and to develop and cultivate patterns of problem-solving communication needed to bring about family problem-solving efforts. Coping refers to the family's strategies, patterns, and behaviors designed to maintain or strengthen the family as a whole, maintain the emotional stability and well-being of its members, obtain or use family and community resources to manage the situation, and initiate efforts to resolve family hardships created by a stressor. Coping refers to a wide range of behaviors that family members use to manage a stressor (M.A. McCubbin & H.I. McCubbin, 1989).

Family Response—Stress and Distress. A stressor produces tension, a response, in the family that calls for management (Antonovsky, 1979). Stress emerges when this tension is not reduced or brought within manageable limits. A state of tension, characterized as family stress rather than as a stressor, arises when there is an actual or a perceived imbalance between the demands placed on the family and the family's resistance resources and capabilities. Family stress is then depicted as a nonspecific demand for adjustment behavior. Therefore the amount of stress in a family varies, depending on the nature of the stressor, the resources and the capabilities of the family to deal with the stressor, and the psychological and physical well-being of its members at the time of onset of the stressor. Family distress describes a negative state in which the family defines the demand-resources imbalance as unpleasant or even destabilizing to the family. In contrast, eustress is a positive state characterized by the family's defining the demands-resources imbalance as desirable and a challenge that family members accept and, in some cases, appreciate (H.I. McCubbin & Patterson, 1983b).

Family Bonadjustment, Maladjustment, and Crises (X). Some stressors do not create major hardships for the family system, particularly when mediated by the family's typology of established patterns, resources, and coping and problem-solving abilities, appraisals, and strengths. In situations of bonadjustment, the family moves through the situation with relative ease, which leads to a positive outcome. In most cases this involves minor adjustments and changes in the family system.

In other stressful situations, however, especially major traumas or catastrophes, hardships are often numerous and severe, demanding more substantial changes in the family system—in its roles, goals, values, rules, priorities, boundaries, and patterns of functioning. Families in this situation are not likely to achieve stability with ease. New patterns of family functioning are called for. In situations involving this disruption in established patterns, the family will, in all likelihood, experience maladjustment and a resulting state of crisis.

Family crisis has been conceptualized as a continuous condition of disruptiveness, disorganization, or incapacitation in the family social system (Burr, 1973). Whereas family stress is a state of tension brought about by the demand-capability imbalance in the family, crisis is a state of disorganization in the family system. Families in crisis are unable to restore stability, are often trapped in cyclical trial-and-error struggles to reduce tensions (which tend to make matters worse), and make only small changes in the family structure and in patterns of interaction where new patterns of interaction and functioning are needed (H.I. McCubbin & Patterson, 1983b). A family in crisis should not carry the stigmatizing value judgment that somehow the family unit has failed, is dysfunctional, or is in need of professional counseling (H.I. McCubbin & Patterson, 1983b). A family crisis may be viewed as an expected, if not necessary, condition for the family to adapt to a difficult situation. Family crisis denotes family disharmony and imbalance in the system and a demand for basic changes in the family patterns of functioning to restore stability, order, balance, and a sense of harmony. This movement to initiate changes in the family system's pattern of functioning marks the beginning of the adaptation phase of the Resiliency Model.

The Family Adaptation
Phase in Ethnic Families

The Resiliency Model, which focuses on family change and adaptation over time, emerged from studies of war-induced family crises

(H.I. McCubbin, Boss, Wilson, & Lester, 1980; H.I. McCubbin & Patterson, 1981, 1982, 1983a, 1983b), the study of families faced with chronic stressors and illness (M.A. McCubbin & H.I. McCubbin, 1987, 1989; Kosciulek, M.A. McCubbin, & H.I. McCubbin, 1993), the study of family transitions and changes over the life cycle (Olson et al., 1983; H.I. McCubbin et al., 1988; H.I. McCubbin & Lavee, 1986), and the study of Native Hawaiian, Filipino, Asian American, and African-American families faced with both normative and non-normative stressors and crises (M.A. McCubbin & H.I. McCubbin, 1988; H.I. McCubbin, M.A. McCubbin, & Thompson, 1992; H.I. McCubbin, Thompson, Thompson, & M.A. McCubbin, 1992; H.I. McCubbin et al., 1993; H.I. McCubbin et al., 1994). The Resiliency Model adds a host of post-crisis or adaptation-oriented components and processes in an effort to explain the family's behavior in the process of adaptation.

1. The additional life stressors and changes that may undermine or curtail the family's ability to achieve adaptation in the face of family crisis;

2. The critical psychological, family, and social resources that families call on, are shaped by, and call into use in their effort to facilitate family adaptation;

3. The unique processes of family appraisal involving culture and ethnicity that gives "meaning" to changes in the family and facilitates coping, functioning, and adaptation;

4. The intrafamily and family-to-community processes families engage in to achieve satisfactory adaptation;

5. The patterns of family functioning that are changed and established to achieve a satisfactory level of adaptation;

6. The range and efficacy of coping behaviors, patterns, and strategies called upon and created to facilitate adaptation;

7. The relational nature of family adaptation unique to each ethnic group of families and that may be common across ethnic groups.

The adaptation phase of the Resiliency Model is outlined in Figure 2. The level of family adaptation in the face of a crisis situation is determined by a number of interacting components.

The *pileup (AA)* of demands on or in the family system created by the situation, family life-cycle changes, and unresolved strains interacts with the family's newly instituted patterns of family functioning and retained established patterns of functioning. These components interact with the *family's resources (BB)* such as strengths and capabilities, which are *supported by family and friends and social support* in the community and by the family's appraisals. A *situational appraisal (CC)* is formed in response to assessment of the total family situation and particularly from the perceived relationship between the family's resources and the demands of the situation. This family appraisal of the crisis situation interacts with the family's *paradigms (CCC)* or specific views or expectations and specific patterns of functioning affecting specific domains of family life (e.g., work and family, child rearing, spiritual orientation, etc.). The family paradigms are in turn shaped by the family's *sense of coherence (CCCC)* or dispositional world view that expresses the family's sense of order. This sense of coherence plays an important part in facilitating the family's need for congruency and harmony. The final and most global level of appraisal is the *family's schema (CCCCC)*. This fifth level of appraisal involves shared values, beliefs, and expectations, facilitates the development of family meanings, and has a direct influence upon the family's sense of coherence. The resource and appraisal components interact with the family's *problem-solving and coping repertoire (PSC)* to facilitate family adaptation to the crisis situation.

Family Adaptation. Since family adaptation becomes the central concept in understanding the family's struggle to manage the crisis created by the initial stressor, it is used to describe the *outcome* of family efforts to bring a new level of balance, harmony, and functioning to a family-crisis situation. In that family bonadaptation involves positive change in the family and positive transactions between the family and the community and its agencies, it is reasonable to argue that the family struggles to achieve a balance and a fit at both the *individual-to-family* and the *family-to-community* levels of functioning. Family efforts directed toward adaptation involve consideration of and response to both levels of functioning because the change at one level of family functioning affects the other (Antonovsky, 1987). Although all components of the adaptation phase interact with one another to shape the level of family adaptation, it nevertheless would also be instructive to examine each of the components separately. The relative importance of these components is described as they relate to adaptation.

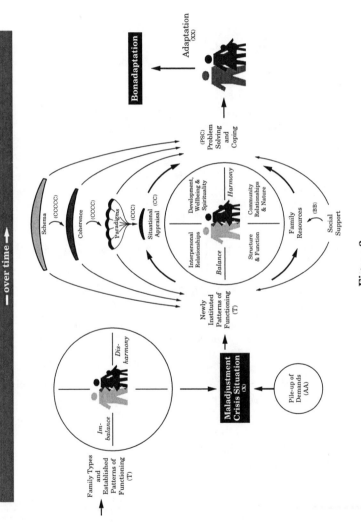

Figure 2

Adaptation Phase of the Resiliency Model of Family Stress, Adjustment and Adaptation and the Relational Processes of Balance and Harmony

Pileup (AA) of Demands. Because family crises evolve and are resolved over time, families are seldom dealing with a single stressor-induced crisis. Our research indicates that the experience of pileup of demands is commonplace and a critical factor that should be taken into account. This is particularly important to do in the case of a prolonged illness, such as caring for a child with a physical disability or family member with a chronic illness (M.A. McCubbin, 1988, 1989).

Because families function over time and in a social context that also changes, at any single point in time, there are at least six broad categories of stresses and strains contributing to a pileup in a family's adaptation in a crisis situation:

1. The initial stressor and related hardships that developed over time;

2. Normative transitions in individual family members and the family as a whole that happened during the same period of time;

3. Prior family strains accumulated over time;

4. Unexpected situational demands and contextual difficulties;

5. The consequences of family efforts to cope;

6. Intrafamily and social ambiguity that provides inadequate guidelines on how families should act or cope effectively with the crisis and its hardships.

The additional hardships associated with a family crisis may include ambiguity solutions, increased marital or sibling relationship strains, community conflicts, parent-child conflicts, and decreased emotional or financial resources depending on the nature of the stressor. These hardships create additional burdens on the family system above and beyond the initial stressor that started the process and that put the family in a crisis situation.

Normative Transitions. The second broad category of stresses and strains leading to pileup is normative transitions. Families are not static social units. They go through predictable transitions as the result of the normal growth and development of their young members (for example, the need for nurturance and supervision, or increasing independence and autonomy), the development of adult members (career development, return to school for more education, returning to the work environment, commitment to a career and independence), the changes in the extended family system (illness and death of grandparents), and the predictable family life-cycle changes (children entering school, adolescence, the empty-nest stage, retirement) (see Olson et al., 1983).

These normal transitions may occur in the same time frame as the family struggles to manage a crisis situation. Families may be experiencing several overlapping crisis situations each demanding changes in the family's patterns of functioning, making adaptations more difficult to achieve. Intervention with families faced with a crisis must take into consideration not only the hardships created by the stressor but also the concurrent normative transitions that may spin the family out of a stable situation into a disturbing, disorienting style of functioning.

Prior Family Strains Accumulated Over Time. The third category of stresses and strains contributing to pileup is prior family strains. Most family systems carry residual strains, which may be the result of unresolved hardships from earlier stressors, transitions, crises, or which may be inherent in ongoing roles, such as parenthood and employment (Pearlin & Schooler, 1978; H.I. McCubbin et al., 1988; H.I. McCubbin & Thompson, 1989). Prior strains may be exacerbated in the face of a new stressor and, consequently, contribute to the pileup of difficulties families are called upon to face.

These prior strains may surface under the pressure of new demands and therefore require management in a crisis situation (H.I. McCubbin & Patterson, 1983a). Prior strains such as incidents of racism and/or discrimination become an important target for professional intervention for two reasons. First, the current or presenting crisis situation when allowed to surface may mask family difficulties (prior strains) that need attention. Second, prior strains may mask the major hardships of the crisis situation which also demand attention.

Situational Demands and Contextual Difficulties. The fourth category of stresses and strains leading to pileup is situational demands and contextual difficulties. Society may create additional demands that undermine the functioning of the family as it attempts to adapt to a crisis situation. Family decisions regarding illness, for example, are often complex, calling for negotiation with several medical agencies and a variety of health professionals. A family crisis may emerge.

Consequences of Family Efforts to Cope. The fifth category of stresses and strains leading to pileup is the consequences of family efforts to cope. These stresses and strains emerge from specific behaviors or strategies that a family may have used in the adjustment phase, such as increased rigidity or suppression of anger, or that the family uses currently in their effort to adapt to the crisis situation (H.I. McCubbin & Patterson, 1983a; M.A. McCubbin, 1990). Some coping strategies, such as taking on a job to handle the financial demands of the family situation or consuming alcohol to manage psychological tension (which may lead to psychological or physical dependency), may produce additional burdens on the already overtaxed family. These demands, some created initially as a result of seemingly positive effort, must also be considered in the assessment of family demands and pileup in a crisis situation. Because successful coping is often the direct result of trial-and-error efforts and the result of individual family members' coping skills and abilities, as well as the family coping as a unit, the professional should not be surprised to discover families struggling with what they perceive to be a good coping effort or strategy, only to discover that the short-run benefits may lead to long-term difficulties. Families who confront and challenge racism or discrimination in society, community or the workplace, however well intended, principled, and factual, may face the long-term consequences of being isolated, ostracized, and ridiculed.

Intrafamily and Social Ambiguity. The sixth category of stresses and strains leading to pileup is intrafamily and social ambiguity. Every crisis situation has a certain amount of ambiguity and uncertainty. Any change in demand for family adaptation, as in the case of the long-term care of a terminally or chronically ill member, has an element of uncertainty because the family needs to alter its structure, rules, roles, and responsibilities. Given the expectation that society will offer families guidelines for coping with crises, it is probable that families will face the additional strain of social ambiguity in those situations where needed social prescriptions for crisis resolution and family adaptation are unclear or absent (H.I. McCubbin & Patterson, 1983a). The prescriptions for coping may not be clear or contradictory.

Family Types and Newly Instituted Patterns of Functioning (R). The Resiliency Model of Family Stress, Adjustment, and Adaptation has also been shaped by David Olson and colleagues at the University of Minnesota (Olson, 1986; Lavee, 1985; M.A. McCubbin, 1990) and by their efforts to introduce and document the importance of various family types, in addition to the Circumplex Model, which may help us understand which instituted and established patterns of family functioning emerge to be of greatest importance under different circumstances. In our research on both normative families and families faced with an illness-induced crises (H.I. McCubbin et al., 1988; H.I. McCubbin & Thompson, 1989; M.A. McCubbin, 1989; M.A. McCubbin & H.I. McCubbin, 1989), several family types or instituted patterns were introduced for consideration, each emphasizing different aspects of family functioning. We introduced the regenerative family type, which involves family coherence (appraisal) and family hardiness (internal strengths and locus of control) as an important set of patterns that instill a sense of integrity and strength in family units faced with a crisis. Additionally, we underscored the importance of a rhythmic pattern of family functioning and introduced the rhythmic family type, which focuses on family time and routines as the family's way of maintaining family life in relatively predictable patterns of family living in an effort to cope with life changes. In the context of families under stress, these instituted patterns provide a process by which family unity and durability are maximized.

These two family typologies gain added importance in assessing and diagnosing family functioning in what might become viable targets for intervention (M.A. McCubbin & H.I. McCubbin, 1989). These typologies represent an attempt to classify families into unique groups that characterize how families function and suggest processes operative within the family system. The literature on family strengths (Curran, 1983; H.I. McCubbin, Patterson, & Lavee, 1983; Olson, H.I. McCubbin, Barnes, Larsen, Muxum, & Wilson, 1983; Stinnet & DeFrain, 1985) points to the importance of family attributes and patterns that emphasize family integrity, unity, flexibility, and predictability.

Newly Instituted Patterns in Adaptation. Families have a wide range of established patterns of functioning that give meaning and stability to the family's way of life. A family's established patterns may not be adequate to manage a crisis in the family system, and so newly instituted patterns are called for to keep the family functioning with a sense of unity and stability while managing the crisis and related hardships. Although we have chosen to focus on critical family strengths and the patterns families adopt to develop and maintain these enduring qualities, we are also interested in what newly instituted patterns of functioning families create and maintain to achieve adaptation.

What new patterns are instituted depends on the nature of the crisis situation and what is called for and needed. In general, new patterns of functioning focus on five domains of family functioning.

1. patterns that involve changes in the family's rules

2. patterns that involve changes family routines and traditions

3. patterns that involve changes in the coalitions in the family unit

4. patterns that alter the family's patterns of communication

5. patterns that alter the family's relationship to the community

Family Resources (BB)—Strengths and Capabilities. In the Resiliency Model of Family Stress, Adjustment, and Adaptation, capability is defined as a potential the family has for meeting all of the demands it faces. We emphasize two sets of capabilities: (1) resources and strengths, which are what the family has, and (2) coping behaviors and strategies, which are what the family does as individual members and as a family unit. Just as there are three sources of demands (individual members, the family unit, and society), there are three potential sources of resources: individual family members, the family working as a unit, and the community. An adaptive resource is a characteristic, trait, or competency of one of these systems (individual, family, community) that facilitates adaptation. Resources may be tangible, such as money or programs, or intangible, such as ethnic identity and self-esteem. A listing of potential resources is nearly infinite. Those resources that have emerged in the family stress literature as being crucial for meeting demands during illness in the family are outlined below.

Personal Resources. Seven categories of personal resources that may be used by the family in adaptation are:

1. The innate intelligence of family members, which can enhance awareness and comprehension of demands and facilitate the family's mastery of these;

2. Knowledge and skills acquired from education, training, and experience so that individual family members and the family unit can perform tasks with greater efficiency and ease;

3. Personality traits (for example, a sense of humor) that facilitate coping;

4. Physical, spiritual and emotional health of members so that intact faculties and personal energy may be available for meeting family demands;

5. A sense of mastery, which is the belief that one has some control over the circumstances of one's life;

6. Self-esteem, that is, a positive judgment about one's self-worth;

7. The ethnic identity and cultural background of family members and the ethnic orientation or world view adopted by the family unit to guide the family's functioning.

These three latter personal resources, a sense of mastery, self-esteem, and ethnic identity, have been emphasized by many researchers of family stress as important factors in the stress process because their presence is critical for effective efforts at managing demands. Yet, these are the resources most threatened when the pileup of demands, which implies a failure at mastery, becomes too large. One of the important pathways that may link stresses and strains to negative family outcomes, such as the psychological depression of its members or intrafamilial conflict, is the weakening of self-esteem (Pearlin, Menaghan, Lieberman, & Mullan, 1981).

Family System Resources. Family resources for family adjustment and adaptation have been intensely studied in the past decade. Social and behavioral scientists and lay people yearn to identify the traits of "healthy, normal, invulnerable, resilient, well-functioning" families. Two of the most prominent family resources identified by several investigators (see review by Olson, Sprenkle, & Russell, 1979) are cohesion (the bonds of unity running through the family life) and adaptability (the family's capacity to meet obstacles and shift course). Other aspects of cohesion that have been emphasized include trust, appreciation, support, integration, and respect for individuality (Stinnet & Sauer, 1977).

Family organization is another resource that has received attention (Hill, 1958; Moos, 1974). Family organization includes agreement, clarity, and consistency (not to preclude fluidity) in the family role and rule structure. Shared parental leadership and clear family generational boundaries are additional resources related to organization (Lewis & Looney, 1984). Communication skill is a critical resource. Different aspects of communication ability such as clear and direct messages (Satir, 1972), instrumental and affective communication capability (Epstein, Bishop, & Baldwin, 1982), and verbal-nonverbal consistency (Fleck, 1980) have been emphasized. Family problem-solving is also significant. Some families adopt a problem-solving style that underscores affirmation of family member's worth and self-esteem, whereas other families adopt an incendiary style that exacerbates family tensions (M.A. McCubbin, H.I. McCubbin, & Thompson, 1987).

Family hardiness also emerges as an adaptation resource. Family hardiness specifically refers to the internal strengths and durability of the family unit. It is characterized by a sense of control over the outcome of life events and hardships, a view of change as beneficial and growth producing, and an active orientation in responding to stressful situations (M.A. McCubbin, 1989). A buffer, a mediating factor in mitigating the effects of stresses and demands, family hardiness helps a family adjust and adapt over time. Family time together and family routines in daily living are relatively reliable indicators of family integration and stability. When faced with a medical crisis, families that make an effort to maintain family routines to create some degree of family continuity and stability have a higher probability of enduring (H.I. McCubbin, Thompson, Pirner, & M.A. McCubbin, 1988).

Social Support (BBB). Community resources and supports include all persons and institutions that the family may use to cope with a stressor situation. Resources and supports include friends and a range of services, such as medical or community services. Schools, churches, and employers are also resources for the family. At the broad social level, government policies that support families may also be viewed as community resources.

In the study of family adaptation, social support is the one community resource that has received the most attention in literature on stress. It is most often viewed as one of the primary buffers or mediators between stress and health breakdown (see reviews by Cassel, 1976; Cobb, 1976; Pilisuk & Parks, 1983). There have been many conceptualizations of social support (see Caplan, 1974; Cassel, 1976; Granovetter, 1973; House, 1981; Pinneau, 1975), but we believe Cobb's (1976) definition is the most useful in the context of the Resiliency Model for the family faced with a crisis situation. Cobb (1976) defines social support as information exchanged at the interpersonal level that provides: (1) emotional support, leading the individual family members in the family unit to believe that they are cared for and loved; (2) esteem support, leading family members to believe that they are respected and valued; and (3) network support, leading the family members to believe that they belong to a network of communication involving mutual support and mutual understanding.

Family Appraisal Processes in Resiliency and Adaptation. The influence of culture on family life has been documented in the family literature. A comprehensive review by Tseng and Hsu (1991) reveals that, over time, culture has influenced family functioning in a great variety of ways: marriage forms, choice of mates, post-marital residence, the family kinship system and descent groups, household and family structures, the primary axis of family obligations, family-community dynamics, and alternative family formations (Nanda, 1980; Tseng & Hsu, 1986; Li, 1968; Berkner, 1972; Pelzel, 1970; Ishisaka, 1992; Mokuau, 1992; Miller, 1969). Historically, the family has been the conduit for cultural transmission, providing a natural atmosphere for traditions to be passed from generation to generation, and it has evolved throughout the ages to keep culture and ethnic heritage alive. In turn, the traditions themselves have given families a sense of stability and support from which they draw comfort, guidance, and a means of coping with the problems of daily life.

Both ethnicity and culture, used synonymously in this chapter, are defined as the customary beliefs, integrated patterns of human behavior (such as thought, speech, and action), social forms, and traits of a racial group. They are nurtured, cultivated, and transferred across generations and among family members through traditions and celebrations, as well as through family problem-solving efforts (McGoldrich, 1989). In solving problems and managing family life, the family's culture fundamentally influences two critical levels of family appraisal involved in the process of adaptation: the family's schema, and family paradigms (M.A. McCubbin & H.I. McCubbin, 1993; H.I. McCubbin, M.A. McCubbin, & Thompson, 1992;

H.I. McCubbin, Thompson, Thompson, M.A. McCubbin, & Kasten, 1993). These processes of family life are the ways in which families give meaning to stressful life events and family struggles, and they appear to play a fundamental role in shaping the family's responses and strategies.

The concept of family schema, integral to the process of appraisal, may be traced to the general literature on the psychology of stigma, which underscores the critical importance of ethnicity and culture (Taylor & Crocker, 1981; Fong & Markus, 1982; Bem, 1981). A family's schema may be defined as a structure of fundamental convictions and values. Shaped and adopted by the family system over time, the family's schema creates the family's unique character and serves as an overriding shared informational framework against and through which family experiences are processed and evaluated. A family schema, expressed through the family's "world view," includes cultural and ethnic beliefs and values and evolves into an encapsulation of experience that serves as a framework for evaluating incoming stimuli and experiences (Martin & Halverson, 1981; Segal, 1988; H.I. McCubbin, Thompson, Thompson, M.A. McCubbin, & Kasten, 1993). Highly resistant to change, a family schema could include values such as respecting and maintaining one's ethnic heritage, and honoring and respecting one's elders. It might include convictions such as caring for the land, valuing the meaning of dance and music, and valuing a native language. Not only does a family's schema give some order and stability to family life, it plays an influential role in shaping and legitimizing the family's established patterns of functioning, rules, and boundaries, as well as the family's problem solving behaviors.

Family Appraisal Processes in Resiliency and Adaptation. The meaningful relationship between the family schema, paradigms, the sense of coherence, and family adaptation is integral to the family's appraisal processes as assessed by the Resiliency Model of Family Adjustment and Adaptation. It is challenging to depict a dynamic family appraisal process that spans a period of time and involves the family unit with its identity and values, the community, and the members acting as individuals. It is vital, however, for behavioral scientists in general, and family scientists in particular, to tease apart the process in order to grasp the elements and processes of appraisal. As diagramed in Figure 2, the family appraisal processes in family crisis situations involve five fundamental levels: schema (5), coherence (4), paradigms (3), situational appraisal (2), and stressor appraisal (1). Stressor appraisal is not depicted in Figure 1 because the current emphasis on family adaptation places the family's initial definition of a stressor aside and focuses upon family schema, coherence, paradigms, and situational appraisal (H.I. McCubbin, Thompson, Thompson, & M.A. McCubbin, 1994).

Level 5. Family schema (CCCCC): A generalized structure of shared values, beliefs, goals, expectations, and priorities, shaped and adopted by the family unit, thus formulating a generalized informational structure against and through which information and experiences are compared, sifted, and processed. A family schema evolves over time and serves as a dispositional world view and framework to evaluate crisis situations and legitimate adherence to and change in the family's established patterns of functioning. While fostering family problem solving and coping, the family schema has as one of its central functions the development of family meanings. This aspect of family appraisal involves the creation of family "stories" or "understandings" shared by family members for the purpose of facilitating the family's adaptation to the crisis situation. The meanings are often described in cryptic phrases or special words such as "God's will" or the Hawaiian *malama*, used to encourage acceptance of adversity. These meanings transcend the immediate stressor and the situation and place the crisis in a larger context of experiences. From this perspective, the family schema facilitates the development of meaning through the processes of: classification (framing the situation in terms of shared values and expectations), spiritualization (framing the situation in context of the family's shared beliefs), temporalization (framing the situation in terms of the long view and long-term consequences as well as the positive aspects of the present), and contextualization (framing the situation in terms of nature and its order of things as well as the community and personal relationships and the interpersonal order of things) (M.A. McCubbin & H.I. McCubbin, 1993; H.I. McCubbin, Thompson, Thompson, M.A. McCubbin, & Kasten, 1993).

Level 4. Family coherence (CCCC): A construct that explains the motivational and cognitive bases for transforming the family's potential resources into actual resources, thereby facilitating coping and promoting the health of family members and the well-being of the family unit. This is a dispositional world view that expresses the family's dynamic feeling of confidence that the world is comprehensible (internal and external environments are structured predictable and explicable), manageable (resources are available to meet demands), and meaningful (life demands are challenges worthy of investment) (Antonovsky, 1979, 1987; Antonovsky & Sourani, 1988).

Level 3. Family paradigms (CCC): A model of shared beliefs and expectations shaped and adopted by the family unit to guide the family's development of specific patterns of functioning around specific domains or dimensions of family life (e.g., work and family, communication, spiritual/religious orientation, child rearing, etc.). Once a paradigm is shaped and adopted and used to interpret phenomena and to guide family behaviors, family functioning in the absence of any paradigm cannot occur (Reiss, 1981; H.I. McCubbin, Thompson, Thompson, & M.A. McCubbin, 1992).

Level 2. Situational appraisal (CC): The family's shared assessment of the stressor, the hardships created by the stressor, the demands upon the family system to change some of its established patterns of functioning. The appraisal occurs in relation to the family's capability for managing the crisis situation.

Level 1. Stressor appraisal (C): The family's definition of the stressor and its severity is the initial level of family assessment (appears in Figure 1). Consistent with the classic work of Reuben Hill (1949), the family's response to a stressor will be shaped by the definition that the family attributes to the situation. In the context of a crisis situation, which places a demand on the family unit to change, this initial level (1) of appraisal becomes secondary to the adaptation process. This shift occurs due to the fact that families faced with changes in functioning are called upon to manage a host of stressors and demands, well beyond the impact of the initial crisis producing event.

The Appraisal Process: A Brief Description. In the case of a stressful situation calling for predictable and straightforward responses, as in the case of a family member with a treatable injury (such as a broken arm), the family's appraisal process is activated with relatively little involvement of the family's schema (dispositional world view of beliefs, values, goals, and meanings) nor the family's sense of coherence (dispositional world view of confidence, comprehensibility, and manageability). This stressful situation involves the family's paradigms (specific beliefs and expectations that guide the family's established patterns of functioning in such areas as marital relationships, child rearing, health care, and intergenerational relationships), the family's appraisal of the stressor, and the related hardships that arise. All of these factors, particularly the family's paradigms, stressor appraisal, and situational appraisal, play central roles in the family's appraisal process and help to shape family behavior and responses.

In contrast, in the face of adversity, such as the birth of a child with a physical disability, the established patterns of family functioning are not adequate to manage the situation (the stressor and related short- and long-term hardships). This situation requires changes in the functioning of the family unit and the fifth (schema), fourth (sense of coherence), third (paradigms), and second (situation) levels of family appraisal are often called into action to guide the family's response to the situation. Working backward from the initial stressor, family situational appraisals are first called into action by the demands of the crisis situation, challenging the way the family will function. Family routines will likely be altered; family roles related to providing physical care will need to be reexamined; family paradigms, which have served as the family framework to guide, affirm, and reinforce the established patterns of family functioning, will be challenged and called into question; and newly instituted patterns and accompanying roles and expectations will emerge. New paradigms will also emerge to reinforce and legitimate the new patterns of functioning—a necessary process to provide family stability and predictability. The family's sense of coherence, always available as a dispositional resource to facilitate adaptation, will be of greater importance in fostering the family's world view in the face of this adversity or challenge. The family's sense of coherence allows the family to maintain its confidence that the world is comprehensible, manageable, and meaningful. Thus the family's level of coherence shapes the degree to which the family transforms its extant or potential resources into actual resources and thereby facilitates the creation of new patterns of functioning, promotes harmony and congruency, and fosters coping and adaptation.

Because the family's established patterns of functioning are threatened, the family's schema, the hub of the family's appraisal process, is also involved. As already noted in the definition of family schema, culture and ethnicity may play a critical role in helping the family derive meaning by placing the family's situation into a broader set of values. This new meaning may result in the family framing the crisis situation as less threatening when viewed over time, when viewed in the context of the cultural acceptance of all children in the community, when viewed as a spiritual challenge, and when viewed as part of the natural ebb and flow of nature. This family world view may foster the adoption of new patterns of functioning and coping. When combined with the three other central processes of appraisal (coherence, paradigms, and situational appraisal), the family's schema serves the family unit by fostering the creation of the family's unique identity and enhancing the development of the family's sense of coherence (H.I. McCubbin, M.A. McCubbin, & Thompson, 1992).

Additionally, the family schema indirectly facilitates the family's shifting of paradigms and thus supports the necessary changes in the way the family functions. These paradigm shifts may be necessary for coping with the long-term needs of the family in managing a disability within the family context. *Family meanings* play a vital role in the transitional process of adopting new patterns of functioning, releasing old patterns, and achieving congruency and harmony between a family's paradigms, schema, and behaviors. Ultimately, culture and ethnicity shape family functioning, particularly in response to the crisis situations in which the family's stability and continuity may be threatened. To further this reasoning, the description of the integration of ethnicity into the family schema, coherence, meanings, and paradigms will draw from research on Native Hawaiian families.

As noted in Figure 2, the family appraisal processes play a critical set of roles in fostering family adaptations. In Adaptation, the appraisal process of schema, coherence, and paradigms fosters the demand for changes in the family's established patterns of functioning. The family may have temporary changes and appear to adapt (pseudo-adaptation) but may find itself in need of future changes, thus creating another process of crisis, appraisal, and change. In the Adaptation Phase, *newly instituted patterns of family functioning* (created by trial and error and planful efforts) may find acceptance and be legitimated and reinforced by emerging and accepted family paradigms, the family's dispositional sense of coherence, the family's schema. Family bonadaptation, characterized by an internal sense of family harmony, balance, stability, and congruity (between schema, coherence, paradigms, and patterns of functioning), is presented as the desirable outcome of the appraisal and change process (M.A. McCubbin & H.I. McCubbin, 1993).

To illustrate the role of ethnicity and culture in shaping a family's schema, the five components of the Native Hawaiians' family schema will be described (Frankl, 1984; Kanahele, 1986). The family's schema includes shared values and convictions regarding family structure, self or group concept, spiritual beliefs, nature and the land, and time orientation. Specifically, the Native Hawaiians emphasize the extended family, or tribal structure. They have a common concern for the social and economic well-being of all individuals, and they have a family support network that encompasses both immediate and extended family. Predictably, the Native

Hawaiians have developed a "we" group orientation where the needs of the whole rise above the needs of the individual (Herring, 1989). In the case of Native Hawaiians, the concept of *malama*, or caring, is the dominant theme that places the family group and the well-being of the community as a whole above the individual.[2]

Spiritual-religious underpinnings also play an important role in shaping the family's response to the challenge of internal conflicts and family hardships. Native Hawaiians view the world in terms of a "Great Spirit"; spirituality is part of the entire world. From the Native Hawaiian perspective, spirits appear in many forms, and the individual strives for unity with the cosmos as the way to achieve spirituality. Native Hawaiians see spirituality as a natural outgrowth of all aspects of life. This spiritual orientation to life facilitates Native Hawaiians' ability to create a family paradigm that cultivates the belief that a "disabled" child or deviant member is "normal" and a valued member of the community, despite any physical, developmental, or psychological handicaps.

The two additional components of family schema that shape family behavior are nature and land, and time orientation. Native Hawaiians view the environment as living. Land cannot be owned and should be respected and preserved. From their point of view, what we do to the land we do to ourselves. The Native Hawaiian world view is that land is the basis for life. *Aloha aina* or *aloha malama* reflects their belief in loving and caring for the land. Resources must be nurtured and preserved for future generations. The Native Hawaiian extends the philosophy of harmony or *Lokahi* with the land to other aspects of life, with emphasis on achieving balance, a sense of wholeness, and harmony with nature (see Table 1).

From the Native Hawaiian perspective, time is relative and life is cyclical. Native Hawaiians, as well as Native American Indians, think of time in the present; families thrive if they take advantage of the positive aspects and the strengths of the moment. Clearly, the family's world view is shaped to some degree by the family's "roots" or ethnic and cultural orientation (see H.I. McCubbin et al., 1992; H.I. McCubbin & E.A. Thompson, 1994).

Ethnicity and Family Paradigms

One's culture and ethnicity has a formative effect on schema-level appraisal, and, whether or not ethnicity is consciously and planfully incorporated into the paradigmatic patterns of family functioning, their effects can be observed (H.I. McCubbin, Thompson, Thomp-

Table 1
Ethnic and Cultural Dimensions of
Family Schema or Family World View

Family Values and Convictions	Native American Cluster	
	Native American Indian	Native American Hawaiian
Family Structure	Extended Family Tribal structure: Concern for social and economic well-being.	Extended Family social support networks
Self/Group Orientation	" We": Group Orientation with emphasis on the needs of the group above that of the individual.	" We": Group Orientation with mutual *malama* (caring) more important that the individual.
Spiritual Beliefs	The Great Spirit is in all: Spirituality is part of the world.	Spirits appear in many forms in the world: The individual should strive for spiritual unity with the cosmos.
Land/Nature	The environment is living: Land should be respected and preserved. What we do to the land we do to ourselves.	Land is the basis for *Aloha aina* or *Aloha Malama* (Love and Care for the Land). Resources must be nurtured and preserved for future generations.
Time Orientation	Present-Oriented: Time is relative. Life is cyclical.	Present-Oriented: Time is relative.

son, M.A. McCubbin, & Kasten, 1993). In a recent study of Navaho children with autism and their families, it was shown that despite some families' conscious choice to follow a less traditional path and thus define themselves as modern (rejection of ethnically based traditional ways) or semi-traditional (living in a non-traditional way, but incorporating some ethnically based traditional ways), the influence of cultural beliefs and definitions of disability had a wide-ranging and powerful effect on the family's paradigm and the family's adaptation to the long term care of their disabled member (Connors, 1992).

As depicted in Table 2, the culturally shaped paradigms of childhood chronic illness or disability for Native American Indians and Native Hawaiians are distinct from those meanings held by Anglo-American families. Although Native American Indian values vary between specific tribes, the overall Native American Indian definition of illness or disability focuses less on the inabilities of the children involved, and centers instead on the function the children, whatever their abilities, can serve within the family and the community.

The wider range of accepted behavior in Navaho culture and their family paradigm, for example, means an individual's function within society is valued regardless of how limited his or her contribution is. "Thus to be able to care for lambs with minimal supervision, to help with chores such as gathering wood or carrying water, to express a flicker of recognition towards a familiar person, and to attempt to communicate through wordless vocalizations or non-verbal gestures, is quite often seen as falling within the broad standards of becoming a socially competent Navaho" (Connors, 1992; H.I. McCubbin & Thompson, 1992).

Whereas the Anglo family paradigm of disability and illness may consider them foreign and intrusive in the family system, the Native American Indian and Native Hawaiian paradigm stresses the wholeness and harmony of life, of which illness is a part. While a Native American Cluster family faced with a serious disability is forced to process the same information and many of the same reactions of sadness and sorrow experienced by an Anglo-American family, the former's assessment and accommodation of the disability also centers around the *restoration of harmony* rather than a singularly focused attempt to "cure" or "fix" the disabled child.

Family Meaning. The Native American (Hawaiian & Indian) Cluster appears to cultivate a family paradigm that gives no "special" meaning to having a child with a chronic illness or disability; the children and their medical conditions are not labeled. Illness and disability are seen as part of a more general world view of wellness and harmony; family members may differ in the degree to which they may be be ill or well, but all members are accepted and valued regardless of their physical condition along the continuum. What the Native American (Hawaiian & Indian) Cluster labels as the source or cause of illness appears to be an extension of their schema. They place responsibility for the child's medical situation upon themselves, as well upon the natural cycle of life characterized by periods of harmony and disharmony. This paradigm places responsibility for care and treatment of the child upon the family and kin system; harmony can best be achieved through shared family and community efforts. The extended family is emphasized as a source of long-term care. By contrast, for Anglo-Americans, illness and disability are foreign to the family unit, and thus become stigmatizing labels, which, in turn, necessitates their receiving "special" treatment. Since the cause for the illness or disability is perceived to lie outside the Anglo-American family unit, the emphasis on medical treatment is likely to become a major strategy for providing ongoing care.

Family Development and Functioning. The Native American Cluster continues to build and be guided by paradigms emphasizing shared responsibility for the chronically ill or disabled member, with a strong emphasis on the extended family and the community playing a prominent role in providing long-term care. The children, regardless of the severity of their medical condition, are valued as functioning members of the community. These paradigms are supported by two complementary paradigms in the realm of work roles and education. Parental roles in providing care for the children are supported by a paradigm which accentuates the value of providing a service or benefit to society. In contrast to the Anglo-American family system, in the Native American Cluster, education and learning are not only shared among family members, but experiential learning is highly valued and affirmed. Essentially, family development and functioning in the Native American family Cluster is underscored in the family paradigms of sharing the responsibilities for long-term care among members and kin, affirming the value of all members and their contributions to the family and its members.

Family Care and Treatment. Clearly, the family's paradigms that give meaning to illness and disability and that shape the family's development and functioning interact with the family's paradigm for providing care and treatment. The Native American Cluster of families uses cultural methods to assist the family in restoring harmony and healing, and these methods often include the immediate family and the kin network of relatives and friends in problem solving. Acceptance and incorporation of the ill or disabled member is an underlying goal of the family's efforts to cope with the situation. The Anglo-American culture places a strong emphasis upon private and professional treatment of the chronically ill or disabled member. In this case the family functions as a closed unit, limiting information and care to select persons and professionals.

Problem Solving and Coping (PSC). The process of acquiring, allocating, and using resources for meeting crisis-induced demands is a critical aspect of family stress, adjustment, and adaptation. Researchers, family practitioners, and health care professionals who use a resource-management framework to view both human and material resources also understand and recognize that resources are limited. Therefore resources must be allocated to manage multiple goals and demands (Deacon & Firebaugh, 1975; Paolucci, Hall, & Axinn, 1977). The Resiliency Model of Family

Table 2
Ethnic and Cultural Dimensions of Family Paradigms

Specific Domains Of Family Functioning	Native American Cluster	
	Native American Indian	Native American Hawaiian
	Specific Beliefs and Expectations	
I. Childrearing	Community-focused childrearing: Children are to be shared: discipline and nurturing are the responsibility of all.	Community-focused childrearing: Each child is a *pua* (flower) representing the future. Extended family has major responsibility.
II. Work roles	Work for the present: Accumulated wealth should be shared with extended family: legitimates and values work roles.	Work for the present: Work should provide a service or benefit to society: legitimates and values different work roles.
III. Education	Education occurs in all facets of life: individuals should learn from one another.	Education is part of the group orientation: learning from one another is more important than individual achievement.
IV. Meaning and Treatment of Chronically Ill and Disabled Members		
Role of Disabled	Viewed as valued functioning members of the society	Absorbed as valued functioning members of the society
Source of Illness	Introspective: illness or disability may be due to misconduct for which family is being punished. Family or kin is responsible.	Introspective: illness or disability reflects an imbalance in the *mana* (energy) or *pono* (harmony). Family or kin is responsible.
Definition of Illness or Disability	Part of the whole: view illness as part of a more general pattern of harmony/disharmony.	Illness is part of wellness; normal
Language of Disability	No words in most Native languages to classify disabled: assimilated.	No words in Hawaiian language to classify disabled: assimilated.
Orientation to Treatment	Public: Medicine involves ritual and spirituality. Aimed at restoration of wholeness and spiritual balance. Community/family involvement.	Family & Community with medicine focused on restoring harmony *(pono)* and wholeness.
Problem-solving and Accommodation	Community oriented: with emphasis on community acceptance and integration: Extended family and tribal social support; emphasis on care of family members.	Community acceptance and integration: Extended family form protective net around individual: *Aloha 'Ohana* (love of kin) and *Ho oponopono* (ritualized family and kin problem-solving).

Stress, Adjustment, and Adaptation characterizes the family system as a resource-exchange network in which problem solving and coping occur. In this model problem solving and coping are the actions for this exchange.

In the context of the Resiliency Model, we define a coping behavior as a specific effort (covert or overt) by which an individual family member or the family functioning as a whole attempts to reduce or manage a demand on the family system and bring resources to bear to manage the situation. Specific coping behaviors may be grouped into patterns, such as coping directed at "maintaining family integration and cooperation," which is one of the coping patterns that has emerged as important for families who have a chronically ill child (M.A. McCubbin, 1984). Coping patterns, on the other hand, are more generalized ways of responding that transcend different kinds of stressful situations. When coping is viewed in the context of multiple demands, it seems more useful and relevant to view coping as a generalized, rather than a specific, response.

Although coping most often has been conceptualized at the individual level, we also consider family-level coping, for obvious reasons. Family coping may be viewed as coordinated problem-solving behavior of the whole system (Klein & Hill, 1979), but it could also involve complementary efforts of individual family members, which fit together in a synergistic whole. This creates a balance between demands and resources and at the same time eliminates stressors and hardships. In our view the function of coping is to maintain and restore the balance between demands and resources and at the same time remove or lessen the intensity of the crisis and its accompanying hardships. In our work with families faced with a crisis, we have identified four broad headings that characterize the ways in which coping facilitates adaptation.

1. Coping may involve direct action to eliminate or reduce the number and intensity of demands created by the illness. For example, a family could decide to place its terminally ill grandmother in a nursing home rather that keep her at home with them. The pressures of home care may often disrupt the family. The placement of the grandmother in a nursing home may reduce the tensions in the illness situation.

2. Coping may involve direct action to acquire additional resources not already available to the family. Finding medical services for a member with a chronic illness or developing self-reliance skills when a spouse dies suddenly are examples of coping to increase resources.

3. Coping may involve managing the tension associated with ongoing strains. This is necessary because of the inevitable residual of family strains resulting from an illness. Physical exercise is a commonly recognized coping mechanism. Taking time out as a family for talking and enjoying each other's company, using humor appropriately, and openly expressing emotion and affect in a

responsible, nonblaming manner are other ways for families to reduce tension.

4. Coping may involve family-level appraisal to create, shape, and evaluate meanings related to a situation to make it more constructive, manageable, and acceptable. This strategy for coping interacts directly with what is labeled as family schema appraisal in the Resiliency Model. It may be directed at changing individual family members or the total family schema of the situation, such as reducing role strain by lowering home expectations of a family member who spends a majority of time at the hospital. Reframing the home environment or sections of it as a "hospital setting" helps the family to label the situation in a manner that has more meaning and thus is more acceptable. Maintaining an optimistic outlook and acceptance of the situation and fostering the belief that this is the best the family can do under the circumstances are also important appraisal-oriented coping strategies.

In summary, coping and problem solving may be directed at the reduction or elimination of stresses and hardships, the acquisition of additional resources, the ongoing management of family system tension, and shaping the appraisal at both the situational and the schema level. These coping strategies are vitally important and often operate simultaneously.

The Family Adaptation Process, Bonadaptation, Maladaptation, and Crisis (XX). Family adaptation is a process in which families engage in direct response to the excessive demands of a stressor and depleted resources and realize that systemic changes are needed to restore functional stability and improve family satisfaction. At one level, adaptation involves the process of restructuring and making changes in rules, boundaries, and patterns of functioning. Once changes are instituted as new family patterns, the family efforts at adaptation are complemented by the family's efforts at the appraisal (schema) level. Family efforts at the appraisal level bring family members to value, accept, and affirm changes over time facilitating bonadaptation (H.I. McCubbin & Patterson, 1983b; M.A. McCubbin & H.I. McCubbin, 1989). On the other hand, families may not achieve a satisfactory level of adaptation (maladaptation). Consequently, they return to a crisis situation (XX) and then must find a new way to adapt.

Relational Process of Adaptation: Native American and Filipino Perspectives. The Native Hawaiian (Kanaka Maoli, or "the true people") perspective on coping and adaptation brings a concept of a relational process of adaptation into sharper focus. The insightful writing of Marsella, Oliveira, Plummer, and Crabbe (1995, see Chapter 4) clarifies the importance of an ethnic perspective in understanding how families adapt to crisis. These authors emphasize the importance of setting aside the Western Eurocentric notions of the individual and the serving of self and the adoption of an ecological or contextual perspective in which the individual, the family unit ('ohana), nature ('aina) and the spiritual world ('uhane, akua, aumakua, kupua) are interconnected and interdependent. The family is an integral part of the social fabric of not only the Native Hawaiian society but also the consciousness or mind of the Native Hawaiian. All of these units are "united and inseparable" from the larger social, natural and spiritual forces in the world (Marsella, Oliveira, Plummer, & Crabbe, 1995).

Within this relational and family ecological perspective, the concept of harmony or what the Hawaiians refer to as *Lokahi* gains prominence and becomes a focal concept underlying adaptation. Marsella and associates (1995) argue, harmony is a state "to be actively pursued in all realms of action and experience." To paraphrase and generalize this concept of harmony to a family level, a family knows when *Lokahi* (harmony) is achieved because the unit experiences a general state of well-being characterized by the presence of energy and vitality, referred to in the Hawaiian culture as *mana*. Adaptation therefore involves both harmony and an energylike force (mana), which are interdependent and, in their presence, the family, the individuals, the spirit, and the social ecology or nature are one—unity.

In the Native Hawaiian context, this ideal state may be referred to as *pono* or as Marsella and associates (1995) refer to as *ma'e ma'e*. This experiential state they argue is what the family unit and the individual strives to achieve through seeking a balance and a purity that is closely related to the unity of the individual family, nature, and the spiritual worlds. When this state is achieved, there is arguably optimal health and well-being and functioning. To achieve this state of harmony and unity, or balance and purity, at the family and community level, the family emphasizes altruism and helping others, and contributing to the common good in a situation in which the group gains higher importance or over one's individual and more self-centered goals. Predictably at the ecological or "nature" level, this state of harmony is achieved through the process of family and individual investment in conservation and protection of the land or what the Hawaiians refer to as the *'aina*. Finally, at the spiritual level, this balance is achieved through reverence and respect for the gods through rituals and prayer (Marsella, Oliveira, Plummer, & Crabbe, 1995).

It is striking that the literature on both the Native American Indian and the Native American Hawaiian, both indigenous people of their native lands, emphasizes the importance of a relational perspective to understanding resiliency in families. The insightful and sensitive writings of Terry Cross (1995), which focuses on the individual rather than the family, makes the relational world view of Native American Indians clear and meaningful. From this perspective, four major forces or set of factors come into play in achieving adaptation. They are the context, the mind, the body, and the spirit. The mind, Cross (1995) contends, is composed of the individual family members' cognitive processes such as thoughts, memories, and knowledge, and emotional processes such as feelings, defenses, and self esteem. The body encompasses all of the physical aspects of the individual such as genetic inheritance, gender, physical condition, nutrition, and substance use. The contextual factors are culture, community, family, peers, work, school, and social history. The spirit includes both positive and negative aspects of teachings and practices and metaphysical or innate forces. These four elements are constantly interacting and changing. "The system is constantly balancing and rebalancing itself as we change thoughts, feelings, our physical state or our spiritual state." Adaptation is defined as the state of balance that contributes to the health of the members of the family and the family unit as a whole. In those situations where the family unit is out of balance cultures provide mechanisms to assist in the process of rebalancing. Native American Indians culturally maintain this balance in many ways, including spiritual teachings, social skills and norms, dietary rules, and family roles.

Cross (1995) argues that from a relational point of view the resiliency in families emerges through an understanding of "the holistic and complex interrelationships that come into harmony and allow a family to not only survive" but also to thrive. He states that the environment in which families of ethnic backgrounds function is filled with resources that promote strength and harmony. For example, Cross calls attention to the impact of oppression and the damage that it does to people of ethnic backgrounds but also emphasizes that this struggle fosters the development of survival skills. Families cultivate a learning experience within the home environment that facilitates the development of what he calls a "sixth sense" about where Native Americans are welcome and where they are not. Parents and siblings teach children to recognize "the subtle clues that may spell danger." These members interpret oppressive events from television or the movies for younger children and in so doing transmit information that cushions "the assaults of the mainstream media." "We learn how to cope with the dynamics of difference and pass our strategies on to our children" (Cross, 1995). In the cognitive arena, family resiliency is enhanced through the process of self-talk and by the stories Native Americans hear about how others have managed life events and change. In this way, family members learn proven strategies for using resources and adapting to change. In "storytelling" families pass on stories of their lives, their skills and in so doing "we parent for resiliency" (Cross, 1995). In the relational world view Cross (1995) describes the importance of the interdependence of all of these factors that must be taken into account in order to reach an understanding of the resiliency in families. It is "the constant change and interplay of the various forces [mental, physical, spiritual, and contextual] that account for resilience" (Cross, 1995). When the family system focuses on achieving harmony, resiliency is advanced by contributing to the balance among these forces.

In Filipino American families, members depend on each other for emotional, psychological, and financial support (Bulatao, 1981; Affonso, 1978; Almirol, 1982) and the family structure is built on cultural values that reflect a system of cooperation and mutual support that members depend upon for a sense of belonging. The community network is an integral and valued part of family life with kinskip relations being highly valued and regarded as familial whether defined by blood, marriage, or fictive kinship (Duff & Arthur, 1973; Guthrie, 1968; Takagi & Ishisaka, 1982). These families place a high priority on dependence, loyalty to, and solidarity with the family and kin group. The interests or desires of the individual are sacrificed for the good of the family, and cooperation among family members is stressed over individualism. Much like the Native Hawaiians, underlying the strong sense of family is the dominant cultural value of smooth interpersonal relationships, which permeates and guides the everyday lives and behaviors of Filipinos; open displays of anger or aggression are discouraged, and passive and cooperative behaviors are encouraged (Varies, 1963; Agbayani-Siewert, 1994). The relational process in Filipino families centers on four factors: reciprocal obligation (*Utang ng loob*), shame (*hiya*), self-esteem (*amor proprio*), and getting along with others (*pakikisama*).

As Agbayani-Siewert (1994) notes *Utang ng loob* evolves in the family unit as a moral principle that dictates that when an individual recognizes a favor or service, he or she must reciprocate; this is a form of social control under the auspices of the family unit. This element of reciprocal obligation is reinforced by *hiya,* which serves to maintain the importance of the group over the individual. *Hiya* or shame emerges when the individual fails to meet an expectation or performs in ways that meet with family disapproval (Almirol, 1982). The family process is shaped further by *Pakikisama,* the relational pressure to go along with others even if doing so contradicts one's own desires. This dimension of family life is complemented by the belief that family members who have *pakikisama* also possesses *pakiradam*—the ability to sense things, especially other people's wants, needs, and expectations (Hippler, 1985). Functionally, *pakikisama* assures that good feelings and cooperation in the family and other relationships are maintained. *Amor proprio,* or self-esteem, is closed linked to shame or *hiya* in the Filipino family system. Filipinos are characterized as being highly sensitive to criticism and are easily humiliated; criticism may be taken as a personal insult (Lynch, 1981) and may prompt an individual to take aggressive action to protect the self. *Hiya* or shame serves to repress this aggressive behavior. It is an expectation in the Filipino family system not to criticize, complain about, or question others.

From the family perspective, the relational process involves a dynamic set of factors emphasizing the family's schema or world view, coherence and paradigms that are shaped by the family's ethnic and cultural background. It is in the process of adaptation that we gain a fuller and richer understanding of the family's relational process of achieving harmony and balance by instituting patterns of functioning that bring often competing if not opposing family forces into order. The family's dimensions of interpersonal relationships, community relationships and relationships with nature, the family's development, well-being and spirituality as well as the family's structure and functioning are taken into account, guided by the goals of harmony and balance. In ethnic families the process of adaptation emphasizes the family's natural and self-healing resources and capabilities.

Efficacy of the Resiliency Model in Ethnic Families

While being beyond the scope of this chapter to present all of the investigations confirming the efficacy and the validity of earlier and current versions of the Resiliency Model of Family Stress, Adjustment, and Adaptation (Lavee, H.I. McCubbin, & Patterson, 1985; Lavee, H.I. McCubbin, & Olson, 1987; H.I. McCubbin et al., 1994; Florian & Dangoor, 1994; E.A. Thompson, H.I. McCubbin, A.I. Thompson, & Elver, 1995) in the study of ethnic families, it is important to describe the results of one investigation that renders empirical support for the framework but more importantly that calls attention to the importance of ethnicity in family adaptation.

The Case of Native Hawaiian Families. The opportunity to examine the relationship between family ethnic orientation, coherence, and family functioning is rare. In 1993, at the invitation of two agencies involved in providing educational and social (prevention-oriented) services to Native Hawaiian families, particularly to families with preschool-age children, social and behavioral scientists from the Center for Family Studies at the University of Wisconsin–Madison were challenged to develop ethnically relevant and culturally sensitive measures of family functioning which could be used in future studies of Native Hawaiian families (H.I. McCubbin et al, 1994).

The importance of studying Native Hawaiians has already been established by virtue of their "at risk" status among minority populations in the United States (Blaisdell, 1989; Mokuau, 1992). The health risks for Native Hawaiians are astounding. Native Hawaiians have the worst health profile in the United States. More than 65% of Native Hawaiians are obese, and their mortality rates from cancer, heart disease, and diabetes are the highest in the nation. The mortality rates for Native Hawaiians, when compared to the average mortality rates for all races in the United States (adjusted for age/sex per 100,000), are striking: 26.4 from infectious diseases (versus 13 for all races); 29 from diabetes (versus 9.8 for all races); 46.1 from strokes (versus 35.1 for all races); 183.9 from cancer (versus 132 for all races); and 273 from heart disease (versus 189 for all races).

In this investigation, one hundred and fifty-five families ($n=155$) of preschool-age children were invited to participate in a study designed to record: (a) the family's "pile-up" of normative and non-normative life events and changes and their assessment of the severity of each of the changes they experienced; (b) the family's level of support from the community in which they lived; (c) the family's world view or schema, emphasizing their involvement in and valuing of their cultural heritage and the meaning they attached to cultural values; (d) the family's problem-solving communication style and the degree to which they were affirming and less inflammatory in their approach to issues and problems; and (e) the criterion for the study, the family's level of dysfunction including having members abusing substances, member(s) having emotional difficulties, and interpersonal abuse.

Structural Equation Test of the Resiliency Model for Native Hawaiian Families. In the trimmed model (Figure 3), family problem-solving communication (-.33) emerges as the critical explanatory variable for family dysfunction (maladaptation). The appraisal processes of family (ethnic) schema (+.29) combined with family hardiness (+.51) explain a significant proportion of the variance in family problem solving communication. Additionally, as outlined in the Resiliency Model, another pathway emerges: Family (ethnic) schema is causally related (+.31) to coherence, which is causally linked (+.48) to family hardiness, which, as already established, is causally linked to family problem-solving communication (-.33). Community social support, contributes to both family (ethnic) schema (+.32) and to family hardiness (+.19) both of which are causally linked to family problem solving and family dysfunction. The unique, independent, but noteworthy contributions of both family (ethnic) schema and family coherence to family dysfunction are affirmed in this investigation.

This investigation attempted to respond to the challenge that research on coherence be inclusive of other important but ethnically relevant variables; to better understand how families remain healthy and recover when confronted with stressful life events, the effects of two or more variables must be considered concurrently, such as hardiness and coherence or coherence and family schema. This effort to combine variables is clearly reflected in the literature: Kobasa, Maddi, and Puccetti (1982) examined hardiness and exercise, and Holahan and Moos (1986) explored personality characteristics and coping strategies, to note a few of the salient studies. The benefit of multivariate investigations, particularly when employing structural equation techniques, is the examination and discovery of the possible causal ordering of variables that would go unnoticed by the more parsimony-seeking efforts to isolate the best set of predictors to explain family dysfunction. Of central importance to this investigation, had the analysis been limited to the traditional paradigm of isolating the "best set of predictors," the central value of coherence and the relative salience of family schema, inclusive of ethnic and cultural values, would have remained relatively obscure.

Figure 3.
Trimmed Family Resiliency Model with Ethnic Schema
and Family Dysfunction Among Native American Hawaiians *(N = 93)**

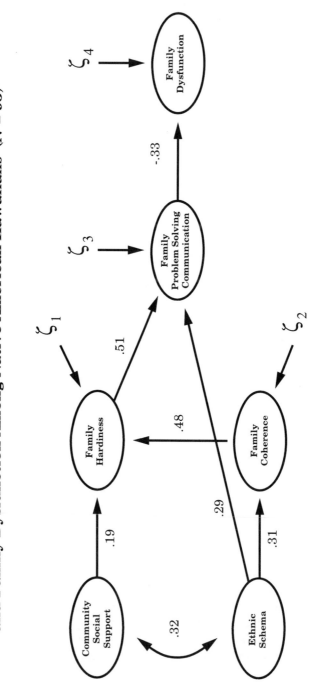

*Coefficients presented are standardized Betas

Coherence emerges as being of paramount importance to explaining, at least indirectly, the variability in family dysfunction. Coherence appeared to have a relatively prominent role in the causal ordering of variables; the family's sense of coherence, influenced by family schema, has an indirect relationship to family dysfunction through family hardiness and family problem-solving communication.

These findings support three general observations. The structured equation model supports Antonovsky's (1987) thesis that one's sense of coherence as a dispositional world view expressing the dynamic feeling of confidence, comprehensibility, manageability, and meaningfulness plays an important role in facilitating adaptation. Second, the findings suggest that the sense of coherence attenuates the severity of family dysfunction or pathology. Third, the findings suggest that the sense of coherence plays a catalytic role in family resiliency by combining with and fostering the family's resistance resources, such as family hardiness (the family's dispositional resource of having a sense of commitment, control, confidence, and challenge) and family problem-solving communication (affirming style of communication) (Antonovsky, 1994). The expectation that the family's sense of coherence would be ubiquitous and have powerful direct effects on family functioning was not supported.

Family schema, an important focus of this investigation, is introduced as a dispositional factor in family appraisal, contributing to family adaptation by fostering coherence and other family resources. Family appraisal, in turn, promotes family adaptation and functioning. This generally stated hypothesis was confirmed. For Native Hawaiian families, family schema with its emphasis on an ethnic world view has three pathways through which it influences family dysfunction. In the most direct pathway, family (ethnic) schema works through or in combination with family problem-solving communication. In the second pathway, family (ethnic) schema works through the family's sense of coherence, family hardiness and family problem-solving communication. In the third and final pathway, family (ethnic) schema works through community social support, family hardiness and family problem-solving communication. The Structural Equation Analysis (EQS) indicated an appropriate fit between the Resiliency Model and the data on Native Hawaiian families with Goodness of Fit indices of: CFI (Comparative Fit Index) = .95, Chi-square = .117, df = 15 and a probability of .20.

Summary and Conclusions

Ethnic families negotiate change and stressful life events with an innate reaction to fight, to remain stable, and to resist changes in the family's established patterns of behavior. Family adjustment, characterized by relatively minor changes in the family system, is a predictable phase in the family's response to a stressor. Many stressors may also require family adaptation, even drastic change in the family system. In these situations families are called upon to expand and to contract, to incorporate and to release, and to achieve stability by disrupting existing patterns of functioning. In these struggles and particularly in the face of an stressor-induced family crisis, families adapt by instituting changes in the family's pattern of functioning, changing its scheme, or blueprint, for functioning, and by changes in the family's relationship to the outside world.

Family stress theory, in particular the Resiliency Model of Family Stress, Adjustment, and Adaptation, attempts to explain this dynamic process by isolating those individual, family, and community properties and processes that interact and shape the course of ethnic family behavior over time and in response to a wide range of stressful situations. The Resiliency Model encourages professionals to recognize family resiliency and the natural healing qualities of family life, which, if understood, could become targets for intervention.

Notes

1. Copyright 1995 by H. I. McCubbin & M. A. McCubbin, "Resiliency in Ethnic Families: A Conceptual Model for Predicting Family Adjustment and Adaptation."

2. Throughout the chapter, some diacritical marks in Native Hawaiian, Filipino, and Native American languages could not be reproduced because of printing limitations.

References

Affonso, D. (1978). The Filipino American. In A.L. Clark (Ed.), *Culture in childrearing health professionals* (pp.128-153). Philadelphia: F.A. Davis.

Agbayani-Siewert, P. (1988). *Social service utilization of Filipino Americans in Los Angeles.* Unpublished manuscript, School of Social Welfare, University of California, Los Angeles.

Agbayani-Siewert, P. (1994). Filipino American culture and family: Guidelines for practitioners. *Families in Society: The Journal of Contemporary Human Services, 75*(7), 429-438.

Almirol, E. (1982). Rights and obligation in Filipino American families. *Journal of Comparative Family Studies, 13*, 291-306.

Antonovsky, A. (1979). *Health, stress, and coping.* San Francisco, CA: Jossey-Bass.

Antonovsky, A. (1987). *Unraveling the mystery of health.* San Francisco, CA: Jossey-Bass.

Antonovsky, A. (1994). The sense of coherence: an historical and future perspective. In *Sense of coherence and resiliency: Stress, coping and health.* Madison, WI: University of Wisconsin System.

Antonovsky, A., & Sourani, T. (1988). Family sense of coherence and family adaptation. *Journal of Marriage and the Family, 50*, 79-92.

Bem, S. L. (1981). Gender schema theory: A cognitive account of sex typing. *Psychological Review, 88*(4), 354-364.

Berkner, L. K. (1972). The stem family and the development cycle of the peasant household: An eighteenth-century Austrian example. *American History Review, 77*, 398-418.

Blaisdell, K. (1989). Historical and cultural aspects of Native Hawaiian health. *Social Process in Hawaii, 32*(1), 1-21.

Bulatao, J. (1981). The Manilino mainsprings. In F. Lynch & A. de Guzman, II (Eds.), *Four readings on Filipino values* (4th ed., pp.70-118). Quezon City, Philippines: Ateneo de Manila University.

Burr, W. F. (1973). *Theory construction and the sociology of the family.* New York: John Wiley.

Caplan, G. (1974). *Support systems and community mental health.* New York: Behavioral Publications.

Cassel, J. (1976). The contribution of the social environment to host resistance. *American Journal of Epidemiology, 104*, 107-123.

Cheung, F., & Snowden, L. (1990). Use of inpatient mental health services by members of ethnic minority groups. *American Psychologist, 45*, 347-355.

Cobb, S. (1976). Social support as a moderator of life stress. *Psychosomatic Medicine, 38*, 300-314.

Connors, J. (1992). *Navajo perceptions of autism and social competence: A cultural perspective.* Madison, WI: University of Wisconsin--Madison, unpublished doctoral dissertation.

Cross, T. L. (1995). Understanding family resiliency from a relational world view. In H.I. McCubbin, E.A. Thompson, A.I. Thompson, & J.E. Fromer (Eds.), *Resiliency in ethnic minority families: Native and immigrant American families.* Madison, WI: University of Wisconsin System.

Curran, D. (1983). *Traits of a healthy family.* Minneapolis: Winston.

Deacon, R., & Firebaugh, F. (1975). *Home management context and concepts.* Boston: Houghton Mifflin.

Duff, D., & Arthur, R.J. (1973). Between two worlds: Filipinos in the U.S. Navy. In S. Sue & N. Wagner (Eds.), *Asian American psychological perspectives* (pp. 202-211). Palo Alto, CA: Science and Behavior Books.

Epstein, N., Bishop, D., & Baldwin, L. (1982). McMaster model of family functioning: A view of the normal family. In F. Walsh (Ed.), *Normal family processes.* New York: Guilford.

Fleck, S. (1980). Family functioning and family pathology. *Psychiatric Annals, 10*, 46-57.

Florian, V., & Dangoor, N. (1994). Personal and familial adaptation of women with severe physical disabilities: A further validation of the double ABCX model. *Journal of Marriage and the Family, 56*, 735-746.

Fong, G. T., & Markus, H. (1982). Self schemata and judgments about others. *Social Cognition, 2*, 191-204.

Frankl, V. E. (1984). *Man's search for meaning: An introduction to logotherapy* (3rd ed.). New York: Simon & Schuster.

Granovetter, M. (1973). The strength of weak ties. *American Journal of Sociology, 78*, 1360-1380.

Guthrie, G. (1968). *The Philippine temperament: Six perspectives on the Philippines.* Manila, Philippines: Bookmark.

Hansen, D., & Johnson, V. (1979). Rethinking family stress theory: Definitional aspects. In W. Burr, R. Hill, F. I. Nye, & I. Reiss (Eds.), *Contemporary theories about the family* (Vol. 1, pp. 582-603). New York: The Free Press.

Herring, R. (1989). The American native family: Dissolution by coercion. *Journal of Multicultural Counseling and Development, 17*, 4-13.

Hill, R. (1949). *Families under stress.* New York: Harper & Row.

Hill, R. (1958). Generic features of families under stress. *Social Casework, 49*, 139-150.

Hippler, A. (1985). Culture and personality studies of the Pilipinos of northern Luzon: A case of pragmatic erosion. *Journal of Psychoanalytic Anthropology, 8*, 115-155.

Holahan, C., & Moos, R. (1986). Personality, coping, and family resources in stress resistance: A longitudinal analysis. *Journal of Personality and Social Psychology, 51*, 389-395.

House, J. (1981). *Work stress and social support.* Reading, MA: Addison-Wesley.

Howard, A. (1974). *Ain't no big thing: Coping strategies in a Hawaiian-American community.* Honolulu, HI: University Press of Hawaii.

Ishisaka, H. A. (1992). Significant differences between Pacific-Asian and Western cultures. In J. Fischer (Ed.), *East-West directions: Social work practice, tradition, and change.* Honolulu, HI: School of Social Work, University of Hawaii.

Kanahele, G. H. S. (1986). *Ku kanaka: Stand tall. A search for Hawaiian values.* Honolulu, HI: University of Hawaii Press.

Klein, D., & Hill, R. (1979). Determinants of family problem-solving effectiveness. In W. Burr, R. Hill, I. Reiss, & I. Nye (Eds.), *Contemporary theories about the family* (Vol. 1). New York: The Free Press.

Kobasa, S., Maddi, S., & Puccetti, M. (1982). Personality and exercise as buffers in the stress-illness relationship. *Journal of Behavioral Medicine, 5*, 391-404.

Kosciulek, J.F., McCubbin, M.A., & McCubbin H.I. (1993). A theoretical framework for family adaptation to head injury. *Journal of Rehabilitation, 59*, 40-45.

Kumbabe, K., Nishida, C., & Hepworth, D. (1985). *Bridging ethnocultural diversities in social work and health.* Honolulu: University of Hawaii Press.

Lavee, Y. (1985). *Family types and family adaptation to stress: Integrating the circumplex model of family systems and the family adjustment and adaptation response model.* Unpublished doctoral dissertation, University of Minnesota, St. Paul.

Lavee, Y., McCubbin, H.I., & Olson, D.H. (1987). The effect of stressful life events and transitions on family functioning and well-being. *Journal of Marriage and the Family, 49*, 857-873.

Lavee, Y., McCubbin, H.I., & Patterson, J. M. (1985). The double ABCX model of stress and adaptation: An empirical test by analysis of structural equations with latent variables. *Journal of Marriage and the Family, 47*, 811-825.

Lavee, Y., & Olson, D.H. (1991). Family types and response to stress. *Journal of Marriage and the Family, 53*, 786-798.

Lewis, J., & Looney, J. (1984). *The long struggle: Well-functioning working-class black families.* New York: Brunner/Mazel.

Li, Y.Y. (1968). Ghost marriage, shamanism, and kinship behavior in rural Taiwan. In *Folk religion and the world view in the Southwestern Pacific.* Tokyo: The Keio Institute of Cultural and Linguistic Studies, Keio University.

Lynch, F. (1981). Social acceptance reconsidered. In F. Lynch & A. de Guzman, II (Eds.), *Four readings on Philippine values* (4th ed., pp.1-68). Quezon City, Philippines: Institute of Philippine Culture, Ateneo de Manila University.

Marsella, A.J., Oliveira, J. M., Plummer, C. M., & Crabbe, K.M. (1995). Native Hawaiian (Kanaka Maoli) culture, mind, and well-being. In H.I. McCubbin, E.A. Thompson, A.I. Thompson, & J.E. Fromer (Eds.), *Resiliency in ethnic minority families: Native and immigrant American families.* Madison, WI: University of Wisconsin System.

Martin, C. L., & Halverson, C. F. (1981). A schematic processing model of sex typing and stereotyping in children. *Child Development, 52*, 1119-1134.

McCubbin, H. I., Boss, P., Wilson, L., & Lester, G. (1980). Developing family invulnerability to stress: Coping patterns and strategies wives employ. In J. Trost (Ed.), *The family and change.* Sweden: International Library Publishing.

McCubbin, H. I., & Lavee, Y. (1986). Strengthening army families: A family life cycle perspective. *Education and Program Planning, 9*, 221-231.

McCubbin, H.I., & McCubbin, M.A. (1988). Typologies of resilient families: Emerging roles of social class and ethnicity. *Family Relations, 37*, 247-254.

McCubbin, H. I., McCubbin, M. A., & Thompson, A. I. (1992). Resiliency in families: The role of family schema and appraisal in family adaptation to crises. In T. Brubaker (Ed.), *Families in transition.* Newbury Park, CA: Sage.

McCubbin, H. I., & Patterson, J. M. (1981). *Systematic assessment of family stress, resources and coping: Tools for research, education and clinical intervention.* St. Paul, MN: Department of Family Social Science.

McCubbin, H. I., & Patterson, J. M. (1982). Family adaptation to crisis. In H. I. McCubbin, A. Cauble, & J. M. Patterson (Eds.), *Family stress, coping and social support.* Springfield, IL: Charles C. Thomas.

McCubbin, H. I., & Patterson, J. M. (1983a). The family stress process: The double ABCX model of adjustment and adaptation. In H. McCubbin, M. Sussman, & J. Patterson (Eds.), *Advances and developments in family stress theory and research.* New York: Haworth.

McCubbin, H. I., & Patterson, J. M. (1983b). Family transitions: Adaptation to stress. In H. I. McCubbin & C. R. Figley (Eds.), *Stress and the family: Coping with normative transitions*, I. New York: Brunner/Mazel.

McCubbin, H. I., Patterson, J. M., & Lavee, Y. (1983). *One thousand army families: Strengths, coping and supports.* St. Paul, MN: University of Minnesota.

McCubbin, H. I., & Thompson, A. I. (1989). *Balancing work and family life on Wall Street: Stockbrokers and families coping with economic instability.* Edina, MN: Burgess International.

McCubbin, H.I., & Thompson, A.I. (1992). Resiliency in families: An East-West perspective. In J. Fischer (Ed.), *East-West connections in social work practice: Tradition and change.* Honoluiu, HI: School of Social Work, University of Hawaii.

McCubbin, H. I., Thompson, A.I., Pirner, P., & McCubbin, M. A. (1988). *Family types and strengths: A life cycle and ecological perspective.* Edina, MN: Burgess International.

McCubbin, H. I., & Thompson, E. A. (1994). Preserving family values in the age of technology. In D. Malcolm (Ed.), *The family in the aquatic continent, cultural values in the age of technology.* Hawaii: Maui Pacific Center.

McCubbin, H. I., Thompson, E. A., Thompson, A. I., & McCubbin, M. A. (1992). Family schema, paradigms, and paradigm shifts: Components and processes of appraisal in family adaptation to crises. In A. P. Turnbull, J. M. Patterson, S. K. Bahr, D. L. Murphy, J. Marquis, & M. Blue-Banning (Eds.), *Cognitive coping research in developmental disabilities.* Baltimore, MD: Paul H. Brookes.

McCubbin, H.I., Thompson, E.A., Thompson, A.I., & McCubbin, M.A. (1994). Ethnicity, schema, and coherence: Appraisal processes for families in crisis. In H.I. McCubbin, E.A. Thompson, A.I. Thompson, & J.E. Fromer (Eds.), *Sense of coherence and resiliency: Stress, coping, and health.* Madison, WI: University of Wisconsin System.

McCubbin, H. I., Thompson, E. A., Thompson, A. I., McCubbin, M. A., & Kasten, A. (1993). Culture, ethnicity and the family: Critical factors in childhood chronic illness and disabilities. *Journal of Pediatrics, 91*(5), 1063-1070.

McCubbin, M. A. (1984). Nursing assessment of parental coping with cystic fibrosis, *Western Journal of Nursing Research, 6*, 4.

McCubbin, M. A. (1986). *Family stress and family types: Chronic illness in children.* Doctoral dissertation, University of Minnesota.

McCubbin, M.A. (1988). Family stress, resources, and family types: Chronic illness in children. *Family Relations, 37*, 203-210.

McCubbin, M. A. (1989). Family stress and family strengths: A comparison of single- and two-parent families with handicapped children. *Research in Nursing and Health, 12*, 101-110.

McCubbin, M.A. (1990). The Typology Model of Adjustment and Adaptation: A family stress model. *Guidance and Counseling, 5*, 6-22.

McCubbin, M.A., & McCubbin, H. I. (1987). Family stress theory and assessment: The T-double ABCX model of family adjustment and adaptation. In H. I. McCubbin & A. Thompson (Eds.), *Family assessment inventories for research and practice.* Madison: University of Wisconsin–Madison.

McCubbin, M.A., & McCubbin, H. I. (1989). Theoretical orientations to family stress and coping. In C. R. Figley (Ed.), *Treating stress in families.* New York: Brunner/Mazel.

McCubbin, M. A., & McCubbin, H. I. (1993). Family coping with health crises: The resiliency model of family stress, adjustment and adaptation. In C. Danielson, B. Hamel-Bissell, & P. Winstead-Fry (Eds.), *Families, health, and illness.* New York: Mosby.

McCubbin, M. A., McCubbin, H.I., & Thompson, A. (1987) Family Problem-Solving Communication Index. In H. I. McCubbin & A. Thompson (1989). *Balancing work and family life on Wall Street: Stockbrokers and families coping with economic instability.* Edina, MN: Burgess International.

McCubbin, M. A., McCubbin, H. I., & Thompson, A. I. (1994). The family problem solving communication index. In A. I. Thompson, *Gender, problem solving communication, and health risk: Considerations for adult education programing.* Unpublished doctoral dissertation, University of Wisconsin--Madison.

McGoldrich, M. (1989). Ethnicity and the family life cycle. In B. Carter & M. McGoldrich (Eds.), *The changing family life cycle* (2nd ed.). Boston, MA: Allyn & Bacon.

Miller, L. (1969). Child rearing in the kibbutz. In J. G. Howells (Ed.), *Modern perspectives in international child psychiatry.* Edinburgh: Oliver & Boyd.

Miranda, M., & Kitano, H. (1976). Barriers to mental health: A Japanese and Mexican dilemma. In C. Hernandez, M. Hauz, & N. Wagner (Eds.), *Chicano social and psychological perspectives* (2nd ed., pp. 242-252). St. Louis, MO: C.V. Mosby.

Mokuau, N. (1992). A conceptual framework for cultural responsiveness in the health field. In J. Fischer (Ed.), *East-West directions: Social work practice, tradition, and change.* Honolulu, HI: School of Social Work, University of Hawaii.

Moos, R. (1974). *Family environment scales.* Palo Alto, CA: Consulting Psychologists Press.

Nanda, S. (1980). *Cultural anthropology.* New York: D. Van Nostrand.

Olson, D., (1986). Circumplex Model VII: Validation Studies and FACES III. *Family Process, 25,* 337-351.

Olson, D., McCubbin, H. I., Barnes, H., Larsen, A., Muxem, A., & Wilson, M. (1983). *Families—what makes them work.* Beverly Hills, CA: Sage.

Olson, D., Sprenkle, D., & Russell, C. (1979). Circumplex model of marital and family systems l: Cohesion and adaptability dimensions, family types and clinical applications. *Family Process, 18,* 3-28.

Paolucci, B., Hall, O., & Axinn, N. (1977). *Family decision making: An ecosystem approach.* New York: John Wiley.

Pearlin, L., Menaghan, E., Lieberman, M., & Mullan, J. (1981). The stress process. *Journal of Health and Social Behavior, 22,* 337-356.

Pearlin, L., & Schooler, C. (1978). The structure of coping. *Journal of Health and Social Behavior, 19,* 2-21.

Pelzel, J. (1970). Japanese kinship: A comparison. In M. Freedman (Ed.), *Family and kinship in Chinese society.* Stanford, CA: Stanford University Press.

Pilisuk, M., & Parks, S. (1983). Social support and family stress. In H. I. McCubbin, M. Sussman, & J. Patterson (Eds.), *Social stress and the family: Advances and developments in family stress theory and research.* New York: Haworth.

Pinneau, S. (1975). *Effects of social support on psychological and physiological stress.* Unpublished doctoral dissertation. Ann Arbor: University of Michigan.

Reiss, D. (1981). *The family's construction of reality.* Cambridge, MA: Harvard University Press.

Satir, V. (1972). *Peoplemaking.* Palo Alto, CA: Science and Behavior Books.

Segal, Z. (1988). Appraisal of the self-schema construct in cognitive models of depression. *Psychological Bulletin, 103*(2), 147–162.

Stinnet, N., & DeFrain, J. (1985). *Secrets of strong families.* Boston: Little, Brown.

Stinnet, N., & Sauer, K. (1977). Relationship characteristics of strong families. *Family Perspective, 11*(4), 3-11.

Sue, S., & Morishima, J. (1982). *The mental health of Asian Americans.* San Francisco: Jossey-Bass.

Takagi, C., & Ishisaka, H. (1982). Social work with Asian- and Pacific-Americans. In J. Green (Ed.), *Cultural awareness in the human services* (pp.138-144). Englewood Cliffs, NJ: Prentice-Hall.

Taylor, S. E., & Crocker, J. (1981). Schematic bases of social information processing. In E. T. Higgins, C. P. Herman, & M. P. Zanna, (Eds.), *The Ontario symposium on personality and social psychology* (Vol. 1). Hillsdale, NJ: Erlbaum.

Thompson, E. A., McCubbin, H. I., Thompson, A. I., & Elver, K. M. (1995). Vulnerability and resiliency in Native Hawaiian families under stress. In H.I. McCubbin, E.A. Thompson, A.I. Thompson, & J.E. Fromer (Eds.), *Resiliency in ethnic minority families: Native and immigrant American families.* Madison, WI: University of Wisconsin System.

Trask, H. (1995). Native sovereignty: A strategy for Hawaiian family survival. In H.I. McCubbin, E.A. Thompson, A.I. Thompson, & J.E. Fromer (Eds.), *Resiliency in ethnic minority families: Native and immigrant American families.* Madison, WI: University of Wisconsin System.

Tseng, W. S., & Hsu, J. (1986). The family in Micronesia. In W. S. Tseng & C. A. Less (Eds.), *Culture and mental health in Micronesia.* Honolulu, HI: Department of Psychiatry, John A. Burns School of Medicine, University of Hawaii.

Tseng, W. S., & Hsu, J. (1991). *Culture and family: Problems and therapy.* New York: Haworth.

Varies, R. (1963). Psychiatry and the Filipino personality. *Philippine Sociological Review, 11*(3-4), 179-184.

Chapter 2

Race, Ethnicity, Families, and Education

Gary D. Sandefur[1]

Published statistics show that American Indians, Blacks, and Hispanics are less likely to complete high school and attend college than are Whites, while Asians are more likely than Whites to complete high school and attend college.[2] These racial and ethnic differences are often the subject of media and cocktail party speculation in which the alternatives of culture and discrimination are offered as possible explanations. Asian success, for example, is attributed to cultural values that promote hard work and education, while the lack of educational success among Blacks is attributed by some to deficient cultural values or by others to persisting discrimination against Blacks in the educational system.

Social science, though sometimes prone to unfounded speculation as well, has uncovered at least some partial explanations of these racial and ethnic differences. A good deal of research over the years indicates that much of the difference in high school graduation and college attendance between Blacks and Whites is due to differences in family background characteristics such as parental education, whether one resides in a nonintact family or not, and number of siblings (see, for example, Hauser & Phang, 1993; Sandefur, McLanahan, & Wojtkiewicz, 1989). In fact, some of the racial and ethnic differences are reversed after controlling for family background. Hauser and Phang (1993) found, for example, that Whites were the most likely and Blacks the least likely to drop out of high school during the 1973–1989 period after controlling for family background. Hispanic dropout rates were intermediate between Blacks and Whites. Alexander et al. (1987) and Thomas et al. (1979) found that Blacks were more likely than Whites to enroll in four year colleges, and Alexander et al. (1982) found that Blacks were more likely than Whites to obtain a bachelor's degree. These studies also controlled for differences in family background.

Although there are some inconsistencies in the findings that may be due, at least in part, to differences in data sets, time periods, and model specification, the weight of the evidence suggests that family background is an important factor in producing Black/White, and to a lesser extent, Hispanic/White differences in high school completion, college attendance, and college graduation.[3]

A good deal of recent research in areas other than the sociology of education has documented the significance of families and family characteristics in determining what happens to people during adolescence or later in adulthood. We do not, however, know very much about racial and ethnic differences in family characteristics other than the major socio-demographic family background measures and how these affect racial/ethnic differences in outcomes. To the extent that there has been research on racial and ethnic variations, the research has focused on African-American families. We know much less about Asian and Hispanic families, and almost nothing about American Indian families.

The purpose of this chapter is to provide more information on racial and ethnic variations in family characteristics and how these affect racial and ethnic differences in educational attainment. To do this, two major questions are addressed: (1) What are the major variations in the structure and functioning of families across the principal racial and ethnic groups in the United States? and (2) Do these variations in families help account for racial and ethnic differences in educational attainment?

More specifically, the research will explore three sets of factors: (1) family socio-demographic characteristics; (2) a specific set of subcultural factors including parenting practices; and (3) secondary school quality. As mentioned previously, one partial explanation of racial and ethnic differences in educational attainment is that these differences in outcomes are due to differences in family background (e.g., family structure, number of siblings, parental education) (Bean & Tienda, 1987; Furstenberg, Morgan, Moore, & Peterson, 1987). For example, the lower educational levels of Black parents account in part for the lower educational attainment of Black children. Blacks, Hispanics, and Native Americans are more likely than Whites to reside in nonintact families at all ages. Adjusting for these differences in family background leads to reduced racial and ethnic differences in certain outcomes.

Subcultural variables include individual attitudes and values, and peer and parental attitudes and values. In this chapter, racial and ethnic differences in parenting practices, including parental supervision and communication, are examined. White and Asian parents may spend more time with their children, and may be more involved in school work than are American Indian, Black, and Hispanic parents. These differences in parenting practices may help account for racial and ethnic differences in educational attainment.

The third source of differences lies in the context within which schooling takes place. American Indians, Blacks, and Hispanics may attend lower quality schools on average, in part because their incomes are lower than those of Whites. If they do, part of their lower educational attainment may be due to differences in the quality of their schools. Gamoran (1992) points out, however, that past research on the effects of schools on educational attainment suggests that school resources have very limited effects on achievement, and certainly a much smaller effect than family background variables. Consequently, it could be that differences in school quality play only a small role in explaining racial and ethnic differences in educational outcomes.

Data

The data for the project were drawn from the sophomore cohort of the High School and Beyond Survey (HSB). The HSB is a nationally representative survey of American high school students undertaken for the National Center for Educational Statistics (NCES) by the National Opinion Research Center (NORC). It is a longitudinal survey of two student cohorts, sophomores and seniors, who were initially surveyed in the spring of 1980 and were re-interviewed in 1982, 1984, and 1986. This report uses the information from all three waves for the sophomore cohort. All calculations, including the multivariate analyses, were done with weighted data.

The HSB data contain a wealth of information on adolescents, as well as their families of origin. These include school performance in high school, dropping out of school, attendance at junior colleges and four-year colleges, junior college completion, four-year college completion, marriage, and fertility. The data contain information on respondents' family and work experience and feelings of self-esteem and efficacy.

The HSB data also contain excellent information on family values, socialization practices, and school characteristics. Respondents were asked about their parents' expectations and influence, parent-child communication, and parental supervision. They were also asked about their peers' aspirations and orientation, and the quality of their schools. Additional information on school quality was obtained from the school survey and includes indicators for student composition, dropout rates, college attendance, and socio-economic status.

Results

Racial and Ethnic Variations in Educational Attainment

Table 1 contains the percentage of men and women in each racial and ethnic group who do not complete high school, who complete high school and do not attend any college by 1986, who complete high school and begin their post-secondary careers at a two-year college, and who complete high school and begin their post-secondary careers at a four-year college.[4] Asian men and women are the most likely to complete high school, the most likely to attend college of any type, and the most likely to begin their post-secondary careers at four-year colleges. American Indian men and women are the least likely to finish high school, the least likely to attend college, and the least likely to begin their post-secondary careers at four-year colleges.[5]

Table 1
First Post–High School College Attendance by Race and Gender

	American Indian	Asian	Black	Hispanic	White
A. Men					
No HS Diploma	25.0%	4.7	19.5	16.1	10.1
HS, No College	51.1	12.6	44.7	50.6	36.7
2 Year College	12.4	33.8	15.7	18.3	19.5
4 Year College	11.5	49.0	20.0	15.0	34.7
B. Women					
No HS Diploma	41.6	3.5	13.7	15.0	7.4
HS, No College	32.8	12.0	37.7	42.3	35.0
2 Year College	9.3	31.1	22.2	22.9	23.8
4 Year College	16.2	53.5	26.3	19.8	33.7
Sample Size	249	389	1793	2870	7935

Source: Author's tabulations with weighted data from the HSB Sophomore Cohort.

**Racial and Ethnic Variations
in Family Structure**

Table 2 contains information on racial and ethnic differences in family background. Chi-square tests indicate that each set of differences is statistically significant. Panel A shows racial and ethnic differences in religion. Hispanics are the most likely of the five groups to be Catholic, while Blacks are the most likely to be non-Catholic. Asians are the most likely of the five groups to have no religion.

Panel B in Table 2 shows that the racial and ethnic groups are distributed differentially across the regions of the United States. Whites are more likely than the other groups to live in the Northeast and the North Central parts of the United States; Blacks are more likely than the other groups to live in the South, and Asians are more likely than the other groups to live in the West.

Panel C provides information on an indicator of residential stability, whether or not a student has changed school districts between grade five and the sophomore year. The results show that Asians are the most likely to have changed school districts at least once, while Whites are the least likely to have changed school districts at least once.

Panels D and E contain information on parental education. Almost half of Black sophomores either do not live with or know the education of their fathers. The fathers of Asian youth are the most educated. Over 37% of these fathers have attended or completed college, compared to 28% of the fathers of White youth. On the other hand, only 12% of the fathers of Black youth have attended or completed college. The mothers of Asian youth are the most educated, while the mothers of American Indian youth are the least educated.

Panel F shows that Asian and White youth are more likely to live in a two-parent family, while Blacks are least likely to do so. Panel G shows that American Indian, Black and Hispanic youth are more likely to have more than one sibling than are Asian and White youth.

Considered as a group, the statistics in Table 2 suggest that the background characteristics of American Indians, Blacks, and Hispanics (especially parental education and family structure) place these groups at a disadvantage relative to Asians and Whites, and may help explain at least some of the differences in educational outcomes observed in Table 1.

Table 2
Family Background by Race

	American Indian	Asian	Black	Hispanic	White
A. Religion					
Catholic	23.5%	28.4	8.0	48.4	34.8
Other	67.1	51.0	82.2	44.2	59.1
None	9.4	20.6	9.8	7.4	6.0
B. Region					
NE	12.8%	14.0	18.6	15.5	23.2
NC	16.7	14.9	16.2	16.6	32.6
S	36.7	18.3	58.9	43.3	28.6
W	33.8	52.9	6.3	24.2	15.6
C. Never Changed School Districts Since Grade 5					
	56.8%	48.5	61.7	61.1	67.1
D. Father's Education(a)					
NA	24.8%	30.2	46.3	30.8	20.4
Less than HS	30.0	12.2	15.6	27.5	16.6
HS Grad	27.8	20.4	26.2	27.1	33.3
Some College	6.0	9.4	5.9	7.1	10.2
College Degree	11.4	27.8	5.9	7.5	19.5
E. Mother's Education(a)					
NA	16.5%	26.2	28.3	20.6	14.0
Less than HS	22.9	18.0	17.1	28.3	13.6
HS Grad	48.4	28.4	37.1	38.3	47.9
Some College	5.2	8.5	9.6	7.2	11.8
College Degree	7.0	19.0	7.9	8.7	12.7
F. Family Structure When Sophomore					
Intact	61.0%	74.2	43.7	66.4	74.3
Single	18.2	16.3	34.8	19.8	13.9
Step	6.7	4.6	10.9	6.7	9.1
Other	7.1	4.9	10.6	7.1	2.7
G. Percentage with More Than One Sibling As Sophomore					
	80.2	71.9	80.9	78.0	67.9

Source: Author's tabulations with weighted data from the HSB Sophomore Cohort. Statistical tests indicate that there are statistically significant differences in each characteristic across racial and ethnic groups.

Note: (a) An NA for parental education indicates that the respondent was not living with that parent at the time of the survey or did not know the education of that parent. The category of HS Grad includes individuals who obtained some vocational training beyond high school.

Racial and Ethnic Differences in Family Functioning

Table 3 contains descriptive information on parenting practices. Chi-square tests indicate that each set of racial and ethnic differences is statistically significant. Over 80% of all youth report that their mothers monitor their school work, with White and Asian youth being the most likely to report maternal monitoring. Over 80% of Asian youth report that their fathers monitor their school work, while only 60% of Black youth report paternal monitoring. These statistics are based on the data for those youth with fathers at home. White youth are the most likely to report that their parents always know what they are doing, while Black youth are the least likely to report parental knowledge of their activities. Asian and White youth talk with their parents more often than youth in the other groups. Finally, Asian youth are most likely and American

Table 3
Parenting Practices by Race and Ethnicity

	American Indian	Asian	Black	Hispanic	White
Mother Monitors Schoolwork	82.8%	86.5	84.3	86.2	87.5
Father Monitors Schoolwork	63.0%	83.5	60.2	69.9	76.7
Parents Always Know What Respondent is Doing	78.3%	79.9	72.0	77.4	82.0
Respondent Talks with Parents Less than Once a Week	65.5%	58.9	60.9	63.5	58.7
Mother Wants Respondent to Finish College	36.0%	68.6	55.0	40.6	46.4

Source: Author's tabulations with weighted data from the HSB Sophomore Cohort. Statistical tests indicate that there are statistically significant differences in each characteristic across racial and ethnic groups.

Indian youth least likely to report that their mother wants them to finish college. Again, these figures suggest that American Indian, Black, and Hispanic youth are disadvantaged relative to White and Asian youth in the quality of parenting that they receive.

Racial and Ethnic Differences in School Quality

Table 4 contains information on the characteristics of the school attended at the time of the first interview as a sophomore. Analyses of variance for each of the four characteristics indicate that the racial and ethnic differences are significant. In general, Asians and Whites attend schools with the most favorable characteristics.[6]

Table 4
Sophomore School Characteristics by Race

	American Indian	Asian	Black	Hispanic	White
Percentage of Students Who Drop Out of School Respondent Attended	68.4%	53.1	55.5	57.0	43.4
Average Score for School Facilities (a) Overall Mean = 2.766; standard deviation = .607	2.65	2.90	2.82	2.77	2.76
Average Score for Peer's Poor Attitudes Toward School (b) Overall Mean = 1.242; standard deviation = .289	1.28	1.17	1.20	1.27	1.24
Average Score for Positive Behavioral Climate in School (c) Overall Mean = 1.938; standard deviation = .441	1.83	2.05	1.84	1.92	1.96

Source: Author's tabulations with weighted data from the HSB Sophomore Cohort. Statistical tests indicate that there are statistically significant differences in each characteristic across racial and ethnic groups.

Notes: (a) This is the average score on questions where the range was from 1 (poor) to 4 (excellent). The questions dealt with the condition of buildings, library facilities, academic instruction, school's reputation in the community, teacher interest in the students, effective discipline, fairness of discipline, and school spirit.

(b) This is the average score on questions where 1 = true (good attitude) and 2 = false (bad attitude). The questions were: does your friend get good grades, is your friend interested in school, does your friend attend class regularly, and does your friend plan to go to college.

(c) This is the average score on questions where 1= often happens, 2 = sometimes happens, and 3 = rarely or never happens. The questions were: Students don't attend school, students cut classes, students talk back to teachers, students don't obey instructions, students fight with each other, and students attack teachers.

Explaining Racial and Ethnic Differences in High School Graduation

Table 5 contains the results of estimating four models of racial and ethnic differences in high school graduation. These models are estimated using logistic regression. The coefficients in the table for categorical variables are the effects of the specified category on the log odds of graduating from high school relative to the reference category. The coefficient for Black, for example, in Model 1 indicates that the log odds of graduating from high school is .418 lower for Blacks than for Whites (the reference category). The coefficients in the table for continuous variables are the effects of a one unit increase in the independent variable on the log odds of graduating from high school. The coefficient for number of siblings, for example, in Model 2 indicates that each additional sibling decreases the log odds of graduating from high school by .093.

Table 5
The Determinants of High School Graduation (Logistic Regression)

Variables	Model 1: Race and Gender	Model 2: Family Background	Model 3: Parenting Practices	Model 4: School Quality
Female	.268*	.318*	.225*	.193*
	(.0542)	(.0568)	(.0586)	(.0592)
RACE AND ETHNICITY (Reference category = white)				
Black	−.418*	.160*	.116	.103
	(.0787)	(.0873)	(.0887)	(.0901)
Hispanic	−.518*	−.164*	−.144*	−.140*
	(.0743)	(.0799)	(.0809)	(.0814)
Asian	.574*	1.015*	.964*	.887*
	(.3364)	(.3466)	(.3503)	(.3527)
American Indian	−.595*	−.137	−.112	−.0888
	(.2331)	(.2455)	(.2456)	(.2466)
FAMILY STRUCTURE AS SOPHOMORE (Reference category = Intact)				
Single Parent		−.429*	−.413*	−.425*
		(.0729)	(.0737)	(.0742)
Step Parent		−.429*	−.386*	−.364*
		(.0921)	(.0934)	(.0942)
Other Family		−.842*	−.785*	−.818*
		(.1097)	(.1112)	(.1116)
Number of Siblings		−.093*	−.070*	−.077*
		(.0229)	(.0233)	(.0235)
REGION OF THE COUNTRY WHEN SOPHOMORE (Reference category = NE)				
North Central		−.054	−.073	−.095
		(.0880)	(.0890)	(.0898)
South		−.202*	−.252*	−.291*
		(.0836)	(.0848)	(.0857)
West		−.351*	−.441*	−.473*
		(.0944)	(.0958)	(.0967)
RELIGION (Reference category = No religion)				
Catholic		.748*	.634*	.618*
		(.0850)	(.0863)	(.0878)
Other Religion		.495*	.417*	.407*
		(.0712)	(.0863)	(.0743)
NUMBER OF CHANGES IN SCHOOL DISTRICT SINCE AGE 5				
		−.274*	−.278*	−.261*
		(.0252)	(.0255)	(.0256)

Table 5 (continued)
The Determinants of High School Graduation (Logistic Regression)

Variables	Model 1: Race and Gender	Model 2: Family Background	Model 3: Parenting Practices	Model 4: School Quality
PARENTAL EDUCATION (Reference categories = Less Than High School)				
Father High School Grad		.270*	.265*	.271*
		(.0778)	(.0785)	(.0790)
Father Attended College		.655*	.548*	.516*
		(.0820)	(.0833)	(.0836)
Mother High School Grad		.403*	.370*	.374*
		(.0681)	(.0691)	(.0695)
Mother Attended College		.637*	.502*	.469*
		(.0823)	(.0838)	(.0843)
PARENTING PRACTICES				
Mother: Schoolwork			.286*	.244*
			(.0854)	(.0861)
Father: Schoolwork			.114	.087
			(.0710)	(.0713)
Parents Aware			.323*	.265*
			(.0693)	(.0699)
Never Talk with Parents			−.229*	−.182*
			(.0592)	(.0599)
Mother: Desires College			.771*	.670*
			(.0748)	(.0766)
SCHOOL QUALITY				
Dropout Rate				−.007
				(.0144)
Composite Facilities				.215*
				(.0357)
Bad Peer Orientation				−.617*
				(.0749)
Positive Behavioral Climate				.247*
				(.0551)
CONSTANT	1.693	1.537	.682	.685

Source: Calculations with data from the Sophomore Cohort of the High School and Beyond Survey.

Note: An * indicates that the coefficient is significant at or below the .10 level.

The first model is simply another way of demonstrating what is shown in Table 1: Asians are more likely to graduate from high school than are Whites, while American Indians are the least likely to graduate from high school.

In Model 2, the data are controlled for family background, including family structure, number of siblings, region, religion, residential mobility, and parental education. The results show that after controlling for these factors, Blacks are more likely to graduate from high school than are Whites, the difference between Whites and Hispanics becomes smaller, the difference between Asians and Whites becomes larger, and the difference between American Indians and Whites becomes insignificant. Obviously, then, the differences in the family characteristics of the racial and ethnic groups account for a good deal of the differences shown in Table 1, except for the difference between Asians and the other groups.

The effects of the family characteristics are what would be expected based on theory and on past research. The probability of completing high school is lower for those from disrupted families, decreases with the number of siblings, is higher for those with a religious affiliation, decreases with residential instability, and increases with parental education.

At least two aspects of the racial and ethnic differences in Model 2 described in Table 5 deserve additional comment. First, although it may seem surprising that Blacks are more likely to graduate from high school after controlling for family background, this finding is consistent with other research on Black/White differences mentioned above. The fact that Blacks are less likely to graduate from high school than are Whites is largely due to Black/White differences in family structure and parental education. Second, the increase in the difference between Asians and Whites is due to the concentration of Asians in the West, where the graduation rate is lower in these data, the greater likelihood of Asians having no religion, and the greater residential instability of Asians. These factors suppress the real difference in Asian and White graduation rates.

The addition of the remaining variables in Models 3 and 4 does little to alter the picture of racial and ethnic differences revealed in Model 2. Most of these additional variables do, however, have significant effects on high school graduation. Those students whose mothers monitor their school work, whose parents are always aware of their activities, who talk with their parents, and whose mother desires them to complete college are more likely to complete high school. All measures of school quality, with the exception of dropout rate, also have significant effects on high school completion.

Racial and Ethnic Differences in the Effects of Family Characteristics on High School Graduation

Table 6 contains the results of estimating Model 4 for each of the racial and ethnic groups separately. This is not a true test of racial and ethnic differences, but it does give us an indication of whether there are any likely differences. A true test involves estimating interactions between race and ethnicity and specific variables in Model 4.

For the purposes of this project, emphasis was placed on whether family structure and parenting practices have different effects for the racial and ethnic groups. The results for family structure show that individuals from other family arrangements, that is, those in which neither parent is present in the home, are significantly less likely than those from intact families to graduate from high school in each of the racial and ethnic groups. There are no significant differences between those in single-parent, step-parent, and two-parent families among American Indians, Asians, and Blacks, and no significant differences between those in step-parent and two-parent families among Hispanics. However, part of this is due to the fact that the sample sizes for the minority groups are smaller than those for whites.

It is computationally intractable to perform a sound test of the complete set of interactions between family structure and race and ethnicity. It is possible to simplify family structure by combining the three nonintact categories into one nonintact category. This procedure was done, and an interaction test to see if the effects of residing in a nonintact family were significantly different across the racial and ethnic groups was performed. The results suggest that the effects of residing in a nonintact family are significantly less for Blacks than for Whites, but do not differ significantly across the other racial and ethnic groups.

An interaction test for racial and ethnic differences in the effects of parenting practices was also performed, and the findings suggest that the effect of mother monitoring school performance was highest among American Indians and that the effect of talking with parents less than once a week was positive for Hispanics.

Table 6
School Quality Model for Each Racial Group (Logistic Regression)

Variables	American Indian	Asian	Black	Hispanic	White
Female	.485	.133	.357*	−.009	.181*
	(.5021)	(.5381)	(.1461)	(.1114)	(.0815)
FAMILY STRUCTURE AS SOPHOMORE (Reference category = Intact)					
Single Parent	−.861	.421	−.066	−.476*	−.524*
	(.6280)	(.7928)	(.1683)	(.1316)	(.1047)
Step Parent	−.373	1.259	.125	−.258	−.467*
	(.7626)	(1.990)	(.2524)	(.2061)	(.1236)
Other Family	−1.487*	−2.040*	−.482*	−.397*	−1.031*
	(.7667)	(.8203)	(.2190)	(.1970)	(.1748)
Number of Siblings	−.255	−.226	−.039	.009	−.101*
	(.1741)	(.2083)	(.0557)	(.0416)	(.0333)
REGION OF THE COUNTRY WHEN SOPHOMORE (Reference category = NE)					
North Central	−2.695*	.995	−.224	.223	−.119
	(1.008)	(1.099)	(.2263)	(.2004)	(.1196)
South	−1.970*	−.537	.204	−.120	−.458*
	(.9345)	(.8354)	(.1884)	(.1631)	(.1196)
West	−1.387	.744	.280	−.363*	−.572*
	(.9546)	(.8151)	(.3308)	(.1723)	(.1331)
RELIGION (Reference category = No religion)					
Catholic	.243	−.836	.331	.727*	.609*
	(.8727)	(.7806)	(.3238)	(.1419)	(.1239)
Other Religion	−.984	−.446	.476*	.829*	.300*
	(.6979)	(.7333)	(.1641)	(.1455)	(.1058)
NUMBER OF CHANGES IN SCHOOL DISTRICT SINCE AGE 5					
	−.636*	−.037	−.174*	−.314*	−.246*
	(.2068)	(.2353)	(.0635)	(.0475)	(.0359)
PARENTAL EDUCATION (Reference categories = Less Than High School)					
Father High School Grad	−.258	−.201	.439*	.153	.291*
	(.6431)	(.7876)	(.2289)	(.1523)	(.1052)
Father Attended College	2.199*	−.489	−.295	.152	.684*
	(.8376)	(.6880)	(.2358)	(.1675)	(.1109)
Mother High School Grad	−.881	.354	.427*	.576*	.319*
	(.5849)	(.6523)	(.1822)	(.1343)	(.0949)
Mother Attended College	.234	1.038	1.003*	.629*	.359*
	(.7178)	(.7151)	(.2350)	(.1730)	(.1122)

Table 6   (continued)
School Quality Model for Each Racial Group (Logistic Regression)

Variables	American Indian	Asian	Black	Hispanic	White
PARENTING PRACTICES					
Mother: Schoolwork	2.516*	–.512	.253	.191	.139
	(.8470)	(.8994)	(.1999)	(.1640)	(.1211)
Father: Schoolwork	–1.130	1.282	.107	.154	.106
	(.7250)	(.8340)	(.1609)	(.1328)	(.1004)
Parents Aware	1.223*	.408	.060	.451*	.214*
	(.6619)	(.6221)	(.1664)	(.1268)	(.0992)
Never Talk with Parents	–1.247*	–.218	.071	.207*	–.292*
	(.5173)	(.5705)	(.1470)	(.1123)	(.0827)
Mother: Desires College	.823	3.000*	.689*	.588*	.683*
	(.6027)	(.8245)	(.2280)	(.1384)	(.1032)
SCHOOL QUALITY					
Dropout Rate	.062	–.134	.081*	–.014	–.013
	(.1327)	(.0913)	(.0453)	(.0244)	(.0198)
Composite Facilities	–.110	.272	.012	.216*	.287*
	(.2608)	(.2948)	(.0748)	(.0607)	(.0537)
Bad Peer Orientation	–.760	–1.034	.166	–.619*	–.843*
	(.6721)	(.8223)	(.1826)	(.1370)	(.1073)
Positive Behavioral Climate	1.165*	.154	.373*	.145	.189*
	(.5216)	(.5264)	(.1154)	(.0952)	(.0822)
CONSTANT	2.518	.006	–.958	.254	.319

Source: Calculations with data from the Sophomore Cohort of the High School and Beyond Survey.

Note: An * indicates that the coefficient is significant at or below the .10 level.

Explaining Racial and Ethnic Differences in College Attendance

Next, racial and ethnic differences in college attendance were examined by, first, estimating models of the determinants of college attendance among those who completed high school; and, second, estimating a multinomial logit model with four possible outcomes: never completing high school, completing high school but never attending college, completing high school and entering a two-year college, or completing high school and entering a four-year college.

Table 7 contains the results of estimating four models, paralleling those in Table 5, of college attendance among those who had completed high school by 1986. The first model shows that Hispanics are least likely to attend college, Asians are most likely to attend

Table 7
The Determinants of College Attendance (Logistic Regression)

Variables	Model 1: Race and Gender	Model 2: Family Background	Model 3: Parenting Practices	Model 4: School Quality
Female	.127	.133	.109	.101
	(.0807)	(.0821)	(.0839)	(.0844)
RACE AND ETHNICITY (Reference category = white)				
Black	−.178	.140	.112	.096
	(.1322)	(.1434)	(.1441)	(.1454)
Hispanic	−.949*	−.662*	−.644*	−.645*
	(.1802)	(.1847)	(.1850)	(.1859)
Asian	.475*	.612*	.602*	.580*
	(.2909)	(.3006)	(.3004)	(.3018)
American Indian	−.110	.190	.223	.249
	(.4277)	(.4335)	(.4348)	(.4395)
FAMILY STRUCTURE AS SOPHOMORE (Reference category = Intact)				
Single Parent		.104	.093	.122
		(.1224)	(.1229)	(.1239)
Step Parent		−.069	−.069	−.029
		(.1594)	(.1599)	(.1604)
Other Family		−.709*	−.701*	−.724*
		(.3597)	(.3602)	(.3614)
Number of Siblings		−.072*	−.067*	−.058*
		(.0347)	(.0377)	(.0380)
REGION OF THE COUNTRY WHEN SOPHOMORE (Reference category = NE)				
North Central		−.041	−.043	−.077
		(.1117)	(.1119)	(.1126)
South		.017	.013	−.018
		(.1144)	(.1148)	(.1154)
West		−.284	−.317*	−.349*
		(.1411)	(.1414)	(.1420)
RELIGION (Reference category = No religion)				
Catholic		.440*	.414*	.560*
		(.1534)	(.1542)	(.1615)
Other Religion		.326*	.308*	.474*
		(.1437)	(.1446)	(.1519)

Table 7 (continued)
The Determinants of College Attendance (Logistic Regression)

Variables	Model 1: Race and Gender	Model 2: Family Background	Model 3: Parenting Practices	Model 4: School Quality
NUMBER OF CHANGES IN SCHOOL DISTRICT SINCE AGE 5				
		−.054	−.055	−.048
		(.0461)	(.0462)	(.0466)
PARENTAL EDUCATION (Reference categories = Less Than High School)				
Father High School Grad		.125	.103	.117
		(.1301)	(.1307)	(.1314)
Father Attended College		.750*	.700*	.689*
		(.1107)	(.1115)	(.1119)
Mother High School Grad		−.032	−.046	−.038
		(.1231)	(.1238)	(.1243)
Mother Attended College		.559*	.487*	.444*
		(.1191)	(.1199)	(.1204)
PARENTING PRACTICES				
Mother: Schoolwork			.117	.186
			(.1661)	(.1723)
Father: Schoolwork			−.070	−.074
			(.1222)	(.1246)
Parents Aware			−.127	−.179
			(.1145)	(.1172)
Never Talk with Parents			−.206*	−.193*
			(.0926)	(.0941)
Mother: Desires College			1.008*	.841*
			(.2550)	(.2564)
SCHOOL QUALITY				
Dropout Rate				−.000
				(.0002)
Composite Facilities				−.123*
				(.0632)
Bad Peer Orientation				−.955*
				(.1400)
Positive Behavioral Climate				.409*
				(.0934)
CONSTANT	−2.811	−3.480	−4.196	−3.564

Source: Calculations with data from the Sophomore Cohort of the High School and Beyond Survey.

Note: An * indicates that the coefficient is significant at or below the .10 level.

college, and there are no significant differences among Blacks, American Indians, and Whites. It is important to remember, of course, that this is based on analyses only of those who have finished high school.

The results for Model 2 in Table 7 show that, after adjusting for differences in family background, the difference between Hispanics and Whites is somewhat smaller, but still statistically significant, while the difference between Asians and Whites actually increases. As was the case with the high school graduation results, the difference in the Asian/White college attendance rates was suppressed by the concentration of Asians in the West, where college attendance rates are lower, and the higher likelihood of Asians having no religion.

Some factors that were significantly related to high school graduation are not significantly related to college attendance. These factors include residential mobility and whether or not a parent graduated from high school. Those students who resided in single-parent and step-parent families as adolescents are just as likely to attend college as those who resided in two-parent families, but those who resided in households with no parent are much less likely to attend college. The number of siblings, religious affiliation, and whether or not the parents attended college are significantly associated with college attendance as well as with high school graduation.

Adding parenting practices or school quality measures to the equations has little effect on the Asian/Hispanic/White differences. Among the parenting measures, talking with parents and mother's aspirations are significantly associated with college attendance. Among the school quality measures, peer orientation and behavioral climate are significantly associated with college attendance, as is the measure of school facilities. The sign of the latter variable, however, is negative, which is not what would be expected nor what is found with high school graduation.

Table 8 contains selected results from estimating a series of multinomial logistic regression models in which the independent variables were those used in Models 1–4 in Tables 5 and 7. The nonintact categories of family structure were combined to create a dichotomous family structure variable: intact versus nonintact.

Panel A shows the "unadjusted" odds ratios in which the odds of a particular educational outcome are compared to those of not finishing high school. These are based on a model in which the only variables were race/ethnicity and gender. These ratios have a fairly straightforward interpretation. The Black/White ratio of .625

for high school graduation only versus not graduating from high school means that the odds of Blacks completing high school only are .625 of those for Whites. In general these odds ratios reflect what one sees in Table 1, that is, that there are not only racial and ethnic differences in high school graduation but also in the likelihood of entering a two-year or a four-year college.

Panel B presents the odds ratios for the alternative educational outcomes after adjusting for family background, parenting practices, and school characteristics. The results show that the differences in the odds of each of the educational outcomes among American Indians, Blacks, Hispanics, and Whites are smaller after these adjustments. In fact, the odds for Blacks and Whites do not differ significantly. On the other hand, the differences between Asians and the other groups are larger *after* adjustments are made.

The results in Panel C can be used to assess which characteristics are important in distinguishing among who finishes high school and who does not finish high school, and which characteristics also influence whether one goes on to college or not. The pattern of

Table 8
Odds Ratios for Initial College Attended
Based on Multinomial Logit Models

	HS Only/ No HS Grad	2 Yr Coll/ No HS Grad	4 Yr Coll/ No HS Grad
A. Unadjusted			
American Indian/White	.648	.324*	.289*
Asian American/White	.583	2.344*	2.276*
Black/White	.625*	.476*	.392*
Hispanic/White	.718*	.492*	.271*
B. Adjusted for Family Background, Parenting Practices and School Characteristics			
American Indian/White	.846	.414*	.560*
Asian American/White	.955	3.115*	4.446*
Black/White	.873	.877	.879
Hispanic/White	.911	.668*	.500*
C. Effects of Selected Characteristics			
Mother High School Graduate	1.613*	1.753*	1.783*
Father High School Graduate	1.305*	1.513*	1.441*
Mother Attended College	1.415*	2.479*	3.580*
Father Attended College	1.148*	2.045*	3.564*
Nonintact Family	.586*	.567*	.466*
Mother Desires College	1.612*	4.438*	8.504*

Source: Multinomial logistic regression models using data from the Sophomore Cohort of the High School and Beyond Survey.

Note: An * indicates that the odds ratio is significant at or below the .10 level.

effects for mother's and father's high school graduation, for example, suggests that this factor is important in determining whether one graduates from high school or not, but does not really distinguish among who goes to college or what kind of college they first attend. The pattern of effects for mother's and father's college attendance, on the other hand, suggests that this not only affects high school graduation, but whether or not someone attends college, and what type of college they first attend. These support the findings about parental education in Table 7.

Whether or not one resided in a nonintact family as a sophomore affects whether or not one finishes high school, but residential status does not distinguish among those who do and do not attend college, nor the type of college first attended. Having a mother who desires her children to attend college affects high school graduation, college attendance, and the type of college first attended.

Summary and Conclusions

This project addressed two principal questions: (1) What are the major variations in the structure and functioning of families across the principal racial and ethnic groups in the United States? and (2) Do these variations in families help account for racial and ethnic differences in educational attainment?

The results show that Black, Hispanic, and American Indian sophomores in 1980 were disadvantaged relative to White sophomores in that their parents were less educated, they were less likely to live in an intact family, and they were more likely to live in larger families. In addition, American Indian, Black, and Hispanic sophomores were significantly less likely than White sophomores to have their school work monitored by their parents. American Indian and Hispanic sophomores talked with their parents significantly less than White sophomores, and had parents whose aspirations were lower than those of White sophomores.

In attempting to answer the second question posed above, the findings suggest that the lower high school graduation rates and college attendance rates of American Indians, Blacks, and Hispanics were in part due to differences in family background, that is, family structure, number of siblings, and parental education. This corresponds with previous research on Black/White/Hispanic differences using other data (Hauser, 1991), and shows that a similar pattern emerges for American Indians. Differences in family background, parenting practices, and school quality do not, however, explain any of the difference in educational outcomes between Asians and Whites.

The results suggest some possible approaches to pursuing racial and ethnic parity in educational outcomes. Given the importance of marital disruption in explaining racial and ethnic differences in educational outcomes, we must ask ourselves as a society what we can do to overcome the effects of marital disruption on children. In other work with my colleague Sara McLanahan, we demonstrate that a good deal of the effect of marital disruption on educational outcomes is due to the differences in the income levels of one-parent and two-parent families (McLanahan & Sandefur, 1994). Other research by economists, sociologists, and other social scientists reaches a similar conclusion. One way to overcome some of the effects of growing up with a single parent is to improve the income and income security of single parents by insuring that non-custodial parents, generally fathers, pay their fair share of support for their children. This would help children in all single-parent families, and because minority children are more likely to live in such families, would also work toward parity in educational outcomes.

Second, parents should recognize that their decisions to bear children out-of-wedlock or divorce after their children are born creates disadvantages for their children. This suggests that a decision to become a single-parent family should be made very carefully and that parents must work hard to overcome the disadvantages created by such a decision.

Finally, we as a society must recognize that parental education and family structure, though in some respects due to the choices of parents, are *ascribed* characteristics for children that affect their likelihood of educational success. We must work to insure that the barriers to educational success created by these traits are erased by providing encouragement, support, and financial assistance to children from disadvantaged backgrounds to allow them to take advantage of the educational opportunities available in American society.

Notes

1. Acknowledgments: The research was supported by grants from the Assistant Secretary for Planning and Evaluation-Department of Health and Human Services and the National Institute of Child Health and Human Development to the Center for Demography and Ecology and the Institute for Research on Poverty at the University of Wisconsin–Madison. I thank Steve Cook and Enilda Arbona for their research assistance, Michael Herrell for his helpful comments and suggestions, and Paul Dudenhefer for proofreading the final version.

2. One must keep in mind that each of these major racial and/or ethnic group-ings contains a very heterogeneous set of people. The Hispanic category, for example, contains people of Mexican, Puerto Rican, Central American, and South American origin, as well as people who have just immigrated to the United States and some whose families have been in the United States for several generations.

3. An example of differences in findings is Hauser's (1991) finding using data from the Current Population Surveys that the chances of college entry were high-est among Hispanics and lowest among Blacks in the late 1980s, while Alexander et al. (1987) and Thomas et al. (1979) using data from the National Longitudinal Survey of the Class of 1972 found that Blacks were most likely and Hispanics least likely to enroll in four-year colleges. Here, both the differences in data sets and the difference in time periods probably help explain the differences in findings. All three studies conclude, however, that family background is an important con-tributor to racial and ethnic differences in educational outcomes.

4. The data from the sophomore cohort do not permit an examination of comple-tion of college since many individuals who were high school sophomores in 1980 will not have had time to complete college by 1986. I am in the process of conducting analyses of college completion using data from the senior cohort.

5. The percentage of American Indian women who do not have a high school diploma by 1986 seems very high and may be due to a few unusual cases in a relatively small sample.

6. One must be cautious in interpreting the effects of the school characteristics in this chapter. This is because the HSB was collected by first sampling high schools, so a good number of individuals in the sample share high schools and, thus, high school characteristics. In this chapter, high school characteristics are treated in the same way as individual characteristics and family background. Social scientists have devised more appropriate ways of including high school characteristics in multivariate analysis. The focus in this chapter, however, is primarily on family background and parenting practices, and school characteris-tics are included primarily as controls.

References

Alexander, K. L., Riordan, C., Fennessey, J., & Pallas, A. M. (1982). Social background, academic resources, and college graduation: Recent evi-dence from the National Longitudinal Survey. *American Journal of Education, 90,* 315–333.

Alexander, K. L., Holupka, S., & Pallas, A. M. (1987). Social background and academic determinants of two-year versus four-year college at-tendance: Evidence from two cohorts a decade apart. *American Jour-nal of Education, 96,* 56–80.

Bean, F. D. & Tienda, M. (1987). *The Hispanic population of the United States.* New York: Russell Sage Foundation.

Furstenberg, F. F., Jr., Morgan, S. P., Moore, K. A., & Peterson, J. L. (1987). Race differences in the timing of adolescent intercourse. *American Sociological Review, 52,* 511–518.

Gamoran, A. (1992, January). Social factors in education. *Institute for Research on Poverty Notes and Comments.* Madison, WI.

Hauser, R. M. (1991). Trends in college entry among Whites, Blacks, and Hispanics, 1972–1988. *Institute for Research on Poverty Discussion Paper 958–91,* Madison, WI: University of Wisconsin.

Hauser, R. M., & Phang, H. S. (1993). Trends in high school dropout among Whites, Black, and Hispanic youth, 1973 to 1989. *Institute for Research on Poverty DP 1007–93.* Madison, WI.

McLanahan, S., & Sandefur, G. (1994). *Growing up with a single parent: What hurts and what helps?* Cambridge: Harvard University Press.

Sandefur, G.D., McLanahan, S., & Wojtkiewicz, R. (1989). Race and ethnicity, family structure, and high school graduation. *Institute for Research on Poverty DP 893–89.* Madison, WI: University of Wisconsin.

Thomas, G. E., Alexander, K. L., & Eckland, B. K. (1979). Access to higher education: The importance of race, sex, social class, and academic credentials. *School Review, 87,* 133–156.

Chapter 3

Factors Promoting Marital Resilience Among Interracial Couples

Anna Y. Chan and Elaine Wethington

Relatively few empirical studies have examined marital relationships among interracial couples. The majority of these studies, moreover, concentrate on the negative aspects of these marriages, such as the expectation that interracial couples will have a greater probability of divorce than same-race couples (e.g., Jeong & Schumm, 1990; Rankin & Maneker, 1987). The assumptions underlying such studies are that interracial marriage is a "stressor" and that exposure to stress undermines marital adjustment (White, 1990), although the latter assumption is not always warranted (see Glenn, 1990). Thus, speculation in the literature on the well-being and stability of such marriages is mostly negative.

The theoretical perspectives asserting that interracial marriages are by their nature more difficult, unstable, and conflictual than other marriages (Gordon, 1964) remain to be supported (Spickard, 1989). Direct empirical tests of the assumptions underlying the traditional stress perspective on interracial marriage are rare, as are detailed descriptions of the processes thought to contribute to less harmonious relations. This chapter develops a theoretical perspective on adjustment in interracial marriage that is based on the concept of *resilience* rather than stress.

A resilience perspective on interracial marriages differs from more traditional approaches by paying as much attention to positive resources brought by individuals to these marriages as to the social and personal circumstances that may threaten marital stability. It also redefines the outcome of interest, shifting the focus from negative emotional adjustment and unhappiness to "competence" and good coping (Luthar, 1993). Resilience is generally viewed as a process encompassing the management of environmental and social challenges that would be expected to threaten well-being and functioning (Werner, 1990). As a consequence, the resilience approach elaborates not only circumstances under which a marriage is likely to be a failure, but also the circumstances that produce success.

From a resilience perspective, this chapter reviews and critiques research on marital relations and stability among interracial couples, focusing on five issues: (1) demographic characteristics and social resources of those who marry interracially; (2) the particular racial combination of the partners, including whether the husband or the wife is a member of a more socially dominant group; (3) challenges facing interracial marriages, including rearing biracial children; (4) personal factors that promote the selection of an individual into an interracial marriage and affect commitment to the marriage; and (5) the social context of interracial marriage, including social prejudice, the availability of same-race marital partners, and social network support for the couple. Throughout, there is a particular focus on Asian-White intermarriage, a major proportion of interracial marriages in the United States.

Traditional Theoretical Perspectives

Traditional perspectives have tended to view interracial marriage as a potential psychological threat. For example, Park (1928) asserted that individuals whose lives spanned two cultures—ethnic or racial—were "marginal" to both, and thus were prone to confusion, loss of identity, alienation, and distress. If one accepts the assumption that undertaking an intimate relationship with someone of another race would produce marginality (or be attractive only to those who are already marginal), it is then not surprising that studies of interracial marriage would focus on instability, conflict, and distress (e.g., Baber, 1937; Rankin & Maneker, 1987). Early psychological studies emphasized the deviant or "marginal" personality characteristics of those who married interracially (for discussions of this literature, see Porterfield, 1978; Cretser & Leon, 1982). Sociological and anthropological studies (e.g., Lee & Yamanaka, 1990) have viewed the "problem" of interracial marriage as arising from an inability to assimilate or acculturate to the culture of one's marital partner, difficulty brought about by demands for rapid assimilation or acculturation (Jeong & Schumm, 1990), or racial prejudice (e.g., Porterfield, 1978). From either an assimilation or acculturation perspective, success or failure in an interracial marriage is predicted to correlate with qualities such as the assimilation status and goals of the minority spouse's group, social distance between the two racial groups represented in the marriage, or the resolution of the status inconsistency between the partner from the dominant racial group and the partner from the subordinate group.

It is curious, however, that theoretical perspectives on adjustment in interracial marriage have not yet thoroughly incorporated major critiques of marginality theory, despite their long-standing history as alternatives. Goldberg (1941), for example, argued that living on the edges of two cultures could provide psychological benefits, such as increased opportunity for the development of social competence, other sorts of personal growth, and social network expansion (but see Gibbs, 1987). Only a handful of the more recent studies of interracial marriage have seriously considered the possibility of positive psychological effects accruing to those in interracial marriages (e.g., Sung, 1990). In contrast, research on the psychological impact of biculturalism on individual development now reflects the view that biracial and bicultural individuals can develop competence rather than suffer loss of social and cultural identity (LaFromboise, Coleman, & Gerton, 1993).

Why is this so? There are a number of methodological reasons that may account for a lack of recent research attention and critical evaluation of traditional assumptions about interracial marital relations. The most important factor is that data are hard to come by. Interracial couples are still relatively rare, despite an increasing prevalence (U.S. Bureau of the Census, 1993). This fact makes systematic sampling through surveys very expensive and difficult. Frequently, census data on divorce are used to make inferences about the marital relations of interracial couples. Unfortunately, census data do not tell us anything directly about marital relationships other than their relative stability over an estimated period of time; moreover, census data may undercount interracial couples (Monahan, 1976). In order to address questions about the quality of marital relationships per se, researchers have turned to methods that produce more detailed, but less generalizable, findings. Most of the more recent studies utilize convenience or snowball samples (e.g., Sung, 1990), gather data from public records in relatively limited geographic areas (e.g., Rankin & Maneker, 1987), or confine recruitment to very specific populations, such as Korean wives of American servicemen (e.g., Jeong & Schumm, 1990) or well-educated New Yorkers (Sung, 1990). Except for the use of public records, these methods have not resulted in the recruitment of widely representative samples, although much useful data have been acquired.

As noted earlier, the community survey approach can be an inefficient way to deal with the respondent selection problem, even in localities where interracial marriages are more common, such as Hawaii and California. (Screening costs would be enormous, given that married-couple households are now less than half of all households, and interracial couples comprise only 2% of all marriages [U.S. Bureau of the Census, 1993].)

Even very large survey datasets, with thousands of respondents, contain only a relative handful of interracial couples for analysis. For example, Chan (1992) examined the satisfaction and perceived future stability reported by interracial couples using the National Survey of Families and Households, a sample of 13,107 households. Consistent with population numbers, less than 2% of the married couples represented were interracial, and for 20% of the total sample, race was not ascertainable for one member of a couple. Such relative numbers severely limited the power to draw inferences.

In addition to such methodological difficulties, there are a number of theoretical issues that have also limited research and new theory development on interracial marital relations. The most salient deterrent is the assumption that interracial contact of any sort is fraught with conflict, misunderstanding, and rejection and as a consequence, is stressful. Many interracial contacts undoubtedly are. Relationship context, however, does make a difference, and it has been asserted that the sort of intimate love relationship that brings about marriage compensates for such difficulties (Mathabane & Mathabane, 1993; Porterfield, 1978).

Adopting a positive or "resilience" perspective, moreover, goes against the grain established in areas of research related to the issues examined in interracial marriages. Most notably, attention to potentially positive aspects or sequelae of stressful situations is almost nonexistent (Schaefer & Moos, 1992). Given that marriage results in positive changes for most who undertake it (Perlman & Rook, 1987), adopting assumptions from the "typical" stress perspective may be inappropriate, if not misleading, as a way to understand the processes leading to adaptation in interracial marriages.

Despite an explosion of research on stress and stress processes, research paradigms typically utilized in the area of stress are remarkably consistent in their assumptions. Stress research in general has neglected to attend to the ways in which challenges, even acutely stressful challenges, can produce social competence and emotional and psychological growth, as well as emotional tension and breakdown (e.g., Schaefer and Moos, 1992).

Some of the neglect may be due to the power of the paradigm itself: stress by definition produces emotional discomfort, and even positive challenging situations such as getting married, moving to a bigger and better house, or being promoted at work are classified as "life changes" by researchers (Holmes & Rahe, 1967) and as "stress" by the public (e.g., Kaminer, 1992). Another similar situation is evident in current social role and mental health research, where the negative impacts of role overload on mental health and psychological functioning (e.g., Hochschild, 1989) continue to be emphasized even though the positive impact of holding multiple roles has been documented (e.g., Thoits, 1983, 1986; Wethington & Kessler, 1989).

Another source of difficulty is the lack of an accepted distinction in the minds of many observers and researchers between environmental stress and individual vulnerability to stressors. Environmental stress is most usefully construed and measured as an objective factor, outside the individual (Dohrenwend & Dohrenwend, 1981). Vulnerability, in contrast, is best defined as a personal or social characteristic that makes a person more likely to experience distress under a particular type of stressor (Brown & Harris, 1978; Luthar, 1993). In everyday speech and thought, as well as in research on "risk factors" (as interracial marriage tends to be viewed), environmental stress and vulnerability to the stress are confounded, leading to the facile conclusion that everyone who marries interracially is inevitably under stress.

The Utility of a Resilience Perspective

Three major advantages arise from the resilience perspective in the analysis of interracial marital relations and stability. First, the resilience perspective automatically frames the research questions to address the long-term process of adaptation involving the development of competence as well as to address short-term negative emotional responses. Studies of resiliency in children have found that these personal properties are distinct (Luthar, 1993). Second, the resilience perspective gives attention to both individual resources and strengths as well as the situation, thus reducing the social and psychological "determinism" that seems to result from using the traditional approach; people are not alike, and do not marry for the same reasons. Third, important life course and historical factors affecting marital relations are easier to incorporate into a resilience perspective; clearly, social contexts also vary among places and times.

Most importantly, the resilience perspective views the intimate marital relationship in an interracial marriage as a resource to the couple, rather than as a basis for conflict. Rather than as a condition producing marginality and distress, the development of an intimate interracial relationship can be construed as a challenge through which an individual or couple can become more adapted to a multiracial society and can develop the capacity to endure and flourish. The processes by which this happens arise from the developing strength of the marital relationship itself, the capacities and strengths that individuals bring to these relationships (primarily through their greater education in comparison to those in same-race marriages), and the relationship that builds through shared adversity and exposure to new ideas.

Factors Promoting Resiliency in Interracial Marriages

This section of the chapter reviews the more recent research on marital adaptation, quality, and stability in interracial marriages. A number of consistent findings have emerged from these studies regarding the demographic characteristics of those who marry interracially, the greater likelihood of some racial combinations achieving stability than others, challenges faced by the interracially married, selection into interracial marriage, and the social contexts that promote and support such marriages. The literature review includes speculations about how current research has contributed to the development of a resilience perspective.

Demographic Factors

A consistent finding in contemporary studies of interracial marriages is that these couples tend to be older, more educated, and they tend to have higher incomes (Kitano & Yeung, 1982; Rankin & Maneker, 1987; Sung, 1990; Tucker & Mitchell-Kernan, 1990) than same-race (minority) couples. These characteristics are, on average, associated with greater marital stability (White, 1990).

It is also possible that some earlier observations of heightened conflict in interracial marriages were inappropriately generalized from marriages where one of the partners was less proficient in

English to all interracial marriages. A number of interracial marriages in the U.S. involve foreign-born spouses (see Rankin & Maneker, 1987). One recent small study ($n = 35$) has found that lower proficiency in English is related to lower marital and overall life satisfaction among interracial couples (Jeong & Schumm, 1990). English proficiency is in turn associated with income, education, and length of residence in the U.S. (Jeong & Schumm, 1990). Hence the interracial couples most vulnerable to marital distress may be those with lower incomes, less education, and shorter residence of the foreign-born partner in the U.S. These factors need to be examined in a larger and more representative sample of interracially married couples.

Differential Stability of Racial Combinations

It has long been known that racial combination is an important factor to consider regarding marital stability. Some particular combinations are more likely to encounter social prejudice and family opposition than others (Baber, 1937; Porterfield, 1978). Physical appearance, the historical relationship between the two groups, and the number of generations the family of the minority partner has been in the U.S. clearly matter (Spickard, 1989). For example, Baber (1937), in one of the earliest studies on black-white interracial marriage, found that interracial couples in which the minority spouse was of darker complexion reported lower marital happiness than marriages involving more light-complexioned minority partners. This study suggests that some combinations are more likely to encounter social prejudice than others, particularly couples where one of the spouses is African-American and the other white. More recently, Rankin and Maneker (1987) found that black husband-White wife marriages are more likely to end in divorce than white husband-black wife marriages. They attribute the difference to greater economic pressure, peer disapproval, and racism directed at black husbands.

Indeed, racial prejudice is usually cited as the reason for why some interracial marriages combinations are relatively rare and others more common. Lee and Yamanaka (1990), analyzing 1980 census data, found that Asian Americans outmarry at a much greater rate than Blacks or Americans of Latin/Hispanic origin (25.4% versus 2.2% and 12.7%, respectively). This is consistent with the expectation that relationships with the dominant social group and social relationships between minority groups may deter certain interracial marriages.

Gender relations also seem to play a role in whether particular combinations come about. Approximately four times as many African-American men marry "out" as do African-American women, with wide regional variations (Tucker & Mitchell-Kernan, 1990). The reasons for the gender differentiation remain unclear because the demographic correlates of outmarriage are virtually identical for both men and women (Taylor, Chatters, Tucker, & Lewis, 1990). Interracially married blacks are likely to have moved away from their place of birth, and to have been raised in a more socially tolerant region of the U.S. (Tucker & Mitchell-Kernan, 1990). In a study of two southern states, Schoen and Wooldredge (1989) reported that interracially married black men were, on average, more highly educated than same-race married black men. Carter and Glick (1976) reported that black men who attended graduate school were the most likely to be married interracially. Taylor and colleagues (1990) have suggested, however, that the gender difference in entering into interracial marriage is related to traditional minority community discouragement of such marriages having more impact on women than men. In contrast, Collins (1985) theorized that black women value their independence and purposefully avoid marriage with white men, to whom they would be doubly socially subservient.

Gender relations also play a particularly large role in the marital choices of Asian immigrants and Asian Americans, although the gender difference in regard to interracial marriages is the reverse of that seen in African-Americans. Asian males are more likely to marry other Asians than are Asian females (U.S. Bureau of the Census, 1972). (For example, 32% of Japanese American women and 27% of Filipino women were married interracially in 1970 [U.S. Bureau of the Census, 1972]). In this case, traditional Asian family customs are probably the most salient factor. Asian males have been responsible for continuing the family line, while the marriages of daughters are considered less important (Chan, 1992; Sung, 1990). This pattern has held true for all generations of immigrants from Asia, persisting well beyond the first generation (Spickard, 1989). Historical development should also not be discounted as an explanation for the high interracial marriage rate for some groups of Asian Americans. The improved image of Asians in the U.S. over this century has resulted in less social disapproval being experienced by white-Asian intermarriages (Spickard, 1989).

It would be instructive to see whether marital adjustment among different interracial marital combinations varies in relationship to the relative frequency of such marriages, in contrast to their normative social acceptability. Unfortunately, few studies have compared marital relations across different interracial marriage combinations, although studies of divorce indicate that divorce rates differ (e.g., Ho & Johnson, 1990). Chan (1992) examined the relationship between racial combination and multiple indicators of marital adjustment in Asian-white, black-white, and other interracial marriages, using data from the National Survey of Families and Households. Contrary to the expectation that, on average, interracial marriages would be reported as less satisfactory and less stable than same-race marriages, a more complicated and interesting pattern emerged. The only combination with significantly worse satisfaction and perceived future stability than same-race marriages involved Asian wives married to white husbands. There was also a tendency (not statistically significant) for the white partners in interracial marriages to report less satisfaction than whites in same-race marriages. Unfortunately, the dataset did not contain measures through which explanations for these patterns could be more carefully examined.

Challenges Facing
Interracial Marriages

A number of unique and threatening problems have been attributed to interracial marriages, situations that are apt to create problems in communication or cause conflict. The most significant of the unique problems are family opposition to the marriage, cultural and gender role expectation differences, and difficulties rearing biracial children (Porterfield, 1978; Spickard, 1989).

Family Opposition. Opposition from family members is typically reported as a significant source of difficulty for all racial combinations of interracially married couples. Family opposition is associated with the number of generations an Asian family has been in the U.S. First-generation Asian immigrants are less likely to marry out, possibly because they are more likely to encounter and be influenced by traditional cultural attitudes and expectations. They are also more likely to experience more parental control during dating and courtship. Lack of proficiency in English and greater residential segregation may also reduce the chance of intermarriage among first-generation immigrants (Kitano, Yeung, Chai, & Hatanaka, 1984; Lee & Yamanaka, 1990; Sung, 1990).

Family opposition may also facilitate divorce as an option to solve marital problems. Interracial couples who lack support and acceptance from their families may experience fewer barriers when considering divorce; in fact, they may be more likely to blame their marital problems on differences between culture of origin (Imamura, 1986). Nevertheless, case studies that considered how partners cope with family opposition found that family opposition abates over time (Mathabane & Mathabane, 1993; Sung, 1990). Imamura (1986) suggested that many families successfully conceal their opposition from the interracial couple.

Cultural and Gender Role Differences. One of the major ways in which cultural differences could produce marital stress and instability is through differences in gender role expectations. These differences are associated with higher distress (Ross, Mirowsky, & Huber, 1983) and marital difficulties (Hochschild, 1989). A study of mixed race marriages in Nigeria (Imamura, 1986) bears out this expectation, where differences in gender role expectations were associated with lower marital happiness.

Differences in gender role expectations may be brought about by differences in upbringing. Conflicts may be particularly upsetting for interracially married Asian wives. For example, Asian American wives may find that their expectations for an egalitarian marriage are violated by husbands who may have expectations of more traditional behavior from them, simply because they are Asian. In couples where Asian wives are traditional and the husbands prefer this gender role division, the marriage is likely to be very stable (Chan, 1992). Premarital socialization among some Asian women, moreover, may also play a part in contributing to marital stability. Connor (1976) suggested that Japanese-born women in interracial marriages weathered marital crises better for having been prepared to believe that the life of a married woman is very difficult.

On the other hand, one small study of Asian-white marriages in which the partners were well-educated suggested that many of these marriages are just as likely to be nontraditional and nonconventional as otherwise (Sung, 1990). Many interracial couples may also be aided by *not* having a traditional orientation. Given that their networks are more likely to contain nonkin (Spickard, 1989), their marital interactions may be less gender-differentiated; they may be more likely to have joint conjugal role relationships where husband and wife share many activities together without the expectation of differentiation (Bott, 1971).

Biracial Children. Some researchers have argued that interracial couples will have fewer children because they are concerned about the social "marginality" of their children (Sung, 1990). It is known that interracial couples tend to have fewer children than same-race couples. In a review of the relevant literature, Sung (1990) found that depending on the sample, 30-49% of interracially married Chinese are childless. Since children are a barrier to divorce, childless couples may be more likely to dissolve their marriages. This relationship, however, has only been established among black-white intermarriages (Rankin & Maneker, 1987).

Concern over the well-being of interracial children, however, may be an overcautious response. Social workers and other related professionals have noticed an increased number of biracial adolescents with behavioral problems (Gibbs, 1987; Lyles, Yancey, Grace, & Carter, 1985; McRoy & Freeman, 1986). This perceived increase in numbers could be due to the nature of the clinical populations studied or a reflection of increasing numbers of biracial children.

An empirical study of child behavioral problems in a sample drawn from a non-clinical population, however, revealed no differences between biracial and uniracial offspring on an index of psychological well-being (Johnson & Nagoshi, 1986). Similarly, a student sample drawn from nonclinical populations (Stephan & Stephan, 1991) found no differences in behavioral problems between biracial and other students. In fact, Stephan and Stephan documented positive outcomes among mixed-heritage students; specifically, they were more likely to engage in intergroup contact and have positive attitudes toward minority groups, display greater language facility, and report more appreciation of the culture of minority groups. It should be noted that Stephan and Stephan's study was done in Hawaii and New Mexico, two states where minority culture may be more appreciated and valued. Thus it is unclear whether the same results would be found in locations where there is greater social prejudice and intolerance.

Selection Into Interracial Marriage

The choice to undertake an interracial marriage is undoubtedly affected by racial prejudice (Taylor, Chatters, Tucker, & Lewis, 1990). As a corollary, it is also possible that those who marry interracially may be resistant to or protected from the effects of social prejudice, immune to family opposition, or simply socially competent and tolerant.

One of the few to measure these personal characteristics, Sung (1990) found that her interracially married respondents were more flexible and resourceful in dealing with individual differences. They were likely to have combatted and overcome strong family objections to the marriage as well as other social sanctions. Moreover, they all had married for love, a finding consistent with

Porterfield's (1978) study of black-white interracial marriages. Marriage for love is associated with greater marital stability (Whyte, 1990).

Social Context as a Resource

There is little research linking differences in social context to adaptation and stability of interracial marriages. Three contextual factors, however, are likely to be associated with marital success: prejudice and community acceptance; availability of same-race marital partners; and the structure of personal social networks.

Prejudice and Community Acceptance. One important factor of social context is community and regional acceptance of interracial marriages. Rates of interracial marriage are found to be higher on the West coast of the U.S., where tolerance of racial differences is somewhat greater (Spickard, 1989).

A number of studies are consistent with this interpretation. Tucker and Mitchell-Kernan (1990) examined black-white interracial marriages in Los Angeles. They found that blacks born in the northern part of the U.S. or in a foreign country were more likely to be married to nonblacks than the sample average. They interpreted this as an indication that moving away from community of origin to a more permissive or tolerant environment (in regard to race) would facilitate interracial marriage.

Similar contextual factors operate to facilitate Asian-white intermarriage. Sung (1990) found that moving away from community of origin may facilitate racial outmarriage since nonacceptance of interracial marriages is just as strong from the minority family as from the dominant race family. Consistent with Sung's observation, Lee and Yamanaka (1990) reported that outmarried Asian American women are more likely to be residing in states other than California and Hawaii, even though Asian Americans are concentrated in those states. Although it may also reflect lack of opportunity to marry someone of Asian origin as well, Lee and Yamanaka suggest that distance from a traditional Asian community increases the chance of interracial marriage. Distance may also contribute to interracial marital stability, because the spouses are emotionally dependent on each other.

Availability of Same-Race Partners. Interracial marriage rates are affected by minority group size and sex ratio (Cretser & Leon, 1982); specifically, when ethnic or racial minority communities are small, the sex ratio is likely to be unbalanced, and more interracial marriages will occur. Group size may also be a relevant variable for explaining marital relations and stability. The size of the minority group and its concentration may reflect how much support or discouragement an interracial couple will experience (Spickard, 1989). If peer discouragement does have a negative impact on marital relationships, then interracial marriages should be more stable outside ethnic enclaves.

Social Networks. It is commonly believed that interracial couples are ostracized and have limited social support, or at least run that risk (Porterfield, 1978). However, the fact that many interracial couples are likely to form among those of higher education attainment (Rankin & Maneker, 1987; Sung, 1990) and outside segregated neighborhoods suggests that interracial couples could, on average, have larger networks (Wellman, 1981). Education is the single most predictive factor of network structure (Cochran, Larner, Riley, Gunnarsson, & Henderson, 1990; Fischer, 1982). People with more education have more numerous and diverse relationships, as well as better social skills. More education also promotes employment, providing more opportunity for network building.

People with more education are also likely to have more nonkin network members (Fischer, 1982). Importantly, nonkin members may (in the absence of kin) provide critical functions of support. Among those interracial couples who live far away from their kin (Tucker & Mitchell-Kernan, 1990), social networks probably tend to be nonkin dominated. This is significant because nonkin relationships are likely to be voluntarily formed and based on friendship. Nonkin-dominated networks may insulate an interracial couple from criticism and peer pressure, particularly by compensating for potential family opposition.

Interracial marriage may also increase the pool of network members available, especially in those cases where both members of the couple are committed to maintaining ties with both racial groups (Spickard, 1989). By having more interaction with people of different races, both spouses may become more tolerant toward different cultures; thus, interracial couples could also develop effective ways to cope with marital differences.

Most importantly, such features of network structure may make it easier to minimize exposure to stress, conflict, and criticism of the relationship, significant sources of perceived network stress. There are reasons to believe that interracial couples will minimize their stress by choosing friends very carefully. Networks are the cause of stress as well as support (Wellman, 1981). By maintaining stronger ties with those who support their marriage, they will enjoy more support.

Components of a Resilience Perspective on Interracial Marriage

A series of preliminary hypotheses drawn from the existing literature deserves serious exploration as a way to understand processes in interracial marriages. First and foremost, researchers should take into account the fact that the majority of interracial marriages are motivated by love (Mathabane & Mathabane, 1993; Porterfield, 1978; Sung, 1990). The relationship formed is an intimate one, and intimate relationships facilitate the development of resilience (Luthar, 1993).

> Hypothesis 1. Interracial marriages are likely to be more stable and less conflictual than other types of interracial relationships (e.g., mentoring, coworker).

Testing this hypothesis will require collecting comparative data across different types of interracial contacts and relationships. Researchers should also take into account the fact that facing and overcoming challenges promotes growth as well as presents negative affect (Schaefer & Moos, 1992).

> Hypothesis 2. The unique challenges of interracial relationships, including enduring family opposition, dealing with cultural differences, withstanding social prejudice, and raising biracial children, facilitate personal growth and the development of mature coping and conflict-resolution styles.

Testing this hypothesis necessitates longitudinal designs. It will also require researchers to study *process* as well as emotional and social outcomes.

Finally, researchers should be aware that the demographic and other personal characteristics of many of those who marry interracially—although certainly diverse—paint a positive picture of their capacity to weather marital difficulties. Social context and racial combination will also shape the ways in which couples can adapt.

> Hypothesis 3. When they have greater than average education (as many possess), interracial couples have better resources for handling problems they encounter, including cross-cultural differences.

Hypothesis 4. More educated interracial couples will also build a strong counter-support network of like-minded friends.

Hypothesis 5. Even in the absence of greater education attainment and the resources that education brings, interracial couples are likely to build strong identifications with each other through shared adversity and other experiences.

Hypothesis 6. The marital quality and stability of interracial couples will vary by racial combination and social context.

Testing these hypotheses will require researchers to adopt a more *comparative* approach across race and class.

References

Baber, R. (1937). A study of 325 mixed marriages. *American Sociological Review, 2,* 705-716.

Bott, E. (1971). *Family and social network.* London: Tavistock.

Brown, G. W. & Harris, T. O. (1978). *Social origins of depression.* New York: Free Press.

Carter, H. & Glick, P. C. (1976). *Marriage and divorce: A social and economic study.* Cambridge, MA: Harvard University Press.

Chan, A. Y. (1992). *Marital satisfaction and marital stability of interracial/interethnic couples.* Unpublished master's thesis, University of Utah.

Cochran, M., Larner, M., Riley, D., Gunnarsson, L. & Henderson, C. R. (1990). *Extending families: The social networks of parents and their children.* New York: Cambridge University Press.

Collins, R. (1985). *Sociology of marriage and the family: Gender, love, and property.* Chicago: Nelson-Hall.

Connor, J. (1976). *A study of the marital stability of Japanese war brides.* San Francisco: R & E Research Associates.

Cretser, G. A. & Leon, J. J. (1982). *Intermarriage in the United States.* New York: Haworth Press.

Dohrenwend, B. S. & Dohrenwend, B. P. (1981). *Stressful life events and their contexts.* New York: Prodist.

Fischer, C. (1982). *To dwell among friends: Personal networks in town and city.* Chicago: University of Chicago Press.

Gibbs, J. (1987). Identity and marginality. *American Orthopsychiatric Association, 57,* 265–278.

Glenn, N. D. (1990). Quantitative research on marital quality in the 1980s: A critical review. *Journal of Marriage and the Family, 52,* 818–831.

Goldberg, M. M. (1941). A qualification of the marginal man theory. *American Sociological Review, 6,* 52–58.

Gordon, A. I. (1964). *Intermarriage:: Interfaith, interracial, interethnic.* Westport, CT: Greenwood.

Ho, F. C. & Johnson, R. C. (1990). Intra-ethnic and inter-ethnic marriage and divorce in Hawaii. *Social Biology, 37,* 44–51.

Hochschild, A. (1989). *The second shift.* New York: Avon.

Holmes, T. H. & Rahe, R. H. (1967). The social readjustment rating scale. *Journal of Psychosomatic Research, 11,* 213–218.

Imamura, A. (1986). Ordinary couples? Mate selection in international marriages in Nigeria. *Journal of Comparative Family Studies, 17,* 325–336.

Jeong, G. J. & Schumm, W. (1990). Family satisfaction in Korean/American marriages: An exploratory study of the perception of Korean wives. *Journal of Comparative Family Studies, 21,* 325–336.

Johnson, R. & Nagoshi, C. (1986). The adjustment of offspring of within-group and interracial/intercultural marriages. *Journal of Marriage and the Family, 48,* 279–284.

Kaminer, W. (1992). *I'm dysfunctional, you're dysfunctional: The recovery movement and other self-help fashions.* Reading, MA: Addison-Wesley.

Kitano, H. & Yeung, W. T. (1982). Chinese interracial marriage. *Marriage and Family Review, 5,* 35–48.

Kitano, H., Yeung, W. T., Chai, L. & Hatanaka, H. (1984). Asian American interracial marriage. *Journal of Marriage and the Family, 46,* 179–190.

LaFromboise, T., Coleman, H. L. K. & Gerton, J. (1993). Psychological impact of biculturalism: Evidence and theory. *Psychological Bulletin, 114,* 395–412.

Lee, S. M. & Yamanaka, K. (1990). Patterns of Asian American intermarriage and marital assimilation. *Journal of Comparative Family Studies, 21,* 287–305.

Luthar, S. S. (1993). Annotation: Methodological and conceptual issues on childhood resilience. *Journal of Child Psychology and Psychiatry, 34,* 441–453.

Lyles, M., Yancey, A., Grace, C. & Carter, J. (1985). Racial identity and self esteem. *Journal of the American Academy of Child Psychiatry, 24,* 150–153.

Mathabane, M. & Mathabane, G. (1993). *Love in black and white: The triumph of love over prejudice and taboo.* New York: Harper Collins.

McRoy, R. & Freeman, E. (1986). Racial identity issues among mixed race children. *Social Work in Education, 8,* 164–174.

Monahan, T. (1976). An overview of statistics on interracial marriage in the United States, with data on its extent from 1963–1970. *Journal of Marriage and the Family, 38,* 223–231.

Park, R. E. (1928). Human migration and the marginal man. *American Journal of Sociology, 5,* 881–893.

Perlman, D. & Rook, K. S. (1987). Social supports, social deficits, and the family: Toward the enhancement of well-being. In S. Oskamp (Ed.), *Family processes and problems: Social psychological aspects* (pp. 17–144). Newbury Park, CA: Sage.

Porterfield, E. (1978). *Black and white mixed marriages.* Chicago: Nelson-Hall.

Rankin, R., & Maneker, J. (1987). Correlates of marital duration and black-white intermarriage in California. *Journal of Divorce, 11,* 51–67.

Ross, C. E., Mirowsky, J. & Huber, J. (1983). Dividing work, sharing work, and in-between. *American Sociological Review, 48*, 809–823.

Schaefer, J. A., & Moos, R. H. (1992). Life crises and personal growth. In B. N. Carpenter (Ed.), *Personal coping* (pp. 149–170). Westport, CT: Praeger.

Schoen, R. & Wooldredge, J. (1989). Marriage choices in North Carolina and Virginia, 1969–1971 and 1979–1981. *Journal of Marriage and the Family, 51*, 465–481.

Spickard, P. (1989). *Mixed blood: Intermarriage and ethnic identity in twentieth-century America.* Madison, WI: University of Wisconsin Press.

Stephan, W. & Stephan, C. (1991). Intermarriage: Effects on personality, adjustment, and intergroup relations in two samples of students. *Journal of Marriage and the Family, 53*, 241–250.

Sung, B. (1990). Chinese American intermarriage. *Journal of Comparative Family Studies, 21*, 337–352.

Taylor, R. J., Chatters, L. M., Tucker, M. B. & Lewis, E. (1990). Developments in research on black families: A decade review. *Journal of Marriage and the Family, 52*, 993–1014.

Thoits, P. A. (1983). Multiple identities and psychological well-being: A reformulation and test of the social isolation hypothesis. *American Sociological Review, 48*, 174–187.

Thoits, P. A. (1986). Multiple identities. *American Sociological Review, 51*, 259–272.

Tucker, M. B. & Mitchell-Kernan, C. (1990). New trends in black American interracial marriage: The social structural context. *Journal of Marriage and the Family, 52*, 209–218.

U.S. Bureau of the Census. (1972). *1970 Census of the Population PC (2) 4C.* Washington, DC: U.S. Government Printing Office.

U.S. Bureau of the Census. (1993). *Statistical Abstract of the United States.* Washington, DC: U.S. Government Printing Office.

Wellman, B. (1981). Applying network analysis to the study of support. In B. H. Gottlieb (Ed.), *Social networks and social support.* Beverly Hills, CA: Sage.

Werner, E. (1990). Vulnerability and resiliency: A longitudinal perspective. In M. Brambring, F. Loesel, & H. Skowronek (Eds.), *Children at risk: Assessment, longitudinal research, and intervention.* Berlin: Aldine de Gruyter.

Wethington, E. & Kessler, R.C. (1989). Employment, parental responsibility, and psychological distress: A study of married women. *Journal of Family Issues, 10*, 527–546.

White, L. (1990). Determinants of divorce: A review of research in the eighties. *Journal of Marriage and the Family, 52*, 904–912.

Whyte, M. K. (1990). *Dating, mating, and marriage.* New York: Aldine de Gruyter.

II. Native Americans

II a. Native Hawaiians

Chapter 4

Native Hawaiian (*Kanaka Maoli*) Culture, Mind, and Well-Being[1]

Anthony J. Marsella, Jill Mokihana Oliveira,
Carol Milani Plummer,
and Kamana'opono M. Crabbe

The purpose of this chapter is to discuss the relationship between Native Hawaiian (*kanaka maoli* or "the true people") culture, mind, and physical/psychological well-being. To accurately grasp the complex relationships among these variables, it is essential to understand the tragic history of the Native Hawaiian people and their current efforts to restore and rebuild their heritage and way of life. The Native Hawaiian people are today struggling to reestablish themselves as a sovereign nation following more than two centuries of colonial exploitation and abuse that decimated their population and destroyed their culture.[2]

Ultimately, their physical and psychological well-being must be understood within the context of the destructive political, social, and economic forces that led to their demoralization, powerlessness, and near decimation. These once proud people, whose ancestors had lived in Hawai'i for more than a thousand years, became strangers in their own land in less than a century following contact with Europeans, and in the process, they became victims of countless physical, psychological, and social pathologies, even as they fought desperately for dignity and survival.

In the history of the Native Hawaiian people are etched fundamental principles regarding the relationship between sociopolitical forces and human health and well-being. In the history of the Native Hawaiian people are etched irrefutable facts which testify that human health and well-being are first and foremost sociopolitical challenges.

The Land

The Hawaiian Archipelago is comprised of shoals, reefs, and more than 132 islands formed by volcanic activity that began at the floor of the Pacific Ocean. The largest islands are Kaua'i, Ni'ihau, O'ahu, Maui, Moloka'i, Lana'i, Kaho'olawe, and Hawai'i. Over the passage of millions of years, they became a lush tropical paradise of flora and fauna that thrived in the isolation provided by their great distance from others lands and peoples (Nordyke, 1989).

The beauty of the Hawaiian Islands is legendary and continues to be so today in spite of development. In 1866, Mark Twain, the American writer and an early visitor to Hawai'i, noted:

> ... the Sandwich Islands—to this day the peacefullest, restfullest, sunniest, balmiest, dreamiest haven of refuge for a worn and weary spirit the surface of the earth can offer.... There they lie, the divine islands, forever shining in the sun, forever smiling out of the sparkling sea, with its soft mottling drifting cloud shadows and vagrant cat's paws of wind, forever inviting you (Frear, 1947, Quoted in Nordyke, 1989, p. xix).

Even today, amidst excessive population growth and industrialization, the Hawaiian Islands remain one of the most beautiful lands on earth, a tropical paradise that continues to fulfill idyllic dreams of tranquility and respite from the burdens of the world. This was the land to which the Native Hawaiian people first came. This was the land that was to offer them an endless bounty and an enviable harmony with nature and the spiritual world. This was also the land that would witness the continuing saga of the Native Hawaiian people's cultural growth, cultural demise, and current cultural resurgence and renewal.

The People

The question of who is a Native Hawaiian has been a topic of perennial debate, and many different criteria have been used in an effort to establish a meaningful definition. The 1959 Statehood Admissions Act defines a Native Hawaiian person as "Any descendant of the aboriginal peoples inhabiting the Hawaiian Islands in 1778." Thus, according to this definition, anyone having any quantum of ancestral Hawaiian blood can be considered a Native Hawaiian.

Other Hawaiians have argued that only certain proportions of blood should define Native Hawaiian status (e.g., 50%). The debate is endless. However, one thing is clear—the issue of who is a Native Hawaiian must go beyond blood quanta to ethnic identity and the support and endorsement of traditional customs and practices if the Hawaiian people are to flourish and survive as a distinct cultural group.

Today, Native Hawaiian people occupy both poles of the socioeconomic and social status spectrum. For the first time in history, the Governor of the State of Hawai'i has Hawaiian blood. A growing number of wealthy and influential professional and business leaders also have Native Hawaiian ancestry. Yet, the vast majority of Native Hawaiians continue to languish at the lower end of the social strata, handicapped by centuries of exploitation, abuse, and racism.

Based on health surveillance statistics, the State of Hawai'i's population consists of more than 942,564 residents, excluding military members and dependents (Honolulu Star Bulletin & Advertiser, January 5, 1992, p. B-1). Of this number, it is estimated that there are approximately 202,134 mixed-blood Native Hawaiians and 9,344 pure-blood Native Hawaiians (less than 1% of the state's population). However, the 1990 federal census indicates that there are approximately 156,812 Native Hawaiians, rather than 211,478, since many Native Hawaiians failed to identify themselves as having Hawaiian ancestry.

In addition to the population that resides in the State of Hawai'i, the 1990 federal census reported that 99,269 people across the mainland United States identified themselves as having Hawaiian blood (Fernandez, 1993). If one combines these totals (211,478 in Hawai'i plus 99,269 out-of-state) there are an estimated 310,747 people of Native Hawaiian ancestry residing in the United States. The majority have less than 50% Hawaiian blood.

A more recent estimate of the Native Hawaiian population according to blood quantum distribution was offered by Miike (1993). This report suggested that there are fewer than 5,000 pure Hawaiian-blood (*piha Kanaka Maoli*) people remaining. Other percentage groupings included 19,200 three-quarters to full, 64,800 one-half to three-quarters, 93,600 one-quarter to one-half, and 52,800 less than one-quarter. Truly, the Native Hawaiian bloodline and the Native Hawaiian culture are highly vulnerable.

Some Historical Considerations

The Arrival of the *Kanaka Maoli*

It is believed that the Native Hawaiian (*Kanaka Maoli*) people came to the Hawaiian Islands more than 2,000 years ago. They sailed northward thousands of miles in doubled-hulled open canoes from the Marquesas, Tahiti, and/or the Society Islands (i.e., Polynesia) navigating by the stars, the winds, and the currents, in a voyage that exceeded the distances and dangers of any comparable Western European voyage of the time (e.g., Emory, 1959; Nordyke, 1989, Stannard, 1989).

For centuries, this migration apparently continued in both directions, until the population of the Hawaiian Islands may have come to exceed 875,000 people (see Stannard, 1989), and the Hawaiian cultural traditions had become strong and well established. It is believed that migration and contact between the people of Hawai'i and the islands of their origin ceased sometime around the 12th century, and that all subsequent growth in population occurred internally (Nordyke, 1989).

The early history of the Native Hawaiian people is largely unwritten, although 19th century newspapers offered numerous historical accounts by Native Hawaiians. However, much of what is known is derived from chants, genealogies, legends, and some early 19th century writing from royalty (*ali'i*) such as King David Kalakaua (1836–1891) (Kalakaua, 1888). One of the most important of all myths is the creation genealogy chant—the *Kumulipo* (Johnson, 1981). Although there is speculation that other groups of people had early contact with the Hawaiian Islands (e.g., shipwrecked Japanese sailors, lost Spanish Galleons), there is no substantive evidence that any other people beyond the original Hawaiian people and possibly some other Polynesian people ever visited or contacted the Hawaiian Islands prior to 1778. A number of scholarly books on Hawaiian social and political history have been written by contemporary historians and are recommended to the interested reader (e.g., Dawes, 1974; Fuchs, 1961; Kame'eleihiwa, 1992; Kuykendall, 1938, 1953, 1967; Rayson, 1984; Stannard, 1989; Trask, 1993).

While the pre-contact population of Hawaii has been the topic of considerable debate, ranging from estimates of 200,000 to 875,000 (see Nordyke, 1989; Stannard, 1989), there is no disagreement that following the first contact with Western people in 1778, the Native Hawaiian population sharply declined, due to communicable diseases, infertility, high infant mortality, emigration, war, intermarriage, the adoption of tobacco and alcohol, and, some say, despair.

Tuberculosis, syphilis, gonorrhea, small pox, measles, whooping cough, mumps, cholera, influenza, and alcoholism were rampant. Infant mortality was extraordinarily high, as was infertility due to scarring of female reproductive organs from venereal disease. Reports indicate that more than 15,000 Native Hawaiian people died in a single small pox epidemic in 1853 (e.g., Nordyke, 1989).

The lowest point in the population decline of the Native Hawaiian people was reached in 1876 when only 53,900 Native Hawaiian people were reported to be living in the Kingdom of Hawai'i. Assuming a compromise figure of 500,000 Native Hawaiians in 1778 (an estimate somewhere between the proposed extremes of 200,000 and 875,000), the first one hundred years following contact resulted in a 90% population decline (e.g., Nordyke, 1989). Is it any wonder that some Native Hawaiian people speak of their history as genocide and as a horror (see Stannard, 1989, 1992)?

The Arrival of Captain James Cook

On January 18, 1778, Captain James Cook, an English sea captain, arrived in the Hawaiian Islands in his tall-masted sailing boats, HMS Resolution and HMS Discovery. This was the Native Hawaiian people's first contact with Europeans and European culture. In the finest tradition of the imperialistic ethic of the times, Captain Cook named the islands he had "discovered" the Sandwich Islands, in honor of his patron and sponsor, John Montagu, the Earl of Sandwich.

The Native Hawaiians at first thought that Cook might be a God (e.g., *Lono,* the God of Agriculture), and offered him extravagant hospitality and welcome. However, within the span of a year, it soon became clear to the Native Hawaiians that Cook was not a god, but rather a harbinger of their destructive destiny and demise. On a subsequent visit in 1779, Cook was killed in a battle at Kealakekua Bay on the Island of Hawai'i. But the die had been cast, and the future of the Native Hawaiian people and culture was to be filled with tragedy.

Missionaries and Businessmen

Contact with Cook was soon followed by contact with other Western groups including whalers, missionaries, and businessmen, all of whom exploited the wealth and beauty of the land and people. The first missionaries arrived on March 21, 1820, from New England. They came to spread Christianity and ended up taking over much of the land and assuming much of the power. In the process of seeking converts and saving souls, they undermined the very tenets and foundations of the ancient Hawaiian people, destroying their will and spirit.

Within decades following contact, the Native Hawaiian people and culture had been overrun by Western religious, military and commercial interests. A way of life that had thrived for centuries was destroyed by disease, demoralization, and violent death. The Native Hawaiian people watched in despair and confusion as their proud past was denigrated by missionaries, exploited by business interests, and suppressed by colonial political interests.

King David Kalakaua, the last King of the Hawaiian people, watched in vain as his people and their culture declined. In 1888, King Kalakaua allegedly wrote:

> In the midst of evidences of prosperity and advancement it is but too apparent that the natives are steadily decreasing in numbers and gradually losing their hold upon the fair land of their fathers. Within a century they have dwindled from four hundred thousand healthy and happy children of nature, without care and without want, to a little more than a tenth of that number of landless, hopeless victims to the greed and vices of civilization. They are slowly sinking under the restraints and burdens of their surroundings, and will in time succumb to social and political conditions foreign to their natures and poisonous to their blood.... finally their voices will be heard no more forever (Kalakaua, 1888, pp. 64-65; quoted in Nordyke, 1989, p. 27).

It is important not to overly romanticize the Native Hawaiian culture prior to European contact. There were, as is the case for all cultures, many practices that were less than admirable by contemporary standards. It has been said that the Native Hawaiians practiced ritual human sacrifice, although some have questioned the accuracy of these statements (see Kame'eleihiwa, 1992). Further, like many Western nations, their societal governance was often very authoritarian and class-structured, leaving little opportunity for disagreement or conflict with those in power. Wars among the various sub-kingdoms did occur, and violent death in battle was not unknown. Yet, even as these cultural elements are noted, it is clear the Native Hawaiians enjoyed a relatively peaceful and bountiful existence, especially when contrasted to the tragic events that followed contact with Europeans (e.g., Dawes, 1974; Kame'elihiwa, 1992).

The Overthrow of the Monarchy

Perhaps the most tragic event in the history of the Native Hawaiian people was the overthrow of the Hawaiian monarchy by a group of American businessmen on January 17, 1893. In the years following Captain Cook's arrival, hundreds of foreign people came to Hawaii's shores in search of wealth, power, and adventure. As we have already noted, the social and health consequences for the Native Hawaiian people were disastrous and the population declined. Yet, the struggle for survival continued and the Native Hawaiians established a monarchy in 1795 under the leadership of King Kamehameha I (1758–1819).

This monarchy continued for almost one hundred years under the leadership of such notable Native Hawaiian figures as King David Kalakaua (1836–1891), who ascended to the throne of the Hawaiian monarchy in 1874. Upon his death, he was followed to the throne by Queen Lili'uokalani (1838–1917) who was crowned on January 29, 1891. The years of the monarchy were difficult for Native Hawaiians as their land was taken away and they were disregarded by the incoming foreigners (see Kame'eleihiwa, 1992, for a more detailed and moving account of this period). The monarchy represented the last and best hope that somehow the Native Hawaiian people could reestablish themselves and reassert their identity. But, even here tragedy would prevail. On January 17, 1893, Queen Lili'uokalani and the Hawaiian monarchy were overthrown by a group of American businessmen and government officials under the leadership of Lorrin Thurston (1858–1931). With the approval and consent of representatives of the American government in Washington, D.C., the annexationists assumed power and formed a provisional government.

Annexation of the Kingdom of Hawai'i

In the following months, debates regarding the future of the Hawaiian Islands flourished, and at one point President Grover Cleveland actually withdrew the annexationists' request and considered restoring Queen Lili'uokalani to the throne. The struggle between the annexationists and the American government continued.

Finally, in a show of force and discontent, the annexationists put down a Native Hawaiian rebellion to restore the Queen and tried and convicted her for treason on January 7, 1895. She was sentenced to five years in jail (she actually served 21 months) in an act designed to humiliate her and her people.

The world was changing for the United States. Like its European counterparts, the United States' imperialistic impulses and actions were becoming commonplace. The Spanish-American War convinced the American government of Hawai'i's strategic location and commercial value, and on July 7, 1898, President William McKinley signed the annexation resolution, and Hawai'i became a territory of the United States without a vote of the Native Hawaiians. On August 12, 1898, the Hawaiian flag was lowered and the American flag was raised over 'Iolani Palace.. On June 14, 1900, the Territory of Hawai'i was established and commercial and political exploitation of the Native Hawaiian continued unabated.

Both prior to annexation and in the decades that followed, thousands of foreign workers of Chinese, European, Filipino, Korean, Japanese, and Puerto Rican ethnicity migrated to Hawai'i to work the plantations as sugar became king of the Hawaiian Islands' economy. The Hawaiians were forgotten. While some intermarried with white business men and missionaries, creating a small elite class, most became impoverished and destitute.

Today, little remains of the ancient ways of the Native Hawaiian people, in spite of a growing cultural renaissance sparked by the interests of young Hawaiians in their past identity. The commercialized versions of their food, dress, dance, and music support Hawai'i's tourist industry, although these commercialized versions bear little resemblance to the ancient customs of their once glorious past. But a Hawaiian renaissance is in the making, and there is a strong movement for sovereignty that promises to restore Native Hawaiian political control over their land, and with it, the dignity, power, identity, and self-determination the Native Hawaiians have been denied.

Native Hawaiian Culture, Mind, and Well-Being

There are many excellent publications on Native Hawaiian culture, mind, and human behavior (e.g., Gallimore, Boggs, & Jordan, 1974; Howard, 1974; Ito, 1987; Kanahele, 1986; Marsella et al., 1985; Pukui, 1983; Pukui, Haertig, & Lee, 1972, 1979; Takeuchi et al.,

1987; Trask & Trask, 1988; Young, 1980). Pukui, Haertig, and Lee's (1972) publication, *Nana I Ke Kumu* (Look to the Source), is a particularly valuable resource. While these articles and books differ in their focus, a review of their contents yields a useful conceptual perspective for understanding the complex relationships between Native Hawaiian culture, mind, and well-being.

Psychic Unity

To understand the Native Hawaiian mind, one must put aside Eurocentric notions of selfhood and personhood and adopt a contextual perspective in which person, family (*'ohana*), nature (*'aina* = land, *kai* = water, *makani* = wind), and spiritual world (*'uhane, akua, 'aumakua, kupua*) are inter-connected and inter-dependent. They are one, and this oneness is experienced by Native Hawaiians as a psychic unity. That is to say, the consciousness that is felt by the Native Hawaiian is not that which is characteristic of a separate, autonomous detached being, but rather one that is united and inseparable from the larger social, natural, and spiritual forces of the world—there is a felt, palpable, experienced sense of psychic unity and cosmological attachment.

Harmony (*Lokahi*) and
Balance/Purity (*Pono*)

The life force that makes for this unity is called *mana*. It is a spiritual force and power that is felt as energy, vitality, and strength. When the *mana* is present and strong, the person feels a special sense of well-being drawn from the harmony and resonance across the family, nature, and spiritual levels. Harmony (*lokahi*) is an important concept in the Native Hawaiian way. It is a state to be actively pursued in all realms of action and experience. A person knows when harmony (*lokahi*) is present because they experience a special state of well-being characterized by the presence of energy and vitality. Thus, harmony (*lokahi*) and life force (*mana*) are interdependent, and in their presence, person, family, nature, and spirit are one—unity.

Native Hawaiians are encouraged, through cultural socialization practices, to strive for a state of balance and purity that is closely related to the unity of person, family, nature, and spiritual world. This is a state that is called *pono* or sometimes, *ma'ema'e*. This experiential state has profound implications for physical and psychological health and well-being. When this state is present, there is optimal health and well-being, and the person feels strong and in harmony (*lokahi*) with their world. It is clear that the Native Hawaiians were aware of the concept of holistic health long before Western peoples. They understood that mind and body are inextricably linked, and that disease is a function of imbalance and disharmony.

There are a number of things that the Native Hawaiian people can do to create and maintain harmony (*lokahi*), and ultimately, balance and purity (*pono* and *maʻemaʻe*). At the familial and community level, this is accomplished by fitting in, helping others, and working for the group over selfish aims. At the nature level, this is done by conservation and protection of the land. And at the spiritual level, this is achieved through reverence and respect for the Gods through rituals and prayer (*pule*).

Caring for and Preserving the Natural World

This idealized construction of the Native Hawaiian normative identity highlights the importance that is assigned to the spiritual dimension of human experience. Life is to be lived with daily awe, reverence, and respect; there is a close attachment to nature. Everything has its own "personality" and can be talked to and interacted with as if it were human, including rocks, trees, animals, and mountains. Places of special beauty are considered to have a special identity of their own and often have a myth or legend describing their creation.

There are no distinctions between the animate and inanimate world. All things contain the same spiritual life force. There is continuity. While there are evil forces in the world that need to be propitiated, they can be handled or kept at bay if a person lives with proper sanctity and respect for the multitude of Gods and spirits that animate and are the natural world.

The Social Formation of the *Kanaka Maoli*

The social formation of the Native Hawaiian (*Kanaka Maoli*) people was built around the family, royalty, and the spiritual world (e.g., Handy & Pukui, 1972). The family structure was organized according to the following hierarchy:

Ke Akua (God)
'Aumakua (Family Guardian Gods)
Kupuna (Family Elders)
Makua (Parents)
Opio (Children)
Moopuna (Grandchildren)

The family structure was, in turn, part of a larger social structure that included royalty and other social sectors:

Ke Akua (God)
Alii Nui (Kings and High Nobles)
Kahuna Nui (High Priests)
Alii (Lesser Royalty)
Kahuna (Specialized Professions and Trades)
Makaainai (Common People)
Kauwa (Servants)

The social structure was well organized and widely known and accepted. Taboo (*kapu*) systems linked to social and spiritual sanctions and punishments kept the social structures strong among the Native Hawaiians. However, when confronted with Christian missionaries, businessmen, and new forms of social organization based on Western ideas of governance and family relations, the traditional ways yielded to the pressures to conform to new ways. The traditional culture could not accommodate the conflicts in values, beliefs, and practices, and cultural disintegration began to occur with all of its pernicious consequences for health and well-being.

Behavior, Mind, and Health and Disease

All individual behavior and societal actions in the Native Hawaiian (*Kanaka Maoli*) culture are directed toward the creation and maintenance of harmony among the different levels of being (i.e., person, family, nature, spirit). By behaving a particular way, one's *mana* is continued and/or enhanced. This way is the "spiritual" way. There is a spiritual guardian that looks after each person. This guardian is called an *'aumakua*. It is a spiritual ancestral god and protector. For this reason, Native Hawaiians respect their ancestors because an offense can lead to punishment and evil.

Through accident or misbehavior, the connections between the person and/or family and the *'aumakua* can be broken with resulting illness, discord, and misfortune. This can occur because of violations of *kapu* (or taboo), non-negotiable rules and guidelines about proper behavior. The *kapu* or taboo rules can be learned from elders (*kupuna*) and healers (*kahuna*). There are scores of taboos covering virtually all aspects of life including eating, fishing, hunting, menstruation, intercourse, funerals, clothing, and so forth.

When *kapu* are violated or when there is behavior that acts against the harmony of the system, the harmonious energy (*lokahi/ mana*) necessary for psychic unity is lost and illness, disease, suffering, or death are possible. Within this context, any act that destroys or interferes with the social/spiritual order can result in negative consequences.

Among the behaviors that can lead to a breakdown in harmony and loss of *mana* are hate (*ina'ina*), jealousy (*lili*), rudeness (*maha'a*), being nosey (*niele*), bearing a grudge (*ho'omauhala*), bragging (*ha'anui*), showing off (*ho'oi'o*), breaking promises (*hua 'olelo*), speaking bitter thoughts (*waha 'awa*), stealing, fighting, and hostile (*huhu*) behavior. In addition to offensive and anti-social behavior, loss of mana and harmony can occur because of an offended ghost (*lapu*), natural spirit (*kupua*), spirit guardian (*'aumakua*), ancestor/ elder (*kupuna*), or because of prayers for death (*ana'ana*) or a curse (*anai*).

Under these conditions, illness, misfortune, and death can arise, including insanity or craziness (*pupule*). The Native Hawaiian language has many words for the various forms of insanity and mental derangement (see Marsella et al., 1985, for an extensive glossary of mental health terms that were prepared by members of the *E Ola Mau* Mental Health Task Force). Some important terms include the following:

1.	*'a 'a*:	Panic stricken; made dumb by anger and fury
2.	*'a aia*:	Demented
3.	*'a ala'ioa*:	Wild, uncontrolled
4.	*hehena*:	Insane, lunatic, crazy
5.	*ho'ohewahewa*:	Deranged (not as strong as *hehena* or *pupule*)
6.	*kaumaha*:	Sad, heavily burdened
7.	*kuloloa*:	Idiotic
8.	*loha*:	Sullen, spiritlessness
9.	*lu'ulu'u*:	Heavily burdened, sorrowful, troubled

10.	*ma'ina loko*:	Sickness from within (caused by misdeeds, family troubles)
11.	*ma'ina waho*:	Sickness from outside (evil forces, external cause)
12.	*ohewa*:	Delirious, incoherent, drunk
13.	*opulepule*:	Moronic, imbecilic
14.	*pupule*:	Crazy, insane, wild, uncontrolled
15.	*uluahewa*:	Crazy, sometimes due to evil spirit
16.	*uluhia*:	Possessed by evil spirits
17.	*uluhua*:	Irritated, vexed, annoyed
18.	*uluku*:	Disturbed, agitated, nervous
19.	*'uhane noho*:	Possessed by a spirit
20.	*wela*:	Angry (hot)

Restoring the Social Order and Well-Being

To restore harmony and health, one can act with kindness, caring, and responsibility toward family, nature and society. A mature Native Hawaiian (*kanaka makua*) should manifest humility (*ha'aha'a*), politeness and kindness (*'olu'olu*), helpfulness (*kokua*), and acceptance, hospitality, and love (*aloha*). These behaviors are the goals of successful childrearing. All of these behaviors are directed toward preserving social order and cohesion.

Behaviors that interfere with social order and cohesion can lead to illness and disease, and even death. By behaving in ways that are socially responsible, one can expect that others will behave in the same way—reciprocity is achieved. Reciprocity provides the glue that holds the community together. I help you, you help me, and everyone is happy. This is the Native Hawaiian way.

The Native Hawaiian Healing Arts *(La'au Kahea)*

If harmony and balance are disturbed, and illness, disease, and misfortune occur, there are many Native Hawaiian treatments that can restore well-being (see particularly Pukui, Handy, & Livermore, 1934). These include physical interventions such as herbal treatments, purification baths (*kapu kai*), massage (*lomi lomi*), special diets, and fasting, all or some of which can be prescribed by a healer or "doctor" (*kahuna lapa'au*).

In addition, the healer (*kahuna*) can also prescribe psychological and spiritual healing methods such as confession and apology (*mihi*), dream interpretation (*moe 'uhane*), clairvoyance (*hihi'o*), prayer (*pule ho'onoa*), transfer of thought (*Ho 'olulu ia*), possession (*noho*), water blessings (*pi kai*), and spirit mediumship (*haka*). Through these methods, advice may be offered and divine intervention can occur. Sometimes there are special rituals such as exorcism of evil spirits possessing someone. After praying over the possessed person, a family member or a kahuna could say "*Ho'i noa 'ai i kou kahu*" (Go back and destroy your keeper!) (see Greenwell, 1958; Pukui, Haertig, & Lee, 1972).

Ho'opono'pono: Family and Group Therapy

One of the powerful methods of therapy is called *ho'opono'pono*, a form of family and group therapy in which troubled social relationships can be repaired through the process of talking out and sharing negative feelings and conflicts. *Ho'opono'pono*, or "making right" through discussion, prayer, and forgiveness, is usually led by an elder (*kupuna*) or healer (*kahuna*), who directs the family members in the group process to tell the truth.

The term *ho'opono'pono* is derived from the words *ho'o*, meaning "to cause," and *pono*, meaning "proper, balanced, moral, righteous." Through a combination of prayer, discussion, confession, repentance, and forgiveness, the good family and community relationships could be restored and *lokahi* could be achieved.

Haertig (see Pukui, Haertig, & Lee, 1972) stated:

> *Ho'oponopono* requires the telling of all the essential material, no matter how painful this may be. No matter if what is told pains others. The point is that the telling must not be done in vindictive ways or with any desire to hurt. Nothing essential must be held back. Actions and errors of omission or commission pertinent to the problem must be totally revealed (Pukui, Haertig, & Lee, 1972, p. 73).

There are a number of stages in the *ho'opono'pono* process: (1) *Pule Wehe*—opening prayer (*pule*) and identification of the problem (*kukulu kumuhana*); (2) *Wehewehe*—period of discussion in which problems are handled one at a time or peeled away (*mahiki*) and the various transgressions (*hala*) and painful emotions that hinder change (*hihia*) are resolved; (3) this is followed by a period of forgiveness, apology, and repentance (*mihi*) and a letting go of ill feelings (*kala*) and a psychological severing or cutting off of the events that caused the problems (*oki*); (4) the *ho'opono'pono* ceremony is closed with a prayer (*pule ho'opau*) and sometimes various acts of purification and offerings (*pani*) (see Shook, 1985, for greater detail about *ho'opono'pono*).

Summary of Views on Health and Well-Being

In summary, Native Hawaiian views on health and well-being are very holistic in that they emanate from the basic assumption that there is a felt sense of psychic unity that emerges from the harmonious interdependency of person, family, nature, and spiritual forces via the life force and power called mana. For the Native Hawaiian, any or all actions, intentional or unintentional, that result in the destruction of harmony among the different levels of being can result in illness, misfortune, or death. Behavior is supposed to preserve harmony in the social, natural, and spiritual orders. Inappropriate and negative social behaviors can upset the harmony, as can black magic and other evil practices such as sorcery.

Healing can be focused on physical, psychological, and/or spiritual levels, but in all instances, healing is directed toward the reestablishment of harmony in the social, natural, and spiritual levels. In these respects, Native Hawaiian health and healing concepts and practices are highly sophisticated and knowledgeable with regard to mind-body-behavior relationships.

The Health and Mental Health Status of Native Hawaiian People

Regardless of the index or indicator used, Native Hawaiian people are either at the top or close to the top of every category of medical disease, social pathology, psychological maladaptation, and economic and social welfare (e.g., Blaisdell, 1993; Blaisdell et al., 1985; Goebert & Kanoa, 1992; Hammond, 1988; Marsella et al., 1985; Native Hawaiian Educational Assessment Project, 1983; Papa O Lokahi, 1987; Takeuchi et al., 1987; United States Congress, 1987; White & Landis, 1982). Based on a concatenation of findings from the above references, the following conclusions can be reached:

Physical and Medical Health

1. Native Hawaiian people exceed the State of Hawai'i and the United States rates for lung cancer for men and women, breast cancer for women, and uterine cancer for women.

2. Native Hawaiian people have the highest rates in the State of Hawai'i for cancer deaths, diabetes, high blood pressure, gout, bronchitis, asthma, emphysema, and obesity.

3. Native Hawaiians exceed the average mortality rates for all races in the United States, adjusted for age/sex per 100,000 population for infectious diseases (26.4 versus 13), diabetes (29 versus 9.8), stroke (46.1 versus 35.1), cancer 183.8 versus 132), and heart disease (273 versus 189).

4. Native Hawaiian people have the shortest life expectancy in the State of Hawai'i.

5. Native Hawaiian people have rates of higher infant mortality, congenital diseases, and sudden infant death syndrome than other groups in the State of Hawai'i.

6. Native Hawaiian preschoolers have diet deficiencies in calcium, riboflavin, and Vitamins A and C.

7. Native Hawaiian people have one of the highest crude injury death rates among all people in the State of Hawai'i (61.7/100,000).

Social Pathologies

1. Native Hawaiian people comprise 40% of the State of Hawai'i prison inmates.

2. Native Hawaiian people have the highest rates of smoking and the second highest rate of chronic alcoholism in the State of Hawai'i.

3. Native Hawaiian young woman have the highest rates of teenage pregnancy and unmarried pregnancies in the State of Hawai'i.

4. Native Hawaiian people have the second highest rate of child abuse and neglect in the State of Hawai'i. Only Samoans show a higher rate.

5. Native Hawaiian people have the highest rates of arrest and prison sentencing in the State of Hawai'i.

6. Native Hawaiian youth have the highest rates of school absenteeism, school drop-outs, and juvenile

delinquency in the State of Hawai'i. Less than 50% of Native Hawaiian people hold a high school diploma, and Native Hawaiians comprise less than 5% of the college students enrolled at the University of Hawai'i at Manoa.

7. Native Hawaiian students score below parity in reading and math national norms on standardized achievement tests.

8. Native Hawaiian juveniles have the highest rates of arrest for forcible rape, robbery, aggravated assault, motor vehicle theft, weapons, prostitution, arson, and drug trafficking.

Mental Health

1. Native Hawaiian people have the highest rates of anti-social behavior, assaultive acts, and family and school problems among admissions to the State Mental Health facilities.

2. Native Hawaiian people have the highest rate of suicide in the State of Hawai'i. The rate is especially high for young men and the elderly. They also have the highest male to female suicide rate in the State (5:1).

3. Native Hawaiian people suffer from high rates of demoralization, alienation, and low self-esteem. Studies of depression and other related disorders have been conducted, but limitations in their research design and methods make it difficult to arrive at accurate figures for these disorders. Nevertheless, it is widely agreed among mental health officials that demoralization is high and quality of life is low for Native Hawaiians.

4. Native Hawaiians have had the highest rate of mental retardation in the state system.

Economic and Social Welfare

1. Native Hawaiian people have one of the lowest income levels in the State of Hawai'i. More than

66% of the Native Hawaiian people have annual gross family income levels of less than $40,000.

2.   Native Hawaiian people have disproportionately higher rates of welfare utilization and social services.

3.   Native Hawaiian people had a per capita income of $7,740 per year in 1986 (see Takeuchi et al., 1987) while non-Hawaiians had a per capita income of more than $10,100. Most of the jobs held by Native Hawaiians were in the service and labor industries.

Some Closing Thoughts

This litany of facts regarding the current physical, psychological, and social well-being of the Native Hawaiian people clearly highlights the tragic state of affairs that has evolved in the years following the near-demise of the Native Hawaiian culture. There is little need for complex theories to account for these results. The answer resides in the social and economic condition of contemporary Hawai'i. In the one hundred years since the Hawaiian Monarchy (*Onipaa*) was toppled, the Native Hawaiian people have suffered severe cultural disintegration and social stress with resulting consequences for their health and well-being.

If one uses the indices of cultural disintegration advanced by Alexander Leighton (1959), the internationally known social psychiatrist, Native Hawaiian society constitutes a classic example of the health and social consequences of cultural breakdown and deterioration. These indices include few and weak leaders, poor communication networks, a history of social and natural disasters, high migration rates, a breakdown in religious and philosophical systems, and poverty. In the presence of these conditions, Leighton suggested, societies will experience cultural disintegration, characterized by high crime, broken homes, alienation, high rates of mental disorders, social deviancy, and physical disease.

The Native Hawaiian people and culture are today at a historical crossroads in which the decisions they make as individuals and as a people will have important consequences for their continued survival and existence. The discontinuities between the lifestyles and values of the traditional Native Hawaiian way and the demands of contemporary Western life are a formidable challenge. Technological and industrial society values materialism, competition, individual autonomy, mastery, and self-sufficiency, oftentimes at the expense of traditional Native Hawaiian spiritual and collectivistic values and lifestyles. The traditional Native Hawaiian way sought harmony among personal, familial, natural, and spiritual domains while the Western way is openly and unabashedly confrontive and discordant in the pursuit of change and unlimited opportunity.

The pursuit of sovereignty by a growing number of Native Hawaiian people may be the only viable pathway for the survival of a culture that is dialectically opposed to Western life in virtually every cultural form and practice. New leaders, many of them women, are emerging who are proud of their heritage and committed to a new Native Hawaiian identity and consciousness. The newly formed School of Hawaiian Studies at the University of Hawai'i at Manoa has become a mecca for young Hawaiian students.

With sovereignty it may be possible to reestablish a new identity that can be source of pride, dignity, and confidence. These can serve as a counterpoint to the destructive historical and cultural forces that came close to ending the Native Hawaiian people and culture. Though the last two centuries in Native Hawaiian history can only be described as tragic, there is reason to believe the future will witness a resurgence and rebirth of Native Hawaiian culture, and with it a reduction in the physical, psychological, and social disorders that have characterized the Native Hawaiian past.

Notes

1. The authors wish to express their deep appreciation to Professor Lilikala Kame'eleihiwa, Ph.D. and Professor Frederick Leong, Ph.D., for their valuable editorial comments and support. This article is dedicated to the memory of Mary Abigail Kawena Pukui (1895-1986)—Native Hawaiian teacher, scholar, and spiritual leader.

2. Due to printing limitations, some diacritical marks in the Native Hawaiian language cannot be reproduced here.

References

Blaisdell, K. (1993). The health status of the indigenous Hawaiians. *Asian American and Pacific Islander Journal of Health, 1,* 116–160.

Blaisdell, K., et al. (1985). *E Ola Mau: The Native Hawaiian health needs study: Vol. 1. Physical and medical health.* Honolulu, Hawai'i: Alu Like, Inc.

Dawes, G. (1974). *Shoal of time: A history of the Hawaiian Islands.* Honolulu, Hawai'i: University Press of Hawaii.

Emory, K. (1959). Origins of Hawaiians. *Journal of the Polynesian Society, 68,* 29–35.

Fernandez, Y. (1993, August 29). Mainland Hawaiians: Out of sight—and out of rights. *The Honolulu Advertiser,* p. 1

Frear, W. (1947). *Mark Twain and Hawai'i.* Chicago: Lakeside Press.

Fuchs, L. (1961). *Hawai'i pono: A social history.* New York: Harcourt, Brace, and World, Inc.

Gallimore, R., Boggs, J., & Jordan, C. (1974). *Culture, behavior, and education: A study of Hawaiian-Americans.* Beverly Hills, California: Sage.

Goebert, D., & Kanoa, K. (1992). Injury mortality in Hawai'i: *The Rehab Journal, 8,* 4–6.

Greenwell, J. (1958). *Aboriginal Hawaiian therapeutics.* Bishop Museum Archives, Document No. 274. Honolulu, Hawai'i.

Hammond, O. (1988). Needs assessment and policy development: Native Hawaiians as Native Americans. *American Psychologist, 43,* 383–387.

Handy, E., & Pukui, M. (1972). *The Polynesian family system in Ka'u, Hawaii.* Rutland, Vermont: Charles E. Tuttle.

Howard, A. (1974). *Ain't no big thing: Coping strategies in a Hawaiian-American community.* Honolulu, Hawai'i: East-West Center Press.

Ito, K. (1987). Emotions, proper behavior, and Hawaiian concepts of self, person, and individual. In B. Robillard & A. J. Marsella (Eds.), *Contemporary issues in mental health research in the Pacific Islands.* Honolulu, Hawai'i: University Press of Hawai'i

Johnson, R. (1981). *Kumulipo: The Hawaiian hymn of creation* (Vol. 1). Honolulu, Hawai'i: Topgallant Publishing.

Kalakaua, D. (1888). *The legends and myths of Hawai'i.* New York: Charles Webster & Co.

Kame'eleihiwa, L. (1992). *Native land and foreign desires: How shall we live in harmony?* Honolulu, Hawai'i: Bishop Museum Press.

Kanahele, G. (1986). *Ku kanaka (Stand tall): A search for Hawaiian values.* Honolulu, Hawai'i: University Press of Hawai'i.

Kittelson, D. (1985). *The Hawaiians: An annotated bibliography.* Honolulu, Hawai'i: Social Science Research Institute.

Kuykendall, R. (1938, 1953, 1967). *The Hawaiian kingdom* (three volumes). Honolulu, Hawai'i: University Press of Hawai'i.

Leighton, A. (1959). *My name is legion: Foundations for a social psychiatry.* New York: Basic Books.

Marsella, A.J., Gomes, K., Higginbotham, N., Kwan, L., Ostrowski, B., Roche, B., Takeuchi, D., & Wight, K. (1985). *E Ola Mau: The Native Hawaiian health needs study: Vol. 2. Mental health.* Honolulu, Hawai'i: Alu Like, Inc.

Miike, L. (1993, February 14). Who is Hawaiian today? *Honolulu Star Bulletin-Advertiser,* p. B-1.

Native Hawaiian Educational Assessment Project. (1983). *Final report.* Honolulu, Hawai'i: The Kamehameha Schools/Bernice Pauahi Bishop Estate.

Nordyke, E. (1989). *The peopling of Hawai'i.* Honolulu, Hawai'i: University Press of Hawai'i.

Papa O Lokahi. (1987). *The Native Hawaiian health data book.* Honolulu, Hawai'i: Papa O Lokahi.

Pukui, M. (1983). *Olelo no eau: Hawaiian proverbs and poetical sayings.* Honolulu, Hawai'i: Bishop Museum Press.

Pukui, M., Haertig, E., & Lee, C. (1972). *Nana i ke kumu* (Vol. 1). Honolulu, Hawai'i: Queen Lili'uokalani Children's Center.

Pukui, M., Haertig, E., & Lee, C. (1979). *Nana i ke kumu* (Vol. 2). Honolulu, Hawai'i: Queen Lili'uokalani Children's Center.

Pukui, M., Handy, C., & Livermore, K. (1934). Outline of Hawaiian physical therapeutics. *Bernice P. Bishop Museum Bulletin, Number 126,* Honolulu, Hawai'i.

Rayson, A. (1984). *Modern Hawaiian history.* Honolulu, Hawai'i: Bess Press.

Shook, V. (1985). *Ho'opono'pono.* Honolulu, Hawai'i: University Press of Hawai'i.

Stannard, D. (1989). *Before the horror: The population of Hawai'i on the eve of Western contact.* Honolulu, Hawai'i: Social Science Research Institute/University Press of Hawai'i.

Stannard, D. (1992). *American holocaust: The conquest of the new world.* New York: Oxford University Press.

Takeuchi, D., Higginbotham, N., Marsella, A. J., Gomes, K., Kwan, L., Ostrowski, B., Roche, B., & Wight, K. (1987). Native Hawaiian mental health. In B. Robillard & A. J. Marsella (Eds.), *Contemporary issues in mental health research in the Pacific Islands.* Honolulu, Hawai'i: University Press of Hawai'i.

Trask, H., & Trask, M. (1988). *Hawaiian's self determination and ethnodevelopment: A Hawaiian perspective.* Unpublished manuscript. Hawaiian and Pacific Collection, University of Hawai'i, Honolulu, Hawai'i.

Trask, H.K. (1993). *From a native daughter: Colonialism and sovereignty in Hawai'i.* Monroe, Maine: Common Courage Press.

United States Congress. (1987). *Office of Technology Assessment Annual Report on National Health Status.* Washington, DC: United States Congress.

White, A., & Landis, M. (1982). *The mental health of Native Hawaiians.* Honolulu, Hawai'i: Alu Like, Inc.

Yim, S. (1992, January 5). Hawaii's ethnic rainbow: Shining colors, side by side. *Honolulu Star Bulletin & Advertiser*, p. B-1.

Young, B. (1980). The Hawaiians. In J. McDermott, W. Tseng, & T. Maretzki (Eds.). *People and culture of Hawaii.* Honolulu, Hawai'i: University Press of Hawai'i.

Chapter 5

Vulnerability and Resiliency in Native Hawaiian Families Under Stress

Elizabeth A. Thompson,
Hamilton I. McCubbin, Anne I. Thompson,
and Kelly M. Elver

The recent increase in social science research on Native Americans reflects the recognition that the social realities of the Native American population are not adequately understood, nor served, by previous research. Although Native Americans have been included in several major national studies on American families, Native Hawaiians are seldom included within the Native American cluster. Due to the geographical separation of Native Hawaiians from other Native American groups, as well as their relatively small numbers, Native Hawaiians have not been adequately identified as Native Americans. However, the importance of studying Aboriginal Native Hawaiians has already been established by virtue of their "at risk" status among minority populations in the United States (Blaisdell, 1989; Mokuau, 1992). It is widely agreed that the physical, psychological, and social realities of Native Hawaiians place them among the most "at risk" populations within the state of Hawai'i, and previous studies of Native Hawaiians suggest that they are faced with the worst health profile of any group within the United States. Blaisdell (1989) asserts that the forced adaptation of Native Hawaiians to European culture, including dietary and lifestyle influences, undermined Native Hawaiians' physical health. Native Hawaiians have the shortest life expectancy and the highest overall death rate of any ethnic group in Hawai'i, and their mortality rates from cancer, heart disease and diabetes are the highest in the nation (Blaisdell, 1989; Marsella et al., 1995).

In addition, to the physical risks of Native Hawaiians, many psychological and social risks have also been noted. Numerous studies have reported high rates of substance abuse, child abuse and neglect, depression and suicide among Native Hawaiians (see Marsella, Oliveira, Plummer, & Crabbe, 1995). Recent assessments of Native Hawaiian children found that they were among the most "at risk" for negative academic outcomes (Native Hawaiian Educational Assessment Project, 1983). Likewise, Native Hawaiians are overrepresented in the lower socioeconomic segments of the State's population as well as in the State's prison system.

Additionally, Marsella and colleagues (1995) report that Native Hawaiians have the highest rate of pregnancy and births to unmarried mothers. Although the existence of single-parent households within the Native Hawaiian population is not uncommon, research on Native Hawaiian families has not given sufficient attention to the particular strengths and vulnerabilities of single-parent families. The dramatic increase in single-parent households in the last two decades has drawn significant attention to issues of parental stress and coping in the one-parent family (McLanahan, 1983; Kissman & Allen, 1993). The role of social support has often been cited in the literature as an important coping resource for single-parent families (Dornbusch et al., 1985; Kissman & Allen, 1993) The social support received by single parents has also been cited as an important factor in the single parents' sense of psychological and emotional well-being (Sev'er & Pirie, 1991; D'Ercole, 1988).

Coping resources are important to the emotional stability and well-being of family members, and the single-parent family's access to social support resources has been shown in the literature to be an important factor in the mediation of parental stress. Kissman and Allen (1993) illustrate the central social support role that extended family networks can fill for single-parent families, and they emphasize the importance of the extended family among many racial and ethnic minority groups. In a study of social support networks, race, and single-parent families, Hofferth (1984) found that regardless of race, single-parent families were more likely to depend upon extended family for social support than two-parent families. Others have argued that the reliance upon the extended family is an extension of the cultural identity within minority communities, and the supportive role of the extended family is a result of cultural values, not a result of close proximity to extended family networks or the result of situational aspects such as poverty (Keefe & Padilla, 1987; London & Devore, 1988). However, none of these studies included Native Hawaiian single parents.

The existing literature on single-parent families' social support has emphasized the role of the extended family, but less attention has been given to the role of friends and community services in the provision of social support. Several studies have suggested that the establishment of a social support network of friends and community resources is difficult for the single parent because of the isolation of the single-parent family (Kurdek, 1988; Sev'er & Pirie, 1991). Additionally, the literature suggests that single mothers' social support from friends is often related to the social support available to their children, and single mothers often experience difficulty in developing social support relationships distinct from the social support relationships developed by or because of their children (Kurdek, 1988; Petronio & Endres, 1985).

Previous studies have not adequately identified salient vulnerability and resiliency factors for Native Hawaiian families. Although the stressors and coping strategies of Native Hawaiian families have been studied, important differences in resiliency and vulnerability between single- and two-parent families were not explored (McCubbin, Thompson, Thompson, Elver, & McCubbin, 1994). Likewise, previous research on Native Hawaiians has not been sensitive to culturally-specific ethnic coping strategies, the resiliency effects of ethnic identity, or the exacerbating stress related to loss of ethnic identity.

In this investigation, which was guided by the Resiliency Model of Family Stress, Adjustment, and Adaptation (McCubbin & McCubbin, 1993), single- and two-parent families of Native Hawaiian ancestry were invited to participate in a study designed to record: (a) the family's "pile-up" of normative and non-normative life events and changes and their assessment of the severity of each of the changes they experienced; (b) the family's level of support from the community in which they lived; (c) the family's coping repertoire in the management of stresses and strains; (d) the family's problem-solving communication style and the degree to which they were affirming and less inflammatory in their approach to issues and problems; and (e) the criterion for the study, the family's level of distress including having members abusing substances, member(s) having emotional difficulties, and interpersonal abuse.

Method

Subjects

Two community organizations that address the issues of Native Hawaiian families collaborated with the researchers to generate the sample. The first agency addresses the needs of impoverished Native Hawaiian families through education and counseling throughout the state of Hawaii. The second agency is responsible for serving the formal educational needs of Native Hawaiian families. Both agencies were created by Trusts which were established in the late 19th century by members of the Hawaiian royal family. These Trusts were established with the mission of serving the needs and well-being of persons of Native Hawaiian ancestry.

A total of one hundred and ninety-seven families ($N=197$) participated in this study. The total sample included 83 respondents from two-parent households and 114 respondents from single-parent households. To maintain confidentiality, families were contacted by the director of each of the agencies and asked to participate. Families were chosen at random by the agencies from their list of eligible families. In selecting the final sample, the agencies did not provide the research team with a complete list of potential families, nor did they systematically record the number of families who refused to participate. However, the agencies indicated that a low percentage of contacted families refused to participate (less than 10 families). Despite the small sample size, the uniqueness of the sample and the data encouraged the research team to examine the data and to share the results, recognizing that generalizability of the findings is restricted by the sampling limitations. The focal questions for this investigation are: 1) What are the resiliency and vulnerability factors that explain variance in family distress for single- and two-parent Native Hawaiian families?; and 2) Are there differences in resiliency and vulnerability factors between single- and two-parent Native Hawaiian families?

Profile of Participants

The majority (95.4%) of respondents were parents, and a small, but noteworthy percentage (2.0%) were grandparents, or significant others (2.5%). The average age of the participants (of which the majority [91.4%] were women) who responded to the questionnaires on behalf of their families was 30 years (range 12 years to 59 years). On average, the respondents had three children (range 1-9 children). Family income ranged from less than $5,000 (9.3%) to $35,000 (25.3%). The majority of families were in the income range of $10,000 to $34,999 (65.4%). A notable percentage (39.5%) were on General Assistance or AFDC (welfare) support. It is interesting to note that slightly less than half (42.1%) of the families were two-adult households while the remaining families (57.9%) were single-parent households.

Profile of Two-Parent Households

The majority (95.2%) of the respondents from two-parent households were parents, while a small percentage (3.6%) were grandparents or significant others (1.2%). The average age of the participants (of which the majority [91.6%] were women) who responded to the questionnaires on behalf of their families was 32 years (range 12 years to 54 years). On average, two-parent households had three children (range 1-7 children). Family income ranged from less than $5,000 (2.8%) to $35,000 (50.7%). The majority of families were in the income range of $10,000 to $34,999 (91.6%). A notable percentage (11.0%) were on General Assistance or AFDC (welfare) support.

Profile of Single-Parent Households

The majority of the respondents from single-parent households were parents (95.6%), and a small percentage were grandparents (.9%) or were significant others (3.5%). The average age of the family members (of which the majority [91.2%] were women) who responded to the questionnaires on behalf of the family was 29 years (range 15 years to 59 years). On average, the respondents had two children (range 1-9 children). Family income ranged from less than $5,000 (13.5%) to $35,000 (9.0%). Almost half of families were in the income range of $10,000 to $34,999 (48.6%). A large percentage (60.2%) were on General Assistance or AFDC (welfare) support.

Measures

Six primary survey instruments were used in this study:

The Family Distress Index (McCubbin, Thompson, & Elver, 1993) is an eight-item self-report instrument with a four-point scale ranging from Not a Problem to Large Problem. The instrument measures the degree to which the family unit is faced with hardships that may be viewed as symptomatic of family distress. This scale includes items such as: A member appears to have emotional problems; A family member is using or abusing substances; and A family member is abusing another member. The overall reliability (Cronbach's Alpha) for the Family Distress Index is .87.

The Family Pressures Index (McCubbin, Thompson, Patterson, & Wilson, 1993) is a 64-item measure with a four-point rating scale (Not a Problem, Small Problem, Medium Problem, and Large Problem). The instrument measures the degree to which life events, called pressures, affected the family during the preceding 12-month period. The reliability of the Family Pressures Index, which evolved out of the Family Inventory of Life Events (FILE) (McCubbin, Patterson, & Wilson, 1996), was .92.

The Hawaiian Family Crisis Oriented Personal Evaluation Scales (McCubbin, Thompson, Larsen, & Olson, 1993) is a 35-item scale that was expanded from the original 30-item structure of the Family Crisis Oriented Personal Evaluation Scales (FCOPES) (McCubbin, Larsen, & Olson, 1983) for this study. The additional five items focused on ethnically oriented coping strategies that emphasize family problem solving, ethnic problem solving, the involvement of elders, and religious leaders. These five items were added to the other five scales emphasizing the acquisition of social support, reframing, seeking spiritual support, mobilizing to acquire and accept help, and passive appraisal. The overall reliability for the scale was .86 with a test-retest reliability of .81.

The Family Problem Solving Communication Index (McCubbin, McCubbin, & Thompson, 1996) is a 10-item instrument with a four-point Likert scale (False, Mostly False, Mostly True, and True). The instrument consists of two five-item subscales, Incendiary Communication and Affirming Communication. Incendiary communication is defined as that type of communication that is inflammatory in nature and tends to exacerbate a stressful situation, while affirming communication conveys support and caring and exerts a calming influence. Incendiary communication is measured by items such as: "When we have conflicts, we yell and scream at each other." Affirming communication is measured by five items such as: "When we have conflicts, we are respectful of each other's feelings." The overall reliability (Cronbach's Alpha) for the instrument is .89.

The Family Coherence Index (McCubbin, Larsen, & Olson, 1982) is a four-item measure that uses a five-point scale ranging from Strongly Disagree to Strongly Agree. This scale is designed to measure the degree to which families call upon their appraisal skills to manage stressful life events, strains, and changes. It includes the items: Accepting stressful events as a fact of life; Accepting difficulties that occur unexpectedly; Defining the family problem in a more positive way so we don't get discouraged; and Having faith in God. The overall reliability (Cronbach's Alpha) for the instrument is .71.

The Community Support Index (McCubbin, Patterson, & Glynn, 1982), also referred to as the Social Support Index, consists of 22 items and uses a five-point scale ranging from Strongly Disagree to Strongly Agree. The scale was used to measure the degree to which families are integrated into the community, view the community as a source of support and feel that the community can provide emotional, esteem, and network support. Some of the items included are: "People can depend on each other in this community" and "If I had an emergency, even people I do not know in this community would be willing to help." The psychometric properties of the Community Support Index include a reliability (internal reliability) index of .82 and a validity coefficient (correlation with the criterion of family well-being) of .40.

Results

A stepwise regression analysis was conducted to explain the variability in family dysfunction. The respondents' age, income, number of children, and marital status were controlled for in all analyses because they were significantly correlated with some of the variables in the model.

Regression Analysis for Two-Parent Families

The initial analysis focused upon isolating the best set of predictors from the Resiliency Model that explains the greatest percentage of the variance on the criterion, family distress. The step-wise regression analysis revealed that there were three predictors of family distress for two-parent families which explain 48 percent (%) of the variance ($F = 24.42$, $p = .006$) (see Table 1). The most important predictor of family distress was the pileup of family pressures ($R^2 = .34$). This is followed in importance by family incendiary problem solving communication (9%). The final predictor in the step-wise regression equation was social support (5%). The first two predictors were positively related to family distress indicating that both family pressures and incendiary communications contribute to family distress. In contrast, the third and final predictor in the equation was social support which appears to mediate the level of family distress.

Table 1
Stepwise Regression Analysis of Family Distress
for Native Hawaiian Two Parent Households
with Predictors of Pressures, Communication and Support (N=83)

Variables	R	R²	Beta	F	p
Pressures (Pile Up)	0.58	0.34	0.51	41.11	0.001
Incendiary Communication	0.66	0.43	0.33	30.14	0.001
Social Support	0.69	0.48	-0.23	24.42	0.006

R=.69   F=24.42   p=0.0001

Regression Analysis for Single-Parent Families

On the criterion of family distress, the step-wise regression analysis revealed that there were four predictors for single-parent families that explain 32% of the variance. (F= 13.27, p=.05) (see Table 2). The most important predictor of family distress was the pileup of family pressures (R^2 = .19). This is followed in importance by family incendiary problem-solving communication (7%). In contrast to the two-parent families, passive coping emerged as the third predictor for single-parent families (4%). The final predictor in the step-wise regression equation for single-parent families was social support (2%). The first two predictors were positively related to family distress indicating that both family pressures and incendiary communications contribute to family distress. The third predictor for single-parent families, passive coping, was positively related to family distress. In contrast, the fourth predictor in the equation was social support, which appears to serve as a buffer to family distress.

Table 2
Stepwise Regression Analysis of Family Distress for
Native Hawaiian Single Parent Households
with Predictors of Pressures, Communication, Coping and Support (N=114)

Variables	R	R^2	Beta	F	p
Pressures (Pile Up)	0.44	0.19	0.39	26.40	0.001
Incendiary Communication	0.51	0.26	0.22	19.87	0.006
Passive Coping	0.55	0.30	0.19	15.97	0.02
Social Support	0.57	0.32	-0.15	13.27	0.05

R=.57		F=13.27	p=0.0001

Overall Differences in Scales Scores

A series of t tests was performed on all of the significant predictors from the regression analyses, to examine whether or not significant mean differences would be found for the single-parent and two-parent families on the key predictors. Of the four primary predictors from the regression models, only two emerged as statistically significant in the test of means; single parents were significantly higher ($t = -1.85$, p=.03) on the pile-up of pressures scale, and single-parent families were significantly higher ($t = 2.20$, p=.01) on the passive coping scale. Likewise, a t test analysis of the Family Distress Index found that there were significant differences between single- and two-parent families on the dependent measure: Single parents were significantly higher than two-parent families ($t = -1.94$, p=.025) on family distress. In the t test of mean differences, no significant differences were identified between single-parent and two-parent families on the incendiary communication and social support predictors.

Isolating Significant Differences Between Single-Parent and Two-Parent Families

While the key distinction among the predictors for family distress in single-parent and two-parent families was passive coping, in order to identify other differences that might exist, a more detailed analysis was conducted. Therefore, the post hoc question was posed: What are the differences between two-parent and single-parent families on the dimensions of family pressures, family coping, problem solving, and support? A chi-square analysis was conducted for each of the items within the scales to identify specific differences, recognizing that statistically one-fifth of the differences could be attributed to chance alone. Given the exploratory nature of this investigation and the need to gain greater understanding of what differences might in fact exist, the analysis was executed and significant differences are presented for the sake of discussion.

Differences in Family Pressures

Nearly one-sixth of the family pressures were significantly different between two-parent and single-parent families. Not surprising, all ten items were significantly greater for the single-parent households. The significant items were: increase in husband/father's time away from family (62.8% for single parents versus 47% for two-parent families); spouse/parent separated or divorced (27.9% vs. 9.8%); increased difficulty in resolving issues with a "former" or separated spouse (37.3% vs. 7.3%); delay in receiving child support or alimony payments (30.1% vs. 6.0%); went on welfare (35.4% vs. 13.3%); an unmarried member became pregnant (20.7% vs. 6.1%); child became seriously ill or injured (22.3% vs. 8.5%); a member could not get a house/apartment because of racial prejudice (11.5% vs. 3.6%); a child member was treated badly because of racial prejudice (18% vs. 4.9%); and we worry that our ethnicity/roots are dying (76.8% vs. 62.2%).

Differences in Family Coping

Out of a total of 35 items, only six items were significantly different between two-parent and single-parent families. Three items were greater for single-parent families: seeking assistance from community agencies and programs designed to help families in our situation (66.4% vs. 50.6%), asking neighbors for favors and assistance (25.7% vs. 12.2%), and showing that we are strong (76.1% vs. 50.0%). In contrast, three of the items were greater for two-parent families: defining the family problem in a more positive way so that we do not become too discouraged (86.4% for two-parent vs. 66.1% for single-parent families), attending church services (56.1% vs. 38.1%), and participating in church activities (48.8% vs. 33.6%).

Differences in Problem Solving

Out of the original ten problem-solving items, only one item emerged as significantly different between two-parent and single-parent families. Two-parent families were significantly higher on the coping item "When we have conflicts, we get upset, but we try to end our conflicts on a positive note" (95.2% vs. 86.7%).

Social Support

Out of the original 22 items on community support, only one item emerged as significantly different between two-parent and single-parent families. Single-parent families were significantly higher than two-parent families on the community support item "If I had an emergency, even people I do not know in this community would be willing to help" (60.2% vs. 51.2%).

Discussion

The pressures facing two-parent and single-parent families provide us the clearest picture of not only commonalities, but also differences between the two family structures. Family pressures, the pile-up of life events and changes that affect families, emerged consistently as a primary predictor and explanatory factor of the criterion, family distress. Measuring not only the types of stresses and strains that occur within a 12-month period but also the severity of the pressures for the family system, the Family Pressures Index provide us an important profile of the demands placed upon the family system and particularly upon the single-parent family unit.

The pressures facing single-parent family households may be organized or conceptualized into three clusters. The first cluster of pressures that are significantly different from the two-parent households appeared to be residuals of the hardships of divorce and separation, as reflected in the increase in husband/father's time away from the family and the resolution of issues with a "former" or separated spouse. This situation is exacerbated by the additional economic pressures associated with delays in receiving child support or alimony payments as well as going on welfare. The additional hardships of an unmarried member becoming pregnant and/or a child becoming seriously ill or injured are added to this already pronounced set of pressures. The third cluster of pressures is related to racial pressures and ethnicity. It was striking to note that single-parent households were significantly different from two-parent households when confronted with the pressures of not getting a house or an apartment because of racial prejudice, a child member being treated badly because of racial prejudice, and the worry that the family's ethnicity and roots, being of Native American Hawaiian ancestry, were dying. The first two clusters, the residual stressor of separation and divorce, and the economic hardship created by this change in status are widely referenced in the literature and therefore, even though this study focused on Native American Hawaiians, the observations and findings are not unique (see, for example, Propst, Pardington, Ostrom, & Watkins, 1986; McLanahan, 1983).

The emergence of racial prejudice and discrimination, however, is particularly noteworthy in this investigation. While there is a common, if not widespread, understanding that people of color are more likely to be subjected to discrimination in a largely Caucasian or White community, data to support this line of thinking are not widely documented or confirmed with any degree of consistency. The statistics become even more important when we consider that the state of Hawai'i is predominantly made up of clusters of ethnic minority groups which are not predominantly Caucasian. It is important to note, however, that Native Hawaiians even in a land dominated by various ethnic groups and people of color are still underrepresented and remain a minority group in their own native land.

The residual effects of the loss of cultural or ethnic identity have also been referred as an important social, psychological, and anthropological phenomena that some argue has contributed to the emotional and physical illness of ethnic populations (Blaisdell, 1989; Native Hawaiian Educational Assessment Project, 1983). The findings would suggest that we have only begun to touch upon the short and long term consequences of prejudice and discrimination in relationship to the criteria for family functioning. It is interesting to note that the issues of ethnic identity and racial sensitivities appear to be more pronounced for single-parents households than it would be for two-parent family units. Part of this difficulty may be the double minority status experienced by racial and ethnic minority single-parent families in a society where two-parent households are held as an ideal. However, this alone would not account for the importance of ethnicity and culture. As we reported in an earlier investigation (McCubbin, Thompson, Thompson, Elver, & McCubbin, 1994) the importance of ethnic identity, the family's schema, appears to be more pronounced in single-parent family units than they are in two-parent families. Thus, the single-parent family may have a stronger emphasis on, if not sensitivity to, ethnic identity and culture as being important to the family unit. It would be instructive to restate our earlier observations:

> Given the inter-racial and thus multi-ethnic nature of native Hawaiian families, the family schema (including culture and ethnic identity) may, in part, be multi-cultural and not singular in its focus even if the families identity themselves as being native Hawaiians. The values and beliefs of the Japanese, Chinese, Filipinos, and Samoans, for example, may well be integral and valued elements of a family schema, resulting in a blended schema—a mixing which is also likely to be apparent in the children of the family unit. The two adult voices may have jointly shaped the family schema creating a mixed multi-cultural world few to guide the family's patterns of functioning (McCubbin, Thompson, Thompson, McCubbin, & Elver, 1994).

In contrast, in single-parent households, the sense of ethnic identity, an understanding of self as Native Hawaiian, may be reflective of a single adult voice forceful in shaping the family's world view. Being Hawaiian or of Hawaiian ancestry may be more pronounced and have greater meaning because of this singular sense of identity and parental influence. It seems reasonable to argue that it is the combination of their minority status by being in a single-parent household combined with their strong sense of Native Hawaiian identity that renders the family not only vulnerable, but also more sensitive to social stressors such as prejudice and discrimination.

The next critical predictor of family distress is incendiary problem-solving communication. This emerges as the second most prominent predictor of family distress in both two-parent and single-parent households indicating that independent of pressures and hardships including racial discrimination, the strategies the families use to handle these pressures, and their patterns of communication can make a difference in how well the family adapts. Clearly, inter-family conflict, which is characterized by yelling and screaming, not being respectful of each other's feelings, and leaving conflicts unresolved, all contribute to, if not exacerbate, the problems of family distress. The only distinction between the two family structures on family problem-solving communication is that two-parent families place a greater emphasis on ending conflicts on a positive note. One could infer, although only tentatively, that conflicts and tensions are less likely to be resolved with ease in a single-parent family.

This finding of problem-solving communication might well be viewed with greater clarity when compared with the finding that passive coping is more pronounced for single-parent households than it is for two-parent units. The tendency to minimize hardships and to accept difficulties as a fact of life is emphasized in single-parent families and predictably is positively related to greater family distress. It is reasonable to wonder whether this strategy for managing hardships may be linked to ethnicity and culture.

One could argue that the circumstances and hardships of the single-parent family place some aspects of life out of the family control to resolve and contribute to a more passive approach to life events. One could also argue that the Hawaiian perspective on coping includes what Alan Howard (1974) calls "ain't no big thing." Hawaiians are viewed as accepting and minimizing in their approach to difficult life situations.

This characterization, may not be an accurate portrayal of Native Hawaiian families, however. While there is an element of truth to passive coping as being important to single-parent families, it is also true that single-parent families are active, if not proactive, about addressing their needs and gathering resources and support to solve problems and to facilitate their adaptation. For example, the findings indicate that single-parent families are more likely to seek assistance from community agencies and programs designed to help them, place a greater emphasis on asking neighbors for favors and assistance and value the importance of showing that they are strong.

The use of community support in coping with difficulties appears to be more prominent for single-parent households than for two-parent families. In contrast, two-parent families were found to emphasize a more positive appraisal of life situations. Two-parent families stressed church service attendence as well as participation in church activities as strategies to manage stressful life events and pressures.

Social support emerges as a common but important predictor for both two-parent and single-parent families. The only difference between the two family structures is the single-parent family's emphasis upon the importance of community support and their feeling that they can call upon the community to help them in case of an emergency. This predictor emerges as the only factor among pressures, coping, and problem solving that appears to work against family distress. Families who view themselves as being integrated into the community, and feel that the community can provide emotional, esteem, and network support to the family unit and its members, appear to be less vulnerable and less distressed. It is also true that while social support is prominent and emerges as an important predictor, in and of itself it is not sufficient to remove the direct effects of family pressures and hardships upon family functioning, and in this case family distress. The literature underscores the importance of social support as a buffer as well as a mediator of stress, and this observation is partially confirmed in this investigation. In the case of Native American Hawaiians, however, and particularly single-parent family units, the positive effects of social support were not as pronounced as expected.

Future Considerations

Although some significant differences did emerge between single- and two-parent Native Hawaiian families, the findings for single-parent families suggest that future research needs to further explore the resilient factors of single-parent families. The single parents in this study demonstrated a creative and resilient approach to buffering the impact of family pressures through their use of community social support. Single-parent households faced a significantly greater impact of family pressures on their families, however, they were able to mobilize community resources to face those pressures. The resilient nature of single-parent households demonstrated in these data suggest that deficit models of family functioning, wherein single parents are compared to the norms for two-parent households, are not sufficient to understand the complexities of coping with stressful life events in the single-parent family. Deficit modeling is stigmatizing to the single parent, and the resilient strategies that are employed by single-parent families are overshadowed. The data on single-parent Native Hawaiian families are further limited by the failure to differentiate between the single-parent families living independently and single-parent families who are embedded within extended family households. Future research is needed to understand within-group differences for Native Hawaiian single-parent families, in an attempt to identify strategies which facilitate resilient adaptation to the pile-up of stressful life events.

These data suggest that traditional ethnic coping strategies as well as pressures caused by feelings of loss of culture and ethnic identity may be significant for understanding Native Hawaiian family functioning. Although ethnically appropriate items were added to several existing measures for use in this study, additional focus on the development of culturally sensitive research instruments is needed.

Although the generalizability of this research is limited by a small sample size and a failure to examine within-group differences for single-parent families, the results point to the value of focusing on the strengths and resiliency of Native Hawaiian households. By identifying the capabilities of resilient Native Hawaiian families, we can begin to uncover culturally appropriate strategies that may be useful for designing programs and services aimed at strengthening the "at risk" population of Native Hawaiian families.

References

Blaisdell, K. (1989). Historical and cultural aspects of Native Hawaiian health. *Social Process in Hawaii*, 32(1), 1–21.

D'Ercole, A. (1988). Single mothers: Stress, coping and social support. *Journal of Community Psychology*, 16, 41-54.

Dornbusch, S.M., Carlsmith, J.M., Bushwall, S.J., Ritter, P.L., Leiderman, H., Hastorf, A.H., & Gross, R.T. (1985). Single parents, extended households, and the control of adolescents. *Child Development, 56*, 326-341.

Hofferth, S.L. (1984). Kin networks, race, and family structure. *Journal of Marriage and the Family, 46*, 791-806.

Howard, A. (1974). *Ain't no big thing: Coping strategies in a Hawaiian-American community*. Honolulu, HI: University Press of Hawaii.

Keefe, S.E., & Padilla, A.M. (1987). *Chicano ethnicity*. Albuquerque: University of New Mexico Press.

Kissman, K., & Allen, J. (1993). *Single-parent families*. Newbury Park, CA: Sage.

Kurdek, L.A. (1988). Social support of divorced single mothers and their children. *Journal of Divorce, 11*, 167-188.

London, H., & Devore, W. (1988). Layers of understanding: Counseling ethnic minority families. *Family Relations, 37*, 310-314.

Marsella, A.J., Oliveira, J.M., Plummer, C.M., & Crabbe, K.M. (1995). Native Hawaiian (Kanaka Maoli) culture, mind, and well-being. In H.I. McCubbin, E.A. Thompson, A.I. Thompson, & J.E. Fromer (Eds.), *Resiliency in ethnic minority families: Native and immigrant American families*. Madison, WI: University of Wisconsin System.

McCubbin, H.I., Larsen, A., & Olson, D.H. (1982). *Family coherence index.* Madison, WI: Family Stress, Coping and Health Project.
McCubbin, H.I., Larsen, A., & Olson, D.H. (1983). Family crisis oriented personal evaluation scales. In H.I. McCubbin & A.I. Thompson (Eds.), *Family assessment inventories for research and practice.* Madison, WI: Family Stress, Coping and Health Project.
McCubbin, H.I., Patterson, J.M., & Glynn, T. (1982). *Family coherence index.* Madison, WI: Family Stress, Coping and Health Project.
McCubbin, H.I., Patterson, J.M., & Wilson, L. (1996). Family inventory of life events and changes (FILE). In H. McCubbin, A. Thompson, & M. McCubbin (Eds.), *Family assessment: Resiliency, coping and adaptation—Inventories for research and practice* (pp. 103-178). Madison: University of Wisconsin System.
McCubbin, H.I., Thompson, A.I., & Elver, K.M. (1993). *The family distress index.* Madison, WI: Family Stress, Coping and Health Project.
McCubbin, H.I., Thompson, A.I., Larsen, A., & Olson, D.H. (1993). *Hawaiian family crisis oriented personal evaluation scales.* Madison, WI: Family Stress, Coping and Health Project.
McCubbin, H.I., Thompson, A.I, Patterson, J.M., & Wilson, L. (1993). *The family pressures index.* Madison, WI: Family Stress, Coping and Health Project.
McCubbin, H.I., Thompson, A.I., Thompson, E.A., Elver, K.M., & McCubbin, M.A. (1994). Ethnicity, schema and coherence: Appraisal processes for families in crisis. In H.I. McCubbin, E.A. Thompson, A.I. Thompson, & J.E. Fromer (Eds.), *Sense of coherence and resiliency: Stress, coping and health.* Madison, WI: Center for Family Studies, University of Wisconsin System.
McCubbin, M.A., & McCubbin, H.I. (1993). Families coping with illness: The resiliency model of family stress, adjustment and adaptation. In C. Danielson, B. Hamel-Bissell, & P. Winstead-Fry (Eds.), *Families, health and illness* (pp. 21-63). New York: Mosby.
McCubbin, M.A., McCubbin, H.I., & Thompson, A. (1996). Family problem solving communication index (FPSC). In H. McCubbin, A. Thompson, & M. McCubbin (Eds.), *Family assessment: Resiliency, coping and adaptation—Inventories for research and practice* (pp. 639-686). Madison: University of Wisconsin System.
McLanahan, S. (1983). Family structure and stress: A longitudinal comparison of two-parent and female-headed families. *Journal of Marriage and the Family, 45,* 347-357.
Mokuau, N. (1992). A conceptual framework for cultural responsiveness in the health field. In J. Fischer (Ed.), *East-West directions: Social work practice, traditions and change.* Honolulu, HI: School of Social Work, University of Hawaii.
Native Hawaiian Educational Assessment Project. (1983). *Final report.* Honolulu, HI: The Kamehameha Schools/Bernice Pauahi Bishop Estate.
Petronio, S., & Endres, T. (1985). Dating and the single-parent: Communication in the social network. *Journal of Divorce, 9,* 83-105.
Propst, L.R., Pardington, A., Ostrom, R., & Watkins, P. (1986). Predictors of coping in divorced single mothers. *Journal of Divorce, 9,* 33-53.
Sev'er, A. & Pirie, M. (1991). Factors that enhance or curtail the social functioning of female single parents: A path analysis. *Family and Conciliation Courts Review, 29,* 318-337.

Chapter 6

Native Sovereignty

A Strategy for Hawaiian Family Survival[1]

Haunani-Kay Trask

In Polynesian cultures, genealogy is paramount. Therefore, I greet you today with my family origins. I am descended of the Pi'ilani line of Maui, on my mother's side, and the Kahakumakaliua line of Kaua'i on my father's side. I am Native Hawaiian, indigenous to Hawai'i.

Genealogically, Hawaiians descend from *Paphanaumoku*—Earth Mother—and *Wakea*—Sky Father—who created the Hawaiian islands. From these islands came the *taro*, and from the *taro* came our chiefs and the common Hawaiian people.

As in all of Polynesia, so in Hawai'i: Younger siblings must care for and honor elder siblings, who, in return, will protect and provide for younger siblings. The lesson of our genealogy is clear: Hawaiians must nourish the land, our ancestor, who will care for us in return. The relationship is more than reciprocal; it is familial. The land is our mother and we are her children. This is the primary lesson of our genealogy.

For a dozen millennia, the vast Pacific has been our home. As island peoples, we have lived in our mother's keeping and she, in ours. Before the coming of *haole*, that is, white people, our *ali'i*, or chiefs, managed and administered the land while our *maka'ainana*, or people of the land, produced the food. To us, all living things have spirit, and indeed, consciousness. Since the land, or *'aina*, is our ancestor, nothing in the natural world is foreign. For us, the cosmos is a universe of familial relations. When I speak of the Hawaiian family, then I refer to the Native people in relation to their Native land. Today, this relationship can only be understood in the context of Euro-American colonialism.

When Captain James Cook stumbled upon our interdependent and wise society in 1778, he began a violent process from which our people have never recovered. Cook introduced capitalism, iron, and Western political ideas, such as predatory individualism. Most destructive of all, he brought infectious diseases: syphilis, gonorrhea, and tuberculosis. With later immigrant gifts of small pox, measles, leprosy, and typhoid fever, Hawaiians were killed by the hundreds of thousands, reducing our Native population (from an estimated 1,000,000 at contact) to less than 40,000 by 1890. A hundred years after Cook's arrival, my people had been dispossessed of our moral order and chiefly government, many of our cultural practices, and most of our lands and waters.

Meanwhile, Calvinist missionaries had converted masses of dying Hawaiians with the promise of everlasting life. While Christianized Hawaiians continued to die off, missionary advisors to the Hawaiian king urged a change in land tenure from common usage to private ownership to guarantee the prosperity of the people and the nation. Instead, the land division of 1820, called the *Mahele,* enabled missionaries and their descendants to buy up whole sections of individual islands for enormous sugar plantations to generate vast profits. Meanwhile, the common Hawaiian people received less than 10% of their birthright. But controlling the bulk of Hawaiian land was insufficient for the *haole* capitalists; they had to control the government.

Thus, U.S. marines under the direction of the American Minister to Hawai'i, John L. Stevens, occupied Honolulu on January 17, 1893. By this action, the United States initiated a diplomatic/military move to overthrow our lawful Native government and replace it with a racist government of *haole* sugar planters. As co-conspirators, the Americans and their local counterparts were committed to U.S. annexation. Total American dominance of Hawai'i was their goal.

No Hawaiians supported the giving up of Hawaiian sovereignty. Our people had tasted American "democracy" at the overthrow: white gang rule supported by white, military thugs. We preferred our own Native government by our own Native people.

No popular vote on annexation was ever taken in Hawai'i. We were forcibly annexed by the United States in 1898, and became a Territory in 1900. At annexation, 2 million acres of Hawaiian public lands were transferred to the United States. Thus was the land base of our people stolen by the great American Republic.

In familial terms, our mother (and thus our inheritance and heritage) were taken from us. The Hawaiian family was sundered from its moorings, the land. Along with population collapse, land dispossession was the greatest catastrophe for our people. Proletarianization followed immediately upon land loss.

Today, such brutal changes in a people's status—their government, their citizenship, their nationhood—are considered the most serious human rights violations by the international community.

As a result of these actions, Hawaiians became a conquered people, our lands and culture subordinated to another nation. Made to feel and survive as inferiors when our sovereignty as a nation was forcibly ended, we were rendered politically and economically powerless by the turn of the century. Hawaiians continue to suffer the effects of white colonialism. Under foreign American control, we have been overrun by settlers: missionaries and capitalists (often the same people), adventurers, and of course, hordes of tourists, nearly seven million in 1993. All these Americans have one belief in common: To them, Hawai'i is as American as hot dogs and CNN. Worse, most Americans assume that if an opportunity arises, they too may make the trip to "paradise," following along after the empire into the sweet and sunny land of palm trees and *hulahula* girls.

Preyed upon by corporate tourism, caught in a political system where we have no separate political and legal status—unlike other recognized Native peoples in the U.S.—to control our land base (two million acres of trust lands), we are, by every measure, the most oppressed of all groups living in Hawai'i, our ancestral land.

Despite the presence of a small middle class, Hawaiians as a people register the same profile as other indigenous groups controlled by the United States: high unemployment, catastrophic health problems, low educational attainment, large numbers institutionalized in the military and prisons, occupational ghettoization in poorly paid jobs, and increasing emigration from Hawai'i amounting to diaspora.

The latest affliction of corporate tourism has meant a particularly insidious form of cultural prostitution. The *hula*, for example, has been made ornamental, a form of exotica for the gaping tourist. Far from encouraging a cultural revival, tourism has appropriated and prostituted the accomplishments of a resurgent interest in things Hawaiian (for example, the use of replicas of Hawaiian artifacts such as fishing and food implements, capes, helmets, and other symbols of ancient power to decorate hotels). Hawaiian women, meanwhile, are marketed on posters from Paris to Tokyo promising an unfettered, "primitive" sexuality. Burdened with commodification of our culture and exploitation of our people and homeland, Hawaiians live in an occupied country whose hostage people are forced to witness, and for some, to participate in, our collective humiliation as tourist artifacts for the First World.

In the meantime, shiploads and planeloads of American military forces continue to pass through Hawai'i on their way to imperialist wars in Asia and elsewhere. Throughout the Second World War and its immediate aftermath, Hawai'i was under martial law, during which time over 600,000 acres of land were confiscated, civil rights were held in abeyance, and a general atmosphere of military intimidation reigned. Now, as we approach the 21st century, Hawai'i is a militarized outpost of empire, deploying troops and nuclear ships to the South and East to prevent any nation's independence from the American New World Order. In Hawai'i, the military is the most privileged segment of the population, enjoying exclusive housing, beach areas, and economic privileges.

In our subjugation to American control, we have suffered what other displaced, dislocated people, such as the Palestinians and the Irish of Northern Ireland have suffered: We have been occupied by a colonial power whose every law, policy, cultural institution, and collective behavior entrench foreign ways of life in our land and on our people. From the banning of our Native language in 1896, to the theft of our sovereignty in 1893, to forcible annexation in 1898, to territorial incorporation in 1959 as a state of the United States, we have lived as a subordinated Native people in our ancestral home.

But now, Hawaiians are demanding some form of self-government on a land base which we govern without the participation of non-Natives or state and federal governments. Exactly a century after the American invasion of our country, my generation of Hawaiians is opposing the United States, the ideology that we are all immigrants and Americans, and the facile imperialism that forces American culture on resisting indigenous peoples the world over.

The Hawaiian sovereignty movement is nearly 15 years old. Simply put, our claims are based in the overthrow and forced annexation. The leading sovereignty group, Ka Lahui Hawai'i, is organized on the principle of American Indian nations, with citizenship roles, a constitution, a governor, legislature, and advisory bodies, including a judiciary. At present, Ka Lahui has over 22,000 members.

The position of Ka Lahui is the most clearly enunciated among sovereignty groups. We lay claim to 2,000,000 acres of land, that is, all the government lands taken at the overthrow and subsequently transferred to the United States government or its agent, the state of Hawai'i. These claims include all water and mineral rights. Money is not to be taken in lieu of land, only as rent or as compensation for lands irreparably lost. Most critically, Hawaiians must be recognized as a Native nation within the purview of federal policy on other Native peoples in the United States.

I have gone to some length to relate our origins and recent history as a people because for Native peoples, the family is the nation, in the most intimate sense of that term. Given that our cosmology is a universe of familial relations, any policies that reconnect us to our lands of aboriginal occupation will aid the survival of the 'ohana, or Hawaiian family.

In the case of my own people, emigration has been directly caused by the theft of our land base and the intense urbanization that has followed on annexation, statehood, and the rise of mass-based corporate tourism. Because diaspora is directly spurred by land loss and the resulting proletarianization of landless Natives, putting our people back on the land is the first policy to ensure that the Hawaiian family survives. Anything short of this—such as cash subsidies, social services, and the general welfare or workfare approaches—leaves untouched the root of the problem while ignoring the process of atomization and family collapse.

Every study on the Hawaiian family has emphasized two defining cultural attributes: the affective nature of Hawaiian families (that is, the willingness of Hawaiians to place affective ties before money-making, career advancement, and other Western individualistic goals), and the continuing desire for many children, including hanai or adopted children, to allow for large families, and thus large kin networks, often called the extended family. I might just add here that Hawaiians adopt or hanai children, both related and unrelated genealogically, and these children continue, in most cases, to spend time with their blood parents, or makua ponoi, as well as their adoptive parents. In other words, no shame or embarrassment, in the Western sense, attaches to hanai status, either for parents or their hanai children.

Undoubtedly, these desires and characteristics are typically Hawaiian. Unlike haole and Asian families in Hawai'i, Native families emphasize large numbers of people and sharing of resources beyond those related by blood. The determining cultural value is one of generosity which thereby ensures reciprocity. Now, we need to recall that reciprocity is a lesson of our genealogy. Large Hawaiian families survive because they are based on reciprocal relationships that include food, housing, money, and children. Hawaiians give children as readily as food to those with whom they are intimately connected.

But for this network of love, or *aloha*, to continue, and thus for the Hawaiian family to continue, a land base under exclusive Native control is essential. Sovereignty—the ability to govern ourselves—is the best assurance of Hawaiian family longevity.

What is perhaps most striking about the contemporary Hawaiian *'ohana* is simply that it has persevered, despite the accelerating ravages of American colonialism. However, *'ohana* survival is constantly endangered by a stark reality: Hawaiians are the fastest emigrating group in Hawai'i. Thankfully, they are also the fastest reproducing group at home. But for how long? While I speak, new immigrants threaten to outnumber us as they crowd into our islands. In the last survey by the State of Hawai'i, the Hawaiian population continued its numerical decline. And not all of this decline is attributable to our high infant mortality rates and the state's lowest life expectancy. Hawaiian depopulation is also caused by emigration, or diaspora. At present, the only policy that can begin to reverse this alarming reality is federal recognition of our nationhood, the transfer of lands, monies, and resources to a Native government, and the rebuilding of our people's lives on their indigenous lands. Indeed, most of the family studies done on Hawaiians have chosen those Hawaiians fortunate enough to live on the few available acres of Hawaiian trust lands. As paltry as these land awards have been, and as unproductive as the land itself has been, the Hawaiian extended family has persisted there, giving support to my argument that returning Hawaiians to their familial origins— that is, to their land—is the only way to ensure the resiliency of the Hawaiian *'ohana*.

Finally let me end by a reiteration of the Hawaiian genealogy. We are children of *Paphanaumoku*—Earth Mother—and *Wakea*—Sky Father. Hawai'i is our mother; rejoining her completes our family circle. In modern terms, then, we must be returned to the lands of our birth. Our ability to survive as a people depends upon it.

Note

1. This chapter is adapted from a keynote address given by Dr. Haunani-Kay Trask as part of the "Resiliency in Families: Racial and Ethnic Minority Families in America" conference, held at the University of Wisconsin–Madison, May 31-June 2, 1994.

References

Boggs, S., Watson-Gegeo, K., & McMillen, G. (1985). *Speaking, relating, and learning: A study of Hawaiian children at home and at school.* Norwood, NJ: Ablex.

Forster, J. (1960). The Hawaiian family system of Hana, Maui, 1957. *Journal of the Polynesian Society, 69*(2), 92–103.

Gallimore, R., & Boggs, J. (1974). *Culture, behavior, and education: A study of Hawaiian Americans.* Beverly Hills, CA: Sage.

Gallimore, R., & Howard, A. (1968). *Studies in a Hawaiian community: Na makamaka o nanakuli.* Pacific anthropological records, No. 1. Honolulu: Bishop Museum.

Handy, E. S. C., & Pukui, M. K. (1972). *The Polynesian family system in Ka'u, Hawai'i.* Rutland, VT: Charles Tuttle & Co.

Howard, A. (1974). Ain't no big thing: Coping strategies in a Hawaiian-American community. Honolulu: University Press of Hawai'i.

Ito, K. (1985). Affective bonds: Hawaiian interrelationships of self. In *Person, self, and experience: Exploring Pacific ethnopsychologies* (pp. 301–327). Berkeley: University of California Press.

Kame'eleihiwa, L. (1992). *Native land and foreign desires.* Honolulu: Bishop Museum Press.

Korbin, J. E. (1990). Hana'Ino: Child maltreatment in a Hawaiian-American community. *Pacific Studies, 13*(3), 7–22.

Native Hawaiians Study Commission Report, Volumes I and II. (1983).

Native Hawaiian Health Data Book. (1992). State of Hawai'i.

Stannard, D. (1989). Before the horror: The population of Hawai'i on the eve of Western contact. Honolulu: University of Hawai'i.

Trask, H. K. (1993). *From a Native daughter: Colonialism and sovereignty in Hawai'i.* Monroe, ME: Common Courage Press.

II b. Native American Indians

Chapter 7

Understanding Family Resiliency From a Relational World View[1]

Terry L. Cross[2]

Good morning. I want to start here at the podium, and then I am going to move down to the floor because I have an overhead which I want to write some things on and share some thoughts with you. But before I do that, I need to tell you some things about the thoughts I want to share. The proceedings from this gathering are to be published, and I have been asked to contribute my words to that publication. That's good. These are important topics for us to discuss, but it is not without some ambivalence that I approach writing what I am going to share with you.

For a lot of Native peoples words have been held as sacred things to be used carefully. We are often gifted from the Creator with the words that we need at the moment we need them. Speaking like that often comes from the heart, not from the mind and so to turn that type of speech into a publishable paper is something quite different. But, I will do it. Part of my ambivalence is about the way that words are used in the mainstream society. Like land, words are owned. They're claimed through copyrights.

In academic settings we are taught to reference and to cite, and I have certainly written like that as any author or graduate student has done. I still write in that manner today. But for this particular presentation, what I am going to share with you comes from different references. It comes from what has probably been my greatest point of reference: my own family, my mother. These ideas are the essential core of a world view taught to me by my relations, planted in my mind by the silent examples and humble stories of my elders, friends, and clients. These obscure beginnings prepared the way for the rich fruition that comes with dreams and visions, so some of what you will hear are things that have come to me in those times of spiritual work through visions and dreams. Dreams and visions take on meaning with experience and then ripen into "knowing" through meditation and examination so I will share with you today some the knowings that have developed for me over time.

When I have been asked to present these ideas in the past people often have asked, "Do you have something in writing? Can you give me a list of references?" The answer is always "no" because I hesitate to write things down that don't belong to me. I don't own them. They were given to me, and to copyright them seems absurd. As I look around at what is happening to Native religions today and at people who are writing things down—people, many of whom are not Indian themselves, who are putting things into books, and are copyrighting the very essence of our belief systems—there is a bitter sadness about that to me. Just as our land had been appropriated in the past, our thoughts and ideas are slowly slipping away into other peoples' ownership through copyright.

So what I am doing today is a telling. Now, a telling is a story. I have described to you my ambivalence about writing things down, but there is another cultural value that brings me here to this discussion. Like the storyteller, like the traditional helper of the past, we are given these things not for own benefit but for those around us. We are obligated, once given the gift, to share it.

And so here I am. Let me start properly by thanking the Creator for the words that I will share with you and ask that my words might be just what is needed here today. I ask also that they go forth from here in their written form, or in your hearts and minds, in a way that will be used for good and that they will touch each of you, that you be able to roll them around in your own mind and add to whatever it is you think about such topics. Let me also give proper thanks that you are all well, that you are here and that our minds are open. I apologize in advance for any words that might invoke offense to anyone. I didn't come to offend anyone, and I hope that no offense is taken. At the end I will tell you a little bit more about why I start that way.

World view is the collective thought process of a people or a cultural group. We have thoughts which can be generated into ideas. Ideas are collected together to become concepts, and concepts get lumped together to become constructs. Constructs become paradigms. Paradigms get linked together to create world view. By the time we get to world view, it is pretty hard to describe. It is pretty hard to know what it is.

On our globe today there are two predominant world views, linear and relational. I will summarize both world views and then try to show how family resilience can be understood from the relational view. Keep in mind that, in speaking, I will grossly oversimplify both world views. There is no way that I can take something as broad as world view and not over-generalize it and oversimplify it. But for the sake of discussion and investigation, it gives us a way to look at their differences. I will also talk about those two world views as if they are very, very different when in fact they are much closer to each other than can be portrayed in writing or in illustration. I am going to talk about world view in the contexts of helping and healing and how we conceptualize problems and solutions to help us narrow our focus. I will talk about what happens when one of those world views is dominant. In this country, the world view of the mainstream is a linear world view.

At this point, let me make a transition to the overhead projector so that I can share with you these two models and go in further to the relation of models. This circle represents the relational world view or the circular world view. This line represents the linear world view. The linear world view is rooted in European and mainstream American thought. It is very temporal, and it is firmly rooted in the logic that says cause has to come before effect. It is based on cause and effect relationships in a temporal relationship (see Figure 1).

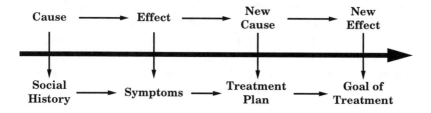

Figure 1
Linear Worldview Model

In human services we are taught that if we can understand the causes of a problem, by taking a social history, then we will better know how to help. Interventions are targeted to the cause, or symptom, and the relationship between the intervention and the symptoms are measured. When we are working in family services, for example, we see a set of symptoms and take a social history. Why? Because we are taught that the more we can learn about that problem or about the person, the more likely it is that we can isolate those factors that have contributed to that set of symptoms and prescribe some kind of treatment. The term "treatment plan" implies another linear cause and effect relationship. Our treatment plan is a new cause and the outcome is the effect. In this series of cause and effect relationships we have to target interventions, as much as possible, to the causes or the symptoms. We are trying to do something to bring about the change.

Through evaluation research, we try as best we can to measure whether this intervention actually brought about the observed outcome. Statistics is a field of study devoted to measuring these linear relationships. If we can demonstrate a linear cause and effect relationship between a helping intervention and the resolution of a problem then we can usually find the support to conduct the service.

The strength of this linear model is that it is measurable. It does tend to drive, or promote, new knowledge and the development of new ideas or theories. It stretches what we know because we are always seeking out better interventions. Its drawback is that it tends to miss the whole person. The linear view is a narrow view. It inhibits us from seeing the whole person. The more education we receive the more we know about a narrower and narrower field of knowledge. In human services, the languages of various specialties are different. Each discipline sees a different set of cause and effect relationships and each believes, first and foremost, in its own view.

Another drawback is that the linear world view tends to encourage a belief that the problem resides in the person. Problems are regarded as largely individual in nature. The person and/or their symptoms become the objects of the treatment, and success is measured by change in individual symptoms. Once you have a diagnosis in this linear model, you have a label that stays with you virtually forever.

This linear world view is the world view of our colleges and universities and of human service professions. I do not mean to judge it as either good or bad. It simply is, and in the U.S. it is dominant.

The relational world view, sometimes called the cyclical world view, finds its roots in tribal cultures. At first, I believed it to be only an American Indian world view, but through working with colleagues from different cultures, I now know that it is the essence of many tribal cultures' world views. It is intuitive, non-temporal, and fluid. The balance and harmony in relationships among multiple variables, including metaphysical forces, make up the core of the thought system. Every event is in relation to all other events regardless of time, space, or physical existence. Health is said to exist only when things are in balance or harmony.

In the relational world view, human service providers are taught to understand problems through the balances and imbalances in the person's relational world. We are taught to see and accept complex (sometimes illogical) interrelationships that can be influenced by entering the context of the client and manipulating the balance contextually, cognitively, emotionally, physically, and/or spiritually. Interventions need not be logically targeted to a particular symptom or cause but rather are focused on bringing the person back into balance. Nothing in a person's existence can change without all others things being changed as well. Thus an effective helper is one who gains understanding of the complex interdependent nature of life and learns how to use physical, psychological, contextual and spiritual forces to promote harmony.

A Relational Model

The relational world view can be illustrated via a four-quadrant circle (see Figure 2). The four quadrants represent four major forces or sets of factors which together must come into balance. They are the context, the mind, the body, and the spirit. The mind includes our cognitive processes such as thoughts, memories, and knowledge and our emotional processes such as feelings, defenses, and self-esteem. The body includes all physical aspects such as genetic inheritance, sex, physical condition as well as sleep, nutrition, and substance use. The context includes culture, community, family, peers, work, school, and social history. The spiritual area includes both positive and negative learned teachings and practices as well as positive and negative metaphysical or innate forces. Of course, I can give only a representative fraction of each quadrant here for sake of discussion.

These four quadrants are in constant flux and change. We are not the same person at 4 p.m. that we were at 7 a.m. Our level of sleep is different, our nutrition is different, and our context is

The things listed below are meant to be examples only. All of life and existence is included in the circle. Balance between all four of these parts brings harmony and harmony is the same as health. Nothing in the circle can change without every other thing in the circle changing as well. The circle is in constant change due to the cycles of the days, weeks and seasons and because of development and changing experience. We are said to be ill if the circle becomes out of balance. Lack of balance causes "dis-ease". In this way of looking at health or mental health, healing may come from any or all of the four parts of the circle.

CONTEXT
Family
Culture
Work
Community
History
Climate / weather

MIND
Intellect
Emotion
Memory
Judgment
Experience

SPIRIT
Spiritual practices / teachings
Dreams / symbols / stories
Gifts / intuition
Grace / protecting forces
Negative forces

BODY
Chemistry
Genetics
Nutrition
Substance use / abuse
Sleep / rest
Age
Condition

Figure 2
Relational Worldview Model

likely to be different. Thus, behavior will be different, feelings will be different, and what we think about will be different. The system is constantly balancing and rebalancing itself as we change thoughts, feelings, our physical state, or our spiritual state. If we are able to stay in balance, we are said to be healthy, but sometimes the balance is temporarily lost. We have the capacity as humans to keep our own balance, for the most part, yet our different cultures provide many mechanisms to assist in this process. Spiritual teachings, social skills and norms, dietary rules, and family roles are among the myriad of ways we culturally maintain our balance.

Take death as an example of an event that threatens harmony. When we lose a loved one we emotionally feel grief, physically we may cry, lose appetite, or not sleep well. However, spiritually we have a learned positive response: a ritual, called a funeral. Usually such events are community events, so the context is changed. We bring in relatives, friends, and supporters. In that context we intellectualize about the dead person. We may recall and tell stories about him or her. We may intellectualize about death itself or be reminded of our cultural view of that experience. Physically we touch others, get hugs and hand shakes; we eat, and we shed tears.

These experiences are interdependent, playing off each other in multi-relational interactions which, if successful, allow us to resolve the grief by maintaining the balance. If we cannot, then we are said, in a western sense, to have unresolved grief or, in some tribal cultures, to have a ghost sickness or to be bothered by a spirit. Different world views often use different conceptual language to describe the same phenomenon.

Helping in the Relational Model

In social work education the question, "Why does the therapeutic relationship work?" is frequently examined. Most introductory textbooks say, "We don't know why it works, but we know it is helpful." From a relational world view, I know why it works. In order to form a relationship with somebody you have to become a part of their context, and by becoming part of their context, you change the balance. If you come into that context in a way that supports, nurtures, or brings about positive changes throughout the balancing process, you are going to do some good, and so for some people just having this context manipulation is enough to feel better. Others need more.

First and foremost, natural helpers, natural healers of native cultures and other cultures around the world become part of the context and, thereby, have an immediate impact no matter what it is they do after that. I know natural helpers who work at an intellectual level. They are advice givers. They will tell you a story, give you an example about how somebody else handled a problem or tell you how historically this was a problem and how it got corrected and thereby give you something to think over. I know natural helpers and natural healers who offer riddles as a way of intervening. Somebody will come to them for help. Sometimes the person is trying a linear, intellectual track of trying to figure out the problem. The helper will give them a riddle, and by the time the person has figured out the answer to the riddle, the problem is gone because the practitioner changed the way the person thinks about the problem and changed the balance. I know natural helpers and natural healers that are great listeners. They might be grandmas or aunties or uncles or grandpas, just good listeners who offer the chance for catharsis. They're often great nurturers. There is nothing like a hug from grandma or a pat on the shoulder and a smile from auntie to kind of bolster you in a difficult time.

Sometimes when I use the term natural helper or natural healer, people say, "What do you mean? Do you mean a medicine man?" No, but I include them. Natural helpers and natural healers are all around us in our cultures. These are people who you turn to for advice, for help, for support, for comfort. They may have specialized skills with spiritual intervention. They may have specialized skills with physical intervention or they may just be good listeners or nurturers.

Some of our spiritual teachers treat a variety of mental health or relationship problems with herbs. Now that may not seem like a linear kind of process, connecting an herbal remedy with a marital problem, but again, they work at trying to manipulate the balance, not attack the issue in a linear way. Some practitioners use fasting, or sweating or use other kinds of physical interventions to bring about change.

Now, there are a variety of spiritual interventions. I know natural helpers, natural healers who teach people how to pray or how to do a particular ceremony. They may teach somebody about the belief system about death and dying for example. There are other practitioners who will perform healing rituals to block negative influences. They may help you set aside some of your own negative actions.

The sweat lodge is a good example of traditional Native American intervention that approaches all of the systems at the same time. Sweat lodges are frequently used in alcohol treatment. When you go to the sweat lodge, you never go alone. There is always the leader. There is always somebody there, and so you come into a context. There is always some amount of teaching that goes on. People instruct you and provide an intellectual framework. Inside the sweat lodge people frequently have emotional reactions, and it is okay to be emotional in that context. People experience vivid memories or visions. The body certainly changes through sweating for an hour and the steam is cleansing. When you come out you feel different. There is this balancing and rebalancing that you go through. So the sweat lodge is used to treat alcoholism, not because it makes the person not drink but because it begins to help the person restore the balance, the harmony.

Family Resilience

This brings me to my description of family resilience from a relational model. When I look for the origins of family resilience within families of color I am not looking for linear cause and effect relationships to isolate the causal factors. Rather I am asking, "What are the holistic and complex interrelationships that come into harmony and allow a family to not only survive but also to grow strong?" The nature of our strengths and challenges becomes evident as we examine family resilience from the relational perspective. What follows are some examples from each quadrant that contribute to the balance. The array of factors is far too great for me to cover and so the examples used are only a small portion of the picture to illustrate the model.

The Contextual

The context within which families of color function is one filled with strength-producing or harmonizing resources. Oppression, for all its damage to us, creates an environment where survival skills are developed and sharpened. We learn to have a sixth sense about where we are welcome and where we are not. We teach our children to recognize the subtle clues that may spell danger. We sit with our children in the movies or in front of the TV and interpret, cushioning the assaults of the mainstream media. We learn how to cope with the dynamics of difference and pass our strategies on to our children.

The richness of our histories and heritage provides an anchor that hold us to who we are. Our relations, relatives, or kin often form systems of care that are interdependent and system reliant. Healthy interdependence is the core of the extended family. It does not foster dependence and does not stifle independence. Rather it is a system in which everyone contributes in some way without expectation of reciprocity. I give my cousin a ride to the store and, while at the store, my cousin buys some items for our grandmother. Our grandmother is home watching my brother's children who are planning to wash my car when I return home. No one person is paying back another and yet the support and help keep cycling throughout the family.

The community provides additional influences. From church to social organizations to politics we all are affected by the events in the world around us. Family resilience is supported by role models, community norms, church structures, and the roles of elders and natural helpers or healers.

The Mental

In the mental area, family resilience is supported intellectually by self-talk and by the stories we hear about how others have managed. Sitting around the kitchen table or the front steps we learn strategies for interacting with the world or how to use resources. In passing on the stories of our lives, we pass on skills to our children, and we parent for resiliency. We instill the values of relationships, of getting by, of not needing, and of hard work for little return. Storytelling is perhaps our greatest teaching resource for communication of identity, values, and life skills. The stories also let us know who our people are and what they stand for, providing role models and subtle expectations.

Emotionally we learn a variety of ego defenses that allow us to deal with overwhelming odds. Denial, splitting, disassociation, and projection are each useful in their own way as mechanisms for surviving oppression. Functionality can only be understood in context. For example, many of our families know real pain and endure grief almost beyond the comprehension of middle America, and yet they give back to their communities. Because of oppression, substance abuse, or poverty, many have learned not to need, not to feel, and not to talk about it. Yet they still help out at the church or at school or by giving sister a break from the kids. These are kindnesses that bring the life-sustaining energy which flows from auntie's approving looks, from a child's laughter, or from a pat on the back.

The Physical

While, for the individual, we think of the physical area as concerning the body in family it also refers to the family structure and roles. Kinship has been discussed, and how we relate to our kin, how we act as a system, and how we sustain each other will greatly influence the balance in our lives.

The role of fathers is part of the balance, one that can contribute strength to the family system whether the father is present in the home or not. In a recent study of Native American families (Nelson, Landsman, & Cross, 1994) that looked at child neglect and the factors that either contributed to or helped prevent it, the role of the father was found to be central. When the father was involved in the family, child neglect was much less likely to be present. The father did not have to be present in the home for the positive effect to be felt. He only had to remain a contributing member of the family and to maintain relationships with his children. Non-custodial dads take note; your continuing relationship with your children contributes to positive outcomes. Families are better able to be resilient if dads positively contribute to the balance.

One thing that kin often do together is eat. Our special cultural or family foods, our use of foods to mark special occasions, and our rituals around eating together are all central contributions to the health of the family.

Family norms about eating and drinking can and do act against harmony at times as when the alcoholic enlists the family in a co-dependent relationship. The harmony of the family is kept by denial and by helping the alcoholic drink, but it is a false harmony that will last until the alcoholic dies or until the family system can no longer support the drinking.

The Spiritual

Spiritual influences in the family include both positive and negative learned practices. The positive practices are those we learn from various spiritual disciplines or teachers: faith, prayer, meditation, healing ceremonies, or even positive thinking. They are the things we learn to do to bring about a positive spiritual outcome or to bring positive spiritual intervention. Negative learned practices are things like curses, the evil eye, or bad medicine. Even things like sin, promotion of chaos, and perpetuation of confusion could be considered learned negative spiritual behaviors. These are things that people do to invoke negative spiritual outcomes or negative spiritual intervention.

Here, folk teachings and the spiritual institutions play a great role. Usually there are learned positive practices meant to counter the negative practices in ourselves or from someone else. Often one person's positive is another person's negative, and the lines between the two become blurred by our emotion. Teachings, community, and family come together to bring about a balance between the two in ourselves and in the family. In communities of color, the church or traditional spiritual disciplines play a significant role in shaping the spiritual practices of the family. The beliefs and the practices that go with them provide a great deal of the energy needed to face adversity.

In the relational world view, human behavior is also influenced by spiritual forces beyond our own making. Luck, grace, positive karma, helping spirits, angelic intervention are just a few of the terms used to describe getting just the right help at just the right time. One does not have to believe in or practice any spiritual discipline to believe in or experience the phenomena. Bad luck, negative karma, ghosts, the devil, misfortune are a few of the terms used to describe the things that bother people no matter what their spiritual practices. These forces are often controlled through prayer, ritual, or ceremony. Some see these influences as driven by external metaphysical forces; others see them as purely driven by chance. Whatever the belief system of the individual, these natural forces are always in play, and thus, challenge and strengthen the family.

All Together

In the relational view, the casual factors are considered together. It is the interdependence of the relationships, with all factors taken at once, that gives understanding of the behavior. It is the constant change and interplay among various forces that account for resilience. We can count on the system's natural tendency to seek harmony. We can promote resilience by contributing to the balance. Services need not be targeted to a specific set of symptoms, but rather services may be targeted toward restoration of balance. Family support services are an example of adding to the balance. Getting in harmony and staying in harmony is the task. So what contributes to family resilience? It is not the extended family. It is not the spirituality. It is not the role of the father. It is the complex interplay among all of those things. It is the balance. It is the harmony that we can achieve in having all of those different things come together. Whenever we try to split it, whenever we try to understand it in a linear kind of way, as we do in current models of research, we lose something in that splitting. My sense is that we have to come up with new models of research and begin to understand the whole; the relationship among all things. I believe that new models of research that are nonlinear are possible and badly needed in our field. Perhaps I am being the heretic here, but to be able to look at interrelationships in multi-causal kinds of ways will be necessary to begin to understand this process.

In the Western European linear world view, we are taught to examine a trait or behavior like resilience by splitting the factors into independent linear cause and effect relationships. This does have value in the development of knowledge of each factor and does tend to further the technology for treating isolated factors. However, such splitting tends to leave us with incomplete knowledge, a "one-size-fits-all" approach to services. Such services fail to acknowledge the spirit. In the linear view the person owns, or is, the problem. In the relational view, the problem is circumstantial and resides in the relationship between or among various factors. The person is not said to have a problem but rather to be out of harmony. Once harmony is restored the problem is gone. In the linear model we are taught to treat the person, and in the relational model we are taught to treat the balance.

Earlier, I addressed the weaknesses of the linear model. The relational model has its weaknesses too. Its downside is that there is this natural tendency to seek harmony even at the expense of the individual in the family. And as already described, if you have an alcoholic in the family, the family will try to compensate by taking care of the alcoholic, often by helping the alcoholic drink. Co-dependent behaviors prevail until the person becomes so sick that the system can't stay in harmony any longer and breaks apart. This weakness also acts as a strength once recovery begins in the family system or community.

I have spoken of the two models as if they are very different, but in reality they are much closer than can be illustrated. There is great overlap between them. For example, my sense is that in the linear approach the lines of thought actually emanate out of the relational circle (see Figure 3). Western helping methods tend to split the person. We give the M.D.s the body. We give the educators and psychologists the mind. We give the social workers the context and the clergy the spirit. We will all look at the same person, with the same symptom configuration, and we will each come up with a different definition of the problem and a different causal relationship or solution to that problem. The M.D. will medicate it away. The educator will teach it away. The psychologist will counsel it away. The social worker will social policy it away, and the clergy will pray it away, and each will be unable to communicate effectively to the other about what the problem is or what to do about it. In addition, we give power to some of those players and not to others. Then we struggle with one another or we stumble over one another.

Today, the linear model dominates delivery of family services, yet almost half the clients nationwide hold a relational world view. Helpers and families are coming to the helping relationship with

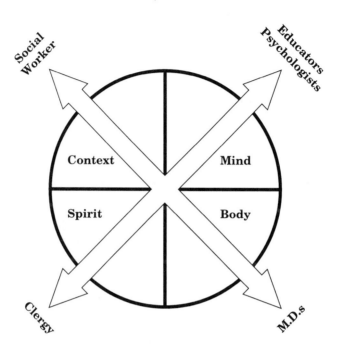

Figure 3
Interrelated Nature of
Linear and Relational Worldviews

different world views, different concepts of the problem and different sets of potential solutions. Unfortunately, in the words of Wade
Nobles (1990), "He who defines reality has power." The mainstream service delivery system has the power of defining the reality,
and currently, reality is linear. As long as the mainstream is unable
to acknowledge the relational model as valid, cultural competence
will remain an elusive goal. Families of color will continue to be
resilient but in spite of the helping system rather than because of it.

I started out by thanking the Creator for the words that I
would share and apologizing for any offense. That model of starting
is traditional in my tribe. It is traditional because it helps keep the
harmony and balance. The constant thanksgiving ensures a good

relationship spiritually. The welcoming with thankfulness and apology helps ensure harmony in relations with people. The Seneca greeting "Nah-weh skeno" means "I give thanks that you are well." It promotes the harmony we have spoken of here. And so, we have this traditional opening whenever we speak. I meant no offense to anyone, and I apologize if my words raised any ill feelings. Any bad feelings that were created by what I said today: I hope that you are able to let go of them. My desire is that you think about what it was I said because I spoke from my heart. I ask that you accept it as information that you might throw around in your own mind. Thank you.

Notes

1. This chapter is adapted from a keynote address given by Terry Cross, M.S.W. as part of the "Resiliency in Families: Racial and Ethnic Minority Families in America" conference, held at the University of Wisconsin–Madison, May 31-June 2, 1994.

2. Mr. Cross is an enrolled member of the Seneca Nation of Indians and is the Executive Director of the National Indian Child Welfare Association.

References

Nelson, K., Landsman, M., & Cross, T. L. (1994). *Family functioning of neglectful families*: Final report. Iowa City: National Resource Center on Family Based Services.

Nobles, W. (1990, April). Untitled Keynote Address given at "Developing Cultural Competence in Health and Human Services" conference, Chicago.

Chapter 8

Walk in Beauty

Western Perspectives on Disability and Navajo Family/Cultural Resilience

Jeanne L. Connors and Anne M. Donnellan

Before the white man came, we were blind [to disabilities].
You brought us the gift of sight. I think we were happier when we couldn't see.
(Elderly Navajo Singer)

We Americans value progress, particularly progress based on science and technology. Many of us grew up with corporate claims that "Progress is our most important product" and "Better living through chemistry." Nowhere is this more obvious than in the world of disability and special education (e.g., Scheerenberger, 1987). As Neville (1994) points out, we are delighted to discuss what science has learned about retardation, and through that knowledge the progress we have made and are making on behalf of the disabled and the people who support them. We are particularly proud to point to changes in laws to benefit children and adults with disabilities (see Gerry & McWhorter, 1991, for a review of recent federal legislation). Kirk and Gallagher (1986) provide a good example: "During the post-World War II era, substantial gains in support have been achieved through the actions of state and federal legislatures, confirming society's determination to provide equity to exceptional children and their families" (p. 30).

Certainly, there is much to appreciate and celebrate. Particularly noteworthy are laws such as PL 94-142 and 99-457 that mandate appropriate educational opportunities for children with special needs. A small percentage of that legislation came as a result of professional knowledge about developmental and other learning disorders. It did not come from our society's "determination to provide equity." Rather, the laws came about as the result of parental advocacy (Dybwad & Dybwad, 1993; Martin, 1991; Skrtic, 1991) with support from some members of the professional community. Not surprisingly, an important part of that legislation is parental involvement in education and rehabilitation for children with disabilities. As with so much of our history in advocacy, however, laws such as these are passed without reference to the socio-political history and the cultural implications of such mandates.

One cannot expect parental involvement to occur, for example, without some concomitant effect on the family who becomes involved with government agencies. Likewise, one cannot expect that professionals will involve families in schools and agencies in ways that are significantly different than their professional training and the formal and informal institutional press mandate. Yet, the language of the laws sets forth an expectation that professionals will involve parents in the process of education and rehabilitation. Not surprisingly, we have had mixed results. The evidence suggests that there is as much frustration and disappointment as there is progress. In the area of early intervention, there is considerable recent interest in re-conceptualizing how to deliver services in a "family centered model" (Bailey, 1987; Bailey, Buysee, Edmondson, & Smith, 1992). In general, however, most families and teachers involved in special education report that the annual review and development of government-mandated individual educational programs are often confrontational and extremely stressful for them (see Cutler, 1993, for a discussion of this issue).

One approach to the problem is to assume that real progress comes not when such laws requiring certain kinds of interactions are passed but when people actually implement them by learning to communicate with one another. In order for that to happen, people, in this case parents and professionals, need to understand more about their respective positions.

This chapter concentrates on two aspects of the parent-professional relationship that are underrepresented in the special education literature: the historical role of the professional in the lives of families with severe disabilities/autism in this country and this century, and the role of families with children with severe disabilities/ autism in a particular subculture, the Navajo nation. We have included the former because professionals are shaped to behave in accordance with the institutions which they serve (Schien, 1968). There is no intent, of course, to suggest that all professionals interact with parents in a certain way.

The people of the Navajo nation are of particular interest, because so little has been written about disabilities, and particularly autism, in non-Western cultures. The roles of the Navajo family and the family of the Navajo disabled child are indicative, in this particular culture, of people attempting to adhere to their own notions of progress. These notions are often discredited by professional attitudes that could actually jeopardize the Navajo family's cultural acceptance of its disabled child. This threat to traditional Navajo family unity points out the necessity for professionals to rethink their own ideas of those roles as the "correct" ones. Few professionals know their own cultural perspective relative to disability, much less the cultural perspective of indigenous peoples. Therefore, this chapter will begin with a brief review of the history of governmental involvement in the lives of individuals with severe disabilities in this century, including cultural issues. The Navajo construct of disabilities within a cultural framework, which offers a very different notion of how disabled individuals are viewed, will also be explored.

Governmental Involvement
With Education and
Professionals

The changing role of government and governmental agents in the lives of children with severe disabilities and their families has both exemplified contemporary societal and professional attitudes and helped to shape those attitudes. Early in this century, the dominant mythology was that America was a melting pot (Glazer & Moynihan, 1963). The goal was to mold all immigrants into some amalgam, which could be called American with Horatio Alger as the model: by hard work and conformity everyone could fit the mold. Once molded into an American, one would prosper.

The molding of new Americans was primarily the responsibility of schools. With immigration at an all time high between 1890 and 1920, the task was formidable. Schools went about this effort with extraordinary zeal and effort (see, e.g., Cavallo, 1970). To their credit, American educators managed to provide basic education to millions of new arrivals in a very short period of time. It must be remembered, however, that this accomplishment had a cost, which is reflected in current dissatisfaction with public education and ongoing calls for school reform (see Smith & O'Day, 1991). Specifically, the emphasis in schooling was on management and efficiency (Callahan, 1962). Management included control of parents and other lay people, mainly by keeping them out of the schooling enterprise (Willower, 1970). Cultural plurality was not even considered. As Leonard Covello, the first Italo-American principal of a major urban public school, wrote of his experience as a turn of the century school boy: "We soon got the idea that 'Italian' meant something inferior...we were becoming Americans by learning how to be ashamed of our parents" (Covello, 1958, p. 6).

These attitudes dominated the boarding schools to which Native American children, including the Navajo, were sent from the early 1900s to the late 1960s. Parental exclusion from the school experience was virtually guaranteed by the practice of sending children to schools hundreds of miles from their home. Within the schools, deliberate attempts were made to break family bonds and destroy any cultural influences that home life might impart on the children, including language, spiritual beliefs, healing traditions, and child-rearing practices. As one Native American told the first author, "When they tell you from the age of six that your Indian ways are wrong and theirs are right, your gods and your spirits are wrong and theirs is good, your Indian people are bad and white people are good, after awhile you start believing it. You want to be white. The only thing is, every morning when I got up and looked in the mirror, I saw an Indian looking back at me!" That the school experience with Native Americans has been a dismal and tragic failure is unquestioned (see, e.g., Crow Dog & Erdoes, 1990), but the managerial approach and efficiency model has remained little changed for the past 100 years of Native American education.

In addition to ignoring the cultural heritage of children and families, efficiency required exclusion of any individual who could not be readily accommodated in the typical fashion (Donnellan, 1980; Skrtic, 1991). Special education, which emphasized that there was something wrong with the child who required individual attention, was the inevitable result of the efficiency model, and it was developed as an isolating and segregating operation. For this population, as for those in regular education, there was no need to accommodate ethnic or cultural differences; the model of education was, after all, based on scientific management principles that were expected to work for all students regardless of cultural background. Teachers learned through the experience of working in schools that, irrespective of the rhetoric, their job was to manage the classroom so that they could get "the class," "the group" through the curriculum (Iannaccone & Button, 1967). Individualization was not part of the pedagogy. Individualization, except for the purpose of management, historically has not been part of the experience in regular or special education (Donnellan, 1980). The resulting conflict was/is inevitable.

Professionals in the disabilities field seldom acknowledge the nature of that conflict. Instead, they frequently write of the "progress" in the field as if progress was part of the natural order, a continuous by-product of science. In fact, the last half of this century has been a continuous battle of parents against school authorities (and other governmental agencies) attempting to get an equal educational opportunity for their disabled children. From the landmark *Pennsylvania Association for Retarded Children vs. The Commonwealth of Pennsylvania* in 1972 to *Holland v. Sacramento Unified School District* in 1994, parents are still having to fight efforts to exclude, isolate and educate children on the basis of disabling conditions (Singer & Irvin, 1991).

More subtle, but equally persistent, are the attitudes of professionals towards their role in relationship to the family. The attitude about the role of professionals in the life of a family with a severely disabled child can be summarized as this: Issues related to children and adults with disabilities are scientific questions. Parents can participate in the discussion, if necessary, but cannot be expected to have the objectivity to make good decisions about educational programs, living situations, or treatment. Parents need to see the problem from the perspective of the professional and make decisions from that perspective. The "doctor/teacher/psychologist-knows-best" is part of the power model from which most professionals have operated (Donnellan & Cutler, 1991).

In the case of one disability group, this attitude of professional knows best became uniquely pernicious. Shortly after autism was first identified by Dr. Kanner, professionals began to see the parents of these children as pathogenic (Bettleheim, 1967). It is easy to trace the origin of this perspective. The children appeared to be quite normal but were not as obviously engaged, bonded, and otherwise attached to their parents as is usually expected. Such serious isolation was seen to have been caused by cold parents, refrigerator mothers, and a recommended treatment was "parentectomy" and psychotherapy for parent and child (see Donnellan, 1985, for a review). It took nearly twenty-five years for professional attitudes to change and for autism to be seen as a developmental disability and not a form of psychosis caused by poor parenting (Rutter, 1978).

Though no longer considered a causative agent, parents of children with autism continue to be blamed for their children's difficulties. In this most recent twist, the parents are blamed for the lack of progress. Beginning in the 1970s, parents were told that if they followed a particular regime exactly, their children would be vastly improved or cured (see Donnellan & Mirenda, 1984, for a review). These regimes often required extraordinary changes in family life and extraordinary effort for all concerned (e.g., Kaufman, 1976; Lovaas, 1978). There was and is a tendency for professionals to assume that progress for the child requires parents to become semiprofessional co-therapists (Schopler & Reichler, 1971). Regardless of the well-meaning attitude of the professional, the underlying message is that the parent must change in his/her fundamental relationship to the child or be blamed for lack of progress. Progress is, of course, defined by the professional (see Skritc, 1991, for a discussion of professional enduction). Thus far, there are no follow-up studies on the effects of these parent-as-therapist regimes on families, marriages, or relationship of siblings to the child who received so much of the family's resources and so different an interaction with the parents.

The professional's training, which emphasizes a child's progress based on an emphasis on "science" and "professional knowledge," also ignores the obvious: what is seen as science or knowledge in one culture may not be recognized as such in another. For example, a Navajo Singer (or medicine man) may pinpoint witchcraft as a cause of autism by finding a dead lizard with eyes and mouth sewn shut under the home of a young man with autism. He is seen, thereby, to have gained important knowledge of this disorder. Further, by performing a prescribed "Sing" (or ceremony) for this particular type of witchcraft, he has utilized the Navajo notion of science. Whether this would be recognized by Western medicine as valid, however, is doubtful. But the point is, of course, that professionals, to be effective, need to acknowledge that knowledge is a cultural construct.

In summary, the role of the state and of state agents in the lives of individuals with significant disabilities has both reflected and shaped a professional perspective that defines children and adults with disabilities as unfit and unworthy unless and until they met some criterion of normalcy, not clearly stated and not readily attainable. Parents have been seen as misguided and emotional, incapable of making rational decisions about issues such as institutionalization and, in fact, life itself (Allen et al., 1989). As the leaders on child affairs, the schools established a model of professionalization that required that parental access to knowledge about the school management as well as the progress of their own children be controlled, and the terms for parental access were determined by the schools (Willower, 1970). Until very recently, these terms did not accommodate cultural differences (see Lynch &

Hanson, 1992). In addition, the professional position assumed that parents were not competent to raise their severely impaired children until and unless they were "trained" to do what professionals believe should be done (Lovaas, 1978; Schopler & Reichler, 1971; Maurice, 1993).

Recently, there has been a broadening of the definition of parent/professional relationships (Donnellan & Cutler, 1991), and in some cases, there have been sincere efforts to develop partnerships. But the dominant message is the same: This child is not acceptable as he/she is. The child must change. You must change to make the child change. And, if the child does not change or you do not change sufficiently, he or she must go someplace else to be changed. It is with this societal attitude in mind that we turn to an alternative view of disabilities, that of the Navajo of northeastern Arizona and northwestern New Mexico.

Navajo Families and Disabled Children

Background

This study involved anthropological research and fieldwork on the Navajo Nation, during which time the first author lived and worked with Navajo staff at a residential facility for exceptional children, all of whom were Navajo or Navajo-Apache individuals.[1] Eight clients (6 male, 2 female, ranging in age from 15 to 29), labeled as autistic and mentally retarded by Western psychologists, were chosen for intensive study because they fit the criteria for a Western-defined disorder (autism). Data were also collected on 24 other individuals without autism but with physical and/or mental disabilities for comparison and discussion purposes. The anthropological training of the first author provided the opportunity to gain a detailed, in-depth "emic" (or insider) view of how the Navajos perceived these individuals and how they were placed in the Navajo social and cultural structures. This goal was in direct contrast to the "etic" (or outsider) view that is most often brought to the study of autism in other cultures; that is, apparently only one anthropological study (Connors, 1992) has investigated non-Western individuals with autism within the context of their own culture to determine how parents perceive and cope with their disabled children.

Staff members and families of the clients with autism or autistic-like behaviors, as well as the families of those diagnosed with mental retardation without autism, were interviewed. In addition, the first author observed daily interactions of the staff with all the clients and, when possible, of family interactions with their children with disabilities. She attended native healing ceremonies, observed normal child/mother interactions throughout the Navajo Nation, interviewed elderly Navajos for a historical background on treatment of the disabled, conducted a community-wide survey to elicit perceptions of autism and mental retardation from those Navajos not directly involved with the disabled, and, in general, immersed herself in the Navajo culture to the greatest extent possible.

Although all of the families that were involved in this research were Navajo, their backgrounds differed considerably. Two of the families of children with autism identified themselves as traditional; that is, they were Navajo-speaking only, derived most of their subsistence from livestock, adhered to traditional practices such as morning and evening prayers, had little or no formal education, and were non-Christian. Both of these families still lived in traditional hogans, one-room circular dwellings made of logs and chinked with clay, with thatch and clay roofs. Two were semi-traditional; that is, they were bilingual, derived some income from wage work, attached less importance to traditional practices, had at least an eighth grade education, and were nominally Christian although they still utilized native ceremonies. They lived on homesteads that might contain a frame house but also included hogans where the grandparents still resided. The remaining families identified themselves as modern; that is, they were English-speaking only, professed Christianity or no religion at all, either renounced or declared ignorance of "Navajo ways," derived all income from wage work, and had high school and/or some college or technical training. These families lived in apartments or trailer homes and tended to live apart from their immediate relatives, having established neolocal residence, but still maintained close obligatory ties with parents, sisters, and brothers. The comparative group were similar in their cultural backgrounds, with a little over half (15) identifying themselves as traditional or semi-traditional and the remainder as modern.

It should be noted that in spite of 200 years of contact with the surrounding Anglo society, the Navajo culture is remarkably stable and enduring. As has been true traditionally on Native American reservations, however, the 25,000-square-mile reservation is an impoverished "third-world colony" and its 150,000 inhabitants, constituting the largest Native American group in the United States, are well below poverty level. Only about one-third of the Nation's 4,500 miles of roads are paved, and less than 50% of the homes have electricity, running water, or telephones. There are no cities on the entire reservation; six major settlements have populations of two to three thousand each and the rest of the Nation is served by small trading posts frequently accessible only by dirt roads, which are impassable during rainy periods. The scattered, isolated, and remote homesteads are the major reason for the endurance of the Navajo culture. Even though border towns such as Gallup and Farmington, New Mexico are somewhat accessible, generally there is little contact with the surrounding Anglo society for much of the Navajo population.

Treatment programs for individuals with disabilities, whether residential facilities or programs to be carried out in the homes by parents with professional guidance, are lacking on the Navajo Nation. Of the facilities that do exist, one accepts only mentally retarded individuals with a relatively high level of functioning and another concentrates efforts on the needs of the physically disabled. A treatment center for the chronically mentally ill accepts only adults and functions mainly as "respite care" during bouts of acute psychosis. Special education classrooms in the day schools are staffed mainly by white teachers who tend to implement Western special education curriculum for the Navajo children with little regard for cultural differences.

Similarly, although the Navajo Nation has five hospitals operated by the Indian Health Service (IHS) that provide free health care to all Navajos, these hospitals and clinics are staffed by white doctors who serve rotations of two years before being transferred to another reservation. It is safe to say that during these two years little knowledge of Navajo culture is gained and many Navajos are reluctant to seek medical care and, when they do, they are hesitant to speak freely.

Thus, most Navajo parents remain relatively unsophisticated about Western notions of biomedicine or of mental retardation and autism, and generally, they encounter the professional attitude only during times of crisis or during yearly Individualized Educational Plan (IEP) reviews at facilities. IEP's are federally mandated plans designed to provide an individualized education to each child in need of special education services. They spell out the child's current state of functioning and the plan for remediation and assessment of progress. The law requires that the plan be evaluated at least annually. These reviews, typically held at the facilities, are often crisis situations for the parents. The result is pervasive misunderstanding between the two opposing cultures.

One incident serves to illuminate the magnitude of this misunderstanding. Several years ago a Navajo child with spinal meningitis was admitted to a hospital where she recovered from her high fever and pain. The parents were then advised to place the child in a residential facility for the developmentally disabled, which they did. Four years later they withdrew her from the school because she had not recovered from mental retardation. "They cured her of the fever in the hospital," said the mother. "I still don't know why that school didn't cure her of thinking slow."

Cultural Constructs of Health and Illness

One factor that often leads Western professionals to misunderstand their indigenous clients is that they often overlook or remain ignorant of the fact that concepts such as causes of illness, treatment of illness, and, indeed, even definitions of illness are cultural constructs. We will briefly examine these constructs from a Navajo perspective.

Causes of Illness. The Navajo maintain a distinct and unique explanation for health and illness, based on identifying and treating causal agents rather than the illness itself. For example, arthritis may result from inadvertently crossing the track of a bear or a feeling of general lassitude and exhaustion may be caused by accidentally coming into contact with an ancient artifact.

The families of the children with autism and mental retardation in this study had their own explanations for their child's disabling conditions irrespective of biomedical ones. Witchcraft was cited by one father who thought that someone jealous of him had placed a curse on his son. A medicine man consulted by the mother of another child with autism suggested that the father may have seen a dead animal while she was pregnant. Another father believed that his disabled son had been conceived by another man because during his autumn hunting season all the animals he had seen had been mating and he had been unable to kill any. It was his belief that this was the animals' way of telling him what was happening back home. His wife, however, strenuously objected to his allegations and pointed out that weaving, herding sheep, and caring for 10 children scarcely gave her time to be unfaithful. As for her husband's hunting skills: "He never brings any meat home because he goes hunting during mating season!"

Another family who sought professional help for a son who exhibited fearfulness and failure to assume responsibility for homestead chores was told that the cause was "generally something the parents did." Since neither parent smoked, drank, or took drugs, they were at a loss to understand their son's difficulties. The father speculated that the disability might have happened because he had worked in a coal mine for eight years prior to his son's birth, but both were left uneasily speculating about the possibility of having done something for which they had been "witched."

In general, families felt dissatisfied with their initial contacts with Western professionals, and often expressed anger. For example, twenty-one years ago the parents of a then-infant daughter, ill with a high fever, sought medical treatment at one of the IHS hospitals near their home. Sent away by the doctor with the advice to return in the morning if she had not improved, the anxious parents took her to another IHS hospital some 45 miles with the same result. After traveling to yet a third hospital and being turned away yet again, at dawn the exhausted parents and dangerously ill child were admitted to an off-reservation hospital where the parents were told, "You waited too long. Your child will never walk or talk. Why didn't you bring her in sooner?" When the father angrily confronted the first doctor for turning them away, he was told to leave the hospital and keep quiet or the doctor would make sure that "none of your family is ever treated here again." Treatment, for this particular child, has consisted mainly of traditional ceremonies since then, and only dire emergencies drive the family to seek Western medical help again.

Treatment of Illness. Once the cause has been determined by a Navajo diagnostician—a crystal gazer, hand trembler, or star watcher—and the proper ceremony has been prescribed, a medicine man, or Singer, is called upon to perform the ceremony, or Sing, to negate the effects of the cause and to restore harmony and, thus, spiritual wellness to the patient. These Sings are exceedingly complex, often lasting for four or five days or even longer, and involve the use of sand paintings, chants, and holy objects such as turquoise stones, bits of coral and shell, medicine sticks, and herbal remedies. For adherents of the Native American Church (NAC), the peyote hallucinogen is also an important ingredient in healing ceremonies. In contacts with the Navajo, it was quite common to observe individuals seeking Western medical treatment for distinct conditions such as a broken bone or a skin rash, while at the same time consulting a Singer to determine what had brought about the accident that caused the broken bone or what had been inadvertently done wrong to cause the rash to appear.

In the case of mental retardation, autism, or such disabling conditions as paralysis from an accident or loss of eyesight due to diabetes, the Singer's responsibility is not to "cure" the condition—to restore the ability to walk or to see or to promise "normal" intellectual capacity. Rather, the Singer assists the individual to accept his or her condition, to integrate mind, body, and spirit, and to allow the individual to live in harmony with that condition. Once this balance has been achieved, the individual is to all intents and purposes a "whole" person again, not only in his or her own eyes but in the perspective of family and neighbors as well.

This sense of harmony, however, often translates into physical improvement. Those families who were interviewed and who had ceremonies performed for their children declared their belief that the Sings had helped their children to become quieter, to have less frequent or severe seizures, to recognize relatives, or to become more alert or mobile. In at least two cases, the parents attributed the survival of their critically ill children to Sings after Western doctors had "given up" on them, and it was not uncommon for parents to remove their children from hospitals to have ceremonies performed and then return them to the hospital to continue Western medical treatment.

In another case, again a crisis situation with a critically ill infant, the mother recalled that her son was snatched away from her by a doctor and "placed in a plastic box with smoke coming out of it. They gave him a shot in the head and told us to get ready to bury him. But my mother had called a peyote prayer meeting. She said they prayed all night, and the next day he woke up and didn't die."

Not all indigenous treatments result in successful recovery, of course. One 16-year-old girl at the residential facility was taken out by her parents for a three-day Sing in which the Singer insisted that she be cleansed of all foreign medications. These included powerful anti-convulsion drugs, the sudden terminination of which resulted in massive seizures on the second day of the ceremony during which the girl died. Her death, however, was not attributed by the parents to the withdrawal from medication, but rather that the evil spirits inhabiting her body had been too powerful for the Singer.

Definitions of Illness. It is important to note that only recently has an attempt been made to translate terms such as mental retardation, autism, and so forth into Navajo, and to the parents in this study, these terms are largely meaningless. Rather, Navajo "ethnosemantics"—that is, what the families and staff themselves called the clients' conditions—are far more indicative of Navajo attitudes toward the disabled. The Navajos tended overwhelmingly to give descriptive labels such as "she runs away" or "he gets excited" or "he's in his own world," whereas the few Anglo staff at the school gave the Western labels of mental retardation or autism. Some families who had received medical diagnoses for their children also used these labels, but further probing such as "What does that mean to you?" revealed that few families accepted or completely understood the implications of mental retardation or autism. Rather, they generally considered the labels in terms of the child not being able to "think like us" or not being able to "take care of herself."

Terms such as mental retardation and autism are, in fact, extremely difficult to explain in the Navajo language without detailed descriptions. A visible disability is often identified by the phrase *Baa da Haz,* which, literally translated, means: "[on one's body] hangs an object [of affliction]." Multiple disabilities are described as *Bich i Niwii Na,* or "toward one are difficult moving times," while a child faced with a major learning problem is conceptually denoted as *Bich i Anahooti,* or "toward one lies a barrier." As an extremely concrete and descriptive language, Navajo is not well-equipped to deal with abstracts such as emotionally disturbed or developmentally delayed; an individual with autism and normal or near-normal intelligence who prefers to be alone, rarely interacts with other, and engages in odd if harmless behavior might be described as "floating on air."

Extensive interviews with elderly Navajo about their recollections of individuals with handicaps when they were children provided a historical perspective to the research. In the past, the only Navajo word for people who were glaringly different was "digiis," a negative term connoting incest (within the family or clan) and generally applied pejoratively. The word itself means "crazy" and was not used to describe individuals who were "slow learners" as long as their behavior was within acceptable social limits. These elderly remembered the term being used for people who were kept apart from other Navajos, who were "screaming and yelling" and "rushing about" and who probably displayed psychotic or schizophrenic breaks. Terms for the physically disabled were conspicuous by their absence in the recollections of these elderly. This is understandable in light of the Navajo notions of wellness, in which a person who is in balance with his or her physical condition is considered a whole person. That is, historically the Navajo did not recognize disabilities as a "handicapping condition," at least to the extent that they felt it necessary to identify and label them. As one elderly Singer said: "Before the white man came, we were blind [to disabilities]. You brought us the gift of sight. I think we were happier when we couldn't see."

From the foregoing, it should be clear that Western practitioners of biomedicine will encounter cultural roadblocks from the very onset, unless the professional is willing and capable of taking into account Navajo definitions and concepts of terms such as health, illness, cure, and progress.

Child-Rearing Practices

One important factor in the role of the disabled Navajo child within the family is the reluctance of Navajos to segregate or isolate children with disabilities. This reluctance stems from the traditional Navajo child-rearing practices. For the white middle-class world (from which most special education professionals come), great emphasis is placed on Western infants from birth to develop regular sleeping and eating routines, to discriminate between objects that can be touched and those that are "hands off," and to conform to a pattern of habits that will eventually lead to academic and employment success. Western children are thus molded from infancy to become a person who can best be integrated into his or her society.

In striking contrast, Navajo infants and toddlers are allowed the first six years of life to become a person in their own right and to develop their own unique identities. They are allowed to eat and sleep precisely when they wish—and where they wish, for that matter. If, for example, a toddler prefers to stay with a nearby aunt or grandmother for the evening and prefers not to go to bed until midnight, it does not occur to any adult to say no or to insist on an appropriate bedtime since, for a toddler, there simply is no "appropriate" bedtime other than the bedtime determined by the child. In addition, a Navajo child rarely, if ever, hears the word "no" or is told not to touch something that belongs to an adult. Mothers with small toddlers who visited the first author's trailer were oblivious to their children handling the tape recorder, cameras, typewriter, notes, and books or wandering off to explore the rest of the trailer by themselves. Because Navajo children do not differ from Western children in excited carelessness, she soon learned to put away valuable equipment when she had visitors as a viable alternative to being compelled to discipline other people's children. This almost total freedom on the part of children, the notion that they can do no wrong in their developmental years, and the tremendous individuality accorded to the child is difficult for Westerners to grasp, but goes a long way toward explaining the Navajo cultural "blindness" to what, in Western culture, would be termed inappropriate behavior or social incompetence.

The notion of what constitutes social competence (an issue of constant concern for Western special educators) can best be described as vague and formless for the Navajo. There are certain expectations, to be sure: one should be able to contribute to the family's well-being, whether by providing financial support (e.g., money for a Sing or for a truck payment) or physical labor (e.g., moving livestock from the mountains to the desert in the fall, helping with sheep shearing, assisting with the preparation of food at a ceremony). One should be able to recognize and apply proper kinship terms and be able to fulfill kinship obligations, and one should be self-sufficient and able to care for his/her self and family. However, the latitude allowed for achieving this social competence is so broad and inclusive that the display of social skills to any degree, however slight it might be, is considered adequate and socially competent.

For the Navajos involved in this study, most of the families overwhelmingly considered their children to be competent. This was, in fact, the case for both children with autism and those without autism. An important signal of competence was conveying to disabled children ownership of livestock, which, among the Navajo, symbolizes the readiness of the family to consider a child capable of assuming adult responsibilities. Even though the children with autism were not capable of fully caring for livestock, ownership of both sheep and goats had been conferred upon them by those families possessing livestock. The children, therefore, were seen as contributing members of the family. In one case, a young man was able to feed the young animals with minimal assistance; in another, the sale of wool from a young man's sheep was sufficient to place him within the family as a financial contributor. For those families who did not possess livestock, skills such as carrying groceries, gathering firewood, or even being able to dress themselves were cited as signs of social competence.

This same tolerance for approximations of social competence was also shown in identifying relatives. Although the clients were unable to correctly apply proper kinship terms to extended family members, it was enough for the families that their children could show a flicker of recognition for a familiar face. Similarly, repetitive, stereotypic gestures such as trickling sand between the hands, finger flicking, or magazine flipping were seen as the ways in which the children amused themselves rather than as representing obstacles to learning more "productive" skills. This unconcern for the stereotypic play in which the clients engaged may be explained by the fact that the Navajo world is "adult-centered"; that is, children are expected to learn to handle and appropriately use adult objects and materials in contrast to the Anglo "child-centered" world where adults enter into children's play by using their child's toys to teach appropriate play skills. Thus, play is not considered as significant for the Navajo as for Anglos, due partly to the fact that Navajo families have far less leisure time to fill because of the sheer labor involved in daily life: hauling water, gathering firewood, herding sheep, or cooking on wood stoves.

The findings from the family interviews were matched by those of the staff who worked closely with both clients with autism or autistic-like behaviors and those with mental retardation without autism. Although the eight clients with autism were strikingly different in their lack of affective response, repetitive language, difficulty in comprehending and generalizing instruction, perseverative routines, and stereotypic gestures, the staff as a whole did not perceive these clients as being all that different from the other clients. While they noted that social skills were lacking in some cases, this was of very little importance and the staff were quick to emphasize the strengths of the clients or to say, "He's okay" or "She's doing fine." As with the families, approximations of appropriate behavior were sufficient to mark the clients as socially competent beings.

Both families and staff overwhelmingly perceived these clients either as babies or little children regardless of their chronological age, as did the Navajo respondents of a community survey. This differed from the Anglo respondents of the survey, who tended to consider individuals with autism or mental retardation as adults in accordance with chronological age. As noted earlier, a great deal of permissiveness is given to Navajo children until the age of six or seven and this pervasive cultural child-rearing practice helps to explain the tolerance accorded to the clients with autism and to those behaviors that are perceived to approximate Navajo notions of social competence. That is, for Navajos to perceive of individuals with autism or autistic-like behaviors as children places them in a category difficult for Westerners to understand.

The effect of these cultural child-rearing practices is strikingly different from the "shaping" and "molding" practices experienced by Western children. Navajo children are allowed approximately six years to form their own identities and to develop their own selves virtually free of constraints. Not until the age of six or seven are they expected to adapt to the group of which they are a part, but even at this point it is the "whole person" who adapts to the group, and to whom the group adapts. When Navajos view individuals with autism as "children," it is not in the sense that they are helpless dependents, but rather that they are perceived as "becoming persons" in the process of defining their own identities. Despite the "non-normalized language" the Navajo perspective is very much in keeping with the notion of individuals with disabilities being "developing human beings" (Wolfensberger, 1972).

This also helps to explain the disregard for the notion of "developmental milestones" displayed by Navajo families throughout this research. For example, a custom of the Navajo is to celebrate a baby's first laugh, and the person who elicits the first laugh is expected to provide a treat such as cake and ice cream for the family. A question was included on the interview form to ascertain how old the child was when his or her first laugh was celebrated in order to determine if the infant's first months conformed to Western-defined development or if the infant had showed signs of developmental delay from birth. The answers to this question, however, ranged from two to eight months and were generally vague. Precise information was difficult to obtain, until one father explained: "Who remembers when a baby laughs? That's not important. What's important is that they laughed and that's what we celebrate."

It is not surprising, then, that tolerance for individuality makes the Navajos less inclined to identify "problem behaviors" and thus less motivated to "fix" or "correct" them, since the behaviors of the clients with autism or autistic-like behaviors were seen as integral parts of who these individuals were. This is also true of children who are physically disabled. One Anglo therapist lamented her difficulty in getting her Navajo staff to carry out "range of motion" exercises on discrete parts of clients' bodies (i.e., arms or legs): "The Navajo seem to interact with the students more, like they were more than just a muscle to restore range of motion to—they see them as whole human beings and don't see any reason to work on an arm or leg." In other words, with a wide tolerance for a variety of behaviors, it is far more difficult to label an individual as not measuring up to cultural standards and norms; rather, the individual is more likely to be accepted as marginally socially competent within his or her own personal limits and abilities and within the wide limits of cultural acceptance.

Residential Placement

It might be argued that placement of Navajo children with disabilities in this residential facility constitutes the practice of segregation and isolation mentioned earlier. To a certain extent, this is true. However, it is important to remember that not until 1974 did any facilities for disabled children exist on the Navajo Nation. Parents unable to cope with the challenges presented by their children were forced to send them hundreds of miles away to state institutions in New Mexico and Phoenix, where visits were difficult to arrange and the child was virtually removed from his or her culture, language, and spirituality. The speed with which parents brought their children back to the reservation when facilities were built to accommodate them is silent testimony to their desire to be reunited with their children.

Reasons for placement of children with autism varied but most often centered around the difficulty of caring for disabled children under physically challenging conditions. One mother reported, "We lived in a hogan and things were rough, with water hauling and we had to chop wood. It wasn't that he was a problem but he wandered off a lot and my life was really hard at that time." Poor parental health was also a factor, with two mothers stating that they were unable to physically restrain, dress, and bathe their grown children. Extended families offered some respite, with aunts, sisters, and grandmothers often assuming primary care for the disabled children, but in one case the grandmother, who had been left with the sole care of her grandson, was herself too frail and ill to meet his needs. In fact, when the first author accompanied the school vehicle taking the young man home for the weekend, we found the grandmother lying on the dirt floor of the hogan, too ill to stand.

Another tragic case involved an alcoholic mother who gave up her autistic daughter to her sister to raise. The aunt, herself an alcoholic, worked in a tavern in a border town and was not above passing the 17-year-old autistic girl around to various male patrons for prostitution. Further research into this case revealed that both the girl's mother and her aunt had severed all cultural ties with their Navajo family and the support of an extended family, exemplifying the breakdown of families caught in the conflict between Navajo ways and Westernization.

For the children without autism but with physical or mental handicaps, other factors were cited as the reasons for placement. In two instances, mothers were faced with a second disabled offspring. One mother had kept the oldest at home and placed her daughter in the residential facility; the other had placed her oldest in the facility and was endeavoring to keep the youngest at home for as long as possible. However, because her responsibility for herding sheep meant long hours outdoors crisscrossing the desert floor and mesas for adequate grazing, she was uncertain how much longer she could withstand the pressure of placement.

It must be remembered that the nomadic lifestyle of the Navajo is still retained, even though their roaming territory has been much reduced by the creation of the reservation. Most families have two or even three homes, one in the desert area during the winter and one in the mountains during the summer when water and grass are more plentiful there than in the lower altitudes. Most often these summer homes are little more than brush shelters and rough cabins, and even the winter homes are cramped hogans into which one or more related families will move to cut down on the amount of wood and coal needed to warm more than one dwelling. Under such conditions, physically unstable children on braces or in wheelchairs can easily suffer burns from stoves, so placement is often seen as offering a safer environment.

For another mother, life with her disabled son simply became too difficult. Fearful that if his condition were discovered he would be forcibly removed from her (a very real fear for Navajo families), she had hidden him at home for 15 years during which time he bit his tongue nearly in half. Too afraid of authorities to take him to a doctor, she had let nature take its healing course, with the result that his tongue had healed in an abnormally large size, effectively preventing him from eating solid food or talking. He had also had a severe eye infection, which had cost him his sight in one eye. He had also broken his leg and improper healing had left him with a severe limp. Finally, she was forced to seek medical treatment when he was bitten by a rattlesnake and spent 42 days in the hospital. Upon his recovery she finally agreed to residential placement, since she was 55 years old and unable to care for him. However, she visited without fail once a month, even though this required the 55-year-old woman to hitchhike 160 miles to the school and 160 miles home again.

Finally, broken homes due to alcoholism and abuse were significant factors for placement. In two cases, a father and a stepfather brutally beat their disabled sons, and for their own protection, the mothers placed them in a residential facility. In another case, both parents had died and an older sister was the only remaining relative of a client at the facility. Because the sister had spent most of her younger years in boarding school, her disabled sister was a virtual stranger to her, and she was completely disinterested in her welfare. She was content to let the school make all decisions "as long as they don't send her home!" Again, these attitudes reflected

Navajos who identified themselves as "modern" and who were struggling with the inevitable cultural conflict.

In general, most parents placed their children out of their home because no other choices were available. They were genuinely concerned about the welfare of their children. They visited the school often and arranged for the children to come home for weekends and during holidays. Unemployment, the necessity to travel long distances to find work, semi-nomadic existences, and rough living conditions contributed to the painful decision to place their children; often this decision was prolonged for several years until the family was simply unable to cope any longer.

No parents, however, reported any extraordinary efforts undertaken on behalf of their disabled children to "fix" their problems or attempt to "normalize" them. This is not surprising given the broad definition of normalcy discussed previously. Once placed in the residential facility, the families seemed indifferent to IEPs and progress charts, often to the dismay of Western staff eager to report any new signs of progress. Again, this is not surprising in light of the tendency to view one's children as competent within their own right. Particularly for those traditional parents who had had Sings performed for their children, progress was measured not in any discrete, visible way but through the restoration of inner harmony and balance, usually through the "Beautyway" that opens and closes nearly every known Sing:

> With beauty before me may I walk
> With beauty behind me may I walk
> With beauty above me may I walk
> With beauty below me may I walk
> With beauty all around me may I walk
> As one who is long life and happiness may I walk
> In beauty it's finished.
> In beauty it's finished.

In spite of increasing pressure to recognize disabilities in Western terms and to "correct" what are perceived as "problem behaviors" in the Western world, the Navajo have continued to adhere to traditional concepts of appropriate and inappropriate behavior. They have remained largely immune from the "deficit model" of exceptionality and the "efficiency model" of education and development. Progress is defined in terms of approximation, if it is defined at all. More often, the children are not seen as being significantly different or problematic. Family members reject the notion that they should be co-therapists and tend not to allow the disabled child to dominate family interactions or resources by the simple expedient of not seeing the necessity for "change" or "progress." Out-of-home placement is seen as a practical issue, driven by difficult living conditions rather than any notion that the children would be "normalized" or "fixed" by the school staff.

Due to the limited sample of the research, the data should be viewed with caution, but it would seem that those families who have rejected traditional ways and accepted the Western world, usually to personal detriment, are more likely to reject their disabled children as well. Whether this is due, however, to acceptance of negative Western labels by Western professionals or indicative of a deeper cultural conflict within the individuals themselves is difficult to judge at this point. The "least dangerous assumption" [2] (Donnellan, 1984) suggests that the traditional Navajo culture provides flexibility and resiliency in the face of disability that makes mental and emotional adjustments somewhat easier for the families to bear. At a minimum it is deserving of respect by Western professionals working with these individuals.

The traditional attitude of acceptance aids greatly in developing a more relaxed attitude toward the role of the disabled child in the Navajo family structure. This is not to say that Navajo families do not have hopes and expectations for their disabled children, some just as unrealistic as those found in other societies, such as an eventual recovery, marriage and family, or complete independence. However, none of the families saw any necessity to radically change their lifestyles to accommodate the disabled child; rather, the child was accommodated into the existing family structure.

As noted earlier, there are recent attempts to rethink family involvement, particularly in early childhood special education where a more family centered approach is advocated (Bailey, Buysee, Edmondson, & Smith, 1992). According to Sontag and Schacht (1994), even in early intervention, the typical professional's model continues to be one of evaluating family values and beliefs without sharing any of the decision-making responsibilities with the family. Typically, such evaluation is done from a dominant culture perspective (Van Willigen, 1986). Not surprisingly, Sontag and Schacht report that the families they interviewed, including Navajo families, preferred that professionals play a consultative rather than decision-making role in their children's lives.

While it is, or should be, obvious that professionals need to consider other models of viewing disabilities in order to be effective in other cultures, it also behooves these same professionals to take a closer look at their own expectations and definitions of progress. Perhaps, for the sake of the family, extraordinary efforts do not need to be taken to fix the child; rather, the family should be allowed to accommodate the child to the degree they think reasonable and to measure progress in ways that make sense to them. Perhaps families should not be forced into the role of co-therapist, but simply allowed to be families who provide love, caring relationships, support, and protection. Perhaps professionals need to be cautious about their own "gift of sight" of disabilities and to practice more selective "blindness." And perhaps, as the Beautyway recommends, we need to focus less on the disabilities and more on helping these and all children to "walk in beauty."

Notes

1. Funds for this research were provided by the Wenner-Gren Foundation and by the National Science Foundation, Grant No. BNS-9007880. Dr. Connors gratefully acknowledges the support of these agencies.

2. The criterion of the least dangerous assumption is a way of addressing the all too common situation in human services, particularly disability-related services where an individual may not be able to assert a clear preference, in which one must make a judgment without having all the information one would ideally wish to have. It suggests that, in the absence of conclusive data, decisions be made based on the assumptions that, if you are wrong, will have the least dangerous effect on outcome for the person with the disability.

References

Allen, W. B., Friedman, M., Berry, M. F., Buckley, E. G., Chan, S.T.S., Destro, R. A., Guess, F. S., & Ramirez, B. C. (1989). *Medical discrimination against children with disabilities.* Washington, DC: U.S. Civil Rights Commission.

Bailey, D. (1987). Collaborative goal-setting with families: Resolving differences in values and priorities for services. *Topics in Early Childhood Special Education, 7*(2), 59-71.

Bailey, D., Buysee, V., Edmondson, R., & Smith, T. (1992). Creating family-centered services in early intervention: Perceptions of professionals in four states. *Exceptional Children, 58,* 298-309.

Bettelheim, B. (1967). *The empty fortress: Infantile autism and the birth of the self.* New York: Free Press.

Callahan, R.E. (1962). *Education and the cult of efficiency.* Chicago: University of Chicago.

Cavallo, D. (1970). The politics of latency: Kindergarten pedagogy, 1860-1930. In B. Finkelstein (Ed.), *Regulated children/liberated children.* New York: Psychohistory Press.

Connors, J. L. (1992). *Navajo perceptions of autism and social competence: A cultural perspective.* Unpublished dissertation, University of Wisconsin, Madison.

Covello, L.C. (1958). *The heart of the teacher.* New York: McGraw-Hill.

Crow Dog, M., & Erdoes, R. (1990). *Lakota woman.* New York: Harper Collins.

Cutler, B.C. (1993). *You, your child and "special" education: A guide to making the system work.* Baltimore, MD: Paul H. Brookes.

Donnellan, A.M. (1980). *The functions of student teaching in special education.* Unpublished dissertation. University of California at Santa Barbara.

Donnellan, A. M. (l984). The criterion of the least dangerous assumption. *Behavior Disorders, 9*, 141-150.

Donnellan, A.M. (1985). *Classic readings in autism.* New York: Teachers College Press.

Donnellan, A.M., & Cutler, B.C. (1991). A dialogue on power relationships and aversive control. In L.H. Meyer, C.A. Peck, & L. Brown (Eds.), *Critical issues in the lives of people with severe disabilities* (pp. 271-312). Baltimore, MD: Paul H. Brookes.

Donnellan, A. M., & Mirenda, P. (1984). Issues related to professional involvement with families of individuals with autism. *Journal of the Association for Persons With Severe Handicaps, 9*, 16-25.

Dybwad, R., & Dybwad, G. (1993). Forward. In B.C. Cutler, *You, your child and "special" education: A guide to making the system work.* Baltimore, MD: Paul H. Brookes.

Gerry, M.H., & McWhorter, C.M. (1991). A comprehensive analysis of Federal statutes and programs for persons with severe disabilities. In L.H. Meyer, C.A. Peck, & L. Brown (Eds.), *Critical issues in the lives of people with severe disabilities* (pp. 495-525). Baltimore, MD: Paul H. Brookes.

Glazer, N., & Moynihan, D.P. (1963). *Beyond the melting pot.* Cambridge: The MIT Press and Harvard University Press.

Iannaccone, L., & Button, H.W. (1967). *Functions of student teaching.* (Research Report No. 1026), Report to Dept. of Health, Education & Welfare. Unpublished manuscript, Washington University, St. Louis, MO.

Kaufman, B. N. (1976). *Sonrise.* New York: Warner.

Kirk, S.A., & Gallagher, J.J. (1986). *Educating Exceptional Children.* Geneva, IL: Houghton Mifflin.

Lovaas, O. I. (1978). Parents as therapists. In M. Rutter & E. Schopler (Eds.), *Autism: A reappraisal of concepts and treatment* (pp. 369-378). New York: Plenum.

Lynch, E., & Hanson, M. (1992). *Developing cross-cultural competence.* Baltimore, MD: Paul H. Brookes.

Martin, R. (1991). *Extraordinary children ordinary lives.* Champaign, IL: Research Press.

Maurice, C. (1993). *Let me hear your voice.* New York: Alfred A. Knopf.

Neville, P. (1994). Genealogy and special education history. Unpublished paper, University of Wisconsin–Madison.

Rutter, M. (1978). Language disorder and infantile autism. In M. Rutter & E. Schopler (Eds.), *Autism: A reappraisal of concepts and treatment* (pp. 141-154). New York: Plenum.

Scheerenberger, R.C. (1987). *A history of mental retardation: A quarter century of promise.* Baltimore, MD: Paul H. Brookes.

Schien, E. (1968). Organizational socialization and the profession of management. *Industrial Management Review*, pp. 1-16.

Schopler, E., & Reichler, R. J. (1971). Parents as co-therapists in the treatment of psychotic children. *Journal of Autism and Childhood Schizophrenia, 1*, 87-102.

Singer, G.H.S., & Irvin, L.K. (1991). Supporting families of persons with severe disabilities: Emerging findings, practices, and questions. In L.H. Meyer, C.A. Peck, & L. Brown (Eds.), *Critical issues in the lives of people with severe disabilities* (pp. 271-312). Baltimore, MD: Paul H. Brookes.

Skrtic, T. M. (1991). *Behind special education: A critical analysis of professional culture and school organization*. Denver: Love Publishing.

Smith, M.S., & O'Day, J. (1991). Systemic school reform. In S.H. Fuhrman & B. Malen (Eds.), *The politics of curriculum and testing* (pp. 233-267). Philadelphia: Falser.

Sontag, J.C., & Schacht, R. (1994). An ethnic comparison of parental participation and information needs in early intervention. *Exceptional Children. 60*, pp.422-433.

Van Willigen, J. (1986). *Applied anthropology*. Westport, CT: Greenwood.

Willower, D. J. (1970). The teacher subculture and rites of passage. *Urban Education*, pp. 103-113.

Wolfensberger, W. (1972). *The principle of normalization in human services*. Toronto, Canada: National Institute on Mental Retardation.

Chapter 9

Social Networks and Systems of Support Among American Indian Navajo Adolescent Mothers

Rochelle L. Dalla and Wendy C. Gamble

Regardless of age, social support received and the perceived quality of social network resources are extremely powerful influences in adjusting to the parenting role (Unger & Wandersman, 1988). Even more than their older counterparts, adolescent mothers rely extensively on social support systems to provide knowledge, material goods, child care, decision making, and emotional encouragement (Zuckerman, Winsmore, & Alpert, 1979). Additionally, the use of support systems indirectly contributes to the health of a young mother's children (Baldwin & Cain, 1980). Consistently, investigations of adolescent parenting populations have found that the most positive outcomes are highly dependent on the quality of a young mother's social support network (Barth, 1988; Boyce, Kay, & Uitti, 1988; Kissman, 1988; Panzarine, 1986). Although this chapter will focus on the networks of social support among young Navajo mothers, no literature currently exists examining this unique population. Thus, a brief review of the support systems among other young, parenting populations is in order.

 Developing and using social supports are central to adapting to teenage motherhood (Unger & Wandersman, 1988). This fact remains consistent across socio-demographically diverse populations (Wasserman, Rauh, Brunelli, Garcia-Castro, & Necos, 1990; Thompson, 1986; Becerra & de Anda, 1984), and support may be especially significant among disadvantaged groups. Parish, Hao, and Hogan (1991) reported that social support networks are important to minority adolescent mothers, particularly African Americans and Hispanics, many of whom live in poverty.

Positive associations among an adolescent's adjustment to motherhood and the availability and use of supportive networks emerge regardless of ethnicity. Differences across ethnic groups have been reported, however, especially concerning the primary providers of support and the types of support received. Wasserman et al. (1990) found that young African-American mothers reported higher levels of guidance and tangible, emotional, social, and prenatal support from family members than reported by their Hispanic peers. Conversely, Dore and Dumois (1990) found that young Hispanic mothers reported significantly closer family ties and stronger feelings of family support than did a comparable group of African-American teen mothers. Compared to Anglo Americans, teenage Hispanic mothers report having more contact with extended family but fewer friends (Codega, Pasley, & Kreutzer, 1990). Finally, Anglo-American teens have been found to rely more on formal sources of support than either African-American or Hispanic teen mothers (Mitchell, Barbarin, & Hurley, 1981).

Because of the traditional extended family structure of many African-American and Hispanic families (Dore & Dumois, 1990), it is not surprising to find that the informal networks of many of these young women are significantly comprised of family members. However, extensive research suggests that, aside from familial sources, support and assistance provided by a spouse independently contributes to positive maternal adjustment (Majewski, 1985; Belsky, Robins, & Gamble, 1984). Teti and Gelfand (1991) found significant, positive associations between perceptions of maternal competence and the quality of the marital relationship. Since the majority of empirical studies have examined associations between marital functioning and parenting behavior, the significance of this research for populations of single adolescent mothers is uncertain. Nonetheless, research suggests that the beneficial effects of a caring, supportive male partner do not diminish in the absence of a marriage license, regardless of that individual's relationship to the child or place of residence (McKenry, Kotch, & Browne, 1991). Thus, despite their single status, young mothers may benefit from the support of a male partner.

Young mothers of various ethnic groups differ in the amount of help and assistance they report receiving from male partners. Young African-American mothers tend to rely almost exclusively on their own mothers, rarely turning to male partners for support (Wilson & Tolson, 1990). In contrast, young Hispanic mothers are much more likely to be married or living with a partner than either African-American or Anglo-American adolescents (Dore & Dumois, 1990).

Investigations as to the amount of support young mothers receive from their peers again reveal ethnic differences. While African-American and Anglo-American teen mothers are likely to turn to friends for support (Garcia-Coll, Hoffman, & Oh, 1987), young Hispanic mothers turn more often to their family or partner (Codega, Pasley, & Kreutzer, 1990; de Anda, 1984).

Aside from these differences, one factor remains constant. Regardless of ethnic group status, teenage parents rarely seek help from formal services. That is, adolescent parents rarely seek assistance outside their informal network systems (Bergman, 1989). However, if informal support is unavailable, formal help is sought. Bergman (1989) noted that young mothers are more likely to seek formal help when they perceive few informal sources available to them or when they perceive weak ties within their informal network system.

In sum, regardless of the population examined, perceptions of having an available network of individuals or institutions willing to offer help and assistance are powerful indicators of teenage mothers' adjustment to the parenting role and subsequent maternal behavior (Unger & Wandersman, 1988; Colletta, 1987). Moreover, although informal sources comprise the majority of all adolescent mothers' support networks, ethnic differences in terms of the most important sources and types of support received have emerged repeatedly. As evident from the discussion above, however, the majority of cross-ethnic investigations of adolescent parenting have focused on Anglo-American, African-American, and Hispanic teens (Wasserman et al., 1990; Lancaster & Hamburg, 1986; Becerra & de Anda, 1984). Studies of other young parenting populations, such as American Indian Navajo teens, are noticeably absent from the literature.

According to the most recent Indian Health Service (IHS) records (IHS Health Statistics, 1992a), in 1990 15.8% of all births among American Indian Navajo women residing on the Navajo Reservation were to adolescents aged 15 to 19 years. National statistics for the same year document an adolescent birth rate (among 15- to 19-year-olds) of 6% (National Center for Health Statistics, 1993). The birth rate among reservation-residing Navajo teens is thus 2.63 times the national average. Conditions that currently exist on the Navajo Indian Reservation, including the lack of formal education, alarming rates of poverty and alcoholism, and pervasive unemployment (see the Indian Health Service, 1992b, Status Summary Reports) may severely challenge a young mother's ability to cope simultaneously with environmental hardship and the demands of motherhood. On the other hand, like African-American and Hispanic families, the traditional Navajo family is characterized as an extended system (LaFromboise & Low, 1991; Lamphere, 1989; Ryan, 1980; Smallcanyon, 1980), a system that potentially offers aid and support to a young mother. Thus, contextual adversities may be "softened" through a strong, supportive interpersonal network.

The purpose of this investigation was to examine, in an exploratory manner, systems of support among young, parenting Navajo women. The primary focus was an analysis of network composition, including size, relationship, frequency of contact, and type of support received (support could be either emotional, parenting, or practical); non-empirical comparisons with the extant data concerning social support systems of adolescent Anglo-American, African-American, and Hispanic mothers were planned. Support was also examined in relation to individual demographic characteristics, such as marital status, age, and place of residence. Finally, the research was designed to determine, for this sample, who was primarily responsible for performing specific, daily, child-related tasks.

Based on the existing literature, several predictions were made. The majority of the young women were expected to be single and living with their families of origin. The extended nature of the traditional Navajo family led to the expectation that the young mothers' networks would be comprised primarily of family members, regardless of marital status or place of residence. It was predicted that family members would be perceived as providing more of each type of support, compared to partner, peers, and formal sources. It was also posited that formal sources of support (e.g., formalized day care or counseling services) would be used infrequently by these young Navajo mothers.

Method

Sample

This study was conducted in a rural, northeastern Arizona community located on the Navajo Indian Reservation. Twenty-two pregnant ($n=5$) or parenting ($n=17$) Navajo women comprised the final sample. They ranged in age from 16 to 19 years (M=17.7 years). One 21-year-old was included because she was the mother of three children and her oldest child was five years old. The majority of the women (73%) were enrolled in high school. Although half of the young women reported having trouble in high school (e.g., problems concentrating on their work or trouble with teachers) only four of the young mothers reported that they had dropped out of school in order to care for their babies but had subsequently returned to school, and only two reported that they had dropped out without future plans of returning.

Most of the young women (64%) reported an annual household income, including all economic resources and benefits, of less than $15,000; five young women were unaware of their annual household income. Eight women (56%) reported being employed. Several reported receiving various forms of public assistance, including Aid to Families with Dependent Children (AFDC) (23%), Medicaid (23%), food stamps (36%), and food supplements for Women, Infants, and Children (WIC) (55%).

Finally, few pregnancy or birth complications were reported; the majority (95%) had received prenatal care, and many (50%) had sought medical attention within the first three months of conception. Seventeen children were included in this investigation. They ranged in age from 1 week to 5 years (M=8.5 months) and 53% were female.

Procedures

Identities and locations of eligible women (parenting or pregnant Navajo teens) were provided by the director of a local, school-based parenting intervention program, by school officials, through word-of-mouth, and through the local prenatal clinic.

All data were collected by a trained graduate student from the University of Arizona; she was accompanied by a young, native, Navajo woman familiar with the local community and fluent in the Navajo language. The purpose of the investigation was explained to each teen contacted, and their participation was requested. The response rate was 100%. After providing their informed consent, each participant completed a series of self-report questionnaires. (The original study had a larger focus, but only information concerning social support will be included here.) Instructions for each measure were explained by the investigator. Although the majority of the women preferred English, one young woman was considerably more fluent in her native tongue. Therefore, all measures and response choices were translated into Navajo for her. All sessions lasted approximately one hour.

Measures

Demographics. Each young woman was asked to provide socio-demographic information, including age, marital and academic status, place of primary residence, and main source of income (i.e., employment, boyfriend, or parents).

Social Support. To assess the size and composition of the social support network, in addition to the type of support received, the Norbeck Social Support Questionnaire (NSSQ) (Norbeck, Lindsey, & Carrieri, 1981) was administered. Respondents were asked to "list each significant person in your life, or who is important to you." Space was provided for listing the names or initials of up to 10 people, including their sex and relationship (e.g., mother, friend, neighbor). Thus, four groups consisting of various sources of support were computed, including the total amount of support perceived from family, partner, peers, and "other."

The type of support (emotional, practical, and parenting) the women perceived was also measured. Respondents answered each question on this instrument for each individual included in their network list, using a five-point Likert-type response scale; response choices ranged from Not at all (1) to A great deal (5). Emotional support, or the expression of positive affect of one person to another, was assessed by asking four questions such as, "How much does this person make you feel liked or loved?" The mean of this subscale was 2.6 (SD=1.7), and the internal reliability, based on Cronbach's test, was .92. Practical support, defined as the giving of symbolic or material aid to another, was assessed by asking two questions, including, "If you needed to borrow ten dollars, a ride to the doctor, or some other form of immediate help, how much could this person help you?" This scale demonstrated a mean of 2.4 (SD=1.7) and an Alpha coefficient of .89. Symbolic or material aid that helps one in the role of parent defined parenting support and was determined by asking two questions, such as, "If you needed advice or information about how to raise your child(ren), how much could this person help you?" The mean of this scale was 2.5 (SD=1.8) and it demonstrated high internal reliability (.90).

The final two questions comprising the typology instrument asked each respondent to rate how long they had known each person on their network list (response choices ranged from Less than six months (1) to More than five years (5) (M = 2.6; SD = 1.7) and their frequency of contact with each person (choices ranged from Once a year or less (1) to Daily (5) (M = 2.5; SD = 1.7). Alpha coefficients were .81 and .80 for each of these scales, respectively.

The Network Functional items (emotional support, practical support, and parenting support) and Network Property items (number of people in network, relationship duration, and frequency of contact) identified earlier, have demonstrated good test-retest reliability over a seven-month period (Norbeck et al., 1981).

Child-Care Support. In order to obtain specific information on child-care support, an additional instrument was administered to the parenting women. This scale was comprised of 12 questions, including, "Who is the primary caregiver of the child? Who feeds the child most often? Who puts the child to bed most often?" Below each question the following list of people was presented: yourself, child's father, maternal grandmother/grandfather, paternal grandmother/grandfather, child's sibling(s), aunts/uncles, other relatives, and other. Mothers were instructed to circle the one person who most often engaged in each behavior. An additional item asked the participants to circle all of the people the child had regular contact with.

Results

Demographic information revealed that, as expected, the majority of the young women (77%) were single, although many (73%) reported involvement with a male partner, such as a boyfriend, who may or may not have been the father of their child. Also as predicted, most (77%) of the young women indicated that they were living with their families of origin (three lived with their husband in a separate residence and two lived with their husband and his family).

Network Composition

In order to determine the primary sources of social support, the number of family members, friends, and formal sources listed by each women was summed, creating a total score for each category. As predicted, family members comprised the largest portion of the social support networks of these young women. Specifically, each participant included at least one family member in her support network, and 63.4% included four or more family members. Thus, similar to other young pregnant and parenting women (particularly African-American and Hispanic youth) family members were considered important sources of informal support.

Although only five (23%) of the women were married, 59% indicated that a male partner was a primary source of social support. Thus, in terms of perceived significance of partner support, these young mothers appear more similar to Hispanic youth than to young Anglo- or African-American mothers.

Also unlike their Anglo-American counterparts, peers appear insignificant in the support systems of these young Navajo women. Specifically, 72% of the respondents did not list a friend or peer as an important source of support; 18% mentioned only one friend, one person identified two friends, and one young women listed three friends as significant sources of support (she was also the only participant who had any previous college experience, having spent one year at the University of Arizona).

As predicted from patterns among their Anglo-American, African-American, and Hispanic parenting age-mates, formal sources appear insignificant in the support systems of these young mothers. Only one young woman spontaneously listed outside, formal agencies as potential sources of help.

Source and Type of Support

Correlational analyses were used to examine associations among sources and types of support. Due to the high degree of intercorrelation between support types (ranging from .96 to .98), a Total Amount of Support variable was created by combining and averaging the three types of support scales (i.e., the total of the emotional, practical, and parenting scores). Correlational analysis revealed that total support was significantly related to number of family members ($r = .90; p < .00$) and marginally related to support from male partner ($r = .35; p < .10$). Male partners were reported as being the most important source of financial assistance for half of the respondents, whereas parents were only mentioned as primary sources of monetary income by 36.4% of the women.

Finally, as one might expect, correlational analyses revealed that total support was also significantly related to both network size ($r = .98; p < .00$) and frequency of contact with network members ($r = .98; p < .00$). However, contact with network members was significantly related only to family members ($r = .88; p < .00$), not to partners, indicating that, although male partners provided substantial support, these young women had less contact with their boyfriends than with their family members.

Support Related to
Individual Characteristics

Analysis of variance techniques were used in order to examine perceptions of social support based on maternal age, marital and parenting status, and place of residence. Previous investigations (Colletta, 1987; de Anda, 1984) have revealed that younger teenage mothers differ from their older counterparts in help-seeking behavior, orientation toward network support, and primary sources of help. Thus, younger (< 17 years) (41%) and older (17 or over) (59%) teens were analyzed separately. Wasserman et al. (1990) reported that child developmental outcome is influenced by a young mother's living arrangements. Thus, young women who reported living with their families of origin (77%) and those who resided elsewhere (23%) were examined separately, as were single and married teens.

Older teens reported receiving more support from "other" sources than did their younger peers. Younger teens reported receiving more support from male partners, although statistical significance was not reached. Married women reported receiving moderately more support from "other" sources than did their single peers [$F(1, 21) = 3.04; p < .10$]. They also reported more total support, although these results were not statistically significant. No differences based on parenting status emerged regarding the primary sources of support, perceived amount of support received from each source, or perceived total support. That is, pregnant and parenting women reported similar amounts of social support, from similar sources.

Analysis of variance techniques also revealed that teens not living with their families of origin reported moderately more support from "other" sources [$F(1, 21) = 3.04; p < .10$]. Females living with their families of origin reported receiving more support from their male partners than did their peers residing elsewhere (i.e., those living with their husband or their husband's family), although these results were not statistically significant.

Childrearing Tasks

One goal of this study was to identify specific people who had frequent contact with these young women's children, in addition to discovering the people who fulfilled the majority of daily childrearing responsibilities. Results revealed that the children had regular (at least three to four times a week) contact with a variety of individuals, including their natural fathers (71%), maternal (94%) and paternal (41%) grandparents, aunts/uncles (59%), and "other" individuals (32%). Although most of the women lived with their own families of origin, the children's fathers appeared to be actively involved in child-care. When asked her response when the baby cried, for instance, one young women commented:

> We usually try to comfort her— if it doesn't work with me
> her father usually likes to try and if it doesn't work with
> him we usually pass her around, someone else like an aunt
> or a grandparent usually tries...

Moreover, despite the apparent availability of many potential child-care "helpers," daily childrearing tasks were reported as being performed almost exclusively by the natural mother; she was the most likely to comfort the child (68%), change the child's clothes (64%), feed the child (68%), put the child to bed (100%), and discipline the child (64%).

When the mother was at school or work, family members were reported as being the primary caregivers for the majority of the children (71%). On the other hand, "other" sources, including individuals or institutions outside the immediate and extended family network (e.g., the school-based day-care facility) were only listed by a minority of mothers (29%) as caring for their child when they were away. These data affirm the earlier hypothesis of infrequent usage of formal support services.

Discussion

Although exploratory in nature, this investigation highlights important information concerning systems of support within a unique population of parenting women. Childrearing is not an easy task; for adolescent mothers who must simultaneously cope with the normative biological, cognitive, and psychological changes that accompany adolescence, the task is made all the more difficult (Codega, Pasley, & Kreutzer, 1990; Thompson, 1986). Raising a child as an adolescent woman, accompanied by the economic and social hardships present on the Navajo Indian Reservation, is likely to be an overwhelming experience. However, the social networks of young Navajo mothers are often comprised of rich, extended networks of informal supports. These support systems may serve as "buffering mechanisms," easing the transition to motherhood and promoting positive adjustment to the maternal role (Wasserman et al., 1990; Dore & Dumois, 1990; Unger & Wandersman, 1988; Colletta, 1987).

The potentially positive consequences of having a strong interpersonal support system do not discriminate; anyone may benefit. However, just as adolescent parenting populations differ, so too do specific aspects of their social networks. Recognizing and attending to subtle differences, both within and across ethnic boundaries, is an important aspect of policy making and successful intervention. Based on the small sample size of this investigation, however, caution must be used when considering the generalizability of the current results. The present data may not reflect the attitudes and beliefs of other Native American parenting youth or the views of Navajo teenage mothers in general. Nevertheless, while multiple statistical comparisons were made without adjusting the level of significance, robust findings emerged despite the small sample size.

As mentioned earlier, regardless of ethnic background, adolescent mothers rarely seek the help of outside, formal support services when informal sources are available; data reported here affirm this position. Indeed, some mothers were suspicious of outside help. For example, a school-based program was available for the young mothers to assist in child-care while they attended classes. However, non-parenting students were employed at the center as aides and several mothers expressed concern about the type of care these student workers provided. One young mother reported:

> Its just the students who watch the kids....I don't know how they take care of the kids and the things they do. Because most of them they don't really read to them or sing to them or stuff like that—they're shy.

Another stated:

> Some students favor some babies the most, sometimes I don't really like that.

Because of adolescents' relative dependence on family members (for financial, emotional, informational, and practical support), it is not surprising to find that young mothers place a considerable amount of importance on support received from family members. This fact also remains consistent across ethnic groups (Wasserman et al., 1990; Garcia-Coll et al., 1987) and was further supported in this investigation. It is important to note that family support may not always be problem-free, as exemplified in the following statement of one young mother in reference to her parents:

> They're always drinking and—and I hate for my daughter to be around them when they're like that. She looks at them—I just don't want her to see them like that.

Most mothers, however, seemed to recognize the importance of family for support, as the following statements illustrate. One mother remarked:

> I like to be around a lot of people—I used to work at a
> grocery store and there were always people around me—but
> my family's pretty big, so [even though I'm not working
> anymore] there's still a lot of people around to play with the
> baby.

In regard to her living situation, another young women reported:

> We spend time with his parents up at Black Mesa some-
> times ...we stay with my parents sometimes too, for like a
> week and then there again [with husband's parents] so we
> kinda just go back and forth.

In addition to family, boyfriends often provide a significant
amount of social support to many young parenting women. One
young woman's daughter had serious birth complications and continued to have seizures. The mother consistently described the
presence and support of her partner throughout the ordeal of the
early days in the neonatal intensive care unit. She said:

> Daniel calls her a name—it's a Navajo name which I cannot
> pronounce, but it means "fighting woman," something like
> that.

Thus, like their Hispanic counterparts, these young Navajo
women reported a significant portion of social support coming from
their male partners; many acknowledge support particularly in the
form of financial aid.

Similarly, findings from this study reveal that pregnant and
parenting Navajo adolescents are also more like their Hispanic counterparts in the infrequency with which they turn to peers or friends
for help—a pattern not observed among African-American and Anglo-
American teen mothers, who report peers as important sources of
support (Garcia-Coll et al., 1987). Several young Navajo mothers
reported feeling hesitant and fearful about their friends' reactions
to their pregnancy. One mother remarked:

> When you first find out you're pregnant you're scared and
> you think, "Oh my God—what if my friends find out— what
> will they say?" You just really don't want anybody to find
> out....The whole point is that you really have to know who
> your friends are and the people who really will care about
> you.

Similar attitudes were reflected in the following statement:

> I know this one friend of mine who was embarrassed of it [her pregnancy] because she said her friends would refuse her after they found out that she's pregnant.... She said after she starts showing she's going to drop out [of school].

One explanation which may account for this apparent lack of trust in peer relationships is that the vast distances between homes and the lack of available transportation among reservation-dwelling teens may obstruct the development and maintenance of kinship ties with same-age peers. Future investigations examining peer orientation among reservation-dwelling youth may provide further insights.

Data analyses revealed that older teens, not living with their families of origin, reported receiving more help from sources besides family and partner than did their younger peers who resided at home. These reports appear consistent with those of other teenage mothers who, because of age and the formation of more extended networks are able to rely less extensively on their family for social support (Colletta, 1987). However, unlike older Mexican-American teens who report more partner support than younger Mexican-American mothers (de Anda, 1984), younger Navajo teens (who are more likely to live with their families of origin) reported receiving more male partner support than did their older peers. Male partners appear to contribute independent support for these young mothers despite the availability of family aid.

An important goal of this investigation was to determine what type of support (emotional, practical, or parenting) young Navajo mothers receive from various sources. However, this proved an impossible task; no distinction was made between each of the three types of support. Two possibilities exist for this lack of discrimination: (a) the participants did not distinguish one type of help from another, that is, they viewed assistance as support, regardless of the particular form that assistance took; or, more likely, (b) the instruments used in this investigation did not adequately distinguish among support types as perceived by this sample of young women. Future studies utilizing more culturally sensitive instruments may indeed identify distinct differences in the perceptions of support types received by young Navajo mothers.

The data presented here speak directly to policy makers and intervention specialists. However, investigators, researchers, and social scientists must step back and determine whether intervention is an appropriate "goal" of research endeavors. From an Anglo-American, dominant culture perspective, adolescent childbearing is often considered a "major social issue" instigating potentially negative economic ramifications for the entire country (Kissman, 1988; Duncan, 1984). Adolescent childbearing, however, may not be viewed in similar terms outside White, middle-class society. For instance, Geronimus (1986, 1987) and others (Geronimus & Bound, 1990; Kleinman & Kessel, 1987) have successfully argued that among certain disadvantaged populations teenage childbearing may be an adaptive strategy. Specifically, bearing a child while young, before the adverse effects of poverty, discrimination, and disease deteriorate a woman's health, may actually be adaptive in maintaining the status quo by ensuring healthier pregnancies and infants. Thus, before it is assumed that adolescent childbearing is an issue requiring intervention from outside sources, there must be a clearer conception of the entire context within which youthful childbearing occurs. Qualitative methods lend themselves to the contextually comprehensive investigations required to meet this end and to further the understanding of teenage childbearing.

If, however, one reaches the conclusion that intervention is indeed a desired and necessary endeavor, implications drawn from the present data may result in more satisfying outcomes for intervention agents and program participants. The importance of family involvement and the significance of partner support and assistance among young Navajo women cannot be ignored or neglected. It is also noteworthy that these women do not appear to bestow child-related tasks upon other individuals, even when others are available and apparently willing to help. Rather, these young mothers assume the greatest amount of responsibility in caring for their young children. Programs offering child development training classes, for not only the mother but the entire family, including the male partner, may yield the most successful results in terms of increased program participation and decreased attenuation.

References

Baldwin, W., & Cain, V. S. (1980). The children of teenage parents. *Family Planning Perspective, 12,* 34.

Barth, R. (1988). Social skill and social support among young mothers. *Journal of Community Psychology, 16,* 132–143.

Becerra, R. M., & de Anda, D. (1984). Pregnancy and motherhood among Mexican-American adolescents. *Health and Social Work, 9,* 106–123.

Belsky, J., Robins, E., & Gamble, W. (1984). The determinants of parental competence. In M. Lewis (Ed.), *Beyond the dyad: Vol. 4. Genesis of behavior.* New York: Plenum Press.

Bergman, A. G. (1989). Informal support systems of pregnant teenagers. *Social Casework: The Journal of Contemporary Social Work, 70,* 525–533.

Boyce, W. T., Kay, M., & Uitti, C. (1988). The taxonomy of social support: An ethnographic analysis among adolescent mothers. *Social Science Medicine, 26,* 1079–1085.

Codega, S. A., Pasley, B. K., & Kreutzer, J. (1990). Coping behaviors of adolescent mothers: An exploratory study and comparison of Mexican Americans and Anglos. *Journal of Adolescent Research, 5,* 34–53.

Colletta, N. D. (1987). Correlates of young mothers' network orientations. *Journal of Community Psychology, 15,* 149–160.

de Anda, D. (1984). Informal support networks of Hispanic mothers: A comparison across age groups. *Journal of Social Service Research, 7,* 89–105.

Dore, M. M., & Dumois, A. O. (1990). Cultural differences in the meaning of adolescent pregnancy. *Families in Society: The Journal of Contemporary Human Services, 71,* 93–101.

Duncan, C. J. (1984). *Years of poverty, years of plenty: The changing fortunes of American workers and their families.* Ann Arbor, MI: Institute for Social Research.

Garcia-Coll, C. T., Hoffman, J., & Oh, W. (1987). The social ecology and early parenting of Caucasian adolescent mothers. *Child Development, 58,* 955–963.

Geronimus, A. T. (1986). The effects of race, residence, and prenatal care on the relationship of maternal age to neonatal mortality. *American Journal of Public Health, 76,* 1416–1421.

Geronimus, A. T. (1987). On teenage childbearing and neonatal mortality in the United States. *Population and Development Review, 13,* 245–279.

Geronimus, A. T., & Bound, J. (1990). Black/White differences in women's reproductive-related health status: Evidence from vital statistics. *Demography, 27,* 457–466.

Indian Health Service. (1992a). *Navajo health status summary: Navajo area Indian health service.*

Indian Health Service. (1992b). *Regional differences in Indian health.* U.S. Department of Health and Human Series: Office of Planning, Evaluation, and Legislation.

Kissman, K. (1988). Factors associated with competence, well-being, and parenting attitude among teen mothers. *International Journal of Adolescence and Youth, 1,* 247–255.

Kleinman, J. C., & Kessel, S. S. (1987). Racial differences in low birth weight. *New England Journal of Medicine, 317,* 749–753.

LaFromboise, T. D., & Low, K. G. (1991). American Indian children and adolescents. In J. T. Gibbs & L. N. Huang (Eds.), *Children of color: Psychological interventions with minority youth.* San Francisco: Jossey-Bass.

Lamphere, L. (1989). *To run after them: Cultural and social bases of cooperation in a Navajo community*. Tucson, AZ: The University of Arizona Press.

Lancaster, J. B., & Hamburg, B. A. (1986). The biosocial dimensions of school-age pregnancy and parenthood: An introduction. In J. B. Lancaster & B. A. Hamburg (Eds.), *School-age pregnancy and parenthood* (pp. 3–16). New York: Aldine.

Majewski, J. L. (1985). Conflicts, satisfactions, and attitudes during transition to the maternal role. *Nursing Research, 35*, 10–14.

McKenry, P. C., Kotch, J. B., & Browne, D. H. (1991). Correlates of dysfunctional parenting attitudes among low-income adolescent mothers. *Journal of Adolescent Research, 6*, 212–234.

Mitchell, R., Barbarin, O., & Hurley, D. (1981). Problem-solving resource utilization and community involvement in a Black and White community. *American Journal of Community Psychology, 9*, 223–246.

National Center for Health Statistics. (1993). Vital statistics of the United States (1990). *Natality, 1*.

Norbeck, J. S., Lindsey, A. M., & Carrieri, V. L. (1981). The development of an instrument to measure social support. *Nursing Research, 30*, 264–269.

Panzarine, S. (1986). Stressors, coping, and social supports of adolescent mothers. *Journal of Adolescent Health Care, 7*, 153–161.

Parish, W. L., Hao, L., & Hogan, D. P. (1991). Family support networks, welfare, and work among young mothers. *Journal of Marriage and the Family, 53*, 203–215.

Ryan, R. A. (1980). Strengths of the American Indian family: State of the art. In F. Hoffman (Ed.), *The American Indian family: Strengths and stresses*. Isleta, NM: American Indian Social Research and Development Associates.

Smallcanyon, R. (1980). Traditional child-rearing practices of the Navajo Indians. *Family Perspective, 14*, 125–131.

Teti, D. M., & Gelfand, D. M. (1991). Behavioral competence among mothers of infants in the first year: The mediational role of maternal self-efficacy. *Child Development, 62*, 918–929.

Thompson, M. S. (1986). The influence of supportive relations on the psychological well-being of teenage mothers. *Social Forces, 64*, 1006–1024.

Unger, D. G., & Wandersman, L. P. (1988). The relation of family and partner support to the adjustment of adolescent mothers. *Child Development, 59*, 1056–1060.

Wasserman, G. A., Rauh, V. A., Brunelli, S. A., Garcia-Castro, M., & Necos, B. (1990). Psychosocial attributes and life experience of disadvantaged minority mothers: Age and ethnic variations. *Child Development, 61*, 566–580.

Wilson, M. N., & Tolson, T. F. J. (1990). Familial support in the Black community. *Journal of Clinical Child Psychology, 19*, 347–355.

Zuckerman, B., Winsmore, G., & Alpert, J. J. (1979). A study of attitudes and support systems of inner city adolescent mothers. *Journal of Pediatrics, 95*, 122–131.

Chapter 10

Enculturation Hypothesis

Exploring Direct and Protective Effects Among Native American Youth[1]

Marc A. Zimmerman, Jesus Ramirez,
Kathleen M. Washienko,[2] Benjamin Walter,
and Sandra Dyer[3]

Enculturation is the process by which individuals learn about and identify with their traditional ethnic culture (Little Soldier, 1985). Wilbert (1976) points out that enculturation is a lifelong learning experience in which cultural awareness and understanding develops. When considered as a state of being rather than a process, enculturation refers to the extent to which individuals identify with their ethnic culture, feel a sense of pride for their cultural heritage, and integrate a traditional cultural lifestyle into their lives. Enculturation is especially relevant for Native Americans because they have been systematically and forcibly assimilated into white majority culture.

Unlike other minority populations, Native Americans did not immigrate to this country. Rather, as original inhabitants of North America, they fought with and lost their homes to invading Europeans. They are, in essence, a conquered group that has experienced an ongoing process of domination by the majority culture. Nicols (1990–1991) points out that "from the days of George Washington to the 1970s the use of missionaries and teachers, boarding schools, allotment, termination, and urban relocation are all examples of federal efforts to disrupt tribal societies and to acculturate individual Indians" (p. 87). In spite of the many efforts to eliminate their traditional societies, Native American culture and traditions remain, and are beginning to experience a revival.

This chapter explores the construct of enculturation and its usefulness for understanding Native American youth development in three major sections. First, a brief review of relevant literature is presented in order to define the enculturation construct. This review distinguishes enculturation from acculturation and differentiates it from cultural identity. A research hypothesis—the enculturation hypothesis—that focuses on the protective potential of enculturation is also discussed. Second, an operational definition for enculturation that has been tested empirically and may be useful for exploring the enculturation hypothesis is described. Finally, data that provides preliminary support for the hypothesis are presented.

Enculturation

While much of the research on adolescent development focuses on problem behaviors, risk factors, and deficits in youths' lives (Dryfoos, 1990; Hawkins, Catalano, & Miller, 1992; Jessor & Jessor, 1977; Newcomb & Felix-Ortiz, 1992), a growing body of work has begun to examine factors that may protect youth from the debilitating consequences of potentially harmful behaviors (Garmezy, Masten, & Tellegen, 1984; Rutter, 1987; Brook et al., 1992, 1990, 1989). Enculturation is one such factor that is culturally relevant and consonant with one's Native American heritage. The enculturation construct focuses on the social niche of Native Americans in a way that does not use mainstream norms as the benchmark for comparison.

Enculturation is especially relevant for adolescents as the adolescent period is marked by fundamental developmental changes such as self-identity formation and experimentation. Consequently, research on the relationship of enculturation with self-esteem and alcohol and substance use among Native American adolescents is vital. Native American youths' identification with and participation in their cultural traditions is expected to have a positive influence on their self-esteem because self-acceptance and self-worth are exemplified in adolescents' affinity to their cultural background. Integration of ethnic identity into one's sense of self is also congruent with self-esteem. Similarly, enculturation is expected to be associated with lower levels of alcohol and substance use because traditional Native American culture provides youth with a spiritual foundation that prohibits such behavior. Guyette (1982) suggests that enculturation is especially significant for Native American adolescent development because it may moderate other factors associated with alcohol and substance use.

Enculturation and Acculturation

Enculturation is an experience that occurs within a single cultural group and involves connection to one's cultural background. It is an affirmation of one's cultural heritage rather than a focus on fitting into the majority culture. Similarly, enculturation refers to association with others in one's cultural group and with its traditions rather than assimilation into mainstream society. Nevertheless, enculturation does not necessarily prevent assimilation into majority culture. One may both identify with and feel pride for one's ethnic cultural heritage and also become integrated into mainstream society. Oetting and Beauvais (1991) have found that identification with one's ethnic culture is unrelated to identification with another culture.

In contrast, acculturation is the process by which an ethnic minority individual assimilates to the majority culture. It is a relational term between groups of people that suggests one group's influence over another, which most typically involves the adoption of the majority group's culture by minority group members (Negy & Woods, 1992). The concept of acculturation is often the term used when studying the experience of Latino populations in the United States.

Buriel (1975) has offered two models of acculturation for Mexican Americans living in the United States: acculturation to the majority culture and acculturation to the culture of the barrio. The latter model approximates the notion of enculturation, but acculturation to the barrio is essentially adaptation of a Mexican-American culture to the cultural context in the United States. It may also be unique to the living conditions found in the barrios of large North American cities. Acculturation to the barrio differs from enculturation, even though it involves the maintenance of some ethnic traditions, as it also involves assimilation into mainstream society. Enculturation is a construct that is independent of a relationship to majority culture.

The research literature on acculturation is vast and has developed over a 75-year period (Padilla, 1980). Common measures of acculturation include the predominant language spoken, citizenship status, and generation level. Researchers have found an association between acculturation and depression (Vega, Warheit, & Meinhardt,

1984), poor health (Boyce & Boyce, 1983), and substance abuse (Burnam, Hough, Karno, Escobar, & Telles, 1987). The stress associated with acculturation has been used as a theoretical explanation for why minority group members report more alcohol and substance use (Drew, 1988; Schinke, Moncher, Palleja, Zayas, & Schilling, 1988). Oetting and Beauvais (1991), however, have not found acculturation stress as an explanatory factor in adolescent substance use.

Enculturation and Cultural Identity

Enculturation differs from cultural identity in several ways. First, although cultural identity has included multiple definitions, it has not typically included multidimensional assessment. Second, while enculturation incorporates cultural identity, it goes beyond that to include pride in one's cultural heritage and participation in traditional activities (see measurement section below). Third, enculturation is both a process of learning about one's cultural heritage and an outcome to measure the extent to which one is enculturated. In contrast, cultural identity is primarily conceptualized as an outcome that does not include the process through which it develops. Finally, enculturation is a construct that is explicitly linked to ethnic culture without concern for comparison to majority culture. Cultural identity is typically conceptualized in relation to majority culture.

In a review of the research on ethnic identity, Phinney (1992) points out that researchers have no widely agreed upon definition of ethnic identity. Phinney suggests that ethnic identity has been defined as the ethnic component of social identity, feelings of belonging to an ethnic group, shared values with an ethnic group, and the performance of cultural traditions. Ethnic identity, in its many forms, has been associated with higher self-esteem (Phinney & Alipuria, 1990), less anxiety (Parham & Helms, 1985), and less substance use (Parker, 1990; Oetting & Beauvais, 1990).

Enculturation is preferred to cultural identity because it is a multidimensional construct and provides a framework for integrating the various conceptualizations of ethnic identity. Several investigators have suggested that cultural identity does not fully capture the construct because it does not include involvement in cultural activities or affinity to one's Native American cultural heritage (Little Soldier, 1985; Oetting & Beauvais, 1991; Trimble, 1983, 1987). The diverse literature on ethnic identity may also be united by a common framework that captures the many forms it has taken in the research literature. The construct of enculturation may provide an integrated framework for organizing the research literature.

Enculturation Hypothesis

One aspect of the enculturation hypothesis predicts that Native American youth who feel pride in their cultural heritage, feel a strong Native American identity, and participate in Native American cultural activities will have improved psychological well-being and reduced problem behaviors. Phinney and Chavira (1992) provide preliminary support for this aspect of the enculturation hypothesis in a small study of African-American, Latino, and Asian-American youth. They found ethnic identity predicted greater self-esteem over a three-year period. Analytically, the enculturation hypothesis would be partially supported if direct main effects of enculturation are found to predict outcomes such as self-esteem and alcohol and substance use.

A corollary to the enculturation hypothesis is that more highly enculturated youth are expected to be more resilient to potentially harmful factors in their lives than youth not as connected to their cultural group. Consequently, the enculturation hypothesis suggests that enculturation will act as a protective factor against influences found to put youth at risk for a deleterious outcome (e.g., low self-esteem, substance use). Enculturation may work through two mechanisms to protect youth from potentially problematic behaviors (Brook, Brook, Gordon, & Whiteman, 1990); a risk/protective mechanism, in which a protective factor works to mitigate the negative effects of a risk factor; and a protective/protective mechanism in which a protective factor works to enhance the effects of another variable found to decrease the probability of a deleterious outcome. Enculturation may act as a protective factor for Native American youth by reducing the effects of family drug problems on their self-esteem (risk/protective mechanism) or by enhancing the effects of self-esteem on reduced alcohol and substance use (protective/ protective mechanism).

Later in this chapter, the relationship between enculturation, self-esteem, alcohol and substance use, and family drug problems is examined. One analysis examines the risk/protective effects of enculturation for family drug problems on predicting Native American youths' self-esteem. Family drug problems are a significant risk factor for youth because unhealthy family influences have been linked with several problem behaviors among adolescents, especially alcohol and substance use (Andrews, Hops, Ary, Tildesley, & Harris,

1993; Johnson, Shontz, & Locke, 1984; Kandel & Andrews, 1987; Lau, Quadrel, & Hartman, 1990; Needle, McCubbin, Wilson, Reineck, Lazar, & Mederer, 1986; Newcomb, Maddahian, & Bentler, 1986).

In another analysis, the protective/protective effects of enculturation on self-esteem for predicting alcohol and substance use is examined. The identification of factors that protect adolescents from alcohol and substance use are especially important for Native American youth because alcohol abuse has been considered the number one health problem of Native Americans (USDHHS, 1986; May, 1986). Researchers have also reported a negative association between self-esteem and alcohol and substance use (Dielman, Shope, Butchart, Campanelli, & Caspar, 1989; Selnow, 1985; Stacy, Newcomb, & Bentler, 1992). A necessary first step in research on enculturation is, however, the development of psychometrically sound measures.

Measurement of Enculturation

Zimmerman, Ramirez, Washienko, Walter, and Dyer (1994) describe three studies that provide empirical support for a three-component measure of enculturation. The three studies included Native American youth from the same Tribe. The first study explored the initial factor structure of the construct with a sample of 121 youth. This sample was used to explore the enculturation hypothesis in the analyses described below. The second study tested the factor congruence over time. The sample for this study included youth who completed a second questionnaire one year after the first data collection ($N = 69$). The final study included 42 Native American youth who completed only the second-year questionnaire. This study explored the consistency of the factor structure in a new sample.

We used confirmatory factor analysis (LISREL VI) to test a conceptual framework of enculturation that included cultural affinity (i.e., pride and interest in one's cultural heritage), cultural behaviors (i.e., involvement in cultural activities), and Native American identity. Table 1 includes standardized and unstandardized factor loadings from the confirmatory factor analyses for enculturation across all three studies.

The measurement model fit indices for all three studies supported the three component framework for enculturation. The Chi-square tests for all three studies were not statistically significant at the .05 level indicating that the hypothesized models were very similar to the observed data. The Comparative Fit Index (CFI), the Normed Fit Index (NFI), and Nonnormed Fit Index (NNFI) were all

Table 1
Unstandardized Factor Loadings and Standard Errors
(and Standardized Factor Loadings and Errors)
for the Confirmatory Factor Analysis*

Variable	Study 1 (N = 120)	Study 2 (N = 50)	Study 3 (N = 40)
Cultural Affinity			
Factor loading	.643	.577	.521
	(.795)	(.585)	(.657)
Standard error	.125	.256	.156
	(.607)	(.811)	(.754)
Family Activities**			
Factor loading	1.0	1.0	1.0
	(.443)	(.421)	(.573)
Standard error	0.0	0.0	0.0
	(.896)	(.907)	(.819)
Native American Identity			
Factor loading	.351	.552	.511
	(.503)	(.583)	(.675)
Standard error	.084	.238	.150
	(.864)	(.812)	(.738)

*All factor loadings are significant beyond the .05 level

**Scalar indicator

used to further assess the measurement model across the three studies. They ranged from .999 to .826 with only one fit index of the nine computed (3 per study) falling below .900.

Validity for the three component measures was supported by correlations in the expected direction (positive) with the youths' perceived Native American identity of their mother and the number of Native American friends they reported. These results were consistent with the theoretical framework of enculturation presented by others (Little Soldier, 1985; Oetting & Beauvais, 1991; Trimble, 1983, 1987). Conceptual and operational definitions for the three components of enculturation are described below.

Several cautions, however, are warranted for the enculturation framework we developed. First, it may be appropriate only for Odawa and Ojibway tribes[4] for which they were developed. In order for the measure to be generalizable to other groups, it needs to be further developed in other Native American Tribes. Differences between tribal groups may be substantial. The scales also reflect a static measure of enculturation and, as Wilbert (1976) suggests, enculturation is a lifelong learning process. Thus, it is important to recognize that the measures used to represent enculturation represent a single point in time and may oversimplify the construct. Finally, the measures may not capture all aspects of enculturation. Ability to speak or understand one's native language may be a useful indicator for enculturation that was not included in this measure. Although a single 5-point Likert item asking youth how well they knew their Native American language was included in the questionnaire, only four adolescents reported any knowledge of their native language so the item was dropped from the analyses.

Test of the Enculturation Hypothesis

The enculturation hypothesis was tested by exploring both risk/ protective and protective/protective mechanisms. The risk/protective mechanism explores the protective effects of enculturation on the risk factor of family drug problems for the prediction of self-esteem. Family drug problems were hypothesized to have a detrimental effect on adolescents' self-esteem (negative correlation); the enculturation measures were expected to have a positive effect (positive correlation); and enculturation was hypothesized to moderate the effects of family drug problems (risk/protective effect). The protective/protective mechanism explored the enhancing effects enculturation may have on self-esteem for predicting alcohol and substance use. Both self-esteem and enculturation were hypothesized to have direct effects on alcohol and substance use (negative correlations), but they were also expected to interact in a way that each amplifies the effects of the other (protective/protective effect). The study of these relationships is described below.

Methods

Youth Recruitment and Survey Procedure

Youth were sampled from several contexts. These included youth aged 7-18 years who: 1) attended a summer camp ($n=50$); 2) attended a social event organized by the Tribe ($n=13$); 3) were recruited from door-to-door canvassing on the reservation ($n=10$); 4) were recruited from a school program list ($n=10$); 5) were selected from the participant list of a federal program of the Bureau of Indian Affairs ($n=9$); 6) were involved in local Upward Bound program questionnaires ($n=14$); and 7) were children of Tribal employees ($n=15$).

The participants completed questionnaires in a variety of locations including the Tribe's satellite offices, the Tribal youth center, the camp setting, churches, the local community college, and the youths' homes. In some instances (n = 20), the children's reading ability was not adequate for completing the questionnaire. A research staff member read the items to these youth and assisted them in completing the questionnaire. The help they received was for clarification of a question or word. They were not coached for their responses and their responses remained private.

Sample

A final sample of 121 adolescents was obtained. Their mean age was 11.5 (SD = 2.8). The sample included 50% females. Twenty-seven youth were omitted from the analyses described below because they were missing data on one or more of the variables included in the analyses. The final sample size for the analyses described below was 94 (44 males and 50 females).

Measures

A collaborative approach between researchers and Tribal members was employed to develop the questionnaire used in this study. This was done to assure the cultural relevance of the questions and to provide the Tribe with as much input as possible in the study. The researchers recommended several standardized scales. The Tribe chose complete scales, selected items from the scales, and offered some of their own items or suggestions for items. Descriptive statistics for all of the measures used in the study are presented in Table 2. All variables were adequately distributed; however, alcohol and substance use was moderately skewed.

Enculturation Measure

Enculturation was operationalized with three scales: cultural affinity, family involvement in cultural activities, and Native American identity. The measures were developed from existing measures, but were modified to be most relevant for the Tribe involved in the study. Although the measures formed a single factor as described above, they were analyzed separately in order to examine their unique influences. This seemed necessary due to the exploratory nature of the study.

Cultural Affinity. Cultural affinity is defined as pride and interest in one's cultural heritage. It was measured by a five-item

Table 2
Descriptive Statistics for Variables in the Study

Self-esteem		
	M	4.10
	SD	.66
	Skewness	-.56
Alcohol & substance use		
	M	3.46
	SD	9.44
	Skewness	2.38
Family drug problem		
	M	1.22
	SD	1.39
	Skewness	.74
Family activities		
	M	2.38
	SD	2.19
	Skewness	1.26
Cultural affinity		
	M	3.93
	SD	.80
	Skewness	-1.21
Cultural identity		
	M	2.40
	SD	.70
	Skewness	-.74

scale that used a 5-point Likert format. Questions included: 1) How important is it to you to maintain your Indian identity, values, and practices? 2) How much do you know about your Native American culture? 3) How interested are you in learning more about your Native American culture? 4) How different do you think Indian culture is from White culture? and 5) I am proud to be a Native American. These items were combined into a scale based upon exploratory factor analytic results. The factor analysis resulted in a single factor that accounted for 47% of the total variance, the factor loadings for items ranged from .52 to .81 (commonalities ranged from .32 to .66). Cronbach's Alpha for this scale was .70.

Family Activities. Respondents were asked to complete a checklist of nine activities they did with their families. The activities included ghost suppers (feasts to honor the deceased), Pow Wows, sweat lodges, seasonal feasts, naming ceremonies, healings, giveaways, fasting, and learning lodge (a lodge where some sessions are held to teach youth about native traditions). Scores on this variable could range from 0 to 9 as respondents were given a score of 1 for each activity checked.

Native American Identity. A single question was used to measure Native American identity: Do you see yourself as American Indian? The question had four possible responses: not at all (0), a little (1), some (2), and a lot (3).

Perceived Family Drug Abuse Problems

Perceived family drug abuse problems were measured by four dichotomous items. Youth were asked if alcohol or substance use by a family member repeatedly caused health, job, legal, or general family problems for the family. Scores on this variable could range from 0 to 4 as respondents were given a score of 1 for each problem checked. The internal reliability for this scale was .72.

Self-Esteem

Self-esteem was measured with nine 5-point Likert items taken from several existing self-esteem scales (e.g., Rosenberg, 1965). Principal components analysis was used to form the measure. The items formed a single factor accounting for 36% of the total variance. The factor loadings' absolute values ranged from .36 to .74 (commonalities ranged from .44 to .73). Cronbach's Alpha for the scale was .76. Sample items include "Overall, I like myself," "I feel I have much to be proud of," and "I am good at making friends."

Alcohol and Substance Use

Alcohol, cigarette, and marijuana use were measured separately using questions from the Monitoring the Future study (Johnston, O'Malley, & Bachman, 1988). A total substance use score (10 items) summing measures of use from all three substances was computed. Alcohol use was measured with a composite index of six frequency and intensity items. Two of the items asked youth to indicate the number of times they drank alcohol in their lifetime and during the last month (0 = none; 1 = 1–2 times; 2 = 3–5 times; 3 = 6–9 times; 4 = 10–19 times; 5 = 20–39 times; 6 = 40 or more times). One item asked adolescents to indicate how many drinks they usually had when they did drink during the last month (ranging from 0 to 7 or more), and one item asked how much was the most they drank in any one day during the past month using a similar scale. Another item asked youth to indicate how often they got drunk (1 = never, 5 = several times per week). The final item in the alcohol use scale asked youth if they ever drank so much they could not remember the next day what they had said or done. Cigarette and marijuana use were measured with two frequency items: lifetime use and use during the last two weeks. The total possible range for the final alcohol and substance use variable was 0–61.

Data Analytic Procedures

The enculturation hypothesis was explored using hierarchical multiple regression. Self-esteem was the dependent variable in the risk/protective analysis. Alcohol and substance use was the dependent variable in the protective/protective analysis. The three enculturation variables were entered as a group in a second step in all analyses. Family drug problems were entered first in the risk/protective analysis and self-esteem was entered first in the protective/protective analysis. The main effects aspect of the enculturation hypothesis was tested by evaluating the direct effects of enculturation for predicting self-esteem or alcohol and substance use.

A multiplicative (interaction) term between the predictor in Step 1 and each of the three variables comprising enculturation were added in the final (third) step of the regression equations in order to test protective effects. Three different regression equations were computed, each with a different interaction term. The risk/protective effect analysis used the interaction of family drug problems with each of the three enculturation measures for predicting self-esteem. The protective/protective effects were similarly tested using the interaction between self-esteem and the enculturation measures to predict alcohol and substance use.

Interaction effect analyses represent moderator effects (Baron & Kenny, 1986) that are the basis for examining protective mechanisms (Stacy, Newcomb, & Bentler, 1992). Thus, the interaction term tests the risk/protective effects of enculturation for the risk factor of family drug problems and protective/protective effects for enculturation and self-esteem. In order to avoid multicollinearity problems when we examined interaction effects, we centered the predictor variables before the multiplicative (interaction) term was computed (Aiken & West, 1991). The individual centered variables were also used in the regression equation.

Results

Table 3 presents the bivariate correlations among the variables included in both of the regression analyses. Self-esteem is correlated with family drug problems and cultural affinity. The three enculturation variables—cultural affinity, cultural identity, and family activities—are all correlated with each other. Cultural affinity, alcohol and substance use, and family drug problems are correlated with self-esteem (in theoretically consistent directions).

Table 3
Correlation Table of all Variables

	1	2	3	4	5	6
1. Self-esteem	––					
2. Alcohol & substance use	-.39[a]	––				
3. Family drug problems	-.24[a]	.13	––			
4. Cultural affinity	.34[a]	-.09	-.02	––		
5. Cultural identity	-.01	.14	.15	.43[a]	––	
6. Family activities	-.04	.07	.08	.30[a]	.20[b]	––

[a] $< .01$
[b] $< .05$

Risk/Protective Analysis

Table 4 presents final equation beta weights, R square, and R square change for predicting self-esteem. The results indicate main effects for family drug problems and enculturation, but no interaction effects. Among the enculturation measures, only cultural affinity predicted the youths' self-esteem.

Protective/Protective Analysis

Table 5 presents final equation beta weights, R square, and R square change for predicting alcohol and substance use. The results indicate main effects for self-esteem, but no main effects for the enculturation measures (although cultural identity falls just beyond the .05 level). Interaction effects between self-esteem and cultural identity were also found.

In order to interpret the interaction effects a simple slope analysis was conducted (Aiken & West, 1991). This enables us to describe the nature of the relationship between the two predictors (i.e., self-esteem and cultural identity). This approach tests the statistical significance of the simple slopes of the regression line at single values (usually the mean and 1 standard deviation above and

Table 4
Step R^2, Final Equation Beta Weights, and R^2 Change for Regression of Self-Esteem

		β	R^2	R^2 change
Step 1:	Family drug problems	-.21	.06[b]	0.00
Step 2:	Enculturation		.20	.14[a]
	Cultural affinity	.42[a]		
	Cultural identity	-.13		
	Family activities	-.12		

[a] < .01; [b] < .05

Note: Three separate interaction terms were computed for each of the enculturation measures with family drug problems and separate regression equations were computed using each interaction term as Step 3. None of the interaction terms were statistically significant at the .05 level.

Table 5
Step R^2, Final Equation Beta Weights, and R^2 Change for Regression of Alcohol and Substance Use

		β	R^2	R^2 change
Step 1:	Self esteem	-.36[a]	.15	0.00
Step 2:	Enculturation		.17	.02
	Cultural affinity	-.05		
	Cultural identity	.18		
	Family activities	.06		
Step 3:	Interaction term*	-.21[b]	.21	.04[b]
	Cultural identity x self esteem			

[a] < .01; [b] < .05

Note: Three separate interaction terms were computed for each of the enculturation measures with self esteem and separate regression equations were computed using each interaction term as Step 3. Interaction terms for cultural affinity and family activities with self esteem were not statistically significant at the .05 level.

below the mean) of one predictor while predicting the dependent variable with the other predictor. The results indicate that the regression of alcohol and substance use on self-esteem is significant only for youth who report average or higher levels of cultural identity (i.e., mean levels or one standard deviation above the mean). High levels of cultural identity interact with self-esteem for predicting alcohol and substance use. Youth with low levels of self-esteem but high levels of cultural identity reported the most alcohol and substance use. Youth with high levels of both self-esteem and cultural identity reported the lowest levels of alcohol and substance use. Table 6 describes the results of these analyses and Figure 1 depicts the interaction effects graphically.

Table 6
Regression of Alcohol and Substance Use On Self-Esteem At Particular Values of Cultural Identity, ŷ For Particular Values of Self-Esteem, Standard Error of the Simple Slopes, and T-Tests for the Simple Slopes

	Standard error of simple slope	t-test for simple slope
Cultural identity = 1 SD		
self-esteem: $\hat{y} = -5.33X_{s-e} + 7.16$	1.38	3.86[a]
1 SD: 1.83		
0: 7.16		
-1 SD: 12.49		
Cultural identity = 0		
self-esteem: $\hat{y} = -3.41X_{s-e} + 5.50$	.915	3.72[a]
1 SD: 2.09		
0: 5.50		
-1 SD: 8.91		
Cultural identity = -1 SD		
self-esteem: $\hat{y} = -1.49X_{s-e} + 3.83$	1.19	ns
1 SD: 2.38		
0: 3.83		
-1 SD: 5.32		

[a]$p < .05$

Note: The X_{s-e} in the regression equations above refers to self-esteem.

Discussion

The results of the regression analyses provide initial support for the enculturation hypothesis in two separate analyses. The main effects for enculturation for predicting self-esteem suggest that it plays an important role in the psychological well-being of Native Ameri-

Figure 1
Interaction Effects Plotted for Particular
Values of Cultural Identity (Cultid)

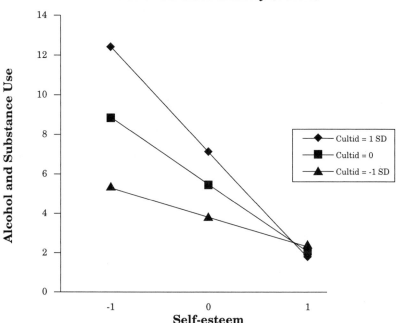

can youths. A risk/protective relationship between these two variables was not found in these analyses because interaction effects were not found. These results should not, however, be interpreted to mean that enculturation is not a risk/protective factor. Rather, enculturation may not be a risk/protective factor for family drug problems in relation to self-esteem. Research that explores other risk/protective mechanisms of enculturation may be more successful.

Future research could explore protective mechanisms of enculturation with risk factors other than a general measure of family drug problems. Enculturation may, for example, protect Native American adolescents' self-esteem from the consequences associated with drug problems of specific family members (e.g., mother, father, and siblings). It may also be useful to explore other social risk factors such as peer influences or more behavioral risk factors such as school failure or delinquency. Similarly, the enculturation hypothesis could be tested on different outcomes than we studied. Other dependent variables might include mental health outcomes (e.g., depression, anxiety), life satisfaction, or active coping behavior.

The results are encouraging as they reflect direct effects of enculturation on self-esteem. One way to enhance Native American youth self-esteem may be to help them develop a greater understanding of and interest in their cultural heritage. One of the most important tasks of adolescence is the development of social roles and socialization into the community and society (O'Keefe & Reid-Nash, 1987; Perry, Kelder, & Komro, 1993). Identification with and affinity toward one's own cultural group may help youth develop social roles that are consistent with their ethnic community. Enculturation also provides them with a sense of community with a group wherein their ethnicity is valued and nurtured. As a result, this may have a beneficial effect on their self-esteem and other aspects of their psychological well-being.

The results of the protective/protective analyses provide some support for the notion that enculturation may be a protective factor for Native American youth. Direct main effects of enculturation were not found, but the results indicated that the influence of enculturation on alcohol and substance use interact with self-esteem. The enculturation hypothesis was supported by the finding that youth with the highest levels of self-esteem and cultural identity reported the lowest levels of alcohol and substance use. Support for the hypothesis is somewhat mitigated, however, by the fact that youth with low levels of self-esteem and high levels of cultural identity reported the most alcohol and substance use. This was an unexpected finding. It was hypothesized that enculturation would have an enhancing effect on self-esteem for predicting alcohol and substance use, but this was only true among youth with high levels of self-esteem.

One explanation for this unexpected finding might be related to the tension that may be created from experiences of racism for youth with a strong Native American identity. Exposure to racist attitudes may have a negative effect on Native American youth self-esteem. These experiences may have the most harmful consequences for youth who also feel a strong Native American identity because they may be struggling to fit into a majority culture that does not welcome the cultural background with which they identify. The use of alcohol and other drugs may be one way youth try to cope with this incompatibility. Anecdotal evidence from observations and comments from youth and Tribal staff suggest that the youth in the sample studied do, indeed, confront anti-Native American attitudes. Future research needs to explore how racist experiences might influence the relationships among enculturation, self-esteem, and alcohol and substance use.

It is interesting that among the three enculturation variables, only cultural affinity predicted self-esteem and only cultural identity predicted alcohol and substance use. Apparently, the different components of enculturation have distinct effects on various outcomes. While this may be a result of the measures used or sample studied, it is theoretically consistent that each component would have unique effects on different outcomes. Cultural affinity, for example, reflects a sense of pride and interest in one's ethnic background, which seems logically connected to self-esteem.

Another explanation for the differential effects of the three components of enculturation may be that different measures were not sensitive enough to detect small effects for different outcome variables. The three enculturation measures may be correlated at varying levels with the outcomes studied, but did not result in statistically significant effects because of the relatively small sample studied. The consequence of a small sample size is limited statistical power which increases the likelihood of failing to find statistical significance (i.e., Type II error). Thus, the study reported in this chapter may have been a conservative test of the enculturation hypothesis. The results should, however, be interpreted cautiously because the study lacked random selection of respondents. In addition, the cross-sectional nature of the analyses precluded determination of causal linkages.

Conclusion

Enculturation appears to be a meaningful protective factor for Native American youth. It is a particularly useful construct for studying Native Americans, and perhaps ethnic minorities more generally, because it helps to focus attention on the social norms and values within a minority group rather than focus on comparisons to mainstream society in which minority group members may not be welcome. Enculturation also provides a theoretical framework that focuses on strengths in the lives of ethnic minority members rather than problems. If enculturation provides Native American youth with a protective mechanism, then interventions designed to prevent deleterious outcomes (e.g., alcohol and substance use, diminished self-esteem) could be designed to help youth learn about and develop pride in their cultural heritage.

The results reported in this chapter provide promise for further research on the role of enculturation for ethnic minority adolescent development. This research could include studies with other Native American Tribes or ethnic groups or other variables such as school attitudes and behavior, mental health outcomes, and family support. Longitudinal research would be especially useful to explore the development of enculturation. Interventions designed to enhance youths' cultural pride, identity, and behaviors could be designed to investigate the causal nature of enculturation. The study reported in this chapter should be interpreted as the commencement of this line of inquiry, and the results are an encouraging sign that this will be a worthwhile endeavor.

Finally, enculturation provides researchers with a more psychologically meaningful perspective of ethnicity than simple demographic indicators such as race (Williams, Lavizzo-Mourey, & Warren, 1994). Williams et al. (1994) point out that simple race comparisons may not be informative because they fail to account for variation within an ethnic group regarding the extent to which an individual feels connected to that ethnic group. This is significant because it advances our knowledge about how ethnicity may influence health and mental health rather than simply offer descriptive information about the fact that groups differ. The construct of enculturation is also significant because it focuses on positive aspects of ethnic minority experiences that emphasize their perspectives in research designed to understand how culture may influence development and behavior within ethnic minority populations.

Notes

1. We would like to thank the Grand Traverse Band of Ottawa and Chippewa Indians for their involvement in this project and especially to the youth and their parents who have agreed to participate in the study. This research was supported by the Center for Substance Abuse Prevention, Grant No. 1 H86 SPO1835–01A1 to the Grand Traverse Band of Ottawa/Chippewa Indians.

2. Kathleen Washienko and Benjamin Walter were research assistants on the project when the data were collected.

3. Sandra Dyer was the Director for the project upon which this study is based at the time of data collection.

4. The Anglicized version of these Tribal names are Ottawa and Chippewa, respectively.

References

Aiken, L.S., & West, S.G. (1991). *Multiple regression: Testing and interpreting interactions*, Newbury Park, CA: Sage.

Andrews, J.A., Hops, H., Ary, D., Tildesley, E., & Harris, J. (1993). Parental influences on early adolescent substance use: Specific and nonspecific effects. *Journal of Early Adolescence, 13*, 285–310.

Baron, R.M., & Kenny, D.A. (1986). The moderator–mediator variable distinction in social psychological research: Conceptual, strategic, and statistical considerations. *Journal of Personality and Social Psychology, 51*, 1173–1182.

Boyce, W.T., & Boyce, J.C. (1983). Acculturation and changes in health among Navajo boarding school students. *Social Science and Medicine, 17*, 219–226.

Brook, J.S., Brook, D.W., Gordon, A.S., & Whiteman, M. (1990). The psychosocial etiology of adolescent drug use: A family interactional approach. *Genetic, Social, and General Psychology Monographs, 116*, 111–267.

Brook, J.S., Whiteman, M., Cohen, P., & Tanaka, J.S. (1992). Childhood precursors of adolescent drug use: A longitudinal analysis. *Genetic, Social, and General Psychology Monographs, 118*, 195–213.

Brook, J.S., Whiteman, M., Gordon, A.S., & Cohen, P. (1989). Changes in drug involvement: A longitudinal study of childhood and adolescent determinants. *Psychological Reports, 65*(3, Pt. 1), 707–726.

Buriel, R. (1975). Cognitive styles among three generations of Mexican-American children. *Journal of Cross-Cultural Psychology, 6*, 417–429.

Burnam, M.A., Hough, R.L., Karno, M., Escobar, J.I., & Telles, C.A. (1987). Acculturation and lifetime prevalence of psychiatric disorders among Mexican-Americans in Los Angeles. *Journal of Health and Social Behavior, 28*, 89–102.

Dielman, T.E., Shope, J.T., Butchart, A.T., Campanelli, P.C., & Caspar, R.A. (1989). A covariance structural model test of antecedents of adolescent alcohol misuse and a prevention effort. *Journal of Drug Education, 19*, 337-361.

Drew, L.L. (1988). Acculturation stress and alcohol usage among Canadian Indians in Toronto. *Canadian Journal of Public Health, 79*, 115–118.

Dryfoos, J.G. (1990). *Adolescents at risk*. New York: Oxford University Press.

Garmezy, N., Masten, A.S., & Tellegen, A. (1984). The study of stress and competence in children: A building block for developmental psychopathology. *Child Development, 55*, 97–111.

Guyette, S. (1982). Selected characteristics of American Indian substance abusers. *International Journal of the Addictions, 17*, 1001–1014.

Hawkins, J.D., Catalano, R.F., & Miller, J.Y. (1992). Risk and protective factors for alcohol and other drug problems in adolescence and early adulthood: Implications for substance abuse prevention. *Psychological Bulletin, 112*, 64–105.

Jessor, R., & Jessor, S.L. (1977). *Problem behavior and psychosocial development: A longitudinal study of youth*. New York: Academic Press.

Johnson, G.M., Shontz, F.C., & Locke, T.P. (1984). Relationships between adolescent drug use and parental drug behaviors. *Adolescence, 19,* 295–299.

Johnston, L.D., O'Malley, P.M., & Bachman, J.G. (1988). *Illicit drug use, smoking, and drinking by America's high school students, college students, and young adults, 1975–1987.* Rockville, MD: National Institute on Drug Abuse.

Kandel, D.B., & Andrews, K. (1987). Processes of adolescent socialization by parents and peers. *International Journal of the Addictions, 22,* 319–342.

Lau, R.R., Quadrel, M.J., & Hartman, K.A. (1990). Development and change of youth adults' preventive health beliefs and behavior: Influence from parents and peers. *Journal of Health and Social Behavior, 31,* 240–259.

Little Soldier, L. (1985). To soar with the eagles: Enculturation and acculturation of Indian children. *Childhood Education, 61,* 185–191.

May, P. (1986). Alcohol and drug misuse prevention programs for American Indians: Needs and opportunities. *Journal of Studies in Alcohol, 47,* 187–195.

Needle, R., McCubbin, H., Wilson, M., Reineck, R., Lazar, A., & Mederer, H. (1986). Interpersonal influences in adolescent drug use---The role of older siblings, parents, and peers. *International Journal of the Addictions, 21,* 739-766.

Negy, C., & Woods, D.J. (1992). The importance of acculturation in understanding research with Hispanic-Americans. *Hispanic Journal of Behavioral Sciences, 14,* 224–247.

Newcomb, M.D., & Felix-Ortiz, M. (1992). Multiple protective and risk factors for drug use and abuse: Cross-sectional and prospective findings. *Journal of Personality and Social Psychology, 63,* 280–296.

Newcomb, M.D., Maddahian, E., & Bentler, P.M. (1986). Risk factors for drug use among adolescents: Concurrent and longitudinal analyses. *American Journal of Public Health, 76,* 525-531.

Nicols, R.L. (1990–1991). Native American survival in an integrationist society. *Journal of American Ethnic History, 10,* 87–93.

Oetting, E.R., & Beauvais, F. (1990). Adolescent drug use: Findings of national and local surveys. *Journal of Consulting and Clinical Psychology, 58,* 385-394.

Oetting, E.R., & Beauvais, F. (1991). Orthogonal cultural identification theory: The cultural identification of minority adolescents. *International Journal of the Addictions, 25,* 655–685.

O'Keefe, G.J., & Reid-Nash, K. (1987). Socializing function. In C.R. Berger & S.H. Chaffee (Eds.), *Handbook of communication* (pp. 419–445). Newbury Park, CA: Sage.

Padilla, A.M. (1980). Introduction. In A.M. Padilla (Ed.), *Acculturation: Theory, models, and some new findings* (pp. 1–3). Boulder, CO: Westview.

Parham, T., & Helms, J. (1985). Relation of racial identity attitudes to self-actualization and affective states of Black students. *Journal of Counseling Psychology, 32,* 431–440.

Parker, L. (1990, Summer). The missing component in substance abuse prevention efforts: A Native American example. *Contemporary Drug Problems,* pp. 251–270.

Perry, C. L., Kelder, S.H., & Komro, K.A. (1993). The social world of adolescents: Family, peers, schools, and the community. In S.G. Millstein, A.C. Peterson, & E.O. Nightingale (Eds.), *Promoting health in adolescents: New directions for the twenty-first century* (pp. 73–96). New York: Oxford University Press.

Phinney, J.S. (1992). Ethnic identity in adolescents and adults: Review of the research. *Psychological Bulletin, 108,* 499–514.

Phinney, J.S., & Alipuria, L.L. (1990). Ethnic identity in college students from four ethnic groups. *Journal of Adolescence, 13,* 171–183.

Phinney, J.S., & Chavira, V. (1992). Ethnic identity and self-esteem: An exploratory longitudinal study. *Journal of Adolescence, 15,* 271–281.

Rosenberg, M. (1965). *Society and the adolescent self-image.* Princeton, NJ: Princeton University Press.

Rutter, M. (1987). Psychosocial resilience and protective mechanisms. *American Journal of Orthopsychiatry, 57,* 316-331.

Schinke, S.P., Moncher, M.S., Palleja, J., Zayas, L.H., & Schilling, R.F. (1988). Hispanic youth, substance abuse, and stress: Implications for prevention research. *International Journal of the Addictions, 23,* 809–826.

Selnow, G.W. (1985). Using a stratified approach in substance intervention and prevention programs among adolescents: An empirical analysis. *Journal of Drug Education, 15,* 327–341.

Stacy, A.U., Newcomb, M.D., & Bentler, P.M. (1992). Interactive and higher-order effects of social influences on drug use. *Journal of Health and Social Behavior, 33,* 226–241.

Trimble, J.E. (1983). Stalking the wily emic: Alternatives to cross-cultural measurement. In S.H Irvine & J.W. Berry (Eds.), *Human assessment and cultural factors* (pp. 259–273). New York: Plenum.

Trimble, J.E. (1987). Multilinearity of acculturation: Person-situation interactions. In D.M. Keats, D. Munro, & L. Mann (Eds.), *Heterogeneity in cross-cultural psychology* (pp. 173–186). Amsterdam: Swets & Zeitlinger.

U.S. Department of Health and Human Services. (1986). *Indian Health Service Alcoholism/Substance Abuse Prevention Initiative.* Washington, DC: Public Health Service, U.S. Government Printing Office.

Vega, W.A., Warheit, G., & Meinhardt, K. (1984). Marital disruption and the prevalence of depressive symptomology among Anglos and Mexican Americans. *Journal of Marriage and Family, 46,* 817–824.

Wilbert, J. (1976). Introduction. In J. Wilbert (Ed.), *Enculturation in Latin America: An anthology* (pp. 1–28). Los Angeles, CA, UCLA Latin American Center for Publications.

Williams, D.R., Lavizzo-Mourey, R., & Warren, R.C. (1994). The concept of race and health status in America. *Public Health Reports, 109,* 26-41.

Zimmerman, M.A., Ramirez, J., Washienko, K.M., Walter, B., & Dyer, S. (1994). The development of a measure of enculturation for Native American Youth. Manuscript submitted for publication.

III. Immigrant Americans

III a. Asian Americans

Chapter 11

Family and Work Roles of Korean Immigrants in the United States

Kwang Chung Kim and Shin Kim

As the proportion of employed married women increases, there is a growing concern about family and work roles in the United States. As Voydanoff (1984) notes, the issue is no longer whether there is any linkage between family and work roles, but rather a recognition of the nature of the linkage and its implications for individuals, families, work organizations, and society. This study focuses on the nature of the linkage with a conceptual model, offering a typology of employed husbands and wives. The model is used to analyze family and work roles of married Korean immigrant adults.

Conceptual Model of Family and Work Roles of Married Couples

Studies of family and work roles of husbands and wives have steadily accumulated in the United States in recent years. Findings of these studies are, however, found to be highly fragmentary and often contradictory (Bird, Bird, & Scruggs, 1984; Blair & Johnson, 1992; Booth, 1977; Burke & Weir, 1976; Ferree, 1976; Kessler & McRae, 1982; Pleck, 1985; Simon, 1991; Vannoy & Philliber, 1992; Wright, 1978). These studies rarely offer a coherent framework for the study of family and work roles of husbands and wives. For a systematic analysis, it is necessary to address two issues: First, a conceptual model, which would offer a systematic or comprehensive perspective on work and family roles is needed; and second, since employed husbands and wives can no longer be considered as a homogeneous group, it is essential to develop a typology to categorize employed husbands and wives.

Toward the development of a conceptual model, a framework that offers a typology of employed husbands and wives based on each spouse's attitude toward the wife's work role (employment) and related family role will be presented. Four family types will be explored. Type I is characterized by a spouse who recognizes that the wife is forced to work outside the home in order to support the family, but who believes that she should stay home as a full-time homemaker. The Type I spouse experiences an uncomfortable discrepancy between his or her expectation for the wife's work role and the reality of her employment (Ross, Mirowsky, & Huber, 1983). The spouse still remains traditional in his or her gender role orientation. The spouse would, therefore, adhere to the traditional belief that "housework and childcare are ultimately wives' responsibility" (Pleck, 1985, p. 93). Pleck's characterization illustrates the Type I husband:

> [A] higher proportion of husbands felt that their wives should not work outside home. Husbands persisted in their belief in spite of the fact that their wives' employment would have reduced the pressure on them as sole breadwinners and increased their family's standard of living (1985, p. 94).

Potuchek describes a group of employed wives, called "helpers," which illustrates the Type I wife:

> There are women who use their employment as a means of contributing to the basic financial needs of their families, but who also subscribe to the traditional norms about breadwinning and who do not interpret their employment as central to the lives of their families (1992, p. 551).

When a spouse acquiesces to or tolerates the wife's employment with a realistic recognition that the wife will need to work for a long period of time to support the family, the spouse moves into the Type II category. For the Type II spouse, his or her tolerance or passive acceptance of the wife's employment represents an attempt to resolve the cognitive dissonance between the necessity of the wife's employment and his or her traditional gender role orientation. This spouse now manages to achieve congruence between the objective and subjective dimensions of the wife's employment by partially modifying his or her expectation for the wife's work role. Since the spouse's attitudinal modification is, however, situationally forced and not accompanied by any change in his or her traditional expectation for the wife's family role, the spouse continues to believe that the wife should perform the traditional family role and maintain her role as a homemaker as much as possible.

If a spouse regards the wife's work role as part of her essential adult role or self-identity, the spouse is in the Type III category. The Type III wife shows some degree of work role commitment. The Type III husband is an individual who accepts or supports the wife's work role commitment. When the wife's work role is so desired or preferred, the traditional family role for the wife needs to be modified and the Type III spouse is likely to believe that the husband should share the family role for the sake of marital equity or balance. Keith and Schafer (1983) clearly express this new role expectation: "Because of the greater salience of family responsibilities for women, commitment to employment represents a departure from the traditional norms, requiring more innovative behavior on their part" (p. 883).

For the Type III spouse, however, the extent of his or her acceptance of the new expectation for the wife is somewhat limited. He or she still maintains the belief that the wife's family role is a more important adult role than her work role. The employed wife's self-identity is defined more by her homemaker's role than by her employment role. The Type III spouse believes that the husband should be the primary provider with the wife as the secondary provider. Although the Type III spouse believes that the employed wife and husband should share household responsibilities, the Type III wife maintains primary responsibility for the family role.

If a spouse believes that the wife's work role is as important as her family role or even more important than the family role, the spouse is classified in the Type IV category. The Type IV spouse believes that the wife's work role is as important as the husband's work role in the family. The employed wife's work role has a significant impact on her conceptualization of self-identity. The employed wife is, therefore, expected to be the primary provider or co-provider and to share the family role equally with her husband. Two-career families and families in which the wife is a co-breadwinner are illustrative of the Type IV category (Bird, Bird, & Scruggs, 1984).

This model offers a typology of employed wives and husbands based on each spouse's attitude toward the wife's work role and the related family role. When the four types of employed wives are cross-classified by the four types of employed husbands, sixteen types of employed couples can be identified. For a systematic analysis of employed wives and husbands, the husband and wife in each family will be classified separately in terms of the typology. The wife and her husband may share the same attitude toward the wife's work role (marital consensus) or they may maintain different attitudes toward her work role (marital dissensus). The antecedent factors (e.g., each spouse's age, family backgrounds, place of birth, education, ethnic status, type of the current occupation, income and other work-related rewards) and/or consequences (e.g., performance of family role, mental health, marital relation, intergenerational relationship, need for closeness and inclusion or dominance) associated with each type of the employed married couples will then be examined (Gilbert, 1985, 1993; Voydanoff, 1984).

In addition to cognitive dissonance, two additional factors may be important antecedents to explain a spouse's classification in the above typology: a spouse's past experience of socialization, and the employed wife's current workplace experience. A spouse may have been socialized to accept a traditional or a modern gender role orientation. Role socialization experiences shape each spouse's attitude toward the wife's work role. At the same time, if the employed wife sees some aspects of her current occupation as rewarding or satisfactory (e.g., earnings, opportunity to work outside the home, chance to meet people, opportunity to use one's education or skills, challenging opportunity), she may begin to prefer her work role to her family role. An employed wife's positive workplace experience may also influence the husband's attitude toward the wife's work role. Conversely, if the wife's work experience is not satisfactory, the husband and wife may maintain a traditional gender role orientation, or if their gender role orientation was non-traditional, they may adopt a traditional gender role orientation,

In studying the consequences of the couples' types, the effects of each spouse's attitude toward the wife's work role will be examined. Each spouse's attitude toward the wife's work role is expected to affect his or her actual performance of the family role (Bird, Bird, & Scruggs, 1984; Vannoy & Philliber, 1992). The employed wife and husband would be obliged to perform the family role to the extent of his or her acceptance of the wife's work role (Barnett & Baruch, 1987). This suggests that the wives in the first two categories (Types I and II) would struggle to perform most of the family role as traditionally expected. Some aspects of the family role may be shifted from the wife to her husband or children when unmanageable pressure caused by work/family overload is experienced by the employed wife (Kim & Hurh, 1988).

Wives in the latter two categories (Types III and IV) face a different situation. As long as the wives think that the work role is part of their essential adult role or self-identity, the employed wives face the issue of equity in addition to the issue of overload (Pleck, 1985). With their sense of equity and overload, these wives may press their husbands to share the family role. From the perspective of equity, Pleck (1985) suggests that the issue is not so much that employed wives are doing too much, but that their husbands are doing too little. The Type III wives would thus press their husbands to perform the family role, but to a less extent than the wives actually do. The Type III husbands would also be willing to accommodate such an expectation. When faced with equity and overload issues, the Type IV spouses would move further and try to share the family role equally.

In addition to an attitudinal effect, the following factors are also expected to influence family role performance, directly or indirectly, through their influence on the couples' attitudes toward the wife's work role: (1) occupational variables (e.g., types of occupation, hours of work, earnings, relative hours of work or earnings of the husband and wife), (2) family variables (e.g., number and age of children, etc.), (3) social status variables (e.g., age, sex, race, education, relative education of the husband and wife), and (4) situational variables (e.g., negative community reaction to non-traditional family role-sharing, or the husband's lack of skill to perform the family role) (Lein, 1984; Pleck, 1985).

The above factors would affect family role performance of spouses in the first two categories (Type I and II) to the extent that the variables severely affect the wife's experience of the double burden of performing family and work roles. But the same variables are expected to affect family role performance of the spouses in the last two categories (Types III and IV) to the extent that these variables create the problem of work overload and raise the issue of equity or fairness in sharing the family role between the husband and the wife. These variables would, therefore, affect the family role performance of the Type III and Type IV spouses more than Type I or Type II spouses. Additionally, wives in the last two categories are likely to press their husbands to perform the family role more than the wives in the first two categories (Barnett & Baruch, 1987; Clark, Nye, & Gecas, 1978).

Family and Work Roles of Korean Immigrant Married Couples

Like many of the current Asian immigrants, recent Korean immigrants came to the United States with a high pre-immigration socio-

economic status as demonstrated by their pre-immigration education, occupation, and residence (Barringer, Gardner, & Levin, 1993;
Hurh & Kim, 1988; U. S. Commission on Civil Rights, 1988). As a
whole, Korean immigration can be characterized as an urban middle-
class migration. Despite their middle-class backgrounds, a great
majority of the recent Korean immigrants are employed in highly
diversified occupations. In spite of the diversity, their current occupations share one common point: As immigrant workers, Koreans
are generally employed in occupations avoided or disdained by the
native-born whites (white males), and, therefore, easily available to
immigrant workers. Occupations that are generally avoided by the
native-born whites include occupations with a short supply of workers, occupations disdained by the native-born workers, and occupations with low earning potential.

Currently, Korean immigrants are heavily concentrated in
the following three types of occupations: (1) professional/technical
occupations, (2) self-employment in small business, and (3) clerical/
service/manual occupations. A high proportion of those who are
currently employed in professional/technical occupations are physicians and nurses. Due to a severe shortage of physicians in the
1960s and 1970s, Korean immigrant physicians had the opportunity
to practice medicine in the United States (U. S. Commission on
Civil Rights, 1992). Most self-employed Korean business owners
primarily serve Korean and other minority customers (African Americans or Hispanic Americans) or are engaged in highly labor-intensive
businesses (e.g., laundry and dry cleaning or fruit and vegetable
shops). These types of small businesses are the kinds of occupations
disdained by native-born whites. Koreans employed in clerical/
service/manual occupations are typically employed in the highly unfavorable secondary labor market characterized by low wages, low
skills, and lack of job security (Doeringer & Piore, 1971; Hurh &
Kim, 1988).

With the exceptions of some of the professional/technical occupations, the occupational distribution of Korean immigrants suggests that many Koreans are employed in highly unfavorable
occupations. Such unfavorable occupations are likely to affect family and work roles in two ways: First, when husbands in Korean
immigrant families are employed in unfavorable occupations, their
occupational situation may require many of their wives to work in
order to support the family; and second, as immigrant workers, a
great majority of employed wives are also employed in unfavorable
occupations. Wives employed in unfavorable occupations are unlikely to experience their current occupations as rewarding or satis-

fying. Unfavorable occupational experiences do not encourage spouses to have a positive attitude toward the wife's work role, nor would husbands be motivated to support the wives' work role or careerism.

While the majority of Korean immigrant wives are employed, most of them are likely to remain in the Type I category due to their traditional gender role orientation and their current unfavorable labor market experiences. As the length of their employment extends, some of them may move into the Type II category although they may not feel rewarded or satisfied in the workplace. Most employed Korean wives would maintain that the family role is the wife's primary responsibility in spite of her employment outside of the home. Most employed wives would be, therefore, burdened by both work and family roles. Furthermore, since their occupational conditions are not likely to improve even with extended residence in the United States, employed wives would continue to experience the burden of dual roles. The following hypotheses are presented for an empirical analysis of Korean employed couples' experiences of family and work roles in the United States:

Hypothesis 1: The majority of the wives in Korean immigrant families are employed out of economic necessity for family support.

Hypothesis 2: The majority of employed couples do not voluntarily accept the wife's employment.

Hypothesis 3: When the employed wives accept their own employment, they do so in order to accept the reality of their employment necessity.

Hypothesis 4: The employed wives are continuously expected to perform housework regardless of length of residence in the United States.

Hypothesis 5: The employed wives actually perform most of housework regardless of length of residence in the United States.

Data Collection

Interviews were conducted with 622 Korean adult immigrants (20 years or older) who resided in the Chicago area. Participants were randomly selected from the *Korean Community Directory of Chicago, 1984-85* and eight telephone directories from the city of Chi-

cago and contiguous suburban communities. A standardized interview schedule was used as part of a larger study of Korean immigrants' adaptation and mental health.[1]

The sample included 334 males (53.7%) and 288 females
(46.3%). The mean age of the total sample was 41.6 with the majority (78.7%) in the age category of 30-50. The average length of
residence in the United States was 8.1 years, although the variance
in length of residence was significant. About 13% ($n=82$) of the
respondents have been in the United States for two years or less,
while a similar proportion of them ($n=78$, 12.6%) have lived in the
United States for 15 years or more.

Data Analysis

Most of the respondents (90.4% of males and 76.2% of females) are
married, and the vast majority of the married male respondents
(91%) and three-fourths of the married female respondents (74.3%)
are currently employed. Among employed husbands, about 40%
($n=116$) are employed in clerical/service/manual occupations, while
the rest are employed in professional/technical occupations (28.2%,
$n=77$) or in self-employed small business (29.3%, $n=80$). Employed
wives are distributed into the above three types of occupations evenly:
professional/technical occupations (30.4%), self-employed small business (31.7%), and clerical/service/manual occupations (37.9%).

If part-time work is defined as less than 35 work hours per
week, few of the employed respondents (5.3% of males and 9.4% of
females) are part-time workers. The work hours of the self-employed small business owners are found to be unusually long; the
majority of them work more than 50 hours a week (Hurh & Kim,
1988). A majority of those currently employed in clerical/service/
manual occupations work under highly unfavorable conditions. Two-
thirds of them (62.9% of males, $n=73$, and 67.2% of females, $n=41$)
indicate that the majority of co-workers are minority workers (e.g.,
Koreans, African Americans, or Hispanics) or mixture of white and
minority workers. These workers are found to be paid less than
those who work mainly with white workers (Hurh & Kim, 1988).

In Korea, traditional gender norms dictate that married
women generally stay at home as full-time homemakers. In the
United States, three-fourths of Korean immigrant wives are currently employed. If their employment reflects their own desire for
work outside the home, it is expected that at the beginning of their
American life, only a small proportion of them would be employed,
but as they stay longer in the United States and become more Ameri-

canized, they would increasingly participate in the labor market (the assimilation model). In contrast, if most wives are employed out of economic necessity, it is expected that a high proportion of wives are employed from the beginning of their immigrant life, and that the proportion of employed wives remains high regardless of length of residence in the United States (the economic necessity model). Table 1 shows the proportion of employed wives classified by length of residence in the United States. Among the newly arrived wives (1-2 years length of residence in the United States), the majority (57.6%, $n=19$) were already employed. Among the wives who have been in the United States for a longer period of time, a higher proportion are employed. This observation empirically confirms Hypothesis 1.

Table 1
Length of Residence and Proportion of Employed Korean Wives

| | Length of Residence | | | | | | |
	1 - 2	3 - 4	5 - 6	7 - 8	9 - 10	11 - 12	13 or more
N	19	20	17	19	24	32	31
%	57.6	80.0	68.0	67.9	80.0	86.5	77.5

The second hypothesis is concerned with whether the husband and wife in Korean immigrant families would accept the wife's work role, when the wife is currently employed. This hypothesis was tested by their response to the statement: "The woman's place is in the home." The respondents who agreed with the statement were classified as having a negative attitude toward the wife's work role, while those who disagreed with the statement were classified as having a positive attitude. For this analysis, only the married respondents from the following two types of families are tested: (1) the single earner family (husband only is employed), and (2) the dual earner family (husband and wife are both employed with no other family members employed). Approximately four-fifths of the married respondents fall into these two categories (83.7%, $n=435$).

Table 2 shows that among the respondents in the dual earner family, only one-third (33.3%, $n=109$) accept the wife's work role, while the remaining two-thirds (66.7%, $n=218$) do not do so (Type I). A higher proportion of the respondents in the single earner family (83.3%, $n=90$) do not accept the wife's work role. No sex

Table 2
Acceptance or Non-Acceptance of the Wife's Work Role Among
Respondents in Two Types of Korean Immigrant Families

		Acceptance	Non-Acceptance	Total
Dual Earner	N	109	218	327
Family	%	33.3	66.7	100
Single Earner	N	18	90	108
Family	%	16.7	83.3	100

difference is observed among the respondents in the dual earner family. These findings show that a great majority of the respondents in the dual earner family are in the Type I category as predicted by Hypothesis 2.

If the respondents' acceptance of the wife's work role is motivated by the employed wives' rewarding or satisfying experiences at their current workplace, those employed wives who accept their own work role are expected to be more satisfied with their current occupation than those who do not (see Table 3). The respondents' job satisfaction is measured by a scale developed by Kallenberg (1977). For each occupational group, no difference was observed in the degree of satisfaction with the current occupation between those who accept the wife's work role and those who do not. This observation does not support the idea that the wives who accept the wife's work role (Type II) feel more rewarded or satisfied with their workplace experience than the wives who do not (Type I). This finding gives empirical support for Hypothesis 3.

As a way to measure the respondents' family role, the married respondents were asked about the division of housework in their families; "Among your family members (e.g., wife, husband and other members), how do you divide housework?" and "In your opinion, how should the housework be divided in principle?" The first question measured the actual division of housework (family role performance), while the second question tests their expectation (family role expectation). Five categories of housework were given: grocery shopping, cleaning the house, laundry, dishwashing, and cooking. The respondents were then asked to rank their family members in terms of their performance of each of the housework categories on a 6-point scale (0="the wife does not perform at all or

Table 3
The Degree of Occupational Satisfaction by
Three Occupational Groups of Employed Women

	Professional/ Technical Workers			Small Business Owners			Service/Manual/ Other Workers		
	n	Mean	SD	n	Mean	SD	n	Mean	SD
Acceptance	24	15.3	4.4	18	17.6	5.3	17	17.1	5.4
Non-Acceptance	19	15.1	5.3	30	18.0	4.3	43	18.2	5.5

is expected to do so" to 5= "the wife performs alone or is expected to do so").

For a systematic analysis, the scores of family role expectation and performance are calculated by adding up the points on the family member's relative performance of the four items of housework, excluding grocery shopping. Only the remaining four items show high factor loadings on the same dimension in the factor analysis. A separate role score was calculated for the wife, the husband, and other family members. The role scores ranged from 0 to 20.

Table 4 shows the scores of both family role expectations and actual performance based on the response of the two groups, the husbands and the wives. In the dual earner family, both groups indicate that it is the wife in the family who is expected to perform the housework and it is the wife who actually performs those tasks. No sex differences between husbands and wives emerged in their scores of the wife's family role expectation and performance. This finding demonstrates that the wife in the dual earner family bears a heavy burden of double role responsibility. In sharp contrast, the two groups of respondents indicate that the husband and other family members (children, grandmother, etc.) are expected to perform and do perform housework to a very limited extent. The two groups of respondents show no sex difference in their scoring of family role expectations and performances for the husband and other family members.

There are greater expectations that non-employed wives in single earner families will perform housework tasks, and non-employed wives actually do perform more housework than the wives in dual earner families. In contrast, the husband and other family members in the single earner family are expected to perform less housework, and they actually do perform less than the husbands and other family members in dual earner families. These findings

Table 4
Family Role Expectation and Performance for
Wives, Husbands and Other Family Members

			Wife's Family Role		Husband's Family Role		Other's Family Role	
			Expectation	Performance	Expectation	Performance	Expectation	Performance
Dual Earner Family	Husband	M	15.0	15.0	5.6	5.6	2.5	3.7
		SD	2.5	3.4	3.5	3.5	4.1	4.9
		n	179	180	180	180	179	180
	Wife	M	15.3	14.8	4.5	4.5	3.3	4.9
		SD	3.2	3.9	3.7	3.7	4.6	5.6
		n	145	143	143	143	145	143
Single Earner Family	Husband	M	16.3	16.7	4.2	4.2	1.7	2.3
		SD	2.1	2.8	3.6	3.6	3.5	4.2
		n	66	66	66	66	66	66
	Wife	M	16.8	17.9	3.5	3.5	1.2	.9
		SD	2.3	2.1	3.7	3.7	2.6	2.6
		n	44	45	45	45	44	45

suggest that when the wife is employed, some burden of performing housework is shifted to the husband and other family members and they are expected to accept increased family role responsibilities.

Table 5
Regression Analysis of Wives' Family Role on Respondent's Attitude Toward the Wife's Work Role, Age, Education and Length of Residence (Only From Dual Earner Family)

	Wives as Respondents Wife's Family Role		Husbands as Respondents Wife's Family Role	
	Expectation	Performance	Expectation	Performance
Attitude	.005	-.05	-.11	-.02
Age	.009	.05	.04	.07
Education	.018	.18*	.10	.01
Length of Res.	-.04	.07	-.13	.05
n	141	139	174	175
R^2	.001	.05	.03	.005

* Significance at the level of .05

The wife's family role in the dual earner family is further examined by the regression analysis (Table 5). The wife's family role is regressed on the attitude (acceptance or non-acceptance of the wife's work role), age, education (college graduates, non-college graduates), and length of residence in the United States. In dual earner families, respondents' attitudes toward the wife's work role, current age and education are not related to the employed wife's family role expectation and performance, with one exception: The findings for employed wives show that a wife with a college degree performs the family role less than a wife with no college degree. The respondents also indicate that the extent of the wife's family role expectation and performance are not related to length of residence in the United States. In conjunction with the findings shown in Table 4, Table 5 shows that there is a high expectation for employed wives in dual earner families to perform housework and that expectation does not diminish regardless of length of residence in the United States. These data confirm Hypotheses 4 and 5.

Discussion

As hypothesized, the data analysis revealed that most wives in Korean immigrant families are currently employed out of economic necessity for family support. At the same time, a great majority of the employed wives and husbands in the sample are found to adhere to traditional gender roles, and they believe that employed wives should stay at home and perform most of the family role (housework). In this respect, the employed wives are no less traditional than the husbands. The Type II wives also do not differ from the Type I wives in the degree of their current job satisfaction. These findings have empirically demonstrated that most of the respondents in the sample remain in the Type I or II category. In Korean immigrant families, the wife's employment signifies the addition of a new role to her traditional family role. Employed wives, therefore, bear a heavy burden of double roles. Furthermore, they do so regardless of length of residence in the United States.

The enduring situation of employed wives' double role burden can be attributed to their past socialization experiences in Korea as well as their current unfavorable labor market experiences in the United States. The two factors jointly sustain or reinforce their adherence to the traditional gender role orientation. This interpretation suggests that employed wives attach meaning to their double role burden. Employed wives themselves accept the traditional family role as part of their current role obligation, and therefore the double burden is not something that is unilaterally imposed on them by their husbands. Rather, the dual work/family role is a system that employed wives voluntarily accept with a sense of obligation.

When employed wives accept the dual work/family role with a sense of obligation, one might wonder how they could manage or cope with the double burden. In his analysis of women's role conflicts, Hall (1972) presents three types of coping strategies. The first coping strategy is referred to as the structural role redefinition. An actor with this coping strategy negotiates with others to redefine their mutual roles or to receive support from others. The second coping strategy is personal role redefinition in which an actor prioritizes his or her roles and concentrates on performing the high-priority roles. This strategy involves dividing or segregating certain roles, overlooking some role demands, reducing standards of performance, eliminating certain roles, and transferring attention from one role to the other roles. The third coping strategy is reactive role behavior. The actor with this strategy plans, schedules, or organizes roles more efficiently and then works harder for a satisfactory performance of roles.

As long as employed wives believe that they have to perform most of the family role, they are not likely to resort to the first coping strategy, unless their double roles are too burdensome. They are extremely unlikely to negotiate actively with or press their husbands and other family members to share the family role. These employed wives would rather assume the second or third coping strategies. In coping with the double burden, employed wives establish priorities for their multiple roles in terms of their importance to the collective welfare of their families (the personal role redefinition) and then work harder for a satisfactory performance of the high-priority roles (the reactive role behavior). Utilization of these two coping strategies involves a considerable degree of sacrifice on the part of employed wives for the collective interests of their families.

As Hall (1972) suggests, these two coping strategies are stress-ridden. Two sources of the stress can be identified in this analysis of Korean wives and husbands: the wives' employment against their own or their husbands' beliefs or preferences, and the employed wives' experience of work overload and energy depletion caused by dealing with the double burden. These two sources of stress suggest that Korean employed wives may experience psychological distress and depression. For a systematic analysis of the implications of the coping strategies utilized, however, the stressful aspects of these coping strategies should be examined in conjunction with the beneficial or rewarding aspects of the strategies in dealing with the double burden of multiple roles (Marks, 1977; Thoits, 1983).

Through the personal sacrifice of employed wives, Korean immigrant families are currently found to maintain a resilient pattern of adaptation in the United States. Since so many immigrant wives contribute financially to their families, Korean immigrants generally maintain a relatively high family income despite the husband's limited employment opportunities in the United States. In 1985, the median annual family income was $27,735 in the United States (U. S. Dept. of Commerce, 1988, p. 427). Two-thirds of the respondents in this current Korean sample who are of an economically active age (age of 55 or less), and who are currently involved in occupations other than self-employment in small business, report that their annual family income in 1985 was $30,000 or more. The family income of small business owners was generally higher than the income of the above respondents.

The relatively high family income of Korean immigrants contributes to the successful image of Asian Americans in the United States (Hurh & Kim, 1989). A high proportion of Korean immigrants in the sample manage to own a home and many of them lived in suburban areas wherein there were good educational opportunities for their children. Home ownership and life in suburban areas symbolizes their achievement of the American middle-class dream.

This pattern of resilient adaptation is likely to continue through the personal sacrifice of the mother/wife in Korean immigrant families, unless some conscious effort is made for an equitable distribution of the family role among family members. Korean immigrant families are currently facing the challenge of developing a new pattern of resilient adaptation for an equitable distribution of the family burden among family members, even though the labor market conditions and other structural conditions in the United States would not encourage them to do so.

This exploratory study has empirically demonstrated the utility of the proposed conceptual model. The model offers a framework to classify employed wives and husbands into meaningful categories. The model also suggests considering both subjective and objective dimensions of employed wives' experiences for a meaningful analysis of the issues related to family and work roles. The model also suggests that family and work roles of employed couples in each type must be examined within cultural (e.g., socialization effect) and social (e.g., workplace experience) contexts. This study has identified the types of family and work roles commonly observed in employed Korean wives and husbands, their distinct role problems, and the current pattern of their resilient adaptation in the United States.

Note

1. This study was funded by the National Institute of Mental Health.

References

Barnett, R., & Baruch, G. K. (1987). Determinants of father's participation in family work. *Journal of Marriage and the Family, 49*, 29-40.

Barringer, H., Gardner, R.W., & Levin, M. J. (1993). *Asians and Pacific Islanders in the United States.* New York: Russell Sage Foundation.

Bird, G., Bird, G., & Scruggs, M. (1984). Determinants of family task sharing: A study of husbands and wives. *Journal of Marriage and the Family, 46*, 345-355.

Blair, S. L., & Johnson, M. P. (1992). Wives' perception of the fairness of the division of household labor. *Journal of Marriage and the Family, 54*, 570-581.

Booth, A. (1977). Wife's employment and husband's stress: A replication and refutation. *Journal of Marriage and the Family, 39*, 645-650.

Burke, R., & Weir, T. (1976). Relationship of wives' employment status to husband, wife and pair satisfaction and performance. *Journal of Marriage and the Family, 38*, 279-287.

Clark, R. A., Nye, F. I., & Gecas, V. (1978). Work involvement and marital role performance. *Journal of Marriage and the Family, 40*, 9-21.

Doeringer, P., & Piore, M.J. (1971). *Internal labor markets and manpower analysis*. Lexington, MA: Heath Lexington Books.

Ferree, M. (1976). Working class jobs: Housework and paid work as sources of satisfaction. *Social Problems, 23*, 431-441.

Gilbert, L. A. (1985). *Men in dual-career families: Current realities and future prospects*. Hillsdale, NJ: Lawrence Erlbaum.

Gilbert, L. A. (1993). *Two careers/one family*. Newbury Park, CA: Sage.

Hall, D.T. (1972). A model of coping with role conflict. *Administrative Science Quarterly, 4*, 471-486.

Hurh, W. M., & Kim, K. C. (1988). *Uprooting and adjustment: A sociological study of Korean immigrants' mental health*. Final Report Submitted to National Institute of Mental Health, U. S. Dept. of Health and Human Services.

Hurh, W. M., & Kim, K. C. (1989). The 'success' image of Asian Americans: Its validity, and its practical and theoretical implications. *Ethnic and Racial Studies, 12*, 512-538.

Kallenberg, A. L. (1977). Work values and job rewards: A theory of job satisfaction. *American Sociological Review, 42*, 124-123.

Keith, P.M., & Schafer, R.E. (1983). Employment characteristics of both spouses and depression in two-job families. *Journal of Marriage and the Family, 45*, 877-884.

Kessler, R. C., & McRae, J. A. (1981). Trends in the relationship between sex and psychological distress. *American Sociological Review, 46*, 443-452.

Kim, K. C., & Hurh, W.M. (1988). The burden of double roles: Korean wives in the USA. *Ethnic and Racial Studies, 11*, 151-167.

Kim, K. C., Kim, S., & Hurh, W. M. (1991). Filial piety and intergenerational relationship in Korean immigrant families. *International Journal of Aging and Human Development, 33*, 233-245.

Lein, L. (1984). Male participation in home life: Impact of social supports and breadwinner responsibility on the allocation of tasks. In P. Voydanoff (Ed.), *Work and family: Changing roles of men and women* (pp. 242-250). Palo Alto, CA: Mayfield Publishing Co.

Lerner, J. V. (1994). *Working women and their families*. Thousand Oaks, CA: Sage.

Marks, S. R. (1977). Multiple roles and role strain. *American Sociological Review, 42*, 921-936.

Pleck, J. H. (1985). *Working wives/working husbands*. Beverly Hills, CA: Sage.

Potuchek, J. L. (1992). Employed wives' orientation to breadwinning. *Journal of Marriage and the Family, 54*, 548.

Ross, C., Mirowsky, J., & Huber, J. (1983). Dividing work, sharing work and in-between: Marriage patterns and depression. *American Sociological Review, 48*, 809-823.

Thoits, P. A. (1983). Multiple identities and psychological well-being. *American Sociological Review, 48*, 174-187.

U. S. Commission on Civil Rights. (1988). *The economic status of Americans of Asian descent: An exploratory investigation.* Clearinghouse Publication 95.

U. S. Commission on Civil Rights. (1992). *Civil rights issues facing Asian Americans in the 1990s.* Washington, DC.

U. S. Dept. of Commerce. (1988). *Statistical abstracts of the U.S.* Washington, DC: U.S. Government Printing Office.

Vannoy, D., & Philliber, W. (1992). Wife's employment and quality of marriage. *Journal of Marriage and the Family, 54*, 337-398.

Voydanoff, P. (1984). *Work and family: Changing roles of men and women.* Palo Alto, CA: Mayfield Publishing Co.

Wright, J. D. (1978). Are working women really more satisfied?: Evidence from several national surveys. *Journal of Marriage and the Family, 40*, 301-313.

Chapter 12

Grandparents as a Family Resource in Chinese-American Families
Perceptions of the Middle Generation

Vicky Chiu-Wan Tam and Daniel F. Detzner

The overall increase in life expectancy for the United States population in the past few decades suggests that there are greater numbers of elderly persons around. Many of the current and upcoming generations of senior family members are physically capable and active. The opportunity therefore exists for the emergence of long-term intergenerational relationships and multigenerational family systems. In fact, it is estimated that 77% of persons aged 65 years or more are grandparents (Hagestad, 1988).

The significance and meaning of grandparenthood vary considerably across families and individuals. The variations are likely to be related to factors such as socioeconomic status, ethnicity, health status, and personality. Barresi (1987) commented that grandparent roles may be more salient in ethnic groups than in the dominant American culture. However, both Kimmel (1980) and Brubaker (1990) indicated that few research studies have examined grandparenthood in ethnic minority families. The existing studies (e.g., Burton & Dilworth-Anderson, 1991; Pearson, Hunter, Ensminger, & Kellam, 1990) typically focus only on African-American families. Therefore, more information is needed about grandparenthood in other ethnic groups.

The present study explores grandparenthood in one ethnic minority group that has received relatively little research attention—Chinese-American families. The interest in understanding

Chinese-American families is triggered by the demographic trend revealed in the 1990 census that Asian Americans are the fastest growing ethnic population in the United States, among which Chinese Americans constitute the largest group. Census data also indicate that more than half of the Chinese-American population are foreign-born, first-generation immigrants (U.S. Department of Commerce, Economic & Statistics Administration, & Bureau of the Census, 1992). The focus of this study is on first-generation immigrant Chinese families in which ethnicity and immigration experiences have an impact on family dynamics. Because there are regional differences in Chinese groups who reside in different parts of the world, this investigation has selected for its focus the group of Chinese immigrants who were originally from Hong Kong. Political uncertainty about the future of this British Colony stemming from its imminent change of sovereignty in 1997 leads to the prediction that immigration from Hong Kong will continue to increase, justifying the need to understand this subgroup of Chinese Americans.

Discussion on family and aging often centers around family caregiving towards the aged and their receipt of assistance from the family. Several scholars (Shi, 1993; Stevens, 1992) have noted that little attention has been directed towards the capability of the elderly family members to provide support for the family. In an era in which grandparents are often in good health and physically capable, it is of interest to examine the contributions of the elderly towards younger family members. Based on a theoretical perspective of family resource management, this study attempts to fill the research gap by exploring the assistance grandparents provide to the family in childrearing.

Family Resource Management Perspective

It has been remarked (Smith, 1991) that most studies on grandparenthood do not have any explicit theoretical perspective; those which do are primarily based on a lifespan development approach, investigating the relationship between the process of aging and the roles of grandparents (e.g., Forsyth, Roberts, & Robin, 1992; Kivnick, 1981; Sprey & Matthews, 1982). This study attempts to understand grandparenthood from a family resource management perspective, focusing on the family's thoughtful adaptation to the opportunities and demands of life through behaviors such as problem-solving, decision-making, and implementation (Rettig, 1993). It draws attention to the study of family resources, which are assets or means that can be used to accomplish goals. Resources available to the family can be human, economic, or environmental (Nickell, Rice, & Tucker, 1976). The present study examines grandparents and their provision of human resources to the family in terms of time, human energy, and competencies. Though economic resources are sometimes provided by grandparents, this study will focus only on human resources. The assistance of grandparents in childrearing is often sought by parents to help produce a new generation of capable offspring. In most cases, parents are the resource managers in the family. The perception of the managers towards resources affects the extent to which the resource is available to the family (Rettig, 1993). Thus, parents' perceptions of grandparents' involvement in childrearing play an important mediating role in the utilization of these human resources.

The perspective of family resource management is placed in context through the human ecological framework, which views the family as exchanging resources with the biological-physical and social environment (Bubolz & Sontag, 1993). The family reacts to internal and external conditions, as well as proacts and initiates action to seek new levels of functioning (Andrews, Bubolz, & Paolucci, 1980). This framework focuses on the relationship of family behaviors to environmental conditions and the effects on families of the institutions and the organizations with which they interact. Attention is thus drawn to the significance of sociocultural context in the study of grandparenthood in an immigrant ethnic group. In particular, immigration experiences and ethnic backgrounds, including values and cultural practices, have enormous impacts on immigrant families' life experiences and their approaches to managing family resources.

Research on Grandparenthood

The present study focuses on Chinese-American families who are straddling two cultures that differ in terms of value emphases and orientation. Grandparent roles in Chinese-American families are expected to share similarities with both Chinese and mainstream American cultures, and at the same time, develop their own unique characteristics. A review of existing studies and literature on grandparenthood in American and Chinese cultures will provide a backdrop for the understanding of grandparents' involvement in childrearing in Chinese-American families.

Intergenerational Relationships in American Families

Research studies have reported a variety of grandparent roles and levels of involvement in American families (Cherlin & Furstenberg, 1985; Neugarten & Weinstein, 1964). The United States is a culture in which individualism and independence are valued. The nuclear family is the dominant family form. Grandparents often do not share a residence with their adult children, and the involvement of grandparents in the family is optional. Intergenerational family relationships are not prescribed as strict obligations, but must be created and recreated by family members throughout their lives (Riley, 1983).

In some families, grandparents are seen as the family's first reserves (Crawford, 1981). They often provide emotional support, encouragement, and assistance with day-to-day or emergent parental needs. Mothers employed full-time outside the home are more likely to seek assistance from grandmothers, among all relatives, in the care of young children (Presser, 1989). Grandparents, as senior family members, represent stability and continuity in family rituals and values (Brubaker, 1990). They are capable of acting as historian, mentor, and role model to the family (Kornhaber & Woodard, 1985).

In other situations, grandparents play a marginal role and have only fleeting contact with grandchildren. A study on grandfathers living in a rural transition area observed low levels of grandfather-grandchild interaction and priority and concluded that the grandfather role was of little relative importance to that sample of older men (Kivett, 1985). Geographical proximity appears to be one of the factors most consistently related to grandparent-grandchild relationships (Cherlin & Furstenberg, 1985; Kivett, 1985; Whitbeck, Hoyt, & Huck, 1993). Another factor affecting the intergenerational connection is the middle generation's expectations for the role of the grandparents (Ramirez-Barranti, 1985; Whitbeck, Hoyt, & Huck, 1993). As a kinkeeper, the adult child has the ability to either facilitate or prevent the involvement of grandparents in their grandchildren's lives.

Ramirez-Barranti (1985) pointed out that American grandparents have the potential to be an important family resource of practical, emotional, instrumental, and informational support. The role of grandparent is clearly of value to grandparents and to the family as a whole (Crawford, 1981). However, the extent to which this resource is mobilized varies from family to family and is affected by factors such as geographical distance and the middle generation's expectations, revealing the optional nature of the position of grandparents in American families.

The Roles of Grandparents in Chinese Families

Currently, there are few published studies on grandparenthood in Chinese-American families in the social and behavioral sciences literature. Discussion on the topic is thus drawn indirectly from the scant research studies conducted in Mainland China, Taiwan, and Hong Kong.

Chinese families in the traditional culture were patriarchal and patrilocal (Wong, 1988). As family solidarity and extended family forms were highly valued, it was common to have multiple generations living together in one household (Baker, 1979). This living arrangement provided an opportunity for Chinese children to grow up amid frequent and continuing contacts with extended family members (Hsu, 1981). In the patrilocal context, paternal grandparents were an essential part of the family. They shared residence with grandchildren and were in daily contact with them. The relationship between maternal grandparents and grandchildren, however, was remote. Building largely upon Confucian philosophy, heavy emphasis was placed on the hierarchical order of society and highly structured role relationships in traditional Chinese culture (Bond & Hwang, 1986). The aged were respected and accorded authority because of their seniority in position in society and the family. Grandparents were often in control of family power and were respected for their wisdom. Family members perceived them as important resources for achieving family goals. While the responsibility of childrearing was primarily shouldered by the mother, the assistance and advice of grandparents were often sought. This exemplifies the reciprocity of dependence between generations for meeting needs, which is another characteristic of Chinese families in the traditional culture (Ho, 1981). The exchange of assistance among family members continued to take place throughout the lifespan as individuals changed from the role of recipient to provider and vice versa, depending on their respective life stages.

Rapid industrialization and urbanization in the 20th century have altered the structure of contemporary Chinese families. Chinese communities around the world, such as People's Republic of China and Hong Kong, have growing numbers of nuclear families, while the numbers of families that consist of more than two generations has been decreasing in the past few decades (China Population Census Office, 1983; Hong Kong Census & Statistics Department, 1991). This phenomenon is the outcome of the family strategy of selective maintenance of kin ties in the attempt to cope with social changes (M.K. Lee, 1991). To meet their expressive and instrumental needs, families choose to maintain close contact with some kin or relatives while loosening their connections with others (M.K. Lee, 1991). At the same time, the erosion of traditional values results in a gradual loss of the importance of the elderly in the family. Grandparents in many families are no longer treated as a treasure or a reservoir of knowledge as they were in the past. As a result of family strategies for managing resources, the involvement of the elderly family members becomes optional. It has also been observed, in contrast to the traditional patrilocal residence pattern, that maternal grandparents sometimes reside with contemporary nuclear Chinese families (Wong, 1975). Again, this illustrates the strategy employed by families to maintain kin ties selectively to satisfy the expressive and instrumental needs of the family.

A few empirical studies on grandparenthood in contemporary Chinese families shed light on the understanding of grandparents' involvement in the family. Shi (1993) surveyed Chinese elderly in rural areas in the People's Republic of China and reported that the aged family members often provided financial and household resources for their adult children. A study on Taiwanese families reported that grandmothers were involved in the rearing of school-age children, although the reliance on their help was not heavy, and their role was only secondary (Olsen, 1976). Lin (1988) also studied grandparenthood in Taiwan and reported that most grandparents believed they might substitute for their adult children in taking care of the grandchildren at least some of the time. However, while most grandparents and parents considered a three-generation household as an ideal family situation, a lower percentage of respondents indicated they would actually choose this type of family arrangement. These conflicting findings reveal the intricate family dynamics involving grandparents and their roles within the family.

A study conducted by Ikels (1983) explored the life experiences of Chinese elderly living in Hong Kong and Boston. Among the aged persons from both cities involved in the study, intergenerational co-residence was not the predominant arrangement. The low level of co-residence in Hong Kong should be examined in the context of urban living, in which the small size of residential dwellings discourages extended family forms (Fan & Lee,

1991). However, the small geographical size of Hong Kong facilitates visits and interaction among family members who live in different households (P.L. Lee, 1991). Several cases reported in Ikels's study revealed that, in spite of having separate residences, elderly parents and their adult children living in Hong Kong continued to provide support to one another. Among the Boston group, some of the Chinese elderly reported they did not want to move in with their adult children until they could not manage living independently on their own. This attitude seems to reflect the assimilation of mainstream American values of independence and privacy. Ikels's study (1983) also reported that many Chinese-American older persons, who are first-generation immigrants, considered living in the United States a less desirable option than living in Hong Kong or China. Their life in the U.S. was handicapped by the lack of English language skills and the loss of a social network established in their country of origin. Because of these impediments, many grandparents stayed in their home country and chose not to come to the United States to join their children. From the findings of Ikels's study, it is hypothesized that the migration experience and cultural adjustment may have weakened the link between grandparents and grandchildren among Chinese-American families.

Chinese-American families live between two cultures and share characteristics with families in the mainstream American and Chinese cultures. They face challenges brought about by migration and cultural adjustment. The goal of this chapter is to explore grandparenthood in Chinese-American families under these challenges. The focal point for this investigation is the perception of the middle generation towards grandparents as a family resource in childrearing from a family resource management perspective.

Method

The goal of this study was to explore the assistance grandparents provided in childrearing in Chinese-American immigrant families. The pool of respondents was drawn from the Chinese-American community in a metropolitan area in the midwest. The Chinese population in the selected metropolitan area is small and represents a non-Chinatown group. Respondents were contacted through a local Chinese language school and personal acquaintances of the author.

The group of respondents consisted of twelve Chinese-American parents, each from a different family. They included eight mothers and four fathers. Each family had at least one child between the ages four and twelve. Families formed from biracial marriages were not included in this study. Respondents were all Chinese immigrants from Hong Kong. They came to this country as adolescents or young adults and had stayed in the United States for an extended period of time, ranging from 9 to more than 25 years. At the time of the interview, these parents were in middle adulthood, with ages ranging from 30 to 42 years. Respondents were engaged in occupations commonly found among Chinese Americans, such as white-collar professionals, restaurant owners, homemakers, and students. As a group, they were well educated, with two-thirds having a college education.

Data for this chapter were drawn from an ethnographic study of childrearing experiences of Chinese-American parents. Ethnographic research attempts to "tell the story" of a community or a culture through the words and customs of its members (Copa, 1989). The goal of this approach is to recreate the shared beliefs, practices, folk knowledge, and behaviors of a group of people (Goetz & LeCompte, 1984). In this study, data were collected from two main sources. First, the author had participated in activities in the Chinese-American community for more than two years. These experiences allowed the author to get to know the respondents and their families in naturalistic settings and created excellent opportunities for participant observation. Second, the bulk of the data for this chapter were collected through semi-structured interviews that lasted from one to two hours. The interviews were conducted in Cantonese, the native dialect of the respondents. An interview guide was used, containing a set of basic questions centered around the respondents' experiences of raising their children in the United States.

Data analysis in this study involved the processes of verbatim transcription and translation from Cantonese to English. Themes regarding childrearing experiences were generated from the transcripts and those that were related to the roles of grandparents in childrearing were selected and analyzed to provide the findings for this chapter.

The scope of this study is limited to the perceptions of the middle generation parents toward grandparents as a family resource in childrearing. Neither the grandparents nor the grandchildren were interviewed. Caution should be used when interpreting the findings; the study employed an ethnographic approach that is based on an interpretive science paradigm and hence is not intended for generalizations about the entire population of Chinese-American families. Instead, the findings offer an opportunity to look into the experiences of twelve Chinese-American families and to understand their life situations.

Availability of Grandparents as a Family Resource: Family Structure and Residence Patterns

The involvement of grandparents in childrearing is first and foremost affected by the availability of that resource. In this section, family structure and residence patterns of the respondents' families are reported.

It has been commented that the structure of Chinese-American families is significantly influenced by immigration policy (Wong, 1985). The process of immigration often breaks up the intact family in the country of origin when immigration occurs in a chain form, starting with one or two family members coming to the United States first. The present U.S. immigration policy favors admission of professionals and reunion of family members. Priority of issuance of immigrant visas is given to applicants with family members who are U.S. citizens or permanent residents, and professionals with at least a college education and specialized skills. In some cases and for a variety of reasons, the family may never be fully reunited in the new country.

Respondents in this study were often among the first ones in their families to migrate to the United States. More than half of the respondents originally came to the United States as college students. They secured professional jobs upon completion of their education and then applied for permanent U.S. residency on the basis of their professional status. The rest of the group came to the United States through family reunion or marriage to a U.S. citizen or permanent resident. Those who came to the United States as students usually came alone while their family members still resided in Hong Kong. This sojourning arrangement sometimes continued after they had secured U.S. citizenship and established their family of marriage in this country.

The typical family structure among the respondents was nuclear as a result of the immigration arrangements. Only two families involved in this study had at least one grandparent living with them at the time of the interview. This pattern of family structure resembles that of the general Chinese-American population, among which nuclear families represent 87% of all households (Wong, 1985). For many respondents, members of the extended family system, including grandparents, still resided in Hong Kong. The geographic distance from the extended family resulted in feelings of isolation and lack of support. This reflects the value of family solidarity and the tendency to rely on the extended family system as a source of assistance and support, especially for childrearing. A mother of two children remarked:

> The reason why I say it is hard [to raise children in the United States] is that people around my age who live in the U.S. are all independent. Neither of us have parents here. We don't have relatives or friends around. When something happens, especially at the time when [my child] was a baby, it was difficult to find help.

The presence of grandparents in the family helped promote grandparent-grandchild relationships, which was considered beneficial to children. One mother made an effort to have her two children get to know their grandparents who lived in Hong Kong by bringing her children back for short visits and arranging phone calls between the two generations. A father of four children said:

> One thing I miss most about raising my children [in the United States] is that my father is not here. [My children] cannot see my parents and [my wife's parents] very often. I think they are deprived in this regard. If their grandparents were here, their growing up experience would be richer through learning and feeling the love of grandparents.

This remark indicated his preference for an extended family and the fact that grandparents were considered an important part of the family.

However, grandparents often lived far away from the respondents, even when they resided in the U.S. Only one-third of the families interviewed had at least one grandparent residing in the same city. The majority of the group had grandparents living outside the same city, with approximately one-third of the families having the nearest grandparents in another city in North America (sometimes more than 1,000 miles away) and another one-third with grandparents residing in Hong Kong. Though family reunion is favored in immigration policy, family members who come to the United States often live in different cities because of job locations. As a result, some grandparents chose to stay with a different adult child and hence lived in another city. Finally, in some families, grandparents decided not to come to the United States but stayed in

Hong Kong. They considered living in the United States a less desirable option than living in Hong Kong, in view of the differences in lifestyle and cultural practices between the two countries. One father of four children reported that both his parents were still living in Hong Kong. Only his mother had come to visit the nuclear family, while the grandfather, who did not enjoy traveling, had never visited. Another father with two children talked about the difficulties that confronted his parents after they moved to the U.S.:

> [My parents] came to live in the United States mainly to help us with child care. They do not really enjoy living here. They do not speak the language. They do not drive, so it is inconvenient for them to go out. For them, life here is like living in prison.

Despite the hardships imposed upon his parents, the fact that they were willing to stay in the United States to help with childrearing demonstrates a commitment to family life and the intergenerational pattern of assistance and interdependence.

It is apparent from the residence patterns that grandparents often did not reside with the nuclear family. This situation was the result of a combination of factors, including immigration strategy, personal preference, job opportunities, and cultural adjustment. Despite the rare incidence of intergenerational co-residence, grandparents still contributed to the nuclear family, which we shall see in the next section. Their contributions reflect thoughtful adaptation to the challenges of the environment and the creative use of human resources in the family.

It should be noted that there are a number of cases in the study in which grandparents had previously lived with the family but had since moved or deceased. Residence patterns clearly change according to the needs and circumstances of the family, revealing the strategy in managing human resources. These past family experiences with grandparents' involvement will be included in the discussion in the next section.

Uses of the Family Resource: Grandparents' Roles in Childrearing

The value of the wisdom, knowledge, and skills of the older generation in Chinese culture is reflected in the perception of the respondents towards grandparents as family resources in the rearing of their children. Most parents mentioned some ways in which grandparents have been or may be helpful in their childrearing. Both paternal and maternal grandparents were reported to offer assistance in childrearing, illustrating the deviation from the patrilocal and patrilineal pattern of the traditional culture. It was also noted that the parents in the study mentioned the assistance of grandmothers more often than that of grandfathers. This might be explained by the fact that childrearing, other than the task of socialization, is still mainly performed by women.

Substitute Parent

The typical form of assistance offered to the family by grandparents was child care. Four parents out of the twelve interviewed reported that grandparents had been their major source of child-care. Another one-third of the families received some help in child-care from grandparents in the form of occasional visits and advice. The rest reported that they had never received any help from grandparents in childrearing, usually because the elder family members were physically far away from the nuclear family.

Respondents reported that grandparents, usually grandmothers, were a source of child-care when both parents were working. In some cases, grandparents helped so significantly that they acted as substitute parents. One mother with two children recounted her experiences in raising her children:

> [My children's paternal] grandmother used to live with us. When my two children were young, Grandmother helped us taking care of them while I went to work.... She went back to Hong Kong when my youngest child was four years old.

Another woman was very grateful towards her mother's assistance in taking care of her children while she worked full-time outside the home:

> [My deceased mother] used to take care of the children till [my eldest son] became a teenager. She lived with us and had been the major person in raising [my youngest two children]. So my children say, "Maternal Grandmother was our mother." ... My mother has been a significant source of help.

Sometimes, the parents were so comfortable with the substitute care arrangement that they allowed their children to stay with the grandparents overseas. A mother with three children who worked full-time in her family business recalled having her six-month old daughter stay in Hong Kong for one year so that the baby could be cared for by her mother. This reflects her level of trust in the grandparent for substitute care and her perception of childrearing as occurring within the context of the extended family system. This perception contrasts with the notion in mainstream American culture of the nuclear family ideal—that parents are supposed to be the best and sole providers of care to their children.

Parental Assistance

Families with grandparents living outside the same city reported that child-care support from the elderly family members would be desirable and that they missed having access to this resource. Some of the parents had attempted to seek alternative forms of child-care assistance from the grandparents. There were cases in which grandmothers traveled the miles for a short visit to offer help, especially in a time of need. A mother of three children described her situation:

> In the period after my children were born, my family members came to help me out because I did not know [how to take care of children] and the baby was very small, like a piece of pastry dough. It was difficult to handle them, especially for bathing.... My mother came when two of my children were born. She stayed for three months each time before she left for Hong Kong again.

For others, grandparents provided assistance in the form of childrearing advice. Respondents called their parents long distance when there was an emergency situation. One mother recalled the times when she sought her mother's help:

> It was a very difficult time [when my son was a baby]. My son cried a lot and I had no idea why. I did not know whether it was because he was hungry, or he had an abdominal pain, or he could not sleep. I called my Mommy [who was in Hong Kong] long distance right away [to seek advice].

Another mother of two children, whose parents and in-laws all resided in Hong Kong, commented:

> It is interesting that you still feel long-distance parenting.... When I was pregnant, my parents told me not to eat this or that. Even though they were not [in the United States], they still gave a lot of messages for you to follow.

This shows that the childrearing knowledge of grandparents continued to be highly valued, even at a distance.

Cultural Socialization

Grandparents were reported to be helpful in cultural socialization and the development of ethnic identity in the children. The socialization of young children in the cultural practices and values of the original country is a significant issue for many immigrant ethnic groups in the United States. It contributes a sense of continuity and identity, but it can sometimes be a source of conflict within families. One of the major means for the development of ethnic identity is language (Gudykunst & Schmidt, 1988). Repeatedly, grandparents were mentioned by the respondents as an important means for children to learn Chinese, especially when the grandparents were non-English speakers. A mother of four children, who worked full-time outside the home, reported:

> After my mother came to the United States, she took care of my children. When I was away from home at work, [my children] asked their grandmother for ice-cream or peanuts. Grandmother did not know what it meant [since she did not speak English] so the children did not get what they want.... As a result, they were forced indirectly to learn the [Chinese] language.

Another mother of three children shared similar opinions:

> The only way to make children speak Chinese is to have an elderly family member who does not speak English at all. In that case, it is possible [for them to acquire the language] and the chance [for them to speak the language] is high.

One mother compared the language development of her two children:

> Their paternal grandmother speaks Chinese. When Grandmother stayed with us, the children talked in Chinese with

her frequently .... Grandmother left for Hong Kong when my son was four years old. As a result, he did not have as much opportunity as my daughter to practice [speaking Chinese]. My daughter spoke Chinese till the age of five when her grandmother left. Now the daughter still speaks some Chinese and she is able to recall many Chinese words.

Another way in which grandparents assisted in the cultural socialization of grandchildren was through the direct teaching of cultural values. One mother was grateful to her father for his teachings:

My father taught [my children] well. Since he lived with us and had time to look after the children at home, he often told them to show filial piety towards their parents because parents worked very hard outside the home. I think [these values] should be passed on from the generation of grandparents.

Furthermore, the mere presence of grandparents could be an opportunity for the children to learn about traditional virtues towards respecting the old. A mother compared her children with their cousins who lived in Hong Kong with their grandparents. The cousins, with the grandparents around, had learned to show respect toward the older generation whereas her own children did not have the opportunity to acquire these virtues. In addition to direct teaching, grandchildren who often see their grandparents have the opportunity to learn cultural practices through observation. Elderly family members often knew more about cultural festive practices and were followers of traditional Chinese customs.

To summarize, among the twelve Chinese-American parents interviewed, there were two major ways in which grandparents were perceived to be family resources for rearing children—child care and cultural socialization. The perception of grandparents as family resource conforms with traditional Chinese values that respect the wisdom and life experiences of the aged and put emphasis on the solidarity of the extended family system.

Perceptions of the Family Resource: When Grandparents Are Not Considered a Family Resource

Discussion so far has focused on positive perceptions towards grandparents as a family resource. It should be noted that there are also neutral or negative perceptions of the involvement of the elderly family members in childrearing. For various reasons, some parents chose not to solicit help from grandparents. Some did not seek grandparents' assistance in child care because they respected the freedom of the elder family members. From their viewpoint, individual freedom and autonomy were valued over the collective good and family needs. Mutual exchange between generations was not seen as a family obligation as in traditional Chinese culture, but rather as an obstacle to personal autonomy. This attitude partially reflects acculturation of American values and is illustrated by the remarks of a father of two children:

> We do not rely on [our parents] to take care of the children. According to our viewpoint, we should not tie them down. We respect the elders' freedom. They should be able to go wherever they like. We don't want them to stay with us just because they have to take care of the children.

Another reason for not seeking grandparents' help was the concern that grandparents, coming from the older generation, did not have much to offer to young children. One father whose extended family did not live in the United States made this remark:

> Many people leave the care of their children to grandparents. Their children turn out to be not bright enough. The old generation of grandmas only spoil the children.... They are concerned with health issues only .... But the problem is: Under grandma's care, your child will never become bright nor learn any substantive knowledge.

His skeptical remark exemplified the differences in values and practices in childrearing between generations and explained the unwillingness to pass the childrearing responsibility on to grandparents. It also conveyed the message that the older generation was not treasured as a source of knowledge and the childrearing practices of grandparents were considered inapplicable to current life situations. Another father of four children expressed his disagreement with childrearing practices of the previous generation:

> Chinese people, especially the generation before us, did not allow their children to argue with the seniors. I think this results in us having a lack of courage to rebel [against things we don't agree to]. This is caused by our parents. They set this rule of no arguing allowed.

Instead of relying on the advice of grandparents, some parents preferred to trust their own decisions on childrearing and to seek other non-familial resources when they needed help. A mother of two children commented:

> The advantage of raising children in the United States is that there are few elders around to offer their unsolicited advice. In Hong Kong, one elder family member gives you one piece of advice and another one gives you another. We don't know who to listen to. Here [in the United States], we make our own decision.... When you don't know what to do or when there are no elders around to give you advice, you can take a parenting class.

Seeking alternative sources of help was possible, in some cases, because of the socioeconomic status of the parents. Middle-class parents have more abundant resources, allowing them to make the involvement of grandparents in childrearing an option instead of the only available alternative.

In summary, some parents did not perceive the involvement of grandparents in childrearing as favorable. One reason was the assimilation of American values, indicated by an emphasis on individual autonomy. Other parents wished to deviate from the ideas of the older generations, which were considered incompatible with present-day situations. These perceptions reveal some parents' attitudes that grandparents were not considered a family resource in childrearing.

Implications

This study explores the involvement of grandparents in childrearing in twelve Chinese-American families, using a family resource management framework. The various strategies and perceptions toward grandparents mobilized as resources reflect the family's thoughtful adaptation to the opportunities and demands of its unique life situations to achieve the goal of producing a generation of capable offspring. This mobilization of grandparents' assistance in childrearing is reported to be influenced by structural and cultural factors in the environment.

The findings of this study will be helpful for human service professionals and policy makers in understanding the needs and resources of Chinese-American families as constrained and strengthened by structural and cultural factors. As revealed in this study, the experiences of immigration and their ethnic cultural background have immense influence on the family dynamics and interactions of the families studied. To understand the experiences of Chinese-

American families fully, analysis should be expanded from focusing on the notion of a nuclear family to the idea of a multigenerational family system in which family members live in separate households spanning thousands of miles while still exerting influence or extending assistance to one another. It will be interesting to investigate whether focusing on a multigenerational family system applies to families of other ethnic groups. The findings of this study should inspire researchers to think beyond Chinese-American families and to consider the roles of the elders in families of all ethnic origins and the strengths of multigenerational family systems in the United States in an era in which the family faces numerous changes and challenges. Contemporary American society is endowed with a generation of healthy and active older people who have great potential to continue to contribute to their families, communities, or society as a whole. Policy makers and human service professionals should discuss the effort to strengthen inter-generational relationships and to mobilize the use of grandparents as a family resource. At the same time, the complexity of family dynamics and interactions that include intergenerational conflicts and differences in values and attitudes need to be considered.

This study is an attempt to use a family resource management perspective in the understanding of grandparenthood in Chinese-American families. It provides an opportunity to understand how the parent generation, often caught in the middle between generations and cultural perspectives, perceives the roles of the older generations in childrearing today. It also helps to explain the strength of family traditions for immigrant populations in this rapidly changing world. Future research on grandparenthood, using a family resource management perspective, should continue to investigate the support and sustenance of families and to pay attention to contextual factors which shape family functioning and interaction.

References

Andrews, M. P., Bubolz, M. M., & Paolucci, B. (1980). An ecological approach to study of the family. *Marriage & Family Review*, 3(1/2), 29-49.

Baker, H. D. (1979). *Chinese family and kinships*. London: Macmillan.

Barresi, C. M. (1987). Ethnic aging and the life course. In D. E. Gefland & C. M. Barresi (Eds.), *Ethnic dimension of aging* (pp. 18-34). New York: Springer.

Bond, M. H., & Hwang, K. K. (1986). The social psychology of Chinese people. In M. H. Bond (Ed.), *The psychology of Chinese people* (pp. 213-266). Hong Kong: Oxford University Press.

Brubaker, T. H. (1990). Families in later life: A burgeoning research area. *Journal of Marriage & the Family, 52,* 959-981.

Bubolz, M. M., & Sontag, M. S. (1993). Human ecology theory. In P. G. Boss, W. J. Doherty, R. LaRossa, W. R. Schumm, & S. K. Steinmetz (Eds.), *Sourcebook of family theories and methods: A contextual approach* (pp. 419-448). New York: Plenum Press.

Burton, L. M., & Dilworth-Anderson, P. (1991). The intergenerational family roles of aged Black Americans. *Marriage & Family Review, 16,* 311-330.

Cherlin, A., & Furstenberg, F. F. (1985). Style and strategies of grandparenting. In V. L. Bengtson & J. F. Robertson (Eds.), *Grandparenthood* (pp. 97-116). Beverly Hills, CA: Sage.

China Population Census Office. (1983). *Ten percent sampling tabulation on the 1982 population census of the People's Republic of China.* Bejing: China Population Census Office.

Copa, P. M. (1989). Viewing competence through the eyes of ethnography. In F. H. Hultgren & D. L. Coomer (Eds.), *Alternative modes of inquiry in home economics research* (pp. 140-158). Washington, DC: American Home Economics Association.

Crawford, M. (1981). Not disengaged: Grandparents in literature and reality: An empirical study in role satisfaction. *Sociological Review, 29*(3), 499-519.

Fan, S. Y., & Lee, S. L. (1991). Xianggang jiating de bianqian [The changes in Hong Kong families]. In J. Qian (Ed.), *Zhongguo jiating ji qi bianqian* (pp. 145-159). Hong Kong: Chinese University of Hong Kong.

Forsyth, C. J., Roberts, S. B., & Robin, C. A. (1992). Variables influencing life satisfaction among grandparents. *International Journal of Sociology of the Family, 22,* 51-60.

Goetz, J. P., & LeCompte, M. D. (1984). *Ethnographic and qualitative design in educational research.* Orlando, FL: Academic Press.

Gudykunst, W. B., & Schmidt, K. L. (1988). Language and ethnic identity: An overview and prologue. In W. B. Gudykunst (Ed.), *Language and ethnic identity* (pp. 1-14). Philadelphia: Multilingual Matter.

Hagestad, G. O. (1988). Demographic change and the life course: Some emerging trends in the family realm. *Family Relations, 37,* 405-410.

Ho, D. Y. (1981). Traditional patterns of socialization in Chinese society. *Acta Psychologica Taiwanica, 23,* 81-95.

Hong Kong Census & Statistics Department. (1991). *Hong Kong 1991 population census: Summary of statistics.* Hong Kong: Government Printer.

Hsu, F. L. (1981). *Americans and Chinese: Passage to difference.* Honolulu: University of Hawaii Press.

Ikels, C. (1983). *Aging and adaptation: Chinese in Hong Kong and the United States.* Hamden, CT: Archon.

Kimmel, D. C. (1980). *Adulthood and aging: An interdisciplinary, developmental view.* New York: John Wiley.

Kivett, V. R. (1985). Grandfathers and grandchildren: Patterns of association, helping, and psychological closeness. *Family Relations, 34*(4), 565-571.

Kivnick, H. Q. (1981). Grandparenthood and the mental health of grandparents. *Aging & Society, 1*, 365-391.

Kornhaber, A., & Woodard, K. L. (1985). *Grandparents/grandchildren: The vital connection.* New Brunswick, NJ: Transaction.

Lee, M. K. (1991). Xianggang jiating de zhuji he bianqian [The structure and changes of families in Hong Kong]. In J. Qian (Ed.), *Zhongguo jiating ji qi bianqian* (pp. 161-169). Hong Kong: Chinese University of Hong Kong.

Lee, P. L. (1991). Xianggang jiating yu qinxutixi de bianqian: Kueigu yu zhanwang [The changes in Hong Kong families and their kinship systems: A reflection and forecast]. In J. Qian (Ed.), *Zhongguo Jiating Ji Qi Bianqian* (pp. 129-143). Hong Kong: Chinese University of Hong Kong.

Lin, M. (1988). *The Chinese grandparent in three generation household in Taiwan.* Unpublished doctoral dissertation, Northwestern University, Evanston, IL.

Neugarten, B. L., & Weinstein, K. K. (1964). The changing American grandparents. *Journal of Marriage & the Family, 26*(2), 199-204.

Nickell, P., Rice, A. S., & Tucker, S. P. (1976). *Management in family living.* New York: John Wiley.

Olsen, N. J. (1976). The role of grandmothers in Taiwanese family socialization. *Journal of Marriage & the Family, 38*(2), 363-372.

Pearson, J. L., Hunter, A. G., Ensminger, M. E., & Kellam, S. G. (1990). Black grandmothers in multigenerational households: Diversity in family structure and parenting involvement in the Woodlawn community. *Child Development, 61*, 434-442.

Presser, H. B. (1989). Some economic complexities of child care provided by grandmothers. *Journal of Marriage & the Family, 51*(3), 581-591.

Ramirez-Barranti, C. C. (1985). The grandparent/grandchild relationship: Family resource in an era of voluntary bonds. *Family Relations, 34*(3), 343-352.

Rettig, K. D. (1993). Family problem-solving and decision-making process of family life: An ecological framework for family relations and family management. *Marriage & Family Review, 18*(3/4), 187-222.

Riley, M. W. (1983). The family in an aging society: A matrix of latent relationships. *Journal of Family Issues, 4*, 439-454.

Shi, L. (1993). Family financial and household support exchange between generations: A survey of Chinese rural elderly. *The Gerontologist, 33*(4), 468-480.

Smith, P. K. (1991). Introduction: The study of grandparenthood. In P. K. Smith (Ed.), *The psychology of grandparenthood: An international perspective* (pp. 1-16). New York: Routledge.

Sprey, J., & Matthews, S.H. (1982). Contemporary grandparenthood: A systemic transition. *The Annals of the American Academy of Political & Social Science, 464*, 91-103.

Stevens, E. S. (1992). Reciprocity in social support: An advantage for the aging family. *Families in Society: The Journal of Contemporary Human Services, 73*, 533-541.

U.S. Department of Commerce, Economic & Statistics Administration, & Bureau of the Census. (1992). *Statistical abstract of the United States 1992: The national data book.* Washington, DC: U.S. Government Printing Office.

Whitbeck, L. B., Hoyt, D. R., & Huck, S. M. (1993). Family relationship history, contemporary parent-grandparent relationship quality, and the grandparent-grandchild relationship. *Journal of Marriage & the Family, 55,* 1025-1035.

Wong, B. (1985). Family, kinship, and ethnic identity of the Chinese in New York City, with comparative remarks on the Chinese in Lima, Peru, and Manila, Philippines. *Journal of Comparative Family Studies, 16*(2), 231-254.

Wong, F. M. (1975). Industrialization and family structure in Hong Kong. *Journal of Marriage & the Family, 37,* 985-1000.

Wong, M. G. (1988). The Chinese-American families. In C. H. Mindel, R. W. Habenstein, & R. Wright, Jr. (Eds.), *Ethnic families in America: Patterns and variations* (pp. 230-257) New York: Elsevier.

Chapter 13

Cross-Cultural and Cross-Generational Differences in Asian Americans' Cultural and Familial Systems and Their Impact on Academic Striving

Paul Y. L. Ngo and Tari A. Malz

Declining school achievement in the United States and the poor mathematics performance of American students in relation to their foreign counterparts, particularly to Asian students, have been sources of legitimate concern. Attempts to reduce this international disparity that have focused on improving secondary education may be misguided because Japanese children have been found to outperform their American cohorts in mathematics as early as in kindergarten (Bacon & Ichikawa, 1988).

Irving Sigel (1988) has suggested that Asian parenting styles play an important role in the academic success of Asian children. Other researchers concur and suggest that cross-cultural differences in Asian children's achievement can be related specifically to their mothers' expectations and beliefs (Bacon & Ichikawa, 1988). However, changing the current state of education in the United States will probably require more than merely changing parental beliefs towards education, given that beliefs exist within and must fit into a cultural context. Therefore, examining the beliefs of Asian American students and their families may help indicate which traditional Asian beliefs or aspects thereof are viable within American society.

Therefore, the purpose of this study was to examine the contribution of Asian American college students' ethnic heritage on the quality of their educational life in the United States. The influence of familial and cultural factors on their attributions and beliefs concerning academic achievement was of particular interest, since some of these factors might represent aspects of Asian culture that are conducive to academic success within a Western society. The ramifications of maintaining a sense of ethnic identity were also investigated by examining students' attributions and aspirations in relation to their self-perceptions. In addition, cross-cultural commonalities as well as differences among the belief systems of various Asian American groups were assessed to ascertain the contribution of such beliefs on reported similarities and differences in academic performance across Asian American groups. Lastly, cross-generational differences were examined to assess the impact of acculturation to life in a Western culture on Eastern-influenced attributions and to determine whether some of these attributions might be sustainable within the United States.

Method

Participants

Eighty-six Asian American students at a large, Midwestern state university volunteered to participate in the study by completing the questionnaire described below. These students differed with regard to ethnicity (e.g., Chinese, Hmong, Japanese, Vietnamese) as well as generation of immigration (Asian immigrants or the offspring thereof). Therefore, the participants' attributions may reflect characteristics of both their Asian and their immigrant heritage, since people who opt to immigrate may be different from those who choose to remain in their homeland. Furthermore, people who opt to immigrate may be unlike others who are forced to do so. It has been suggested that Asians who have elected to immigrate tend to be highly motivated to succeed, which may in part explain their accomplishments (Gibson, 1987; Ogbu, 1990).

Research Instrument

A 158-item questionnaire consisting of items based upon three existing scales as well as original items was constructed to assess the role of cultural factors, such as aspects of one's family life, on students' attributions and beliefs about themselves, primarily in the area of academics. Likert-scale items based on the Suinn-Lew Asian Self Identity Acculturation scale (SL-ASIA) provided students with a means of indicating how traditionally "Asian" they perceived their lives to be in different domains (e.g., their ideals, family and friend relations). Items based on the Sydney Attribution Scale (SAS) were used to assess the nature of their attributions, such as the extent to which they made internal or external attributions with respect to success/failure in various academic areas (e.g., math, English, and history) and the degree to which they attributed success/failure to ability versus effort. Self-concept in academic (e.g., verbal, mathematical) and nonacademic areas (e.g., physical appearance, parent and peer relationships) was assessed via items based upon the Self-Description Questionnaire III (SDQIII) (Marsh, 1994).

Original open-ended and Likert-scale items addressed students' family life and upbringing, their educational attitudes and aspirations, and their actual academic achievement and work record. Items focused primarily on the students themselves, although information regarding their parents' and grandparents' educational levels, occupations, attitudes in relation to achievement, and reasons for and generation of immigration was also requested so that the amount and type of support that family members provided could be indirectly assessed.

Results

Analysis of the data collected in this study is ongoing; the following reflect the results of preliminary analyses. Frequency distributions of students' responses to Likert-scale items were obtained for the group as a whole as well as for subsets of the sample, sorted by ethnicity and generation. The significance and strength of relationships across subjects' responses to various items were assessed via correlational analyses (Pearson's r). Finally, examining students' responses to open-ended questions (e.g., "What factors related to your ethnic heritage do you believe were important in influencing the person you are today?") provided a more "qualitative" impression of students' thoughts and feelings.

Discussion

The family characteristic mentioned most frequently by students as being predictive of their own academic success was the academic performance of their parents, a result that is not altogether surprising given the benefits associated with being reared by knowledge-able models. Perhaps more interesting is the fact that many of the family characteristics mentioned were intimately related to aspects of the students' ethnic heritage. In addition, many of these charac-teristics were shared by members of different Asian American groups, such as their beliefs concerning the importance of education, hard work, persistence, delaying gratification, sacrificing for one's family, and respecting one's elders. All of these beliefs reflect traditional cultural values that, according to the "cultural variation" hypoth-esis, are said to predict academic success (Chen & Uttal, 1988; Lin & Fu, 1990). Furthermore, it makes intuitive sense that these values would exist together, given that doing well in school typically requires hard work, which can in turn entail persistence. Persis-tence may necessitate the delay of gratification, such as when one makes sacrifices for the good of the family and out of respect for parents and elders. Interestingly, such sentiments are more repre-sentative of the collectivistic thought generally found in Eastern cultures than the more individualistic beliefs of Western cultures (Hui & Triandis, 1986).

Moreover, some second- as well as first-generation students made collectivistic statements ("Values such as respect for elders and authority, self-discipline, and importance of family (real respect for parents) are positive influences from Confucian traditions"), sug-gesting that some Eastern values are transmitted and sustained across generations. However, the maintenance of traditional mores can often be difficult, particularly when they conflict with Western ideals. Furthermore, the more typically Western pattern of pursu-ing one's dreams might sometimes be at odds with what is perceived as being best for the family. In other words, identity issues, which are difficult for most young Americans (Erikson, 1968), may be further complicated by Asian Americans' cultural heritage—the pur-suit of individual interests may collide with their sense of responsi-bility to the family (Phinney, 1990). Some Asian American students appear to be "resolving" this conflict by trying to be as American as possible. This behavior may be consistent with Maslow's belief concerning one's need to identify with and be accepted by others, given that lack of belonging can lead to feelings of rejection and loneliness (Maslow, 1970). However, this may be difficult for Asian Americans because they typically possess physically distinguishing traits that make them in essence "non-meltable."

These features serve to make all sorts of differences, physi-cal and otherwise, more salient to others. Others' perceptions of them can in turn cause Asian Americans to be even more attuned to how they differ from other Americans, which has the net result of magnifying the extent of these differences within their own minds. This can influence their self-concept and, when combined with other factors like parental pressure, could contribute to the disproportionately high number of Asian American students in the natural sciences or engineering (35% versus about 3% for European Americans), one aspect of the model minority myth that bears some semblance of truth (Toupin & Son, 1991). Asian American students indicated that technical positions appear to be less subject to racial bias, and suggested that worth in such positions is more a function of performance than of verbal skills, how assimilated one is, or how attractive one is. Interestingly, those students who rated themselves as more attractive were also more likely to select careers in law, government, and the social sciences, career paths more commonly selected by European Americans.

Another factor that may contribute to Asian American students' selection of majors and careers in mathematics and science could simply be that mathematics is easier for some of them, not necessarily because of proclivities but because of their parents' beliefs regarding early mathematics training. Stevenson, Lee, and Stigler (1986) have suggested that this is because Asian parents, like the Japanese, believe in a lower age of understanding or readiness, and, as a result, tend to expose children to math education at an earlier age than their European American counterparts. This contrasts sharply with European American beliefs concerning the wisdom of pushing children academically at an early age.

Japanese parents and teachers strive to develop children's critical thinking skills early on, perhaps so that later education can be efficient without being unduly aversive. They nurture children's thinking skills by being less directive with regards to helping them solve problems. Children struggle not only to solve problems but also to assess the validity of their solutions. Asian parents are more likely to educate in this fashion because they weigh the role of effort in achievement more heavily than their European American counterparts, who tend to believe that achievement is as much a function of ability as it is effort (Stevenson, Lee, & Stigler, 1986). This helps Asian children develop a strong work ethic and encourages them to be persistent—what some have called an acquired resistance to learned helplessness in academics (Sue & Okazaki, 1990). Believing that achievement is in large part due to effort may bestow upon individuals some sense of control over their destiny.

Where do parents acquire these beliefs? It seems plausible that these ideals are passed from one generation to the next, with religion serving as a potential vehicle. Indeed, several students mentioned the importance of Buddhism, Christianity, Confucianism, and Taoism in relation to their academic achievements. For example, one of the main tenets of Confucian thought postulates that individuals have the potential within themselves to achieve fulfillment and happiness. It seems that those who endorse such notions of human plasticity or malleability are more likely to believe that accomplishments and self-improvement can be attained through effort and persistence.

It may be beneficial then to determine which, if any, of these traditional values are more resistant to decay as Asian Americans become more acculturated to life in the United States, since they may represent less culturally specific beliefs. That is, they may be less rooted within the larger societal framework of their country of origin, and may be similar enough to Western beliefs to be accepted by other Americans. Students who struggle, academically or otherwise, may benefit from the sense of direction that such beliefs can provide.

This suggests that Asian groups whose beliefs are more divergent from that of Western cultures may have more difficulty making the transition to American life. For example, it has been reported that Southeast Asian Americans (primarily Cambodian, Hmong, Laotian, and Vietnamese) are as a group more likely to struggle academically than other Asian Americans (Kitano & Daniels, 1988). This differential in performance is undoubtedly due to a multitude of factors, such as access to education in their country of origin and time of immigration. However, it may also be compounded by the distinct sociocultural experiences of each ethnic group, which can lead to cross-cultural differences in beliefs and practices. Therefore, an attempt was made to explore the relationship between holding certain beliefs and actual academic achievement by asking students to provide information concerning their current grade point average as well as how they had fared on a standardized test (i.e., the SAT or ACT). Unfortunately, an insufficient number of students provided these academic performance indices, precluding a meaningful interpretation of this data.

Comparing students' beliefs with reported performance profiles is still insightful, however, particularly if one examines the belief and performance differences of two Southeast Asian groups, the Hmong and the Vietnamese. Westermeyer, Neider, and Callies (1989) have described the Hmong as suffering from some of the worst adjustment problems among Southeast Asians. Examination of their sociocultural history suggests some possible explanations for their difficulties. The academic difficulties that some Hmong American students experience may in part be due to their traditional reliance on an oral as opposed to a written tradition, since their written language was developed only in the relatively recent past (Strouse, 1986). This makes the transition to American schooling, with its emphasis on writing, more difficult. This transition is further hampered by Hmong Americans' tendency to rely on less extroverted acculturation strategies (Berry, Kim, Power, Young, & Bujaki, 1989). Hmong Americans appear to have a strongly developed sense of community, and seem to be more willing to seek help for educational and emotional problems from within their community than what has been reported for other Asian American groups (Atkinson, Whiteley, & Gim, 1990). This strategy is consistent with respect to their sociocultural history, since they have traditionally opted to preserve the integrity of their community, electing to avoid conflict by migrating to less desirable mountainous regions.

The academic performance of Vietnamese Americans may also be related to their sociocultural history. Shared values, words, and symbols reveal a Chinese influence, while Vietnam's Western character reflects the impact of a French and American presence. Exposure to Chinese values (e.g., such as the importance of education) and Western culture may help explain Vietnamese Americans' generally smoother transition to American schools in relation to their Southeast Asian counterparts. However, Vietnamese Americans may have weaker social support systems than Chinese Americans, perhaps because it is more difficult for people from a country ravaged by over a thousand years of war to trust in one another.

Cross-generational comparisons revealed that values that are transmitted from one generation to the next tend to be those that are less culturally distant from those of the mainstream culture, perhaps because Asian American students may be less willing to maintain extreme attitudinal and behavioral differences. Similarly, more peripheral and external signs of ethnic identity, such as behaviors (e.g., customs and traditions) and knowledge (e.g., of their native tongue) that contribute to the trappings of culture, are more prone to decay (Constantinou & Harvey, 1985) than invisible core elements of ethnic identity, such as one's attitudes toward ethnic group membership (Rosenthal & Feldman, 1992; Bond & Yang, 1982; Triandis, Kashima, Shimada, & Villareal, 1986). More importantly, having and holding attitudes about one's ethnic identity can encourage current and/or future explorations of one's ethnicity. In other words, there is some loss of knowledge and/or behaviors due to acculturation, but this does not necessarily imply a rejection of ethnicity or even a lack of ethnic pride. Rather, it appears that many Asian American students maintain an emotional commitment to their family's culture of origin that persists over time.

Therefore, it seems important to distinguish between core versus more peripheral facets of identity. As mentioned earlier, the attrition of more external aspects of ethnic identity may in part reflect an individual's desire to fit in with the culture at large and may not necessarily reflect a lack of commitment to one's cultural heritage. In other words, a distinction should be made between how Asian Americans appear to others (i.e., their peripheral aspects) as opposed to how they perceive themselves (i.e., their core attributes). This appears to be a shortcoming of many existing acculturation instruments, which tend to assess more peripheral and external aspects. Asking respondents to provide information with regards to how they see themselves and how they would like to relate to their ethnic heritage may be a means of measuring more central aspects of ethnic identity.

This is not to say that core values do not change over time. Some degradation of educational beliefs and values was observed in the present sample, although it was not always accompanied by reported decrements in academic performance. This could in part be artifactual because the students in this sample were all drawn from a highly selective institution and voluntarily elected to participate in the study. It could very well be a different state of affairs in the general population, with declines in performance accompanying an erosion of traditional values. The evolution of Asian gangs may be such an example, although it is questionable whether traditional values (e.g., the importance of hard work, education, and respect for elders) were ever truly inculcated in these youths. In fact, the degree to which such values are internalized could help explain why one finds Asian Americans across the academic spectrum (Hartman & Askounis, 1989).

Lastly, some modification in beliefs was also observed in this sample, mostly in terms of a blending of Eastern and Western values. Exposure to certain aspects of American culture appears to cause certain Eastern beliefs to evolve. For example, some students indicated that they valued competition, that they would reason with their children when they became parents, and that they succeeded academically because of their ability, statements that reflect a Western influence. In fact, belief and value modification may in part explain why changes in values were not necessarily accompanied by decrements in performance; such evolved values may be more apropos and conducive to academic success in this Western cultural environment.

References

Atkinson, D.R., Whiteley, S., & Gim, R.H. (1990). Asian American acculturation and preferences for help providers. *Journal of College Student Development, 31,* 155-161.

Bacon, W. F., & Ichikawa, V. (1988). Maternal expectations, classroom experiences, and achievement among kindergartners in the United States and Japan. *Human Development, 31*(6), 378-383.

Berry, J. W., Kim, U., Power, S., Young, M., & Bujaki, M. (1989). Acculturation attitudes in plural societies. *Applied Psychology, 38,* 185-206.

Bond, M. H., & Yang, K. S. (1982). Ethnic affirmation versus cross-cultural accommodation: The variable impact of questionnaire language on Chinese bilinguals in Hong Kong. *Journal of Cross-Cultural Psychology, 13,* 169-185.

Chen, C., & Uttal, D. H. (1988). Cultural values, parents' beliefs, and children's achievement in the United States and China. *Human Development, 31,* 351-358.

Constantinou, S., & Harvey, M. (1985). Dimensional structure and intergenerational differences in ethnicity: The Greek Americans. *Sociology and Social Research, 69,* 234-254.

Erikson, E. H. (1968). *Identity: Youth and crisis.* New York: Norton.

Gibson, M. A. (1987). The school performance of immigrant minorities: A comparative view. *Anthropology and Education Quarterly, 18,* 262-275.

Hartman, J. S., & Askounis, A. C. (1989). Asian-American students: Are they really a "model minority"? *School Counselor, 37*(2), 109-112.

Hui, C. H., & Triandis, H. C. (1986). Individualism-collectivism: A study of cross-cultural researchers. *Journal of Cross-Cultural Psychology, 17,* 225-248.

Kitano, H. H. L., & Daniels, R. (1988). *Asian Americans.* Englewood Cliffs, NJ: Prentice Hall.

Lin, C., & Fu, V. (1990). A comparison of child-rearing practices among Chinese, immigrant Chinese, and Caucasian-American parents. *Child Development, 61,* 429-433.

Marsh, H. W. (1984). Relations among dimensions of self-attribution, dimensions of self-concept, and academic achievements. *Journal of Educational Psychology, 76,* 1291-1308.

Maslow, A.H. (1970). *Motivation and personality* (2nd ed.). New York: Harper & Row.

Ogbu, J. U. (1990). Minority education in comparative perspective. *Journal of Negro Education, 59,* 45-57.

Phinney, J. S. (1990). Stages of ethnic identity development in minority group adolescents. *Journal of Early Adolescence, 9,* 34-49.

Rosenthal, D. A., & Feldman, S. S. (1992). The nature and stability of ethnic identity in Chinese youth: Effects of length of residence in two cultural contexts. *Journal of Cross-Cultural Psychology, 23,* 214-227.

Sigel, I. E. (1988). Commentary: Cross-cultural studies of parental influence on children's achievement. *Human Development, 31*(6), 384-390.

Stevenson, H. W., Lee, S., & Stigler, J. W. (1986). Mathematics achievement of Chinese, Japanese, and American children. *Science, 231,* 693-699.

Strouse, J. (1986). Educational responsibility: The Hmong experience. *Equity and Excellence, 22,* 115-118.

Sue, S., & Okazaki, S. (1990). Asian American educational achievements: A phenomenon in search of an explanation. *American Psychologist, 45,* 913-920.

Toupin, E. S. W. A., & Son, L. (1991). Preliminary findings on Asian Americans: "The model minority" in a small private east coast college. *Journal of Cross-Cultural Psychology, 22,* 403-417.

Triandis, H. C., Kashima, Y., Shimada, E., & Villareal, M. (1986). Acculturation indices as a means of confirming cultural differences. *International Journal of Psychology, 21,* 43-70.

Westermeyer, J., Neider, J., & Callies, A. (1989). Psychosocial adjustment of Hmong refugees during their first decade in the United States. *Journal of Nervous and Mental Disease, 177,* 132-139.

III b. Latino/Hispanic Americans

Chapter 14

The Family and Work Experiences of Puerto Rican Women Migrants in Chicago

Maura I. Toro-Morn

Feminists have made major contributions to the rethinking of the family (see Baca Zinn, 1990; Glenn, 1986, 1987, 1992; Thorne & Yalom, 1982). This new scholarship has challenged the ideology of the monolithic family, the view of the family as natural or biological, and, most importantly, the language of roles that had been so pervasive in family studies (Thorne & Yalom, 1982, p. 3). By exposing how gender has shaped family relations both within and outside the family, feminists have revealed a new system of gender stratification.

The feminist critique of the family has also had an impact on the study of racial and ethnic families. Maxine Baca Zinn (1990, p. 73) argued that by incorporating many feminist insights, current studies of race and ethnic families have dropped the culturally deviant perspective that depicted minority families as deficient or backward. The focus of study has shifted to understanding how race and gender interact to condition the material and subjective experiences of families. The problem, however, is that when it comes to family patterns, race and ethnicity are seen as elements of culture, not social structure. In other words, one of the challenges facing current feminist analyses of ethnic families is to see race as a power system that affects families throughout society. In addition, social scientists need to pay more attention to the adaptive and survival strategies racial and ethnic families employ to adapt in a changing political economy.

This chapter contributes to this emerging literature by exploring the experiences of Puerto Rican women migrants and their families in Chicago. This chapter takes a feminist perspective to explore the migration and adaptation of Puerto Ricans in Chicago. The objectives are to examine how working-class women entered the migration process and to study the adaptive strategies they have used to settle in Chicago. Placing women at the center of the analysis allows descriptions of their contributions to family and community life to be heard. This chapter is based on 30 in-depth interviews collected in the Puerto Rican community between March 1989 and July 1990. Different respondents will be identified by pseudonyms.

Drawing on the work of Louise Lamphere (1987), this chapter distinguishes between strategies of resistance and those of coping or accommodation. Strategies of resistance refer to tactics and actions Puerto Ricans use as a group or as individuals to deal with a racially and socially stratified society. Discussion will focus on how these working-class Puerto Ricans confronted and resisted the prejudice and discrimination they encountered in securing a place to live. Strategies of coping and accommodation refer to actions and tactics used in the allocation of productive and reproductive labor (Lamphere, 1987). In this study, women's work outside the home had become a family strategy for surviving and improving economic position. The second part of this chapter will discuss the coping strategies married working-class women used in different family arrangements to juggle family and work.

Balancing family and work is not a problem unique to immigrant women. What is unique is the possibility of bringing into question the traditional ideologies about the proper role of women. This chapter explores the question: To what extent do the strategies families develop in the process of adapting to life in the city challenge the traditional division of labor within the household? Interviews suggest that husbands may have accommodated to their wives' temporary employment, but that did not change the traditional division of labor within the household. Instead, women developed strategies to accommodate their roles as working wives. Finally, the struggle to adapt to life in the city was complicated when husbands became irresponsible and abandoned their wives. The last part of this chapter examines how married Puerto Rican women dealt with marital problems.

Puerto Rican Migration to Chicago

Puerto Rican migration to Chicago dates back to the post-World War II wave of migration that brought thousands of Puerto Ricans to the United States (Padilla, 1987). In the late 1940s, the impact of U.S. investment and modernization of the economy transformed Puerto Rico from a predominantly agricultural to an industrial economy. Operation Bootstrap—as the development model is popularly known—attracted labor-intensive light manufacturing industries like textiles and apparel to Puerto Rico by offering tax incentives, cheap labor, and easy access to U.S. markets (Dietz, 1986; Pantojas-Garcia, 1990). These changes in Puerto Rico's economy had profound consequences for Puerto Rican families. The development model was unable to create enough jobs, and working-class Puerto Ricans began to leave the island, heading for familiar places like New York City and new places like Chicago. News about jobs in Chicago spread quickly throughout the island as an informal network of family members, friends, and relatives told people of opportunities and helped families migrate.

By 1960, the U.S. Census of Population documented that Chicago was home to 32,371 Puerto Ricans.[1] Seventy-two percent of that population was of Puerto Rican birth, and 28% was of Puerto Rican parentage (U.S. Census, 1960). Internal population growth and continued migration from Puerto Rico continued over the years.[2] As of 1980, Chicago's largest Puerto Rican communities were West Town (28,469), Logan Square (23,792), and Humboldt Park (17,769). More recent settlements have developed in Waukegan City (2,451), Aurora (2,244), and Elgin City (1,495) (U.S. Census, 1980). Although Puerto Ricans have lived in the city for the past fifty years, very little has been written about Puerto Ricans in Chicago.

The interviews collected for this research suggest that over the years Puerto Rican women and their families have used migration as a strategy for dealing with both economic and personal problems. Working-class married women talk about migration as a family project. The political economy that rendered their husbands unemployable forced them to migrate to Chicago as part of a family strategy. Migration took place in stages. Husbands moved first, secured employment and housing arrangements, and sent for the rest of the family later. Given traditional gender roles in Puerto Rican culture, women left the island to be with their husbands, even though some reported they had been working before they left. Their responsibilities as wives and mothers took precedence over any role as wage earner. In other words, gender relations within the family shaped the migration of married working-class women to Chicago. Some married women went willingly, thinking that the move would improve their families' financial situation. Others resisted, but ultimately their roles as mothers and wives compelled them to follow their husbands to Chicago.

Living Arrangements

One of the first problems Puerto Rican families faced upon arrival in Chicago was living arrangements. Puerto Ricans who moved to Chicago often had a period of temporary living arrangements with the family members who had facilitated the move. For some working-class women the transition was easy. A crowded apartment with lots of family members provided a sense of continuity and security. When Alicia arrived in Chicago in the 1950s to get married, she shared an apartment with a cousin and her family. In those days, she recalled, "You rented the apartments with furniture," and "We lived like one big family." Shortly after establishing economic solvency, families moved into their own apartments.

More frequently, working-class migrant women talked about the difficulties adjusting to living with other relatives. Temporary living arrangements ranged from six months to a year, depending on how fast the family could survive on their own and were able to find adequate housing. Within this context, informal reciprocity norms in Chicago dictated that the newly arrived wife would help clean and prepare food for those who were employed. In the 1950s, Rita and her family came to live with her sister-in-law:

> My husband took us to my sister-in-law's house. There *pase la salsa y el guayacan* [popular expression denoting a very hard time]. We had four kids and no house of our own. Imagine? We had to wait to shower after everyone in the other family had taken their shower. If I had my little girl in the bathtub and one of her [sister-in-law] children wanted to shower I had to hurry up and leave them use the shower. For cooking it was worse. I suffered a lot.

At this point, the interview was interrupted because Rita started crying in uncontrollable sobs. She took a deep breath and continued describing that first year of her arrival in Chicago, which for her seemed like a century:

> I used to do everything for her. I cooked, I cleaned the house. You see, because she worked and after work she went to school. She had a house with eight rooms and we rented one room. You had to see all the things that happened to believe it. I shared everything with her, but she did not. She used to buy "cakes" for her children and would not share it with ours. She used to tell me things about my husband that were very hurtful and painful.

Similarly, Victoria described living with her in-laws as the source of numerous problems:

> I stayed home and took care of the children. I cleaned the house. It was very difficult. On top of that I was very shy. I did not dare even to open the refrigerator to get something to drink. I tried to keep a low profile and not be a bother to them.

Agnes went to live with the relatives who had persuaded her and her husband to move from Puerto Rico. She worked for a while but stopped when she became pregnant. Unemployed, she spent much of her time in the house. She found herself baby-sitting and doing chores as if she were a maid, and the living arrangements that she thought were going to be temporary began to seem permanent. Discomforted, she confronted her husband and proclaimed: "Either you find me an apartment or I'm going back to Puerto Rico." Within the framework of the family structure, these women confronted their husbands in a manner that did not threaten traditional family arrangements. In this context, confrontation becomes a strategy of resistance to deal with inadequate living arrangements.

But finding an adequate apartment was no easy task. Padilla (1987, p. 117) wrote that Puerto Ricans "were trapped in the most run-down residential sections in their communities not only because of poverty but also because of a stringent pattern of housing discrimination." Teresa and her husband experienced the effects of this discrimination and poverty:

> When we went apartment hunting if they saw that we were Hispanics and the rent was $60.00, they asked us $90.00. We could never find an affordable apartment. It was very difficult to find decent housing.

Others were asked, "Are you Puerto Rican?" and were told, "We don't rent to Puerto Ricans." Agnes remembered the kind of problems she confronted:

> When I was looking for apartment around Kildare and
> Potomac I found a lot of problems. That area was an area
> where a lot of Europeans lived and when I inquired about
> apartment openings they closed the door on my face. And
> you know what? I did not understand why they would do
> something like that.

As a group, Puerto Ricans devised a number of strategies to resist
the housing discrimination they confronted in Chicago. One strategy of resistance families used to deal with discrimination was looking for apartments with more than one unit available. Other family
members were told about the vacancies so that they might move
together. Some families talked to landlords and found apartments
for family or friends who were still in Puerto Rico. Occasionally,
members of families pooled their resources to buy a multiunit building, enabling families of brothers and sisters to occupy the same
apartment building. Daniela's sister and her family lived on the
first floor of a building they share-bought; Daniela and her family
lived on the second floor, and her sister's family lived on the third.
By living close together, they could help one another more easily.

In addition to these issues, Puerto Ricans struggled with the
idea of buying property because it implied a commitment to making
Chicago their permanent home. Consequently, families often moved
from residences of relatives, to rental properties, to ownership, and
back to Puerto Rico.

Juggling Family and Work

In Puerto Rican culture there is a gender-specific division of labor
which consists of men's work (*trabajo de hombre*) as providers and
women's work (*trabajo de mujer*) as the caretakers of the home and
the children (Rogler & Cooney, 1984). Underlying this gender division of labor is a patriarchal ideology, *machismo*, which emphasizes
men's sexual freedom, virility, and aggressiveness and women's
sexual repression and submission (Acosta-Belen, 1986). *Machismo*
represents the male ideal and plays an important role in maintaining sexual restrictions and the subordination of women. This ideology rationalizes a double standard where a woman can be seen as *la
mujer buena o de la casa* (a good woman) or as *una mujer mala o de
la calle* (a bad woman and a woman of the streets). Men have to
show that *el lleva los pantalones en la casa* (he is the one who wears
the pants in the family) and they are free to *echar una canita al aire*
(literally meaning, blow a gray hair to the wind, culturally it means
to have an affair).

The counterpart of *machismo* is *marianismo,* in which the Virgin Mary is seen as the role model (Espín, 1992). Within this context, a woman's sexual purity and virginity is a cultural imperative. Motherhood, in Puerto Rican culture, lies at the center of such ideology as one of the important roles a woman plays. A woman is viewed in light of her relationship to her children and, as Carmen, one of the respondents, put it, in her ability to *dar buenos ejemplos* (provide a good role model).

Safa (1976) observed that among working-class Puerto Ricans, gender roles are very rigid. Although industrialization and the entrance of women in the labor force completely contradicts the ideal of *la mujer es de la casa* (women belong to the home), in Puerto Rico the domestic role of working-class women remains intact. Working mothers are primarily responsible for the care of the home and the children.

In Chicago, in keeping with this ideology surrounding family values, some husbands resisted the idea of their wives working and took a double shift so that wives could stay home, take care of the children, and do housework. Most often, economic necessity obliged other husbands to accept women's work roles outside the home. Like Lucy said: "I did not come here to work, but I had to." Alicia elaborated:

> In those days one pay check was like nothing. We put together both paychecks and there were times that he had very little or next to nothing left. By that time there were other relatives living with us and there were lots of mouths to feed.

In the 1950s, Chicago's economy offered new immigrants plenty of job opportunities in the booming manufacturing sector. In fact, the same network of family and friends that helped in the process of migration helped working wives find employment in Chicago factories. Josefa, Lucy, Luz, Rita, Teresa, and even Lupe, as a single woman, all reported to have worked in factories.

For most married working-class women, employment was a temporary necessity. The way women talked about their work experiences reflected this attitude. In fact, working-class married women often gave in to their husband's wishes of staying home. However, Rita's experiences illustrate how a woman could resist those traditional roles and seek to change them. Rita's husband did not want her to work. According to Rita:

> After I got to Chicago my husband didn't want me to work. But I wanted to work. I wanted to work because you can meet people, learn new things and one can also leave the house for a while. I saw all the women in the family, his sisters and cousins, working and earning some money and I wanted to work too. They used to tell me that I should be working. But I had four children and who was going to take care of them?

Rita started working secretly. She worked *a la escondida* (in hiding) for about three months. When asked how she managed to work without her husband knowing, Rita replied:

> Since he left to work very early I found someone to take care of my smallest child, and the others went to school. My work hours were from 9:00 to 3:30 so by the time my husband got home I had everything done. I had the house clean, the children were cleaned and had eaten, and I was all put together. My husband did not like when I was not put together.

Rita eventually told her husband about her work escapades because she did not like doing things *a la escondida*. When asked how she managed to tell him, she replied:

> One night when he came home I had fixed him his favorite dish and he was sitting on the couch and I told him that I was working. I told him that I had talked to Maggie and that she told me that they were recruiting. I told him that I went [to the factory site] just to see if I could do that kind of work. He told me: "I don't think so, I don't think you are going to keep it because I want you to take care of the children. What if something happens to you, who is going to take care of you, you don't know English."

Her husband's traditionalism was too great, and Rita gave up working. The money she had earned had gone to clothe the children and to purchase a sewing machine:

> With the money I earned I was able to buy my sewing machine and I felt so proud of myself that I was able to buy it with my own money. We saved a lot of money afterwards. I sew for the family, I felt so proud.

As Rita's case illustrates, she gave in to her husband's traditionalism, but even within the confines of the house she could still find a source of pride. She may have stopped working, but her contributions to the household continued as she was able to sew her children's clothing and other items for the house and the family.

Puerto Rican men may have accommodated to their wives' employment but the traditional division of labor within the family did not change. Lucy articulated the problems of working women:

> It was very hard work because I had to take care of the house, the children and the store. Since my husband never learned how to drive I had to learn to drive. I had to go to the warehouse, do the bookkeeping, everything. In the store I used to do everything. My husband helped but I was practically in charge of everything.

Puerto Rican working mothers, regardless of whether they worked outside the home or with their husbands in the family business, were still responsible for the care of the children and housework. Child care first became a problem at the time of migration as they could not afford to travel all at once. Instead, women had to accommodate their roles as working wives and mothers. In Chicago, women developed short-term accommodation strategies to deal with the daily problems of child care. Shift work represented one strategy couples used to allow these women to stay home with the children. The husband worked the day shift and the wife the night shift. Haydee's father worked the day shift in a factory while her mother worked the evening shift as a cook in a hotel. Josefa worked the night shift in a candy factory, and her husband worked the day shift. Josefa was asked if she ever switched with her husband, so he worked nights and she worked days. She replied that they hadn't, because her current work routine allowed her to take care of her daughter during the day.

When children were old enough for school, both husband and wife might be able to work during the day. For wives, however, there was always the added responsibility of returning home to care for the children and do the household chores. Here, girls were introduced to the household responsibilities very early and were left to care for younger brothers and sisters. When Claudia reached age nine she acquired household responsibilities. She was given keys to the apartment, and after school she was expected to clean the kitchen, pick up around the house, and start dinner. This was one way mothers trained their daughters in the traditional gender roles.

Given the ease of migration, other working-class women brought over relatives with them to help care for the children. Lucy and Daniela brought their mothers to help take care of their children. Teresa brought her younger sister to Chicago so that she could help take care of the children.

Sanchez-Korrol (1983, p. 98) found the same kind of informal child-care practices in the early *colonias* in New York City in which "child-care tasks previously undertaken by relatives defaulted to friends and acquaintances outside the kinship network who provided the services in exchange for a prearranged fee." This grassroots system served both those who were employed and those who had to stay at home. The arrangement usually consisted of bringing child, food, and additional clothing to the "mother-substitute" and collecting the child after work. This system provided a practical way to increase family earnings and was an extralegal system with advantages not found in established child-care institutions. These informal child-care arrangements allowed children to be cared for in a familiar environment, in which there was mutual trust, agreement between the adults involved, and flexibility. Children were cared for in a family settings where the language, customs, and Puerto Rican traditions were reinforced.

When Teresa stopped working she became a child-care provider for the women in her building. Now, she no longer cares for other people's children but instead cares for her own grandchildren. Teresa's history represents a typical cycle of care: placing her children with a neighborhood while she worked, caring for other neighbor's children while they worked, and finally caring for her own children's children, perpetuating such care practices in another generation.

Marital Problems

In addition to juggling family and work, four married working-class women reported a range of problems with their husbands, including alcoholism, infidelity, and desertion. Rita reported that her husband had started drinking and being unfaithful to her. Rita was aware of his problems but chose not to leave him. Instead, she endured the affairs and her husband's alcoholism. He brought her considerable pain and stress until he died suddenly from his alcoholism in 1980.

Interviewing elderly women in Massachusetts, Sanchez-Ayendez (1986) found that as long as men's behavior did not upset the balance in the household where men are the providers and women the center of the home, married women endured such behavior. Ana, one of her respondents, knew her husband was having an affair but believed that success in marriage depended on the woman's ability "to make it work."

In fact, since her husband was becoming less and less involved with the family affairs, Rita took charge and began to go around her husband's authority. She rationalized her moves in terms of her family responsibilities. She had limitations (a major one being her husband), but that did not prevent her from aggressive action. The home was her domain and it was her right to make decisions about it without the intervention of her husband, who had abdicated his authority anyway because of his drinking. In the absence of her husband's authority, Rita became very resourceful. The story of how she bought a home illustrates the kind of strategies Puerto Ricans forged as individuals and as a group.

> I went to the bank and I asked for a loan. But they would not give it to me without my husband's signature. I kept thinking how can I buy this house? I told my husband again and I asked him to come to the bank with me, I waited all morning long for him and he did not show up. I was so disillusioned. I really liked the house and I saw a lot of potential. I went back to the landlord and I told him that I was really interested and that I wanted to buy the house if he gave it to me for $10,000. Some people that lived in the building that knew me supported me and told the landlord that I was a good person. I had done a little bit of work and I had some money saved but not enough.

Faced with this problem, Rita took an alternative route: Ask a friend for a loan:

> I had this friend and she told me about this Cuban man who could lend me the money. I went talked to him and I asked him to loan me $5,000. But that it had to be through a lawyer. I wanted to do it legal. The lawyer told him how are you going to loan this woman all that money? I was furious. I told the Cuban that I give him my word that if I did not respond that he could the take the house from me.

In the process Rita not only had to face the institutional discrimination in the banking industry but also the gender bias from the lawyer who discouraged her friend from lending her the money. Eventually, he lent her the money and with some savings from her children, she bought the house:

> Now, the problem was how to tell my husband about it.
> Well, I fixed the house very nice before we moved. One
> night he came home drunk laid on the couch and I told the
> kids that tonight we are moving to the new house. We
> borrowed a big truck and moved overnight. The following
> morning when my husband woke up, everything was gone.
> [Laughing] I was fixing breakfast in the new house and
> suddenly I remembered that we had left him behind. I
> rushed to the house, talked to him and told him that this
> apartment was old, that I did not like it, and that we should
> sell it. I told him that I had rented out a little house and we
> had moved overnight.... He paid the rent and he did not
> know the house was ours. He gave me the money for the
> rent and I invested it. I rented a house in the back and
> within a year I had the house paid. One day I was going to
> tell him but he got sick. We took him to the hospital on
> Friday and by Sunday he had died. Imagine, he died and
> never knew I had bought the house we were living in.

Years after her husband died, Rita married her husband's best friend
(Carlos), whose wife had abandoned him and his children. She had
helped him raise his family while he had helped her deal with her
husband's alcoholism. Rita and Carlos went through a lot together
with their respective families. In old age they found themselves
alone and decided to stay together.

Nellie, on the other hand, was conscious of her subordination
to her husband and endured it for a good part of her marriage. He
was a gambler, even taking her paycheck to pay for his habits, and
he turned abusive as his drinking increased. Nellie remembered the
fateful day when her marriage came apart:

> He picked me up at work and when we got home he wanted
> me to help him carry some bags. I was very tired and did
> not want to. He hit me right there in the street. That was
> it. I left him and went to my mother's place. I lived with
> my mother for a week. But one day he showed up at work,
> put a knife to my neck and told me that he was going to kill
> me if I did not go back with him. So, I told him I would, but
> first we must go to my mother's to pick up my stuff. That
> was the trick—when we got there I told him that I was not
> going with him. That was on a Friday, the following Satur-
> day he got in trouble with the police and fled to New York.

Nellie became a single mother and had to take two jobs in
order to support herself and her family. She recalled:

> It was so hard to find someone to take care of the children while I was at work. One day my mom was gone to New York for a short trip and the police came and took my children. I was lucky because the two ladies that lived next to me went with me to the police station and helped me. They told the police that I was a good and responsible mother. They gave them back to me and I had to leave a job.

The lack of child care was a major barrier to Nellie's search for work and she was forced to rely on the welfare system for survival. Nellie remembered that the day she went to the welfare office, a welfare officer lectured her in English about her responsibilities as a mother. Nellie left the office before the caseworker was finished and took a factory job. This time she asked a woman in her building to help her with her children for a small fee.

Victoria and Agnes had similar problems with their husbands and, like Nellie, became single mothers, having to rely on welfare to survive. Victoria's husband could not hold a job and disappeared for long periods of time. According to Victoria:

> We were legally married for eleven years and in that period we had four children. Within that period he took off more than twenty-five times, leaving me stranded with the children.

She divorced him and in order to support herself she went on welfare. Victoria recalled the day her sister-in-law took her to the welfare office:

> I felt so ashamed. I was not raised to beg for money. In Puerto Rico, we had very little but we never asked for anything. My mother worked and even though she earned very little we stretched it. When I went to the welfare office my English was not very good. That's why my sister-in-law went with me. Social workers were so rude. They asked my sister-in-law whether I knew that there were contraceptives so that I could avoid having so many children. She fought with them. She later told me what had happened.

Victoria lived on welfare for a number of years, but it was not very reliable. She remembered a particular crisis which, in a way, helped her leave welfare. For some reason, the welfare office had started reviewing her case and stopped sending her money. For seven months she had no means to support herself and her family.

Finally, she lost control and became very ill, or as she put it, *me enferme de los nervios*. Pelto, Roman, and Liriano (1982) found that Puerto Rican single parents in Hartford also reported suffering from this condition of nervous breakdown. They describe this condition as a mental illness that ranges from mild anxieties, to uncontrollable outbursts, to depressions and suicidal tendencies. *Nervios* is perceived as a situational illness and is not seen as the fault of the victim. While Victoria was in the hospital, a Lutheran pastor came to see her at her mother's request. According to Victoria, "He spoke Spanish beautifully and perfectly. He seemed to care about Hispanic problems. He rescued me. When I left the hospital, he offered me a part-time job." Since her children were in school, she was able to work her schedule around them and continued taking welfare while working part-time. She attended a GED program with her church and passed the state examination. Victoria reflected on her choices and what they meant to her:

> It is very difficult to raise your family here just working by yourself. I was on welfare but I was able to raise my children without the drug problem or the gang problem. That's what makes me feel good.

Agnes' problems with her husband started after they moved to Chicago. Puzzled by the marital problems, she attempted to rationalize what had happened. Agnes felt that:

> People come here with the dream of working hard, saving some money and returning to one's homeland. But something happens to men. Couples arrive in this country and their marriages fall apart... I think it has to do with their work. They come to work in those factories and they lose control. They lose their sense of reality. They think that their only responsibility is to provide for the family. They come put the food on the table and off they go to the streets.

Agnes' husband loved to spend money on automobiles. The family's savings were squandered on cars and car parts. Agnes tried to cope by confronting him about the spending and reminding him of their original goals of saving to return to Puerto Rico. But it was hopeless, and they divorced in 1978. Unable to support herself, she turned to welfare. Her daughters were still very young when she divorced and that was one of her considerations for staying alone and not remarrying. She said:

> I always thought of my daughters. I used to tell myself how I am going to allow a stranger to come into our house and take charge of our lives. Sometimes children do not adapt well to a stepfather. Me, no, no, I prefer to raise my daughters alone. I am a person who is very independent I like to depend on my own, and I realized that in order for me to able to move forward and give something to my children I was going to go back to school. I did not want to work all my life in a factory. So, I took public aid and started going to school.

School, however, "was not very stable." So she moved from work to welfare and back to work. At the time of the interview, she worked part-time and received food coupons.

Some husbands abandoned the family altogether. Ivan, now a community leader, and one of the respondents, remembered his mother's struggle to survive on her own. Within a year after relocating to Chicago, his family was abandoned by his father. It was the most traumatic event in his life:

> After my father abandoned us my mother was left with the responsibilities of taking care of us. It was the most difficult time of our lives. We were so poor. Really, I don't have words to describe the kind of situation we lived in. But my mother suffered the most. She was a very proud woman. Even in the most difficult situations, she always found happiness and pride. She always tried keeping us clean and neat—that was her pride.

As these cases reflect, when confronted with marital problems, working-class Puerto Rican women developed a number of strategies. They divorced their husbands, but unable to support themselves, they had to rely on welfare. These interviews show how migration affects family relations, resulting in the emergence of single-headed households.

Concluding Thoughts

This chapter has only begun to explore how working-class Puerto Rican women worked to maintain family life among the tensions and adversities of adjusting to life in Chicago. As family units and as individuals, Puerto Ricans developed both resistance and accommodating strategies to deal with the "darker side of migration." However, much empirical work needs to be done to fully understand how other groups of Puerto Ricans in different family arrangements and across class backgrounds have adapted to life in the United States and survived.

Puerto Rican women—like other immigrant women—confront a basic duality in relation to the family. Families provide economic and emotional support; the family is the only area where people are free to be themselves, and where people come for affection and love. But the family is also an institution that has historically oppressed women. When individuals and families confront economic deprivation, legal discrimination, and other threats to their survival, conflict within the context of the family is muted by the pressure of the family to unite against assaults from the outside. This duality can be seen in the problems women confronted with living arrangements. Living with relatives was both a family strategy to deal with housing discrimination and a source of problems between husband and wife, and even between women. In fact, as families wrestled with the idea of making Chicago their permanent home, life in Chicago became even more complicated. As Rita's story suggests, older working-class women saw their homes as personal domain, one in which decisions about it actually empowered them.

Often, the focus on the family as a site of resistance underestimates how certain family arrangements can be oppressive to women. In particular, an area often misunderstood by scholars is the reproductive work of women on behalf of the family and the benefits such work brings to men (Glenn, 1987, p. 192). As in Puerto Rico, married working-class women in Chicago joined the labor force, albeit temporarily. Like other immigrant women, Puerto Rican women took jobs at the bottom of the labor hierarchy. Their husbands accommodated to their wives employment, but the gendered division of labor within the household did not change. Housework and the care of children continued to be the major responsibility of women. Instead, working-class women had to develop strategies to accommodate their roles as working wives. The area of child care best reflects the resourcefulness of working-class women migrants.

Women tried to provide continuity in the process of forming and recreating family life in Chicago even when husbands deserted them. Older working-class women resisted divorce as a strategy to dealing with abusive or irresponsible husbands. Perhaps for them to openly challenge the Puerto Rican patriarchal system may not have been possible, since they also had a stake in the existing system of authority. Respect and authority in Puerto Rican culture is accorded first to the husband-father, then to the wife-mother. When husbands neglected their responsibilities as fathers, women took charge of the household, providing for their children and family.

For other women, however, divorce was the only way out of a marriage that had turned bad. For these women, this meant becoming heads of household, slipping into poverty, and having to rely on the welfare system to be able to survive. Much maneuvering was required to keep the family together.

In general, the evidence that emerges from these accounts contrasts with the prevailing view of Puerto Rican women as passive and unimportant to the building of Puerto Rican culture and community in Chicago. Instead, it shows women as resourceful, inventive, and determined to overcome the obstacles that confronted them both as families and as individuals. Puerto Rican women were not resigned but were always actively devising strategies to improve their situation and that of their families.

Notes

1. Prior to the 1960s, the U.S. Census of Population did not collect any data about Puerto Ricans in Chicago. Senior (1947) stated that in 1910 the Census Bureau reported only 15 Puerto Ricans living in Illinois' largest city. By 1920, it had increased to 110. Two decades later it had doubled to 245.

2. In 1970, the Puerto Rican population of Chicago had reached an unprecedented 79,582. Sixty-one percent were of Puerto Rican birth, and 39% were of Puerto Rican parentage. As of 1980, Chicago was home to over 116,000 Puerto Ricans, mostly concentrated in the city's northwest side (U.S. Census, 1970).

References

Acosta-Belen, E. (1986). *The Puerto Rican woman: Perspectives on culture, history, and society*. New York: Praeger.

Baca Zinn, M. (1990). Family, feminism, and race in America. *Gender and Society*, 4(1), 68-82.

Dietz, J. L. (1986). *Economic history of Puerto Rico: Institutional change and capitalist development*. Princeton, NJ: Princeton University Press.

Espín, O. M. (1992). Cultural and historical influences on sexuality in Hispanic/Latin women: Implications for psycotherapy. In M. Andersen & P. Hill Collins (Eds.), *Race, class, & gender*. Belmont, CA: Wadsworth Publishing.

Glenn, E. N. (1986). *Issei, Nisei, war bride: Three generations of Japanese women in domestic service*. Philadelphia: Temple University Press.

Glenn, E. N. (1987). Women, labor migration, and household work: Japanese-American women in the pre-war period. In C. Bose & G. Spitze (Eds.), *Ingredients for women's employment policy.* Albany: State University of New York Press.

Glenn, E. N. (1992). From servitude to service work: Historical continuities in the racial division of paid reproductive labor. *Signs, 18*(1), 1-43.

Lamphere, L. (1987). *From working daughters to working mothers: Immigrant women in a New England industrial community.* Ithaca: Cornell University Press.

Padilla, F. (1987). *Puerto Ricans Chicago.* Indiana: University of Notre Dame Press.

Pantojas-Garcia, E. (1990). *Development strategies as ideology: Puerto Rico's export-led industrialization experience.* Boulder, CO: Lynne Rienner Publisher.

Pelto, P., Roman, M., & Liriano, N. (1982). Family structures in an urban Puerto Rican community. *Urban Anthropology, 11(1),* 39-57.

Rodriguez, C. (1989). *Puerto Ricans: Born in the U.S.A.* Boston: Unwin Hyman.

Rogler, L., & Cooney, R. S. (1984). *Puerto Rican families in New York: Intergenerational processes.* Maplewood: Waterfront.

Safa, H. (1976). Class consciousness among working-class women in Latin America. In J. Nash & H. I. Safa (Eds.), *Sex and class in Latin America.* New York: Praeger.

Sanchez-Ayendez, M. (1986). Puerto Rican elderly women: Shared meanings and informal supportive networks. In J. Cole (Ed.), *All-American women: Lines that divide, ties that bind.* New York: The Free Press.

Sanchez-Korrol, V. (1983). *From colonia to community: The history of Puerto Ricans in New York City, 1917-1948.* Westport: Greenwood Press.

Senior, C. (1947). *Puerto Rican immigration.* Rio Piedras: University of Puerto Rico, Social Science Research Center.

Thorne, B., & Yalom, M. (1982). *Rethinking the family: Some feminist questions.* New York: Longman.

U.S. Census of Population. (1960). Subject report: Puerto Ricans in the United States PC(2)-ID. Washington, DC: U.S. Department of Commerce.

U.S. Census of Population. (1970). Subject report: Puerto Ricans in the United States PC(2)-IE. Washington, DC: Department of Commerce.

U.S. Census of Population. (1980). Detailed populations characteristics: Illinois. Washington, DC: U.S. Department of Commerce.

Chapter 15

Exploring Adolescents' Vulnerability to Life Stress and Parental Alcoholism

The Role of Ethnicity and Family Conflict

Manuel Barrera, Jr., Susan A. Li, and Laurie Chassin[1]

Questions concerning individuals' reactions to stressful life events are fundamental to our understanding of psychological distress and human development. Determining the nature of the adversity, identifying who is touched by it, and studying the range of human reactions to it are relevant steps in understanding the psychological adjustment of individuals and families. Researchers who study ethnic minority groups in the United States are particularly attracted to the study of life stress because it captures the daily upheavals of adverse living conditions that characterize the lives of many ethnic minorities. Some aspects of adversity are not event-like, but are more chronic strains such as poverty, unemployment, neighborhood crime, and educational disadvantage that are correlated with minority group status. For children, important forms of strain include conditions that result from their parents' experience with alcohol abuse, psychopathology, substance abuse, or involvement with the criminal justice system. These chronic strains not only represent a direct threat to individuals' well-being, but they provide a context that can exacerbate the negative effects of more specific stressful events.

Beyond the general relations between life stress, strain, and psychological distress that are often observed, many are intrigued by diathesis-stress theories that assert that adversity does not affect individuals uniformly (Monroe & Simons, 1991). Whether the stress conditions are as extreme as the horrors of warfare or as common as job stress, some individuals have access to resources of resiliency that appear to protect them from harsh consequences while others have vulnerabilities (diatheses) that render them susceptible to negative outcomes. Both the epidemiology of psychological disorders and the development of interventions to prevent or treat the consequences of stressful events are informed by a keener explication of resiliency and vulnerability.

This chapter is concerned with research that investigated two characteristics, ethnicity and parental alcoholism, and their influence on adolescents' reactions to stressful life events. It integrates the findings of two reports from a longitudinal study of Hispanic and non-Hispanic Caucasian adolescents who were interviewed over three annual assessments (Barrera, Li, & Chassin, 1993, in press). The chronological sequence of these two studies is maintained in this chapter to reflect the research process that included: (a) an initial cross-sectional analysis that found evidence that Hispanic and Caucasian adolescents had different vulnerabilities to life stress and parental alcoholism, (b) unsuccessful attempts to explain this differential vulnerability, (c) subsequent analyses with two additional waves of data that replicated the differential vulnerability effects, and (d) another attempt to explain vulnerability by examining the role of family conflict.

Ethnicity as a Vulnerability Characteristic

Research questions concerned with ethnic minority group members' *exposure* to stress need to be differentiated from questions concerned with their *vulnerability* to stress (Dohrenwend & Dohrenwend, 1981; Monroe & Simons, 1991). Ethnic minorities are thought to have greater exposure to stressful life conditions and strains than majority group members (Golding & Burnam, 1990; Kessler, 1979). Stressors associated with minority group status, adaptation to a different culture, and low socioeconomic status are all thought to be more prevalent for ethnic minorities.

A separate question concerns ethnic group differences in resiliency or vulnerability to stress. Somewhat surprisingly, of the few studies that explored race and ethnicity as vulnerability characteristics, several showed that Caucasians were more vulnerable to stress than were adults of Mexican heritage (Mirowsky & Ross, 1980), and African Americans and Puerto Ricans (Kessler, 1979).

Even a rare study that examined race/ethnicity as a vulnerability characteristic for adolescents found that Caucasian adolescents were more vulnerable to stress than were African Americans, but Caucasians were not more vulnerable than Hispanics (Dornbusch, Mont-Reynaud, Ritter, Chen, & Steinberg, 1991). Unfortunately, none of the studies identified factors that could account for Caucasians' greater vulnerability (i.e., the resiliency of ethnic minority groups). It is also apparent that there have been few tests of ethnic group differences to stress vulnerability, particularly with minority adolescents and children.

Parental Alcoholism as a Vulnerability Characteristic

Parental alcoholism is a characteristic that appears to increase children's and adolescents' exposure to stress (Brown, 1989; Chassin, Pillow, Curran, Molina, & Barrera, 1993; Roosa, Sandler, Gehring, Beals, & Cappo, 1988) as well as their vulnerability to stress (Sher, 1991). Children of alcoholics (COAs) are exposed to life stress because, in part, of the upheavals that result from their parents' alcohol involvement (e.g., a parent's loss of job, arrest, or marital separation). Increased exposure to stress presumably contributes to adolescents' emotional distress as well as to their own problematic alcohol use (Chassin, Pillow, Curran, Molina, & Barrera, 1993). In this sense, life stress is viewed as *mediating* the relation of parental alcoholism to adolescent problem behaviors such as externalizing symptoms and precocious alcohol use.

As noted earlier, however, there is a separate question concerned with *vulnerability* to stress that might be associated with parental alcoholism. As part of a broader theoretical model, Sher (1991) identified factors related to parental alcoholism that could render COAs more *vulnerable* to the experience of stress. In this model, parental alcoholism is a moderator (i.e., vulnerability characteristic) of life stress' relation to adolescents' problem behaviors. Parental alcoholism's moderating effects are viewed as working through additional moderators. These moderators include deficits that are associated with parental alcoholism such as maladaptive temperament/personality, coping abilities, alcohol expectancies and parenting behaviors. Although there is evidence to support some of the linkages between parental alcoholism and the other hypothesized moderators, there is little evidence that COAs are more vulnerable to life stress than are children of non-alcoholic parents.

Focusing on parental alcoholism is particularly relevant in research that involves Hispanic adolescents and their parents. Alcohol abuse is one of the few behavioral disorders on which Hispanics and Caucasians differ. Although there are not extensive epidemiological data that compare the true prevalence of Hispanics' psychological disorder to the prevalence of psychological disorders of Caucasians, research has shown that the rates are remarkably similar for almost all forms of psychopathology (Burnam et al., 1987; Karno et al., 1987). However, in the Los Angeles Epidemiological Catchment Area Study (LA ECA), Caucasian women had higher rates of alcohol and drug use disorders, and major depression than Hispanic women (Karno et al., 1987). For men in the LA ECA study, there were two disorders that differentiated Hispanics from Caucasians. Caucasian males had higher rates of drug abuse/dependence (14.6% vs. 5.9%), but Mexican American males had significantly higher rates of lifetime diagnoses of alcohol abuse/dependence (31.3% vs. 21%). Furthermore, the lifetime prevalence of alcohol abuse/dependence was by far the most prevalent psychiatric disorder for Hispanic males—three times more prevalent than any other disorder. These findings were consistent with several other studies and reviews that concluded that Hispanic males, particularly Mexican Americans, have a high prevalence of alcoholism and alcohol related problems compared to Caucasian males (Gilbert & Cervantes, 1986).

An Initial Cross-Sectional Study

The purpose of the initial cross-sectional study was to compare Hispanic and Caucasian adolescent children of alcoholics to adolescents whose parents were not alcoholic on multiple measures of adolescents' psychological distress and alcohol use. These analyses tested whether Hispanic and Caucasian adolescents had comparable vulnerability to the effects of parental alcoholism and life stress events. In anticipation of possible differential vulnerability effects, ethnic group differences in the effects of social support and parental substance use were explored as possible explanations. There has been much speculation that Hispanics have access to extensive support networks that protect them from adversity (e.g., Keefe & Casas, 1980), but there is not adequate support for this assertion (Barrera, 1982; Barrera & Reese, 1993). Parental substance use is another factor that might lead to differential vulnerability. As noted in the discussion of the LA ECA study, Hispanics (particularly women) had lower rates of substance abuse/dependence diagnoses than Caucasians. If the parents of Hispanic adolescents experience less impairment because of lower use of illicit substances, then Hispanic adolescents might be more resilient to the effects of life stress and parental alcohol abuse.

Method

Participants

Participants for these analyses were drawn from a larger study (Chassin, Rogosch, & Barrera, 1991) that assessed a total of 454 families (246 adolescents who had at least one alcoholic parent and a comparison sample of 208 demographically matched adolescents whose parents were not alcoholics). Two subsequent annual assessments were successful in retaining 449 of these adolescents at Time 2, and 444 at Time 3. Participants in the current study were a subsample of the larger study.

Because the analyses contrasted adolescents of Hispanic and non-Hispanic Caucasian ethnicity, 31 adolescents who could not be identified unambiguously as either Hispanic or Caucasian were eliminated from the larger sample. Adolescents were included in the Hispanic sample if they self-identified as Hispanic and had at least one parent who could be identified as Hispanic. The non-Hispanic group consisted of adolescents who self-identified as Caucasian and who had no Hispanic parents. The study was restricted further to families in which both parents participated at Time 1. This was done to reduce the ambiguity of any differences between father- and mother-reports that might have emerged, and to permit fathers and mothers to directly report on their own alcohol and substance use.

At the Time 1 assessment, participants were 161 families that had at least one alcoholic parent (COAs) and 145 that had fathers and mothers who were not alcoholic (Controls). All families contained at least one adolescent. Adolescent participants included 142 females and 164 males with a mean age of 12.8 years. There were 69 Hispanic (42 COAs and 27 Controls) and 237 Caucasian (119 COAs and 118 Controls) adolescents. Of the 306 adolescents assessed in Time 1, 305 were assessed in Time 2 and 301 in Time 3. Of the 306 mothers assessed at Time 1, 302 and 299 were retained at Time 2 and Time 3 respectively. Of the original 306 fathers, 292 and 285 participated at Time 2 and Time 3, respectively.

Measures

Background Variables. Parental education and adolescents' age and gender were demographic variables used in the data analyses. Parental education was an average of mothers' and fathers' educational attainment, which was self-reported on a 7-point scale ranging from grade school (1) to graduate or professional school (7).

Parental Alcoholism. Parents' lifetime diagnoses of alcohol abuse or dependence were determined with a portion of the Diagnostic Interview Schedule (DIS, version III; Robins, Helzer, Croughan, & Ratcliff, 1981; Robins, Helzer, Ratcliff, & Seyfried, 1982) that was administered at Time 1 only. The DIS is a highly structured interview that was designed for use by lay interviewers in epidemiological research with general community samples. In the DIS validity studies that examined almost all DIS diagnoses, alcohol abuse/dependence had one of the highest levels of inter-interviewer agreement (kappa=.86) and had excellent sensitivity (.86) and specificity (.98). The DIS and Spanish translations of the DIS have been used extensively with Hispanic populations on the U.S. mainland and in Puerto Rico.

Life Stress. Adolescents reported whether or not 18 life events had happened to them within the past 3 months. Eleven of these events were taken from the General Life Events Schedule for Children (GLESC; Sandler, Ramirez, & Reynolds, 1986), and the remaining seven items from other life events schedules used with children and adolescents. The GLESC; items were previously rated by experts as negative and outside of children's control (Sandler & Reynolds, 1987). The events added to the GLESC items also were negative and uncontrollable (e.g., parent arrested, parent lost job, family moved, close friend died). To avoid content overlap with parental alcoholism, items that made explicit reference to parents' alcohol abuse were omitted (e.g., you saw your mom or dad drunk in public). Similarly, items that referred to explicit family conflict were omitted to avoid content overlap with the family conflict scale (which is described later).

Parent Report of Adolescents' Psychological Symptomatology. Adolescents' psychological distress was assessed with items from the Child Behavior Checklist (Achenbach & Edelbrock, 1983), which is used extensively in clinical work and research with children and adolescents. Parents reported on adolescents' behaviors during the past three months. For the present study, parents reported on 35 internalizing symptoms (e.g., depression and anxiety symptoms) and 31 externalizing symptoms (e.g., conduct disorder symptoms).

Adolescents' Alcohol Use. Adolescents' self-reported heavy alcohol consumption was assessed with two questions that asked about the frequency of drinking to intoxication and drinking five or more drinks on one occasion during the past three months. Each item was rated on an 8-point scale that ranged from not at all (0) to every day (7). These two items were summed. Because the distribution of this sum was skewed positively, it was adjusted by a power (.25) transformation.

Parent Substance Use. Mothers and fathers were asked to report their highest frequency of using several illicit substances over their lifetime: marijuana/hashish, cocaine/crack, tranquilizers, barbiturates, amphetamines, hallucinogens, opiates, and inhalants. Frequency was rated on a 9-point scale that ranged from 0 (never) to 8 (every day). Parent drug use was the average frequency of use of these substances. This measure was used only in the Time 1 cross-sectional analyses.

Social Support. The social support scale was adapted from one developed by Furman and Buhrmester (1985). Adolescents responded to six questions concerning the types of social support they received over the preceding three months from key social relationships. For the present study, six relationships were of interest: mother, father, closest sibling, best male friend, best female friend, and closest non-parental adult. The six social support types corresponded to six domains of social relationships that had been identified by Weiss (1974). These were companionship, instrumental aid, intimacy, affection, admiration, and reliable alliance. Furman and Buhrmester (1985) reported extensive reliability and validity information on their original scale. The original scale development did not attempt to evaluate the equivalence of the scale's psychometric properties across several ethnic groups. Like the measure of parental substance use, the measure of social support was used only in the Time 1 cross-sectional analyses.

Procedures

Participants were given the choice of being interviewed in their homes or the project offices. In most cases interviews were conducted in private homes. Each participating family member was interviewed by a separate interviewer. Measures were programmed into laptop computers so that all skip patterns (including the complex patterns in the DIS) were implemented automatically. Interviewers read each item aloud while participants looked at the items and response scales as they appeared on the screen. All responses were closed-ended and entered directly into the computer. To minimize the possibility of being overheard, participants had the option of using computer keys for entering their own responses rather than verbalizing them to the interviewer. Furthermore, participants were informed that a Certificate of Confidentiality had been obtained from the Department of Health and Human Services. Interviews required between 1 and 2 hours for each family member, and families were paid for their participation.

Results

Ethnic Group Comparisons on Background Variables and Parental Alcoholism

A series of chi-square analyses and t tests were conducted to compare Hispanic and Caucasian adolescents on age, gender, parents' education, and parental alcoholism. The groups did not differ on parental alcoholism, age or gender composition. Mothers, t (304) = 4.58, $p < .001$, and fathers, t (304) = 4.67, $p < .001$, of Caucasian adolescents had significantly higher educational attainment than the mothers and fathers of Hispanic adolescents. In subsequent regression analyses, the adolescents' ages and gender were used as predictors because of their importance as correlates of externalizing problems and alcohol use. Parents' education was included as a predictor because it was related to ethnicity. Table 1 shows the means and standard deviations for predictors and criteria for each ethnic group.

Ethnic Group Comparisons on Exposure to Stress

Life stress scores were regressed on parents' education, adolescent's age, adolescent's gender, ethnicity, parental alcoholism, and the interaction of ethnicity and parental alcoholism. Ethnicity was unrelated to life stress, but parental alcoholism was related to life stress, F (1, 298) = 5.06, $p < .05$. The lack of a relation between ethnicity and life stress suggested that Hispanics and Caucasians did not differ in their exposure to life stress events.

Differential Vulnerability to Parental Alcoholism

Multiple regression analyses were conducted in which the following were predictors: parental education, adolescent's age and gender,

Table 1
Descriptive Statistics for Predictors and Criteria

	Hispanics		Caucasians	
	Mean	SD	Mean	SD
Age	12.81	1.42	12.73	1.48
Paternal education[a]	3.70	1.59	4.68	1.53
Maternal education[a]	3.64	1.58	4.53	1.38
Stress	2.59	2.07	2.34	2.10
Social support[b]	-.07	.80	.08	.70
Paternal drug use[c]	.39	.80	.70	1.31
Maternal drug use[c]	.14	.36	.36	.75
Heavy alcohol use	.11	.37	.13	.40
Internalizing (mothers)	.28	.19	.34	.22
Internalizing (fathers)	.29	.25	.29	.20
Externalizing (mothers)	.27	.18	.33	.24
Externalizing (fathers)	.27	.22	.31	.24

[a] Education levels were: 1 = grade school, 2 = some high school, 3 = high school graduate, 4 = technical school, 5 = some college, 6 = college graduate, 7 = graduate or professional school

[b] Social support scores for individual network members were standardized and then averaged to form a composite score.

[c] Response scale points ranged from 0 (never) to 8 (every day).

Table 2
Relation of Parental Alcoholism, Ethnicity, Stress, and
Their Interactions to Adolescent Problem Behaviors

	Alcohol Use Adolescent Report		Internalizing Mother Report		Internalizing Father Report		Externalizing Mother Report		Externalizing Father Report	
	Beta	F	Beta	F	Beta	F	Beta	F	Beta	F
Parental Alcoholism (COA)	.13	5.81*	.05	.79	.13	5.06*	.11	3.91*	.14	5.98*
Ethnicity (Eth)	.03	.32	.18	9.79**	.00	.00	.16	8.41**	.08	2.08
Stress	.10	3.24+	.24	18.52***	.22	14.55***	.27	23.59***	.22	16.27***
COA X Eth	.12	4.42*	-.02	.12	.00	.00	.01	.07	.08	1.90
COA X Stress	.10	3.37+	.02	.16	.06	1.05	.13	5.32*	.10	3.60+
Eth X Stress	.10	3.24+	.11	4.11*	.08	2.22	.05	.74	-.01	0.0

Note: Standardized betas and F's are taken from the full regression model which also included adolescent age, adolescent gender, and parental education.

+ p <.10; * p <.05; ** p <.01; *** p <.001

ethnicity (0=Hispanic, 1=Caucasian), parental alcoholism (0=Control, 1=COA), life stress, and the two-way interactions between ethnicity, parental alcoholism, and stress. Criteria were mother and father reports of internalizing and externalizing symptoms, and adolescent reports of heavy alcohol use.

As shown in Table 2, parental alcoholism was significantly related to all criteria except mothers' reports of internalizing symptoms. These same regression analyses showed that ethnicity was related to mothers' ratings of internalizing and externalizing symptoms. For both criteria, Hispanic adolescents were rated as less distressed than Caucasians.

The interaction between ethnicity and parental alcoholism was one test of differential vulnerability. Of the five criteria, adolescents' ratings of heavy alcohol use showed a significant interaction, $F (1, 294) = 4.42, p < .05$. To interpret this interaction, an analysis of simple slopes was conducted (Aiken & West, 1991). For Caucasians, there was a significant regression of heavy alcohol use on parental alcoholism, beta=.21, $F (1, 297)=10.71, p < .001$. For Hispanics, the slope of the regression line was not significantly different from zero, beta = $-.04$, $F (1, 297) = .14$, NS. A graph of this interaction indicated that Caucasian COAs reported more heavy

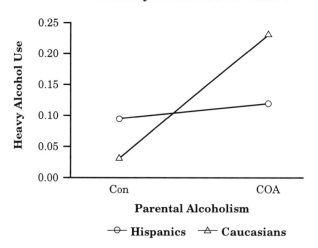

Figure 1
Interaction Between Ethnicity and
Parental Alcoholism for Adolescents' Reports
of Heavy Alcohol Use at Time 1

alcohol use than Caucasian Controls; there was little difference between Hispanic COAs and Hispanic Controls (see Figure 1).

Differential Vulnerability to Life Stress

These regression models also showed that life stress was significantly related to all of the criteria except heavy alcohol use (see Table 2). In tests of differential vulnerability to stress, the interaction between ethnicity and stress was significant for mothers' ratings of internalizing symptoms, F (1, 295) = 4.11, p < .05. The shape of this interaction was similar to that for the interaction of parental alcoholism and ethnicity (see Figure 2).

The analysis of simple slopes for Caucasians showed a significant regression of mothers' reports of internalizing on stress, beta=.31, F (1, 297) = 23.96, p < .001. The corresponding analysis for Hispanics was not significant, beta = .02, F (1, 297) = .03, NS. This interaction suggested greater vulnerability to stress by Caucasian adolescents.

Figure 2
Interaction Between Ethnicity and
Life Stress Events for Mothers' Reports
of Internalizing Symptoms at Time 1

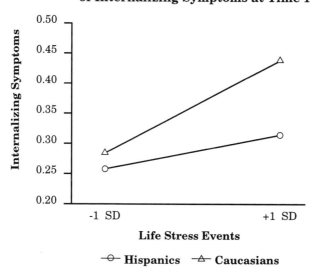

Interactions Between Parental Alcoholism and Stress

The regression analyses included tests of the interaction between parental alcoholism and life stress. As shown in Table 2, this interaction was significant for mothers' reports of symptoms, F (1, 296) = 5.32, p < .05. As shown in Figure 3, the relation of stress to mothers' reports of externalizing symptoms was stronger for COAs than for Controls. The test for the simple slopes showed a significant effect for COAs, beta = .39, F (1, 297) = 30.47, p < .0001, but not for Controls, beta = .13, F (1, 297) = 2.39, NS.

Figure 3
Interaction Between Parental Alcoholism and Life Stress Events for Mothers' Reports of Externalizing Symptoms at Time 1

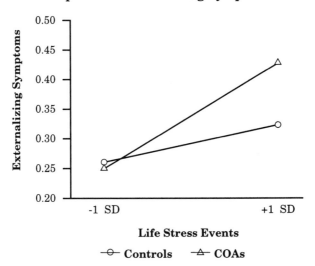

Exploring Explanations for Differential Vulnerability

Social Support. In an initial analysis, social support was regressed on background variables, ethnicity, parental alcoholism, stress and the interaction of these last three variables. Regression analyses showed that stress was negatively related to social support, F (1, 299) = 4.82, p < .03, but social support was not related to ethnicity, parental alcoholism, or to any of the interactions between ethnicity, parental alcoholism, and stress.

In tests to determine if Hispanics' social support could account for their lower vulnerability to stress and parental alcoholism, social support was entered into the regression models that predicted the criteria. Social support was significantly related to mothers' reports of internalizing symptoms, F (1, 294) = 6.64, p < .02, however, all of the significant interactions shown in Table 2 remained significant after accounting for the effects of social support. From these tests, social support did not explain differential vulnerability.

Parental Substance Use. Because the LA ECA study (Karno et al., 1987), found that Hispanic men and women reported less illicit substance use than Caucasian men and women, a similar analysis was conducted with the present data. If parents of Caucasian adolescents had more co-occurring substance use than parents of Hispanics, this could explain the greater vulnerability of Caucasians. In separate analyses, mothers' and fathers' illicit substance use were regressed on ethnicity, parental alcoholism, stress, and their interactions. For mothers' substance use, stress, F (1, 296) = 7.36, p < .01; parental alcoholism, F (1, 296) = 15.03, p < .001; and ethnicity, F (1, 296) = 6.90, p < .01; showed significant effects. Mothers of COAs and Caucasians reported more substance use than mothers of Hispanic adolescents and Controls. For fathers' substance use, parental alcoholism, F (1, 296) = 30.36, p < .001; and ethnicity, F (1, 296) = 7.26, p < .01; showed similar effects.

To explore the possibility that mothers' and fathers' substance use could account for differential vulnerability effects, regression models were re-run with the addition of mothers' and fathers' substance use. The significant interaction between ethnicity and parental alcoholism, ethnicity and stress, and parental alcoholism and stress all remained statistically significant after the inclusion of parental substance use. Thus, parental substance use did not account for differential vulnerability.

A Longitudinal Extension

The initial study had several limitations and raised questions that called for additional research. First, because interactions between life stress, ethnicity, and parental alcoholism were infrequently examined in previous research, it was important to replicate the effects. Second, the initial study was cross-sectional and, therefore, was unable to determine if life stress and its interactions with ethnicity and parental alcoholism were prospectively related to psychological distress and alcohol use. Finally, the initial study failed to identify factors that could explain the greater stress vulnerability of Caucasians and adolescents who had alcoholic parents. The second set of analyses addressed these issues by evaluating the initial sample of families in two more annual assessments. This allowed (a) replication of the initial cross-sectional analyses and (b) prospective prediction of adolescents' alcohol use and psychological distress from prior assessments of life stress.

We also evaluated family conflict as a variable that might explain differential vulnerability. Although no clear link between Hispanic ethnicity and family conflict had been established in prior research, previous studies had found an association between parental alcoholism and family conflict (Benson & Heller, 1988; Roosa, Beals, Sandler, & Pillow, 1990). The presence of conflict in a family should impair its ability to communicate effectively and engage in problem solving. Consistent with this argument, impaired problem solving has been reported in alcoholic families (Sher, 1991). Thus, elevated levels of family conflict might at least account for COA's heightened vulnerability to stress.

To include family conflict as a predictor in analyses of Time 2 and Time 3 data, a 4-item, adolescent self-report scale was constructed from family items that Bloom (1985) used in his factor analytic study of family functioning. The items "we fought a lot in our family," "family members sometimes got so angry they threw things," "family members hardly ever lost their tempers" (reversed scored), and "family members sometimes hit each other" were rated on 5-point scales that ranged from strongly agree to strongly disagree. The internal consistency reliabilities of the scale at the two waves of measurement were .73 and .71.

Results

Cross-Sectional Analyses at Time 2 and Time 3

Table 3 shows descriptive statistics for predictors and criteria separately for Hispanic and Caucasian participants at Time 2 and Time 3.

Table 3
Descriptive Statistics for Continuous Predictors and Criteria: Statistics for
Hispanic and Caucasian Adolescents at Time 2 and Time 3

| | Hispanics | | | | Caucasians | | | |
| | Time 2 | | Time 3 | | Time 2 | | Time 3 | |
	Mean	SD	Mean	SD	Mean	SD	Mean	SD
1. Age	13.79	1.47	14.79	1.49	13.67	1.45	14.64	1.46
2. Parental Education	3.83	1.29	3.77	1.31	4.66	1.19	4.66	1.19
3. Stress	3.78	2.60	3.07	2.36	3.38	2.58	3.09	2.48
4. Family conflict	3.55	.76	3.79	.69	3.73	.84	3.84	.76
5. Adolescent alcohol use	.14	.43	.23	.52	.13	.40	.23	.51
6. Internalizing - mother report	.28	.22	.28	.21	.33	.24	.31	.23
7. Internalizing - father report	.28	.23	.28	.26	.29	.21	.27	.20
8. Externalizing - mother report	.27	.22	.25	.19	.33	.26	.32	.26
9. Externalizing - father report	.27	.20	.28	.21	.31	.25	.31	.26

Regression analyses of cross-sectional data included the same predictors used in the Time 1 analyses: (a) background variables of adolescent's age and gender, and parental education, (b) parental alcoholism (control=0, COA = 1), (c) ethnicity (Hispanic=0, Caucasian=1), (d) life stress, and (e) all two-way interactions between ethnicity, parental alcoholism, and stress. Separate regression models were tested for each of the five criteria (mother and father reports of internalizing and externalizing, and adolescent reports of heavy alcohol use). Cross-sectional analyses at Time 2 showed that parental alcoholism was related to all criteria and stress was related to all criteria except adolescents' alcohol use (see Table 4). These effects replicated those found at Time 1 with one exception. A significant relation between parental alcoholism and maternal reports of internalizing symptoms was found at Time 2 that had not been observed at Time 1.

Ethnicity was significantly related to maternal reports of both internalizing and externalizing criteria, just as it had been at Time 1. Caucasian adolescents were rated as more distressed than Hispanic adolescents. In addition to these average effects, four significant interactions were observed. Similar to the results at Time 1, stress interacted with parental alcoholism in the prediction of maternal reports of externalizing, and stress interacted with ethnicity in the prediction of maternal reports of internalizing. These interactions showed that Caucasian adolescents were more adversely affected by stress than Hispanic adolescents (see Figure 4), and adolescent COAs were more adversely affected by stress than control group adolescents (see Figure 5). Tests of simple slopes (Aiken & West, 1991) confirmed that stress was significantly related to mothers' reports

Table 4
Cross-Sectional Analyses At Time 2: Relation of Parental Alcoholism, Ethnicity, Stress, and Their Interactions to Adolescent Problem Behaviors

	Alcohol use Adolescent Report		Internalizing Mother Report		Internalizing Father Report		Externalizing Mother Report		Externalizing Father Report	
	Beta	F	Beta	F	Beta	F	Beta	F	Beta	F
Parental Alcoholism (COA)	.20	13.45***	.14	6.12*	.20	12.70***	.18	9.73**	.18	9.88**
Ethnicity (Eth)	.02	.09	.12	3.94*	.02	.17	.13	5.52*	.10	3.37+
Stress	.10	3.04	.14	5.92*	.22	14.60***	.17	8.95**	.22	15.38***
COA X Eth	.07	1.46	-.05	.66	-.03	.42	.03	.39	.08	2.30
COA X Stress	.04	.56	-.05	.83	.10	3.17+	.11	3.86*	.16	7.89**
Eth X Stress	.03	.20	.12	4.31*	.11	3.60+	.12	4.13*	.07	1.64
	R	F	R	F	R	F	R	F	R	F
Full Model	.41	6.67***	.28	2.83**	.38	5.31***	.38	5.46***	.43	7.27***

Note: Standardized betas and F's are taken from the full regression model which also included adolescent age, adolescent gender, and parental education.

+ p <.07; * p <.05; ** p <.01; *** p <.001

Figure 4
Interaction Between Ethnicity
and Life Stress Events for Mothers'
Reports of Internalizing Symptoms at Time 2

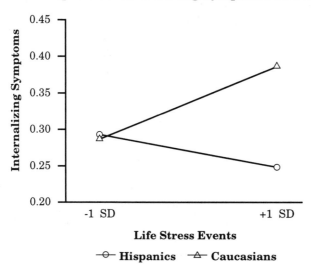

of externalizing for COAs, but not for controls. Similarly, stress was significantly related to mothers' reports of internalizing for Caucasians, but not for Hispanics.

In addition to these interactions that replicated Time 1 findings, two interactions were found at Time 2 that were not found at Time 1. Parental alcoholism interacted with stress in the prediction of fathers' reports of externalizing, and ethnicity interacted with stress in the prediction of mothers' reports of externalizing symptoms. Like the other interactions, these results showed that COAs and Caucasians were more vulnerable to stress than controls and Hispanics.

With the Time 3 analyses, none of the interactions observed at Time 1 and Time 2 was found. However, similar to findings at Time 1 and Time 2, stress was related to all criteria and parental alcoholism was related to the father- and adolescent-report criteria (see Table 5).

Figure 5
Interaction Between Parental Alcoholism
and Life Stress Events for Mothers'
Reports of Externalizing Symptoms at Time 2

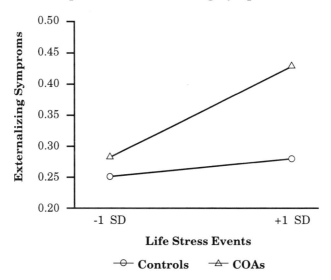

Prospective Analyses

Prospective analyses of criteria at Time 2 included the Time 1 predictors used in the cross-sectional models and the Time 1 measure of each criterion. Thus, these analyses used predictors that were assessed one year prior to the assessment of the criteria and statistically adjusted for prior symptomatology. Results showed that parental alcoholism was prospectively related to all criteria with the exception of fathers' reports of externalizing (see Table 6).

In addition, there were three significant interactions. Significant interactions were found between parental alcoholism and stress for fathers' reports of externalizing, and internalizing. Ethnicity and stress interacted in the prediction of fathers' reports of symptomatology such that stress was significantly related to symptomatology for Caucasians, but not for Hispanics. Also, stress was related to internalizing for COAs, but not for controls.

The prospective analyses of Time 2 and Time 3 data showed only one prospective effect. Time 2 stress was related to fathers'

Table 5
Cross-Sectional Analyses At Time 3: Relation of Parental Alcoholism, Ethnicity, Stress, and Their Interactions to Adolescent Problem Behaviors

	Alcohol Use Adolescent Report		Internalizing Mother Report		Internalizing Father Report		Externalizing Mother Report		Externalizing Father Report	
	Beta	F	Beta	F	Beta	F	Beta	F	Beta	F
Parental Alcoholism (COA)	.15	7.64**	.07	1.40	.17	8.29**	.06	1.20	.16	7.72**
Ethnicity (Eth)	.01	.05	.08	1.64	.00	.00	.16	7.33**	.07	1.53
Stress	.28	26.38***	.13	4.74*	.19	10.76**	.22	14.75***	.24	18.17***
COA X Eth	.10	3.32+	.01	.02	-.02	.10	.08	1.96	.09	2.93+
COA X Stress	.07	1.61	.02	.15	.09	2.15	.05	.70	.08	1.94
Eth X Stress	-.04	.60	.04	.36	.01	.05	.08	2.04	.07	1.59
	R	F	R	F	R	F	R	F	R	F
Full Model	.43	7.32***	.22	1.68	.31	3.39***	.37	5.24***	.42	6.52***

Note: Standardized betas and F's are taken from the full regression model which also included adolescent age, adolescent gender, and parental education.

+ p <.09; * p <.05; ** p <.01; *** p <.001

ratings of externalizing symptoms at Time 3, F (1,268) = 5.68, p < .05. None of the interactions was significant.

Testing Family Conflict as an Explanation for Vulnerability Effects

Tests to determine if family conflict could account for the stress vulnerability of Caucasian and COA adolescents were guided by Baron and Kenny's (1986) description of mediated-moderation and moderated-mediation. Figures 6 and 7 illustrate the distinction between these two mechanisms and the hypothesized causal chains. Each of the models is tested in several steps that specify different regression equations showing significant relations between (a) stress and the criteria, (b) stress and family conflict, and (c) family conflict and the criteria. Moreover, to establish mediated-moderation, the inclusion of family conflict into the regression model should eliminate or substantially reduce the statistically significant interaction between stress and the relevant moderator (parental alcoholism or ethnicity). The stress vulnerability of Caucasians, for example, could be explained by family conflict if the relation of stress to family conflict was stronger for Caucasians than for Hispanics. Within a model of mediated-moderation, family conflict, in turn, would lead to adolescents' problem behavior (see Figure 6).

To establish moderated-mediation, the inclusion of the *interaction* between family conflict and the moderator (e.g., parental alcoholism) should eliminate the significant interaction between stress and the moderator. In this example, family conflict's relation to adolescent problem behavior would be greater for COAs than for controls (see Figure 7).

Cross-Sectional Analyses

As a preliminary step in testing family conflict's role as a mediator of interaction effects, family conflict at Time 2 was regressed on ethnicity, life stress, parental alcoholism and the 2-way interactions between the predictors. This analysis showed that life stress, and the interaction between ethnicity and life stress were significant predictors of family conflict (see Table 7). The relation between stress and family conflict was stronger for Caucasians than for Hispanics. Tests of simple slopes showed that stress was not significantly related to family conflict for Hispanics, F (1, 297) = 2.70, NS, but it was highly significant for Caucasians, F (1, 297) = 32.04, p < .0001.

Table 6
Prospective Effects of Time 1 Predictors and Symptoms on Time 2 Criteria

	Alcohol Use Child Report		Internalizing Mother Report		Internalizing Father Report		Externalizing Mother Report		Externalizing Father Report	
	Beta	F	Beta	F	Beta	F	Beta	F	Beta	F
Parental Alcoholism(COA)	.16	10.47***	.09	4.10*	.11	7.11**	.08	4.89*	.06	3.27+
Ethnicity (Eth)	-.01	.05	.02	.32	.02	.18	.01	.04	.03	.70
Stress	-.01	.07	.05	1.20	.03	.56	.03	.62	.04	.90
COA X Eth	.02	.17	-.01	-.10	.03	.64	.02	.41	.03	.60
COA X Stress	.02	.26	.00	.00	.09	4.64*	.05	1.51	.10	7.60**
Eth X Stress	-.04	.84	.02	.16	.08	3.27+	.06	2.96+	.10	7.70**
	R	F	R	F	R	F	R	F	R	F
Full Model	.57	13.95***	.71	29.02***	.74	35.06***	.79	47.08***	.82	58.52***

Note: Standardized betas and F's are taken from the full regression model which also included child age, child gender, and parental education.

+ p <.09; * p <.05; ** p <.01; *** p <.001

Figure 6
A Model of Mediated-Moderation

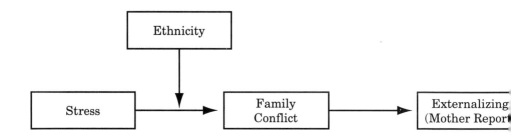

Figure 7
A Model of Moderated-Mediation

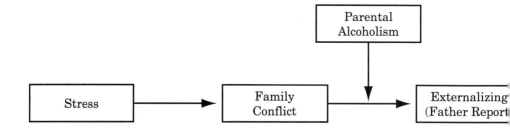

As a second step in the test of mediation, family conflict was included in the regression model with ethnicity, life stress, parental alcoholism, and their interactions in the prediction of only those criteria for which stress vulnerability effects were found (mothers' ratings of internalizing and externalizing symptoms, and fathers' ratings of externalizing). For mothers' ratings of internalizing symptoms, family conflict was a significant predictor, F (1, 294) = 5.05, $p < .03$. When family conflict was entered into the regression model, the effects of life stress and the interaction between life stress and ethnicity were reduced to nonsignificance. As a result, family conflict *did* appear to account for both the effects of stress and the differential vulnerability of Caucasians to life stress (i.e., mediated-moderation).

In the regression analysis of mothers' ratings of externalizing, family conflict was a significant predictor, F (1, 294) = 25.74, $p < .0001$. When family conflict was entered into the regression model, the effects of life stress and the interaction between ethnicity and life stress were reduced to nonsignificance. Identical to the findings for mothers' ratings of internalizing, family conflict accounted for both the effects of stress and the differential vulnerability of Caucasians to life stress (i.e., mediated-moderation).

When fathers' ratings of externalizing was the criterion, family conflict was a significant predictor, F (1, 284) = 26.11, $p < .0001$. Introducing family conflict into the regression model did not eliminate the significant interaction between parental alcoholism and stress. Thus, this analysis did not provide evidence of mediated-moderation. In contrast, the interaction between parental alcoholism and family conflict in the prediction of fathers' reports of externalizing was significant, F (1, 283) = 11.19, $p < .001$, and did reduce the interaction of parental alcoholism and stress to nonsignificance. In the language of Baron and Kenny (1986), this was evidence of moderated-mediation. Tests of simple slopes showed that family conflict was not significantly related to fathers' ratings of externalizing for controls, F (1, 283) = 2.62, NS, but it was significant for COAs, F (1, 283) = 37.40, $p < .0001$.

Prospective Analyses

There were three significant interactions in the prospective analyses shown in Table 6: (a) parental alcoholism and stress in the prediction of fathers' reports of externalizing, (b) ethnicity and stress in the prediction of fathers' reports of externalizing, and (c) parental alcoholism and stress in the prediction of fathers' reports of

Table 7
Regression Models to Assess Family Conflicts' Role in Mediating Stress and Stress Vulnerability: Tests of Mediated-Moderation and Moderated-Mediation at Time 2

	Internalizing Mother Report			Externalizing Mother Report			Externalizing Father Report			Family Conflict
	1[a]	2[b]	3[c]	1[a]	2[b]	3[c]	1[a]	2[b]	3[c]	
Parental Alcoholism (COA)	.14*	.13*	.14*	.18**	.15**	.16**	.18**	.15**	.15**	.10
Ethnicity (Eth)	.12*	.12*	.12*	.13*	.15**	.14**	.10	.12*	.11*	-.05
Stress	.14*	.09	.09	.17**	.06	.04	.22***	.10	.08	.39***
Family Conflict (Conf)		.12*	.12+		.28***	.28***		.30***	.30***	
Conf x COA			.06			.07			.16**	
Conf x Eth			.04			.10			.11*	
COA x Eth	-.05	-.04	-.05	.03	.05	.04	.08	.09	.09	-.05
COA x Stress	-.05	-.05	-.05	.11*	.10	.07	.16**	.14**	.08	.05
Eth x Stress	.12*	.10	.08	.12*	.07	.05	.07	.04	.00	.15*

* p<.05, ** p<.01, *** p<.001

NOTE: All numbers are standardized beta coefficients taken from the final regression model at each step.

[a] This regression model included child's age, gender, and parental education in addition to the predictors shown.

[b] This regression added just family conflict to the regression model in step 1.

[c] This regression added family conflicts' interactions with ethnicity and parental alcoholism to the regression in step 2.

internalizing. However, there was no evidence that family conflict could explain any of the prospective interaction effects for stress, parental alcoholism, and ethnicity. Family conflict was not prospectively related to these criteria. Furthermore, neither family conflict nor family conflict's interactions with ethnicity and parental alcoholism were prospectively related to the criteria.

Discussion

This research began with the basic aim of determining if Hispanic and Caucasian adolescents would show different vulnerabilities to stress and parental alcoholism. Consistent with the spirit of this volume, our research did demonstrate the resilience of Hispanic adolescents to life stress. This is one of the few direct demonstrations of stress resilience for Hispanics, particularly for Hispanic adolescents (cf. Dornbusch et al., 1991). Furthermore, the differential vulnerability to stress that was observed at Time 1 was largely replicated at Time 2 and in prospective analyses based on Time 1 and Time 2 assessments. Obviously, this replication and longitudinal extension were important additions to the Time 1 results because tests of stress resilience with Hispanic youth are so rare in the literature. The prospective analyses were particularly valuable because they lacked the limitations of cross-sectional tests. We also were careful to avoid the ambiguities of analyses based entirely from measures drawn from a single reporter. A central predictor, life stress, was taken from adolescents' reports, but the psychological distress criteria were all drawn from parents' reports. The prospective analyses and the use of multiple reporters provided compelling support for the contention that life stress and its interaction with parental alcoholism and ethnicity contributed to the development of adolescents' problem behaviors.

In addition to demonstrating Hispanic adolescents' resilience to stress, the study also identified a possible explanation for it. Unlike earlier studies of ethnic minorities' resilience to stress that did not find a viable mechanism, we found limited evidence for one possible pathway whereby stress contributed to adolescents' symptomatology. Family conflict accounted for stress' interactions with ethnicity in the Time 2 cross-sectional analyses. This suggested the possibility that Caucasian youth were more vulnerable because stress was more likely to lead to family conflict for them than it was for Hispanics. Family conflict, in turn, was related to externalizing symptoms. Why should stress and family conflict be more firmly linked for Caucasians than they are for Hispanics? Our research did not answer this question. Caucasian adolescents did not report more stress or family conflict than Hispanic adolescents. If Caucasians had inferior skills for preventing stress from developing into family conflict, we would have observed more family conflict in Caucasian families than in Hispanic families. This was not observed. Instead, these findings suggest the presence of other moderating conditions that prevent stress and family conflict to be highly related processes in Hispanic families. This is a topic for future research.

There were other limitations to our research methods and results. Because this research did not account for any of the effects found in the prospective analyses, family conflict was only a partial explanation for differential vulnerability. In the future, there are certainly other factors besides family conflict that might be explored as explanations for differential vulnerability. In a study of substance use initiation of Caucasian, African- and Asian-American fifth graders, racial group differences were found in a variety of family management, discipline, and involvement variables (Catalano et al., 1992). The three racial groups showed different patterns of relations between substance use and some of these family and parenting variables (e.g., revocation of privileges, attachment to parents, selection of friends). It is possible that some of the family factors explored by Catalano et al. (1992) might explain interactions between ethnicity and stress in the same way family conflict did in the present study.

An alternative explanation for the stress resilience we found in this research is that Hispanic adolescents experienced important stress events that were not assessed by the general stress measure we used. Because Hispanics showed relatively weaker relations between stress and measures of both family conflict and psychological distress, it is possible that the stress measure lacked the same "validity" that it had for Caucasians. A goal of future research should be to identify not only potential moderators of ethnicity's interaction with life stress, but to re-evaluate how well we sample the relevant stress events that occur to Hispanic and Caucasian adolescents. One aspect of conducting culturally sensitive community research on this topic is to determine those stress events that are unique to Hispanics (the emic aspects of stress) as well as those aspects that Hispanics share in common with others (the etic aspects) (Barrera, Zautra, & Baca, 1984).

These analyses drew crude distinctions between Hispanic and Caucasian adolescents as an initial demonstration of stress vulnerability and resilience. They did not explore cultural factors per se or variability within the Hispanic subgroup that might have provided further insights into the source of Hispanics' resilience to stress. In future research it would be advantageous to have a large sample of Hispanic adolescents who were heterogeneous on acculturation. If culture played a role in shaping parents' patterns of alcohol use (e.g., the extent to which heavy drinking is done in the home), expression of affect in response to stress, parenting practices or family communication around problem solving, having variability in acculturation should provide for good tests of its influence.

Despite the need for additional research on questions that were not answered by this study, these results have several implications for interventions directed at stress prevention and adaptation to stress. Preventing the occurrence of parental alcoholism and stress events that stem from it are difficult, but worthwhile goals. The events included in our life stress measure were uncontrollable from the adolescent's perspective, but many could have been prevented by parents. Even when parental alcoholism cannot be prevented, there is value to secondary and tertiary prevention approaches that are directed at reducing the many problems that can be associated with a parent's alcoholism. These problems are the stressful life events that are not controlled by children (e.g., parent lost job, parent arrested), but that have substantial effects on their psychological distress.

Interventions designed to reduce family conflict might also be effective ways to prevent the deleterious consequences of parental alcoholism and life stress. In the various regression models that were tested, family conflict appeared to function as a mediator of stress, and as a variable that exacerbated the effects of stress and parental alcoholism. Although the models differed somewhat, they all had a common implication; reducing family conflict would reduce adolescents' problem behavior and psychological distress. Family conflict is, presumably, a problem that is amenable to preventive interventions. Whether effective preventive interventions that focus on family conflict can be developed for ethnically diverse communities or for families that contain alcoholic parents has yet to be determined. One hope is that a better understanding of the resilience of Hispanics and other ethnic minority groups will inform the development of such interventions.

Note

1. This research was supported by Grant DA05227 from the National Institute on Drug Abuse to Laurie Chassin (principal investigator) and Manuel Barrera, Jr. (co-principal investigator). Susan Li was supported by an American Psychological Association Minority Fellowship Award. The tables and figures appeared previously in the *American Journal of Community Psychology* (Plenum Press).

References

Achenbach, T., & Edelbrock, C. (1983). *Manual for the Child Behavior Checklist and Revised Child Behavior Profile.* Burlington, VT: University of Vermont, Department of Psychiatry.

Aiken, L. S., & West, S. G. (1991). *Multiple regression: Testing and interpreting interactions.* Newbury Park, CA: Sage.

Baron, R. M., & Kenny, D. A. (1986). The moderator-mediator variable distinction in social psychological research: Conceptual, strategic, and statistical considerations. *Journal of Personality and Social Psychology, 51,* 1173–1182.

Barrera, M., Jr. (1982). Raza populations. In L. R. Snowden (Ed.), *Reaching the underserved* (pp. 119–142). Beverly Hills, CA: Sage.

Barrera, M., Jr., Li, S. A., & Chassin, L. (1993). Ethnic group differences in vulnerability to parental alcoholism and life stress: A study of Hispanic and non-Hispanic Caucasian adolescents. *American Journal of Community Psychology, 21,* 15–35.

Barrera, M., Jr., Li, S. A., & Chassin, L. (in press). Effects of parental alcoholism and life stress on Hispanic and non-Hispanic Caucasian adolescents: A prospective study. *American Journal of Community Psychology* (accepted with revisions).

Barrera, M., Jr., & Reese, F. (1993). Natural social support systems and Hispanic substance abuse. In R. S. Myers, B. L. Kail, & T. D. Watts (Eds.), *Hispanic substance abuse* (pp. 115–130). Springfield, IL: Charles C Thomas.

Barrera, M., Jr., Zautra, A., & Baca, L. M. (1984). Some research considerations in studying stress and distress of Mexican Americans. In J. L. Martinez & R. H. Mendoza (Eds.), *Chicano psychology* (2nd ed., pp. 223–247). New York: Academic Press.

Benson, C. S., & Heller, K. (1988). Factors in the current adjustment of young adult daughters of alcoholic and problem drinking fathers. *Journal of Abnormal Psychology, 96,* 305–312.

Bloom, B. (1985). A factor analysis of self-report measures of family functioning. *Family Process, 24,* 225–239.

Brown, S. A. (1989). Life events of adolescents in relation to personal and parental substance abuse. *American Journal of Psychiatry, 146,* 484–489.

Burnam, M. A., Hough, R. L., Escobar, J. I., Karno, M., Timbers, D. M., Telles, C. A., & Locke, B. Z. (1987). Six-month prevalence of specific psychiatric disorders among Mexican Americans and non-Hispanic Whites in Los Angeles. *Archives of General Psychiatry, 44,* 687–694.

Catalano, R. F., Morrison, D. M., Wells, E. A., Gillmore, M. R., Iritani, B., & Hawkins, J. D. (1992). Ethnic differences in family factors related to early drug initiation. *Journal of Studies on Alcohol, 53,* 208–217.

Chassin, L., Pillow, D. R., Curran, P. J., Molina, B. S. G., & Barrera, M., Jr. (1993). Relation of parent alcoholism to early adolescent substance use: A test of three mediating mechanisms. *Journal of Abnormal Psychology, 102,* 3–19.

Chassin, L., Rogosch, F., & Barrera, M., Jr. (1991). Substance use and symptomatology among adolescent children of alcoholics. *Journal of Abnormal Psychology, 100,* 449–463.

Dohrenwend, B. P., & Dohrenwend, B. S. (1981). Socioenvironmental factors, stress, and psychopathology. *American Journal of Community Psychology, 9,* 128–159.

Dornbusch, S. M., Mont-Reynaud, R., Ritter, P. L., Chen, Z., & Steinberg, L. (1991). Stressful events and their correlates among adolescents of diverse backgrounds. In M. E. Colten & S. Gore (Eds.), *Adolescent stress: Causes and consequences* (pp. 111–130). New York: Aldine de Gruyter.

Furman, W., & Buhrmester, D. (1985). Children's perceptions of the personal relationships in their social networks. *Developmental Psychology, 21,* 1014–1024.

Gilbert, M. J., & Cervantes, R. C. (1986). Patterns and practices of alcohol use among Mexican Americans: A comprehensive review. *Hispanic Journal of Behavioral Sciences, 8,* 1–60.

Golding, J. M., & Burnam, M. A. (1990). Stress and social support as predictors of depressive symptoms in Mexican Americans and non-Hispanic Whites. *Journal of Social and Clinical Psychology, 9,* 268–286.

Karno, M., Hough, R. L., Burnam, M. A., Escobar, J. I., Timbers, D. M., Santana, F., & Boyd, J. H. (1987). Lifetime prevalence of specific psychiatric disorders among Mexican Americans and non-Hispanic whites in Los Angeles. *Archives of General Psychiatry, 44,* 695–701.

Keefe, S. E., & Casas, J. M. (1980). Mexican Americans and mental health: A selected review and recommendations for mental health service delivery. *American Journal of Community Psychology, 8,* 303–326.

Kessler, R. C. (1979). Stress, social status, and psychological distress. *Journal of Health and Social Behavior, 20,* 259–272.

Mirowsky, J., & Ross, C. E. (1980). Minority status, ethnic culture, and distress: A comparison of Blacks, Whites, Mexicans, and Mexican Americans. *American Journal of Sociology, 86,* 479–495.

Monroe, S. M., & Simons, A. D. (1991). Diathesis-stress theories in the context of life stress research: Implications for the depressive disorders. *Psychological Bulletin, 10,* 406–425.

Robins, L. N., Helzer, J. E., Croughan, J., & Ratcliff, K.S. (1981). National Institute of Mental Health Diagnostic Interview Schedule: Its history, characteristics, and validity. *Archives of General Psychiatry, 38,* 381–389.

Robins, L. N., Helzer, J. E., Ratcliff, K. S., & Seyfried, W. (1982). Validity of the Diagnostic Interview Schedule, version II: DSM-III diagnoses. *Psychological Medicine, 12,* 855–870.

Roosa, M., Beals, J., Sandler, I. N., & Pillow, D. R. (1990). The role of risk and protective factors in predicting symptomatology in adolescent children of alcoholics. *American Journal of Community Psychology, 18,* 725–741.

Roosa, M., Sandler, I., Gehring, M., Beals, J., & Cappo, L. (1988). The Children of Alcoholics Life Events Schedule: A stress scale for children of alcohol-abusing parents. *Journal of Studies on Alcohol, 49,* 422–429.

Sandler, I., Ramirez, R., & Reynolds, K. (1986). *Life stress for children of divorce, bereaved, and asthmatic children.* Paper presented at the 94th Annual Convention of the American Psychological Association, Washington, DC.

Sandler, I., & Reynolds, K. (1987). *Controllability and desirability ratings of life events.* Unpublished manuscript, Arizona State University, Tempe.

Sher, K. J. (1991). *Children of alcoholics: A critical appraisal of theory and research.* Chicago: University of Chicago Press.

Weiss, R. S. (1974). The provisions of social relations. In Z. Rubin (Ed.), *Doing unto others.* Englewood Cliffs, NJ: Prentice-Hall.

Chapter 16

Parental Support for Mexican-American Children's School Achievement[1]

Lynn Okagaki and Peter A. Frensch

Despite efforts to improve the educational status of minority students in the United States, numerous studies continue to find that Hispanic children are not doing as well in school as their Euro-American counterparts (see Fernandez, Paulsen, & Hirano-Nakanishi, 1989; Humphreys, 1988; Rumberger, 1987). Hispanic students in the United States are more likely to leave school prior to high school graduation, to be overage for their grade in school, and to score below national norms on school achievement tests at both elementary and secondary levels (see Cortes, 1986; Garcia, 1992; Sue & Padilla, 1986; Walker, 1987). What is often overlooked is that many Hispanic children are doing well in school. This chapter will examine the relation between home and school environments for Mexican-American children. What factors need to be considered to understand how the home environment influences Mexican-American children's school achievement? While we recognize that the relation between home and school is a dynamic one and that both home and school environments need to be examined, the focus of this chapter is on the contributions parents make to their children's school achievement. First, empirical evidence on various facets of parental support will be discussed, and then the major theoretical perspectives on minority children's school achievement will be considered.

Facets of Parental Support

Five aspects of parental support for children's school achievement will be examined: educational values, educational expectations, instrumental support for schoolwork, understanding the educational process, and beliefs about barriers to success.

Educational Values

Ethnographic case studies (see Delgado-Gaitan, 1987, 1992; Goldenberg, 1987, 1989) have found that Mexican-American parents provide emotional support and encouragement for their children's schoolwork and are concerned about how their children are doing in school. In Delgado-Gaitan's (1987) study of three immigrant families, parents indicated that a good education was very important for their children's futures. Similarly, in their interviews with 123 Hispanic mothers, Stevenson, Chen, and Uttal (1990) reported that the mothers believed that getting good grades was very important. (Note: In this study, the Hispanic families were not identified by country of origin.)

In our own work (Okagaki, Frensch, & Gordon, 1994), we have examined the beliefs and behaviors of Mexican-American parents to gain a better understanding of family influences that are correlated with school success and failure among Mexican-American elementary school children. The focus has been on parents' educational values and expectations, their perceptions of their children's ability to do schoolwork and their own ability to help their children with schoolwork, beliefs about education, and their perceptions of racial barriers that their children might encounter in life. To examine parental beliefs that may encourage school achievement, we examined the beliefs of 82 parents of fourth- and fifth-grade Mexican-American children in northern California. In this study, high achievers ($n=33$) consisted of those children who scored in stanines 7-9 on their school achievement tests. Low achievers ($n=49$) were those children who scored in stanines 1-3 on their achievement tests. Children in special education classes were excluded from the sample. Parents were given questionnaires in English and in Spanish. We found that parents of high- and low-achieving Mexican-American children did not differ in their belief that education is very important in general, and more specifically, that having a good education was important for their own child as a means to obtaining a good job as an adult. Similarly, parents of high and low achievers did not differ in the amount of the education they *ideally* wanted their child to attain. Most parents indicated that they hoped their child would graduate from college and even obtain a graduate or professional degree.

A consistent finding, then, in the literature is that Mexican-American parents believe education is important for their children. They value education and want their children to do well in school.

Educational Expectations

Even if parents believe that education is important, they may not have very high standards or expectations for their children's school achievement. Stevenson and his colleagues (Stevenson & Lee, 1990; Stevenson, Lee, & Stigler, 1986) have argued that children are not likely to do better if their parents are satisfied with their current performance. In our study of high- and low-achieving Mexican-American children, parents did not differ in their expectations for their children's educational attainment. Specifically, both groups expected their children to graduate from college. However, parents of high-achieving Mexican-American children were more likely to set a higher minimum boundary on school attainment. About half of the parents in each group maintained that they would not allow their child to quit school until the child had obtained at least a college degree. However, of those parents who did not set a minimum educational level at having a college degree, more parents of high achievers wanted children to get at least some vocational or college training after high school than did parents of low achievers.

Another indication of the educational expectations that parents hold is their response to children's grades. We asked parents of high and low achievers how they would feel if their child brought home an A, B, C, D, or F on his or her schoolwork. Parents of high achievers set a higher standard for their children. While there were no differences between parents of high and low achievers in their responses to grades of A's, B's, or F's, parents of high achievers were more likely to say they would be upset if their child brought home C's or D's than parents of low achievers were.

Clearly, parents' responses to grades may be a function of the child's prior school performance. To determine if lack of concern on the part of parents of low achievers for grades of C's and D's was the result of children's past performance, parental responses to C's and D's were crosstabulated with the parents' account of the grades their children receive (i.e., we asked parents to report the child's language, reading, math, and science grades). If *only* children who received A's and B's on their schoolwork are considered, then the parents of high achievers who received A's and B's on average are still more likely to report that they would be upset if their children brought home C's and D's than parents of low achievers who received A's and B's. In other words, parents of low achievers were more likely to be satisfied with grades of C's and D's than were parents of high achievers. This satisfaction was *not* related to the parents' reports of the grades their child typically receives. It seems that parents of low achievers were satisfied if their child made passing grades. Thus, even though parents of high and low achievers did not differ in the degree to which they valued education or in the level of schooling they expected their children to attain, by setting a higher minimum level of schooling and by not being satisfied with grades of C's and D's, parents of high achievers may establish higher educational standards for their children. Obviously, an alternative explanation, which we could not rule out in this data set, is that the parents were not accurately reporting the grades that their children receive. However, even if this were the case, the parents of low achievers would still be indicating more acceptance of lower grades than parents of high achievers.

Thus a characteristic of families of successful Mexican-American children is that the parents have higher expectations for their children's school performance than do parents whose children are having difficulties.

Instrumental Support for Schoolwork

Apart from what parents might believe, what do they actually do to help their children with schoolwork? Some researchers have found that although Mexican-American parents believe education is important and help children with their homework, the quality of their instrumental help varied greatly (e.g., Delgado-Gaitan, 1992; Goldenberg, 1987, 1989). In an ethnographic study of six Mexican-American families, Delgado-Gaitan (1992) found that some parents were frustrated as they tried to understand what the teacher wanted on the homework assignments and they often misguided their children in attempting to help them complete assignments. Similarly, in a case study of three Mexican immigrant families, Delgado-Gaitan (1987) reported that although the parents expected their children to do well in school and to study at home, they felt limited in their ability to instrumentally help their children with many of the homework assignments.

In our study of high and low achievers, parents were asked three questions about their role in helping children with schoolwork: (1) what role should parents take in helping children do their schoolwork; (2) how capable do they feel they are in helping their children do well in school; and (3) how confident do they feel about being able to help their children with their homework. Most parents indicated that parents should play a role in helping their children with their schoolwork. There was no reliable difference in the responses of parents of high and low achievers. Most parents felt they could help their children do their homework most of the time (82% parents of high achievers; 66% parents of low achievers). However, parents of high and low achievers differed in the degree to which they felt they were able to help their child do well in school. The majority of parents of high achievers (79%) indicated that there were many things they could do to help their children; only 21% felt there were only some things they could do. Of the parents of low achievers, 55% felt there were many things they could do; while 45% said there were only some or few things they could do to help their children do well in school.

Almost all parents felt they should help their children with their homework, and over half felt they could be of assistance. However, there was some evidence that the parents of high achievers were more confident about their ability to help their children succeed in school. This finding is in accord with the view that Hispanic parents are supportive of their children's school achievement but that some may lack the knowledge or skills to help children with their schoolwork (Delgado-Gaitan, 1992; Laosa, 1982; Trueba, 1988).

We also asked parents what they did to help their children with their schoolwork. Parents of high and low achievers did not differ in their reports of how frequently they helped their children with homework (e.g., show child how to do a homework problem; help child study for a test). Nor did they differ in their reports of how many days in the previous week they had helped their child with homework after school. However, they did differ in the amount of personal reading they did at home. The parents of high achievers reported doing activities that model reading in the home (e.g., read a magazine, check information in a book, such as a cookbook, dictionary, or encyclopedia) more often than did parents of low achievers. This finding is consistent with Laosa's finding (1978, 1982) that the amount of time mothers spent reading to their children was related to the development of literacy skills in Mexican-American preschool children.

Thus, with respect to parents' instrumental help, it seems that parents of high- and low-achieving children help their children with schoolwork equally, but parents of high achievers are more confident about the effectiveness of their help. Moreover, they model the importance of school-related skills, such as reading, more frequently. Parents of successful children demonstrate to their children that skills learned in school will be useful outside of school.

Understanding the Educational Process

In addition to providing help on basic school tasks (e.g., long division problems, writing a book report, identifying adverbs and adjectives), parents can help their children in school by understanding how school works. In all social contexts, there are rules that guide behaviors, establish social roles, and set expectations for interpersonal interactions (Moore, 1981). Some of these rules are explicitly explained. For example, there might be a chart on a classroom wall that lists "No pushing, hitting, or name calling" as one of the classroom rules. However, other rules are generally not explained and form a body of practical knowledge about schooling that is tacit or implicit (Okagaki & Sternberg, 1993a). For example, in some classrooms, the teacher does not readily entertain questions at all times during a lesson. Rather, the teacher signals that students may ask questions by pausing in her speech, looking up and scanning the class (Green & Weade, 1985).

Delgado-Gaitan (1992) reported excellent examples of what happens when schools do not make all of the rules and procedures known in an explicit way for the parents and parents are not familiar enough with the school system to have important tacit knowledge about schooling. In her study of expert and novice readers, Delgado-Gaitan (1992) described a mother whose son was having disciplinary problems at school. Although she would punish the child for getting into trouble, the boy continued to have problems at school. This particular mother did not realize that: (1) the school was a resource for her to use, (2) she could initiate a contact and make an appointment to talk with her son's teacher to discuss the problem, and (3) the school staff would likely view her as a more caring and concerned parent if, in fact, she did initiate a contact with them about her child. Similarly, Delgado-Gaitan observed that the parents of children who were having trouble learning how to read were not always aware that their children were not doing well or what skills were particularly difficult for their children to master. Although the parents received the negative reports on their children's reading progress and disciplined their children, they did not realize that they could call the teacher and get suggestions for specific ways to help their children with their reading.

In our own work, we observed that parents' expectations for their children's educational attainment did not match their children's elementary school performance. Most parents of low achievers expected their children to graduate from college, and half of these parents set the minimum boundary for school attainment at college graduation. Given that the low achievement group was selected from children who scored in the bottom third on their school achievement tests and given that currently only half of the adolescents in this country continue their schooling past high school (William T. Grant Foundation Commission on Work, Family, and Citizenship, 1988), expecting that their children will graduate from college may not be reasonable for parents of low achievers. In light of their responses to grades of C's and D's, it seems that the parents of low achievers may have had a false perception that their children were doing satisfactory work in elementary school because their children were receiving passing grades. Parents may not realize that in their children's schools passing grades of C's and D's actually meant that their children were not doing very well at all. These children were falling behind their classmates and scoring below grade level on their achievement tests.

Thus, another characteristic of families of successful children is that the parents may have more tacit or practical knowledge about the school system. Consequently, they are better able to effectively use the school system as a resource and to determine when they should take more initiative in seeking help for their children. In essence, the parents of high achievers are better consumers of the school system.

Beliefs About Barriers to Success

Beliefs about the benefits of education may be tempered by beliefs that the society is not structured to allow minorities to succeed (Ogbu, 1992). We asked parents of high and low achievers to indicate the degree to which they agreed or disagreed with statements about minority children facing prejudicial treatment in the classroom and, later on, having a harder time getting jobs because of their ethnicity. Most parents in both groups reported that they did not believe that teachers treated minority and majority children differently or that their child would have a harder time in life because of their minority status. However, parents of high achievers disagreed to a greater extent with the racial barrier items than did the parents of low achievers. Thus, parents of successful children may more strongly affirm to their children that there will be opportunities for achievement in their futures and that their hard work will make a difference.

Summary

What are the characteristics of families of academically successful Mexican-American children? Both qualitative and quantitative researchers have obtained fairly consistent findings indicating that Mexican-American parents believe that education is important for their children and they spend time helping their children with their schoolwork. However, parents of successful students set higher standards for their children with respect to their school grades and to the lower boundary for their children's educational attainment. Parents of successful children are more confident about their ability to help their children, more familiar with how the school system works, and more likely to seek help from the school staff when their children are having difficulties in school. In our view, parents of successful children are better consumers of the school system and are better able to access the resources the school system has for families. Finally, it also seems that in successful or resilient families, the parents are more confident that their children will not encounter barriers to their success in life because of their ethnicity. They are more optimistic about their children being able to succeed.

Theoretical Frameworks

Having highlighted empirical evidence on ways in which Mexican-American parents support their children's schooling, discussion now turns to the theoretical models that explain Mexican-American school achievement. The two dominant perspectives on minority children's school achievement are the primary and secondary cultural discontinuity theories. The primary cultural discontinuity view or context-specific approach (e.g., Tharp, 1989; Trueba, 1987, 1988; Vogt, Jordan, & Tharp, 1987; Weisner, Gallimore, & Jordan, 1988) focuses on differences between the minority and majority cultures (e.g., language, behavioral norms) that interfere with the teaching-learning process in the classroom. In contrast, according to the secondary cultural discontinuity theory or cultural-ecological approach (e.g., Gibson & Ogbu, 1991; Ogbu, 1986), important differences between majority and minority people evolve when minority groups develop strategies in response to the oppression imposed on them by the majority group.

Secondary Cultural Discontinuity View

Ogbu (1986, 1992; Ogbu & Matute-Bianchi, 1986), a major proponent of the secondary cultural discontinuity view, argued that certain minority groups are treated at the institutional and policy levels within our society in ways that limit their ability to succeed economically, professionally, socially, and politically. These "involuntary" minority groups, including Mexican Americans, became part of the United States through conquest or slavery and are "regarded and treated by the dominant white group as inferior and are ranked lower than whites as desirable neighbors, employees, workmates, and schoolmates" (Ogbu, 1986, p. 28).

Ogbu posited that poor school achievement by involuntary minorities is a conscious choice, an active response to a system that has failed to work for a particular group of people. According to his analysis, educational policies and practices at both the societal level and local community level have prevented involuntary minorities from gaining access to educational opportunities. Similarly, institutionalized barriers have kept involuntary minorities from gaining economic benefits from their educational achievement that are comparable to the benefits gained by their Euro-American counterparts. In response to negative treatment and institutionalized barriers, involuntary minorities actively reject the low status attributed to them by the majority group and seek ways to change the system, rather than to work within the system. This rejection may involve the development of behaviors and attitudes that are in opposition to majority practices and beliefs. Thus, a consequence of recognizing a job ceiling and lack of social mobility through educational achievement may be that parents, seeing that their efforts may not result in later rewards, will not encourage children to work hard at school. Ultimately, children may develop behaviors that directly conflict with those that are deemed socially appropriate for school by the majority culture. When involuntary minority children do not do well in school, their poor school performance may be understood as a chosen response to a system that does not reward their efforts to achieve within the dominant culture's framework.

Although his extensive writings cannot be summarized here, it is important to note that Ogbu acknowledged within-group variations in minority children's school achievement. Involuntary minority children who want to do well in school adopt various strategies that enable them to succeed. For example, some students drop their own cultural norms and replace them with "White" attitudes and behaviors (called "acting White," Fordham & Ogbu, 1986). According to Ogbu, these minority students suffer from isolation from their minority peers. Other students "camouflage" their desire to achieve in school by being the class clown, while they study secretly and get good grades. Some students adopt an alternation strategy in which they adopt "White" behaviors to succeed in school but maintain ethnically appropriate attitudes and behaviors outside of school.

Primary Cultural Discontinuity View

According to the primary cultural discontinuity perspective (see Delgado-Gaitan, 1992; Laosa, 1982; Tharp, 1989; Trueba, 1988), the lower school achievement of Mexican-American children stems neither from their parents' lack of encouragement for school achievement nor from a low valuation of education. Building on a contextual view of cognition (see Laboratory of Comparative Human Cognition, 1982; Okagaki & Sternberg, 1991; Rogoff, 1990), researchers have argued that: (1) cultural context affects the development of social and cognitive processes; (2) there are important differences between the Mexican-American culture and the majority culture; and (3) these cultural differences lead to the development of different sets of cognitive and social behavioral repertoires. The end result is that children have difficulty decoding the cues that are presented in the classroom and actively engaging in the teaching-learning process.

These researchers have challenged Ogbu's contention that there is a weak link between education and occupational achievement for Mexican Americans. Trueba, citing McCarthy and Valdez's report on Mexican immigration in California (McCarthy & Valdez, 1985, 1986; cited in Trueba, 1988), argued that the observed upward socioeconomic mobility of Mexican immigrants was the result of increases in education. Similarly, Laosa (1982) purported that the lower occupational status of Mexican-American adults in general was related to their lower educational attainment and not to a differential occupational return for schooling between Mexican Americans and non-Hispanic whites. Using the U.S. Census Bureau Current Population Survey data collected in 1979, Rong and Grant (1992) examined educational attainment in successive generations of Hispanic adolescents and youth. In this sample of 1,354 Hispanic adolescents and youths (16-24 years old), the proportion completing high school increased with successive generations from immigrant adolescents (i.e., adolescents who were foreign-born and had immigrated with their parents) to children of immigrants (i.e., adolescents who were the American-born children of immigrant parents) to "native" adolescents (i.e., adolescents who were the American-born children of American-born parents). They interpreted these findings as supporting the primary cultural discontinuity thesis.

Discussion

The mechanisms posited in the primary and secondary cultural discontinuity theories by which parents potentially influence children's school performance are not mutually exclusive. Both may in fact be operating simultaneously. We suggest that both primary and secondary cultural discontinuities affect Mexican-American children's school achievement, but that the ways in which they operate are affected by generational and developmental status.

Generational Differences

One of the difficulties in understanding the contribution of family support to Mexican-American children's school adaptation is that Mexican-American families are not a homogeneous group. Perhaps more than any other group of immigrants to the United States, Mexican Americans have had a continuing stream of newly arriving immigrants who have intermingled with second-, third-, and later generation families (Connor, 1985). Generational differences may affect the ways in which Mexican-American parents support their children's schooling. For example, Buriel (1984; Buriel & Cardoza, 1988) argued that Mexican-American families need to be understood within their generational status, because processes that lead to success differ across generations. According to Buriel, immigrants are a selective group who have a strong motivation to improve their lives. The personal characteristics that give immigrants the motivation and abilities to leave their own countries and adapt to a new environment may make them unique in other ways. Using the National Center for Educational Statistics High School and Beyond longitudinal survey of high school sophomores and seniors, Buriel and Cardoza (1988) examined responses of over 1,000 students who identified themselves as "Mexican," "Mexican-American," or "Chicano." These students were categorized into first-generation students whose parents immigrated to the United States, second-generation students whose parents were born in the United States, and third-generation students whose grandparents and parents were born in the United States. The first-, second-, and third-generation Mexican-American adolescents did not differ on their school achievement test scores. Buriel and Cardoza reasoned that the first-generation students were able to overcome any problems that might have resulted from their parents not being as able to provide instrumental help because they were influenced by their immigrant parents' strong motivations to achieve and improve their lives. Thus, the personal characteristics of immigrants may be one way in which generations differ.

To more closely examine how each generation might differ in the processes that are associated with achievement, Buriel and Cardoza did a stepwise forward regression analysis to identify the variables that predicted school achievement. In all three groups, the students' personal aspirations for the amount of education they expected to complete were related to their math, reading, and vocabulary test scores. Where the groups differed was in the importance of Spanish language usage. Interestingly, language spoken at home and language spoken as a child were not consistent predictors of achievement test scores for first- and second-generation students. This primary cultural difference did not seem important for these students. However, the predominant use of Spanish as a child was negatively related to all three test scores for third-generation students. Because it is atypical for third-generation adolescents to grow up speaking Spanish at home, Buriel and Cardoza posited that it was likely that these adolescents were from families that had not been economically mobile and were still living in low-income neighborhoods. These adolescents might have observed their parents' and grandparents' struggles to succeed and become disillusioned about their own prospects. For whatever reason, Spanish-language usage was related to academic achievement for one group but not for the others. This is evidence that processes or behaviors in one generation of Mexican-American adolescents may be associated with differential outcomes in a different generation.

In our own research, we have examined the ways immigrant and non-immigrant parents of Mexican descent differ in their parenting (Okagaki & Sternberg, 1993b). Specifically, beliefs about childrearing and the conceptions of intelligence of Mexican-American parents who immigrated to the United States and Mexican-American parents who were born and educated in the United States were examined in a sample of parents of kindergarten-, first- and second-grade children. Immigrant parents were found to place more emphasis on developing conforming behaviors in their children than Mexican-American parents who had been born in the United States. Non-immigrant Mexican-American parents more closely resembled Euro-American parents than first-generation Mexican-American parents. That is, both Euro-American and non-immigrant Mexican-American parents gave higher importance ratings to autonomous-behavior items than to conforming-behavior items. This finding is consistent with descriptions of contemporary American culture as one that values children who are intellectually and socially independent, autonomous individuals. In contrast, for the immigrant parents, encouraging conformity to external standards items had higher importance ratings than autonomous-behavior items.

We also examined parents' conceptions of intelligence. In particular, parents were asked how important three types of cognitive (i.e., problem-solving skills, verbal abilities, and creative abilities) and three types of non-cognitive (social skills, motivation, and practical skills) traits were to their conceptions of an intelligent child. The two groups of Mexican-American parents were similar to each other and different from Euro-Americans. Among the non-cognitive attributes, importance ratings of social skills were not significantly different from the average ratings of motivation and self-management skills for both groups. The relatively high ratings of the social skills items occurred within the context of the other items that had, from our perspective, a stronger school orientation. The items in the motivation and self-management subscales were more explicitly school oriented (e.g., gets good grades, studies hard and does homework, learns from mistakes) than were items in the social skills subscale (e.g., plays well with other children, shows respect to others, is sensitive to other people's needs). Hence, we found the importance of social skills to the parents' conception of intelligent first graders to be especially salient and interesting. Others (see Reese, Balzano, Gallimore, & Goldenberg, in press) have found that among Mexican-American immigrants, the concept of education encompasses both academic learning and moral upbringing.

This examination of different generations of Mexican-American parents included their perceptions of the importance of various skills that children learn in first and second grade. The primary difference between non-immigrant parents and immigrant parents was that non-immigrant parents believed that it is more important to teach academic thinking skills, such as how to ask questions and how to be creative, than it is to teach children to print and write neatly. In contrast, the immigrant parents rated learning to do work neatly and orderly as being more important than learning basic facts, developing problem-solving skills, and developing creativity.

The differences in immigrant and non-immigrant parents' beliefs about childrearing and education are examples of ways in which generations of Mexican-American parents differ. Exploration of other beliefs, attitudes, and practices may yield a fruitful way of understanding why general family factors (e.g., parent education; see Buriel & Cardoza, 1988) do not consistently predict Mexican-American children's school performance.

Developmental Differences

A second consideration in understanding the influence of family and parenting variables on Mexican-American children's school achievement is the age of the child in question. Parent-child relationships change as children and parents develop. Consequently, one should expect that the influence of the family on school achievement may differ between elementary school and high school. Much of the research supporting the importance of parents' (typically immigrant parents) lack of tacit or practical knowledge about school and their ability to provide effective instrumental help on schoolwork has been conducted with elementary school children (e.g., Delgado-Gaitan, 1987, 1992; Goldenberg, 1987, 1989; Vogt, Jordan, & Tharp, 1987; Weisner, Gallimore, & Jordan, 1988). Adolescents are less dependent on parents for help with schoolwork. For children born in the United States of immigrant parents, parental help in understanding school tasks and in adapting to the social context of the classroom may be more important in elementary school. This hypothesis is consistent with Buriel and Cardoza's (1988) explanation that the reason they did not find a relation between parent education or family income and school achievement for high school seniors, when others have obtained such a relation, is that socioeconomic factors may be more important in earlier grades.

Conclusions

Returning to the original question, what factors should be considered to explain the influence of the home environment on Mexican-American children's school achievement? First, there are ample data to support the thesis that the experiences of minority groups within the United States differ. To understand the home-school relation, the larger societal context must be considered. Second, when the immediate contexts are examined, it also seems clear that primary cultural differences influence children's school achievement. The skills and behavioral norms of children at home may differ from the behavioral patterns and expectations of the classroom. Consequently, Mexican-American students may have difficulty processing information and decoding cues. Third, these context-specific differences may have more impact on young children than on adolescents. Finally, the heterogeneity of the Mexican-American population affects the adequacy of any explanation of Mexican-American children's school achievement. Whether or not primary cultural differences are critical factors in any particular child's school experience may depend on the parent's generational status in the United States, as well as their attitudes toward the majority culture and their attitudes toward their ethnicity.

Finally, although the focus of this chapter has been on parents' contribution to their children's school achievement, responsibility for understanding cultural differences and developing strategies to more effectively work with children of minority cultures lies predominantly with educators and researchers. Excellent demonstrations (e.g., Moll & Diaz, 1987; Tharp, 1989; Vogt, Jordan, & Tharp, 1987; Weisner, Gallimore, & Jordan, 1988) have already been provided that document that specific changes in instructional practice and classroom organization can be very effective in improving minority children's learning.

Note

1. We would like to thank Karen Diamond for comments on earlier drafts. Preparation of this chapter was supported by a grant from The Spencer Foundation. The views expressed are solely the responsibility of the authors.

References

Buriel, R. (1984). Integration with traditional Mexican-American culture and sociocultural adjustment. In J. L. Martinez, Jr. & R. H. Mendoza (Eds.), *Chicano psychology* (2nd ed., pp. 95-130). New York: Academic Press.

Buriel, R., & Cardoza, D. (1988). Sociocultural correlates of achievement among three generations of Mexican-American high-school seniors. *American Educational Research Journal, 25*(2), 177-192.

Connor, W. (1985). Who are the Mexican Americans? In W. Connor (Ed.), *Mexican Americans in comparative perspective* (pp. 3-28). Washington, DC: The Urban Institute Press.

Cortes, C. E. (1986). The education of language minority students: A contextual interaction model. In California State Department of Education (Ed.), *Beyond language: Social and cultural factors in schooling language minority students* (pp. 3-33). Los Angeles: Evaluation, Dissemination, and Assessment Center, California State University.

Delgado-Gaitan, C. (1987). Parent perceptions of school: Supportive environments for children. In H. T. Trueba (Ed.), *Success or failure? Learning and the language minority student* (pp. 131-155). Cambridge, MA: Newbury House Publishers.

Delgado-Gaitan, C. (1992). School matters in the Mexican-American home. *American Educational Research Journal, 29*(3), 495-513.

Fernandez, R. M., Paulsen, R., & Hirano-Nakanishi, M. (1989). Dropping out among Hispanic youth. *Social Science Research, 18*, 21-52.

Fordham, S., & Ogbu, J. U. (1986). Black students' school success: Coping with the "Burden of 'Acting.' " *The Urban Review, 18*(3), 176-206.

Garcia E. E. (1992). "Hispanic" children: Theoretical, empirical, and related policy issues. *Educational Psychology Review, 4*(1), 69-93.

Gibson, M. A., & Ogbu, J. U. (Eds.). (1991). *Minority status and schooling: A comparative study of immigrant and involuntary minorities.* New York: Garland Publishing, Inc.

Goldenberg, C. N. (1987). Low-income Hispanic parents' contributions to their first-grade children's word-recognition skills. *Anthropology and Education Quarterly, 18*, 149-179.

Goldenberg, C. N. (1989). Parents' effects on academic grouping for reading: Three case studies. *American Educational Research Journal, 26*(3), 329-352.

Green, J. L., & Weade, R. (1985). Reading between the words: Social cues to lesson participation. *Theory into Practice, 24*, 14-21.

Humphreys, L. G. (1988). Trends in levels of academic achievement of Blacks and other minorities. *Intelligence, 12*, 231-260.

Laboratory of Comparative Human Cognition. (1982). Culture and intelligence. In R. J. Sternberg (Ed.), *Handbook of human intelligence* (pp. 642-719). Cambridge: Cambridge University Press.

Laosa, L. M. (1978). Maternal teaching strategies in Chicano families of varied educational and socioeconomic levels. *Child Development, 49*, 1129-1135.

Laosa, L. M. (1982). School, occupation, culture, and family: The impact of parental schooling on the parent-child relationship. *Journal of Educational Psychology, 74*(6), 791-827.

McCarthy, K. F., & Valdez, R. B. (1985). *Current and future effects of Mexican immigration in California: Executive summary.* The Rand Corporation Series. R-3365/1-CR. Santa Monica, CA: RAND.

McCarthy, K. F., & Valdez, R. B. (1986). *Current and future effects of Mexican immigration in California.* The Rand Corporation Series. R-3365-CR. Santa Monica, CA: RAND.

Moll, L. C., & Diaz, S. (1987). Change as the goal of educational research. *Anthropology & Education Quarterly, 18*(4), 300-311.

Moore, D. T. (1981). Discovering the pedagogy of experience. *Harvard Educational Review, 51*(2), 286-300.

Ogbu, J. U. (1986). The consequences of the American caste system. In U. Neisser (Ed.), *The school achievement of minority children: New perspectives* (pp. 19-56). Hillsdale, NJ: Lawrence Erlbaum Associates.

Ogbu, J. U. (1992). Understanding cultural diversity and learning. *Educational Researcher, 21*(8), 5-14.

Ogbu, J. U., & Matute-Bianchi, M. E. (1986). Understanding sociocultural factors: Knowledge, identity, and school adjustment. In California State Department of Education (Ed.), *Beyond language: Social and cultural factors in schooling language minority students* (pp. 73-142). Los Angeles: Evaluation, Dissemination and Assessment Center, California State University.

Okagaki, L., Frensch, P.A., & Gordon, E.W. (1994). Encouraging school achievement in Mexican-American children. Manuscript submitted for publication.

Okagaki, L., & Sternberg, R. J. (1991). Cultural and parental influences on cognitive development. In L. Okagaki & R. J. Sternberg (Eds.), *Directors of development: Influences on the development of children's thinking* (pp. 101-120). Hillsdale, NJ: Erlbaum.

Okagaki, L., & Sternberg, R. J. (1993a). Putting the distance into students' hands: Practical intelligence for school. In R. R. Cocking & K. A. Renninger (Eds.), *The development and meaning of psychological distance* (pp. 237-254). Hillsdale, NJ: Erlbaum.

Okagaki, L., & Sternberg, R. J. (1993b). Parental beliefs and children's school performance. *Child Development, 64*, 36-56.

Reese, L., Balzano, S., Gallimore, R., & Goldenberg, C. (in press). The concept of Educación: Latino family values and American schooling.

Rogoff, B. (1990). *Apprenticeship in thinking: Cognitive development in social context.* New York: Oxford Press.

Rong, X. L., & Grant, L. (1992). Ethnicity, generation, and school attainment of Asians, Hispanics, and Non-Hispanic Whites. *The Sociological Quarterly, 33*(4), 625-636.

Rumberger, R. W. (1987). High school dropouts: A review of issues and evidence. *Review of Educational Research, 57*(2), 101-121.

Stevenson, H. W., Chen, C., & Uttal, D. H. (1990). Beliefs and achievement: A study of Black, White, and Hispanic children. *Child Development, 61*, 508-523.

Stevenson, H. W., & Lee, S. Y. (1990). Contexts of achievement. *Monographs of the Society for Research in Child Development, 55*(1-2), (Serial No. 221).

Stevenson, H. W., Lee, S. Y., & Stigler, J. W. (1986). Mathematics achievement of Chinese, Japanese, and American children. *Science, 231*, 693-699.

Sue, S., & Padilla, A. (1986). Ethnic minority issues in the United States: Challenges for the educational system. In California State Department of Education (Ed.), *Beyond language: Social and cultural factors in schooling language minority students* (pp. 35-72). Los Angeles: Evaluation, Dissemination and Assessment Center, California State University.

Tharp, R. G. (1989). Psychocultural variables and constants: Effects on teaching and learning in schools. *American Psychologist, 44*(2), 349-359.

Trueba, H. T. (Ed.). (1987). *Success or failure? Learning and the language minority student.* Cambridge, MA: Newbury House Publishers.

Trueba, H. T. (1988). Culturally based explanations of minority students' academic achievement. *Anthropology & Education Quarterly, 19,* 270-287.

Vogt, L. A., Jordan, C., & Tharp, R. G. (1987). Explaining school failure, producing school success: Two cases. *Anthropology & Education Quarterly, 18,* 276-286.

Walker, C. L. (1987). Hispanic achievement: Old views and new perspectives. In H. T. Trueba (Ed.), *Success or failure? Learning and the language minority student* (pp. 15-32). Cambridge, MA: Newbury House Publishers.

Weisner, T. S., Gallimore, R., & Jordan, C. (1988). Unpackaging cultural effects on classroom learning: Native Hawaiian peer assistance and child-generated activity. *Anthropology & Education Quarterly, 19,* 327-353.

William T. Grant Foundation Commission on Work, Family, and Citizenship. (1988). *The forgotten half: Non-college youth in America.* Washington, DC: William T. Grant Foundation Commission on Work, Family, and Citizenship.

Chapter 17

Parenting and Child Adjustment in Single- and Two-Parent, Euro- and Mexican-American Families

Wendy C. Gamble and Rochelle L. Dalla

More than a decade ago, reviewers of the father absence literature argued that absence per se was less significant in understanding the adjustment of children living in single-parent, mother-headed families than were a variety of other family and personal factors (Blechman, 1982; Shinn, 1978). Empirical investigations have supported this perspective (Amato, 1993), resulting in information about specific life circumstances common to single-parent families that can disrupt effective parenting and place children "at risk" for maladaptation. Disruptive factors linked directly to less effective parenting include increased significant life changes, decreased financial resources (Colletta, 1983; Compas & Williams, 1990; McLanahan, 1983; McLanahan, Wedemeyer, & Adelberg, 1981; Weinraub & Wolf, 1983; Weitzman, 1985), and the absence of adequate social support (Colletta, 1978; McLanahan & Booth, 1989; Weinraub & Wolf, 1983). A substantial body of literature has shown that high maternal stress is associated with irritable and restrictive parenting (e.g., Colletta, 1983; Lahey, Conger, Atkenson, & Treifer, 1984; Longfellow, Zelkowitz, & Sanders, 1982; Patterson, 1983). For example, Simons, Beaman, Conger, and Chao (1993) recently reported that negative life events and inadequate social support were associated with psychological distress and the use of ineffective parenting practices among single mothers.

Advances have been made in the conceptualization of single parenting as a function of the potential effects of stress, support, and parental adjustment, and in the recognition of variation in parenting and the subsequent effects on how children cope and adapt. The existing literature, however, has drawn a majority of its samples from Caucasian or European-American populations (e.g., Hetherington, Clingempeel et al., 1992; Olson & Banyard, 1993; Weinraub & Wolf, 1983; Simons et al., 1993), despite the fact that the incidence of single-parenting among these groups is below the national average (Laosa, 1988).

The present study focuses on significant factors in understanding how children adjust in single- and two-parent, Euro- and Mexican-American families. Almost one-quarter of Hispanic families with children under 18 years of age are headed by a woman with no husband present (U.S. Bureau of the Census, 1992). The goal of this study was to compare the mean scores for key explanatory variables across four groups that were defined by the number of parents available in the home and by ethnicity. The results of these analyses would be used to determine whether significant group differences exist and whether the same explanatory variables are adequate for understanding processes of child functioning in diverse samples of single-parent, female-headed households. Comparisons of the amount of stress, the amount of contact with support networks, the amount of support received, maternal adjustment, and parenting variables across ethnic groups are necessarily preliminary until more is known about each population and researchers can feel confident that a priori hypotheses based on the emerging strain perspectives are appropriate for more diverse samples. In addition to examining characteristics placing single mothers and their children at risk for negative outcomes, these comparative analyses would allow investigators to examine the conditions that enable these single women and their children to be resilient—conditions that may reduce the risks and probabilities of negative outcomes.

The current study addressed the following questions concerning the effects of growing up in a single, Euro- or Mexican-American mother-headed household.

(1) Do children in family environments that differ in terms of ethnicity and the mother's relationship status show different levels of adjustment, specifically on externalizing and internalizing behaviors as reported by mothers?

(2) Do single mothers face more life changes and potential stresses and have fewer social supports than married (or coupled) mothers?

(3) Do single mothers report experiencing more emotional difficulties and fewer personal resources than married (or coupled) mothers, influencing the child's adjustment directly or indirectly through their effects on parenting?

(4) Do single mothers describe relationships with their children in different ways, specifically in terms of less positive rapport, less monitoring, and more punitive and demanding discipline strategies than married (or coupled) mothers?

These questions were based on the strain perspective of adaptation to single parenting; as previously discussed, this perspective has thus far been developed without attention to differences across ethnic groups. The literature on differences between the two cultural groups of interest, Euro- and Mexican-Americans, has been full of inconsistencies and negative stereotypes about Hispanics (Vega, Hough, & Romero, 1983). Until research is conducted with more conceptual sensitivity to issues of diversity, the existing empirical findings will remain suspect as a base from which to make predictions. However, given this background, the existing literature suggested that one group—single, Mexican-American women—may be at particularly high risk for experiencing strain. It is hypothesized that single Mexican-American women will report harsher parenting practices and that their children will demonstrate more behavioral problems. These hypotheses were based on the assumption that Mexican-American women experience higher levels of stress and financial strain regardless of marital status. Female-headed Hispanic families have median incomes of only 22% of the median income of White two-parent families.

The existing literature also reflects the controversial theory that Hispanics are more family oriented than European Americans and thus have greater access to an extended family support network. According to this theory, single, Mexican-American mothers may be at high risk for experiencing strain if strongly valued kin relationships and extended family networks are fractured by a separation or divorce. Transitions in close relationships may undermine the core value of family which is assumed to be central to Hispanic culture and the Catholic religion.

Conjectures about gender role differences in Mexican-American and Euro-American families are related to these differences in cultural family values. Wilkinson (1987) noted that families of Spanish descent tend to be characterized by the functional dominance of males, complemented by a positive and traditional role for women. In Hispanic families, sex-role distinctions are often reinforced through child-rearing practices and the precedent for a male to be head of the household. If these gender patterns are indeed widespread, then single, Mexican-American women may be ill-prepared to assume the position of head of household. They may receive little community support if their role as household head is perceived as different or unacceptable.

As noted, it is difficult to generate hypotheses about cultural differences given the general shortage of empirical studies of the Hispanic family. Since the present study was designed to examine components of a strain perspective, or variables that have often been interpreted within a deficit model, the difficulty of generating cultural hypotheses was compounded by the potential for reporting results that project negative images about the adjustment of single, Mexican-American women and their children. By assuming that families can be resilient, hypotheses can be framed in a more positive manner. A resiliency hypothesis can be used to examine why some of these women are successfully adapting to their roles as heads of their households.

Finally, diversity in parenting, both within and across ethnic groups, must be interpreted within the socioeconomic context. Socioeconomic status levels have been demonstrated to influence parenting practices in a myriad of ways (Conger, Elder, Lorenz, Simons, & Whitbeck, 1992; McLoyd, 1990). Beyond the obvious difference in the number of parents available for caregiving, one of the most fundamental differences between single- and two-parent families is level of income. Since single-parent women are more likely to experience economic stress, it is commonly assumed that, as a consequence, they employ less sensitive parenting practices and they use more authoritarian discipline. Bank, Forgatch, Patterson, and Fetrow (1993) observed that socioeconomically disadvantaged single mothers employed less effective discipline and their sons were at greater risk for antisocial behavior problems. Because the sampling procedures in the present study were not designed to match participants on the income variable and income differences were anticipated in the sample, it was determined that differences in income would be adjusted for thorough analysis of covariance procedures.

Methods

Participants

The sample of 88 mother-child pairs consisted of: 24 single, Euro-American mothers and their children; 20 married, Euro-American women and their children; 22 single, Mexican-American mother-child pairs; and 22 married, Mexican-American mother-child pairs. The single parents reported their marital status as never married (39.1%), divorced (43.5%), and separated (17.4%). All of the women who lived in households where there were two parents present reported being married. None of the single parent mothers reported having been widowed. Information was not available about circumstances surrounding divorce nor the length of time since separation or divorce. The mothers' ages ranged from 22 to 46 years, with a mean of 32.53. Eighty-eight children were also included in the investigation. The ages of the children ranged from five to eight years, and approximately one-half of the children (49.4%) were female. The mean ages of the children did not differ significantly across the four groups. Seventy-seven percent of the children included in the sample were either first- or second-born in their family. Family sizes varied from one to eight children, with a mean of 2.6.

Measures

Family Demographic and Acculturation Information. Participating mothers responded to demographic questions regarding their own ages, years of education, annual income, family size, and target children's ages, genders, and birth orders. Mothers were asked to describe the target child's contact with his or her natural father, stepfather, and other influential adults in the child's life (Amato, 1987; Dornbusch et al, 1985; Furstenberg & Nord, 1987), and mothers were also asked to indicate with whom the target child has regular contact (three or four times a week). Information about the length of time spent together or the nature of shared activities was not requested.

Participating mothers who identified themselves as Mexican-American were asked to complete the Short Acculturation Subscale for Hispanics (Marin, Sabogal, Marin, Otero-Sabogal, & Perez-Stable, 1987). This 12-item scale was developed for use with different His-

panic subgroups, and it includes items that assess language preference and proficiency, use and preference for English/Spanish language media, and preferred ethnicity of friends and acquaintances.
The scale demonstrates good reliability and validity, and item totals
are highly correlated with validation criteria, including respondents'
generation, length of residence in U.S., ethnic self-identification,
and other acculturation indices. The internal reliability for the
present sample was .92.

   Risk and Life Events. Risk conditions do not exist in isolation. The effects of multiple, nonspecific risk factors or stressor
events may be cumulative, and a greater number of risk factors or
stressors is related to a higher probability of a negative outcome
(Seifer, Sameroff, Baldwin, & Baldwin, 1992). For this reason, two
risk scores and a summative life event score were used in subsequent analyses. The risk scores were generated from information
provided by the mothers on a questionnaire about family and child
characteristics. The first risk score was comprised of variables representing family circumstances associated with potential developmental problems. If the mother reported that the indicated risk
factor was present, a score of one was assigned, and these scores
were summed and averaged. The total family risk score was calculated from information about specific risk-related variables. The
Department of Health and Human Services Low-Income Poverty
Guideline (1991) sets the poverty level at $16,750 for a household of
four (the mean family size for this sample). For this investigation, a
score of one was assigned if the mother reported a family income of
less than $15,000 (51.7%). A score of one was also given if the
family: had been referred for counseling (21.8%); had contact with
Child Protective Services (4.6%) or the Department of Economic
Security (13.8%); had been homeless (1.2%); or had four or more
children in the home (16.5%). Additionally, scores of one were
assigned if the mother reported that anyone in the household was
regularly using alcohol, cocaine, marijuana, heroin, PCP, or amphetamines.

   The second risk score was calculated from the number of
child-specific characteristics and past or present experiences of the
child that may be associated with less than optimal developmental
outcomes. The information used to create this score was specific to
the child and did not include general family problems or parental
dysfunction. The child risk factor was generated from an average of
scores on seven items. A score of one was assigned if the child could
be described by any of the following characteristics: birth order
greater than 2 (23%); experience of a serious illness (e.g., asthma,

chronic ear infections) (43%); disability (e.g., epilepsy, bone malformation, hearing or vision problems) (9.3%); premature birth or low birth weight (8.2%); and serious complications during the mother's pregnancy (12.9%). Additionally, since boys are often considered to be at higher risk for the effects of stressful experiences during early childhood (Garmezy & Rutter, 1983), a score of one was assigned if the child was male (50.6%).

To assess life events or life stressors, the Family Inventory of Life Events and Changes (FILE) was used (Olson, McCubbin, Barnes, Larsen, Muxen, & Wilson, 1982). The FILE is a 71-item self-report instrument designed to record the number of life events or transitions experienced by a family during the preceding six-month period. Mothers indicated whether or not (and the number of times) each event had occurred. From these responses, a total summary score was computed, representing the total number of events experienced (Mean = 7.92, range = 0 – 38). The authors of this instrument reported good reliability for the overall scale score. For this sample, the estimated reliability was .73.

Social Support. To assess the size, composition, and types of social support received, the Norbeck Social Support Questionnaire (NSSQ) (Norbeck, Lindsey, & Carrieri, 1981) was administered. This scale was developed to measure multiple dimensions of social support including emotional affirmation, aid, network size, frequency of contact, and duration of relationships. Each respondent was initially asked to "list each significant person in your life, or who is important to you." The respondent was asked to list up to 10 people, by first name or initial. Next, the participant was instructed to indicate the gender of each person and her relationship with that person (e.g., spouse, mother, neighbor).

Eight questions assessed the types of support the respondent received from her social network. Emotional support was assessed by asking, "How much does this person make you feel liked or loved?" and "How much does this person respect or admire you?" Items designed to assess immediate or practical support included, "If you needed to borrow ten dollars, a ride to the doctor, or some other form of immediate help, how much could this person help you?" Finally, in order to measure the amount of parenting support the participants perceived receiving, the following questions were asked: "If your child were sick for several weeks, how much could this person help you?" and "If you needed information or advice on how to raise your child(ren), how much could this person help you?" Response choices were based on a five-point Likert-type scale (1 = Not at all to 5 = A great deal). The final questions asked the respondent to indicate how long they had known each member of their social support network (responses ranged from 1 = Less than six months to 5 = More than five years) and how often they had contact with each individual (responses ranged from 1 = Once a year or less to 5 = Daily).

The Network Functional items (emotional, immediate, and parenting) and the Network Property items (number in network, duration of relationship, and frequency of contact) were reported by the scale's author to have a high degree of test-retest reliability, ranging from .85 to .92 over a one-week period (Norbeck, Lindsey, & Carrieri, 1981), and from .58 to .78 over a seven-month period (Norbeck et al., 1982). In the present investigation, each of the social support subscales demonstrated a high degree of internal reliability, estimated by Cronbach's Alpha. Specifically, the internal reliability estimates for each type of support (emotional, immediate/practical, and parenting) were .96, .89, and .92, respectively. The mean score of each subscale was 1.98, 1.20, and 2.0, respectively (range 1 to 5).

Maternal Adjustment, Personal, and Social Resources. Perceived self-competence was assessed with Messer and Harter's Self-Perception Profile for Adults (1987). Although the scale is comprised of twelve subscales, only the five-item Global Self-Worth subscale score was included in the analyses. Each item consists of two descriptions from which respondents are asked to identify the description that best describes them. The subscale mean score was 3.05 (range 1 to 4), and internal reliability proved adequate at .86.

In order to assess the participants' severity of depression, a revised version of the Beck Depression Inventory (BDI) (Beck, 1967) was administered. The original BDI is a 21-item scale that assesses the presence and severity of affective, cognitive, motivational, vegetative, and psychomotor components of depression. The short form (comprised of 13 of the original 21 items) was utilized in the present study. Respondents indicated the presence and severity of each symptom on a scale from 0 to 3. Item scores were summed, producing a range from 0 to 39, with higher scores reflecting greater severity of depression.

Beck (1967) reported good to very good test-retest reliability, ranging from .48 for psychiatric patients after a three-week period to .74 for undergraduate students after three months. Research has shown significant correlations between the BDI and a number of other depression measures, indicating strong concurrent validity. Additionally, the BDI correlates significantly with clinicians' ratings of depression. Using Cronbach's Alpha as an estimate of internal reliability, the reliability analyses produced a coefficient of .86.

The anxiety scale of the Costello-Comrey Depression and Anxiety Scales (CCDAS) (1967) was administered. This is a nine-item instrument designed to measure an individual's predisposition for developing anxious affective states. Example items include, "I am calm and not easily upset," and "I get rattled easily." For the present investigation, a revised four-point Likert-type response scale was utilized (1 = Almost never, 2 = Rarely, 3 = Sometimes, and 4 = Most of the time). Total anxiety scores were created by summing each item (four were reverse coded), producing possible anxiety scores ranging from a low of 9 to a high of 36, with higher scores reflecting greater anxiety. Costello and Comrey (1967) reported a split-half reliability of .70 and a test-retest correlation of .72. The anxiety scale is reported to have fair concurrent validity; it is moderately correlated with the Taylor Manifest Anxiety Scales (Costello & Comrey, 1967). For this sample, an Alpha coefficient of .79 resulted.

The Coping Resources Inventory–Form D (Hammer & Marting, 1987) was employed to identify personal resources the mothers may have available for managing stress. Personal coping resources were defined as characteristics that enable the individual to cope more effectively, experience fewer or less intense symptoms linked to stress, or recover faster from stress exposure. This 60-item instrument was designed to measure resources in five domains: cognitive, social, emotional, spiritual/philosophical, and physical. A total resource score was computed by summing the five subscale scores, with higher scores indicating more resources available. The authors reported good internal reliability and moderate to high test-retest estimates. A multitrait-multimethod technique was used successfully to provide evidence of convergent and divergent validity. The Alpha for this sample's total score was .93.

Parental disciplinary practices and quality of parent-child interactions. To assess parenting practices, mothers were asked to complete the Parent Perception Inventory (PPI) (Hazzard, Christensen, & Margolin, 1983). The PPI is divided into positive and negative parental behavior dimensions. The positive parental dimension includes behaviors such as positive reinforcement, comfort, talk time, involvement in decision making, and time together. High scores on the negative dimension indicate more parental criticism, physical punishment, yelling, threatening, neglecting, and ignoring. Ten positive and ten negative items comprise the mother's scale and each was rated on a five-point Likert-type scale (1 = Never, 5 = A lot). Mean composites were created for both the positive and negative dimensions by summing across the ratings for the ten items. Internal reliability as estimated by Cronbach's Alphas were .76 and .79 for the positive and negative subscales, respectively.

The Parenting Practices scale is an 18-item instrument adapted from one developed by Hetherington et al. (1992). The form asks the parents to rate different aspects of their parenting style, including warmth, affection, responsiveness, quality of communication, and involvement. A single factor emerged from a factor analysis and was subsequently labeled as a parent-child Rapport dimension. Hetherington et al. (1992) reported good internal reliability and estimates of test-retest. For the present sample the internal reliability as estimated by Cronbach's Alpha was .93.

The Child Monitoring measure was adapted from Hetherington et al. (1992) . For each item, mothers were asked to rate "how closely they watch, keep track of, or how much they are aware of their child's behaviors" with regard to 16 areas of functioning. They rated each behavior on a five-point Likert-type scale ranging from "Never aware or watching" (1) to "Always aware or watching" (5). Examples of the behavior areas described include: "Whether my child does chores," "What sorts of clothes my child wears to school," "Which friends my child spends time with," and "What my child watches on television." The Cronbach's Alpha for this sample was .81.

Child Adjustment. Mothers completed the parent version of Achenbach's (1991) Child Behavior Checklist (CBC) for all of the target children. The CBC is a 113-item scale designed to assess the functioning of children ages 4 to 16. Mothers were asked to rate whether each statement was "not true," "somewhat or sometimes true," or "very true or often true" for each child. In these analyses, the items were summed and averaged to create two subscale scores labeled "internalizing" and "externalizing." The internalizing subscale includes the withdrawn, somatic complaints, and anxious/depressed syndrome scale scores. The syndrome scales designated as delinquent behavior and aggressive behavior are aggregated under the heading of the externalizing subscale. This instrument is widely used and demonstrates good reliability and validity. The mean for the entire sample of children was .46 for the internalizing scale and .85 for the externalizing scale. Estimates of internal reliability were good; Alpha = .91 for the internalizing scale, and Alpha = .92 for the externalizing scale.

Procedure

This investigation was conducted in a mid-sized southwestern urban community. Women were eligible to participate if they were either Euro- or Mexican-American, single or married, with at least one child between the ages of 5 and 8. Participants were recruited through local primary schools, community-based service agencies, announcements in classes at a local community college, and an advertisement in a local newspaper. All the mothers completed a battery of self-report questionnaires in their own homes. A trained research assistant administered all questionnaires in random order, and explained the procedure for completing each scale. Each respondent took approximately 75 minutes to complete the entire packet.

Results

Group Comparisons

ANOVA or chi-square analyses were employed to examine whether the four family groups, married and single, Euro- and Mexican-American mothers and their children, differed with regard to a number of demographic or family characteristic variables that might influence or even confound group differences on the major variables of interest. Three significant differences emerged. The analysis showed that Mexican-American mothers tended to report significantly larger numbers of children living in their homes. The single and married Mexican-American women reported a mean of 3.3 and 3.1 children, respectively, compared to the single, Euro-American women who reported a mean of 1.8 children, and married, Anglo, non-Hispanic mothers who reported a mean of 2.3 children.

Chi-square analyses revealed a significant difference with regard to employment status (chi-square $= 15.423, p < .001$). Fifty-five percent of the single, Euro-American mothers and 59% of the single, Mexican-American mothers were employed. Twenty-nine percent of the married, Mexican-American mothers, and 10% of the married, Euro-American mothers reported being employed outside of their homes. Additionally, and as anticipated, the groups differed significantly with regard to reported annual income; the non-Hispanic, married mothers reported significantly higher incomes than any of the other three groups ($F = 13.758, p < .000$). Because a number of investigators have argued that socioeconomic status differences between single and married mothers may obscure other differences, and because a significant difference resulted when income was compared for this sample, all analyses comparing group mean scores were conducted with income entered as a covariate. No group differences emerged with regard to maternal age, child gender, or birth order.

Levels of Adjustment

A multivariate analysis of variance covarying the effects of income, or a MANCOVA, was generated for the internalizing and externalizing subscale scores, yielding a significant multivariate F-value ($F = 7.87, p < .001$). The externalizing scale score was associated with a significant F-value resulting from the univariate analysis. Children in single-parent families, regardless of ethnicity, were reported to exhibit the greatest number of externalizing problems and

Table 1A
Means and Standard Deviations of Explanatory and Outcome Variables for Groups Defined by Ethnicity and Marital Status and Results of Univariate Comparisons

| Variable | | Euro-American | | Mexican-American | | |
		Single ($n = 24$)	Married ($n = 20$)	Single ($n = 22$)	Married ($n = 22$)	Univariate F-Value
Child adjustment						
Internalizing	M	−.04	.03	−.05	.13	
	(SD)	(.42)	(.23)	(.40)	(.30)	
Externalizing	M	.44[a]	.22[ab]	.43[b]	.31	15.60***
	(SD)	(.34)	(.21)	(.32)	(.22)	
Stress						
Family risk	M	1.35[ad]	.53[abc]	2.27[cd]	1.40[a]	6.28***
	(SD)	(.93)	(.92)	(1.42)	(1.39)	
Child risk	M	2.55	2.87	3.05	2.45	
	(SD)	(1.32)	(.99)	(1.13)	(1.10)	
Life events	M	8.0	4.27	7.55	6.95	2.24[+]
	(SD)	(3.93)	(3.67)	(5.01)	(5.03)	

[+]$p < .10$
***$p < .001$

[a,b,c,d] Superscripts indicate results from post hoc Tukey comparisons of adjustment means. Means with the same superscripts are significantly different at the .05 level.

significantly more problems than children in married, Euro-American families. The group means associated with each of these variables, the significant F-values resulting from univariate comparisons, and the results of post hoc Tukey comparisons of the adjusted mean scores are reported in Tables 1A, 1B, and 1C.

Table 1B
Means and Standard Deviations of Explanatory and Outcome Variables for Groups Defined by Ethnicity and Marital Status and Results of Univariate Comparisons

Variable		Euro-American		Mexican-American		
		Single (*n* = 24)	Married (*n* = 20)	Single (*n* = 22)	Married (*n* = 22)	Univariate F-Value
Social support						
Immediate	M	2.22	1.91	2.37	2.50	
	(SD)	(1.10)	(1.30)	(1.08)	(1.05)	
Emotional	M	1.90	2.25	2.00	2.08	
	(SD)	(.92)	(1.60)	(.90)	(.92)	
Parenting	M	2.00	1.90	2.16	2.17	
	(SD)	(1.00)	(1.13)	(1.10)	(1.00)	
Total contact	M	2.34	2.07	2.70	2.60	
	(SD)	(1.15)	(1.50)	(1.30)	(1.13)	
Maternal adjustment						
Depression	M	1.41[a]	1.25[abc]	1.40[b]	1.50[c]	12.50**
	(SD)	(.50)	(.31)	(.40)	(.41)	

[+] $p < .10$.
[*] $p < .05$.
[**] $p < .01$.
[a,b] Superscripts indicate results from post hoc Tukey comparisons of adjustment menas. Means with the same subscripts are significantly different at the .05 level.

Life Changes, Potential Stresses, and Social Support

A univariate MANOVA was generated where the family risk, child risk and the total life events scores were entered as dependent variables. The group variable consisted of four groups defined by number of adults parenting (one or two) and ethnicity (Euro- or Mexican-American). These analyses were not generated controlling for income differences since variations across income were built into the construction of the stress and risk variables. A significant multivariate difference resulted (Pillais, $F = 8.04$, $p < .000$). The

Table 1C
**Means and Standard Deviations of Explanatory and Outcome
Variables for Groups Defined by Ethnicity and Marital Status
and Results of Univariate Comparisons**

		Euro-American		Mexican-American		
Variable		Single $(n = 24)$	Married $(n = 20)$	Single $(n = 22)$	Married $(n = 22)$	Univariate F-Value
Maternal adjustment						
Anxiety	M	2.10	2.10	2.30	2.44	3.75[+]
	(SD)	(.50)	(.43)	(.54)	(.52)	
Self-esteem	M	3.35[a]	3.21[b]	3.18	3.11[ab]	6.33[*]
	(SD)	(.50)	(.56)	(.60)	(.85)	
Coping resources	M	3.00[a]	2.90	3.00[b]	2.83[ab]	15.60[**]
	(SD)	(.37)	(.32)	(.32)	(.50)	
Mother's parenting reports						
Positive PPI	M	4.16	4.02	4.30	4.13	
	(SD)	(.45)	(.43)	(.54)	(.40)	
Negative PPI	M	2.60[a]	2.30[ab]	2.60[b]	2.41	7.17[**]
	(SD)	(.65)	(.45)	(.60)	(.47)	
Rapport	M	3.80	4.16	4.21	4.18	3.51[+]
	(SD)	(1.16)	(.62)	(.41)	(.48)	
Monitoring	M	4.70	4.50	4.53	4.51	
	(SD)	(.21)	(.35)	(.30)	(.50)	

[+]$p < .10$.
[*]$p < .05$.
[**]$p < .01$.
[a,b] Superscripts indicate results from post hoc Tukey comparisons of adjustment means. Means with the same subscripts are significantly different at the .05 level.

univariate results suggest that the groups experienced significantly different numbers of family risk characteristics. Single, Mexican-American women reported the most conditions associated with family risk $(M = .19)$. The married, non-Hispanic women experienced the fewest conditions associated with risk $(M = .04)$. The univariate analysis was marginal for the total life events scores; however, the single, Euro-American and two Mexican-American groups reported approximately the same number of life events, and they experienced almost twice as many stressors as Euro-American, married women.

With regard to social support, no group differences emerged from a MANCOVA comparing group means across the three different kinds of social support (emotional, parenting, or practical) or the total contact variable while adjusting for differences in annual incomes. Of interest, however, is the fact that the single, Mexican-American mothers do not appear to be in any way disadvantaged, and in fact, like their married counterparts, have more contact with network members and receive both more instrumental support and advice about parenting than the Euro-American mothers.

Emotional Difficulties and Personal Resources

A MANCOVA was computed controlling for differences in income, with the maternal depression, anxiety, global self-worth, and coping resources entered as the dependent variables analyzed by group. A significant multivariate difference resulted (Pillais, $F = 5.33$, $p <$ .001). The univariate ANOVA comparisons revealed significant differences for the depression, global self-worth, and coping resources scores. Contrary to the expectation that the single mothers would be experiencing more personal adjustment problems, it was the married, Mexican-Americans who reported more depression, more anxiety, lower levels of self-worth, and fewer coping resources. Also contrary to expectations, the Euro-American, single women reported slightly higher levels of self-worth than their married, Euro-American counterparts, and they reported equal numbers of coping resources.

Mean scores from the acculturation scale were compared for the two groups of Mexican-American mothers. A statistically significant difference did not result even though the single women reported slightly higher acculturation scores. (3.85 versus 3.48).

Mother-Child Relationships: Rapport and Discipline

A MANCOVA, covarying the effect of income with the four maternal reports of parenting as dependent variables, resulted in a highly significant F-value (Pillais, $F = 3.1664$, $p < .05$). An examination of the univariate results suggested that, once the effects of income were accounted for, significant group differences existed in maternal reports of harsh parenting practices and rapport with their children. The single, Mexican- and Euro-American mothers reported employing the greatest number of negative parenting practices ($M = 2.6$). Euro-American, married mothers reported the fewest negative parenting practices ($M = 2.30$).

Results from analyses of the parent-child rapport measure revealed that the single, Mexican-American mothers also reported the most rapport in their relationships with their children, while the single, Euro-American mothers reported the least rapport.

Discussion

In recent years, there has been an increasing convergence of results in the identification of factors influencing variability in parenting among single mothers and the subsequent developmental outcomes for their children. The purpose of this project was to examine these variables in a more diverse sample of single and married mothers of Euro- and Mexican-American descent. The results of the analyses presented, despite relatively small numbers of respondents in each of the four groups examined, revealed some statistically significant and important group mean differences. Results also revealed a lack of differences where expected, which may have important implications for using the emergent "strain" model of the effects of single parenting on children's developmental outcomes for more diverse samples. The findings will first be discussed with regard to the tentative answers provided to each of the four research questions.

A number of existing studies examining behavioral adjustment difficulties among children have implicated single parenting as a potential source of these problems (Bank et al., 1993; Hetherington, 1988; Zill, 1988). In the present study, children from single-parent homes were more likely to exhibit externalizing behavior problems as reported by their mothers, regardless of their ethnic background. Eyberg, Boggs, and Rodriguez (1992) reported that regardless of marital status, mothers of children whose disruptive behaviors are within a clinically significant range find these behaviors stressful. However, if the frequencies of child disruptive behaviors are within the average range, single-parent mothers, but not married mothers, continue to report these behaviors as stressful. Several of the factors examined in this investigation may contribute to single mothers' reports of heightened levels of externalizing behaviors.

One factor that contributes to child problems in single-parent homes is stress. The two single-parent groups, both Euro- and Mexican-American, reported experiencing almost twice as many life events in the previous six-month period compared to mothers in coupled, Euro-American households. These findings confirm the expectation that, compared to married mothers, single parents face more stressful life circumstances, which are assumed to diminish their ability to be effective parents and contribute to increases in child behavioral problems. An unexpected finding, however, showed that the married, Mexican-American women reported more life events than married, Euro-American women, although these differences proved to be only marginally statistically significant. Significant differences did emerge for the family risk variable, and in contrast to the expectation that single-parent mothers might be experiencing more risk, differences appeared to be more closely associated with ethnicity than number of parents in the household. Mexican-American single mothers reported the greatest number of family risk factors. Married, Mexican-American mothers reported the second highest number—almost three times as many risk factors as described by the married, Euro-American mothers. As Seifer et al. (1992) have argued, risk factors tend to accumulate, and in addition to being members of ethnic minorities or living in single-parent homes (neither of which individually is sufficient to infer risk), the lives of children in these families may be characterized by a number of additional conditions capable of disrupting developmental paths. These results would seem to suggest that among Anglo, non-Hispanic, single and married women, there may be large and statistically significant within-group differences in the number of life changes experienced or in access to economic resources following the breakup of marriages or close personal relationships. For Mexican-American women, these within-group differences may not exist, and therefore, are not as clearly implicated in child-adjustment problems.

Contrary to expectations, significant group differences did not emerge from reports of support received or in the total amount of contact with support network members. One study has suggested that over time, the networking styles of Euro- and Mexican-American divorced women become more similar following a divorce (Wagner, 1987). When differences between these groups emerged, they tended to be in terms of network composition or sources of support, rather than amounts of support, with Euro-American women reporting lower levels of support from relatives and higher levels of support from friends. The lack of statistical differences in amount of support received could be due to the fact that sufficient time had passed since marital or relationship dissolution, and the social support networks had become more alike over time. This possibility seems highly likely given that 39.1% of the single women in the present sample reported never having been married, so a divorce or significant transitional event affecting support may never have occurred.

Although no statistical differences emerged, the results of comparing the single and married Euro-American mothers' reports of support are comparable to results reported by other investigators (e.g., Weinraub & Wolf, 1983) that suggest that single mothers receive less emotional and parenting forms of support. Fewer differences in support networks were observed between the single and married Mexican-American mothers' reports. Given the small sample size and the preliminary nature of these findings, this discussion can only speculate about the apparent similarity between the two groups of Mexican-American women. It is possible that social support may be equally available to both groups, and therefore, may not be a useful variable for discriminating among these women's parenting and the adjustment of their children. Support was not diminished for the single, Mexican-American women, although the composition of their networks may have changed following marital or relationship disruption. Social support seems to be both available and readily accessible for single, Mexican-American women. The support network may absorb some of the stress of single parenting, buffering the parent and her children from the negative effects of stress, but this possibility needs to be examined empirically.

In terms of maternal adjustment and personal resources, the group differences observed were unexpected. The married, Mexican-American women tended to report higher levels of depression and anxiety, fewer personal resources, and lower perceived self-competencies than any of the other three groups. These women also tended to report lower levels of acculturation than the single, Mexican-American mothers. These unexpected findings led to the consideration of several alternative explanations. As described above, the stress/strain model assumes that stress is higher in single-parent families. Married, Mexican-American women reported higher levels of stress and symptomatology than any other group in this investigation, indicating that marital status per se is not by itself a sufficient predictor of distress. For these women, other family characteristics might need to be considered. The centrality of the family in one's daily life, referred to as "familism," is often assumed to be a protective factor. Yet familism often means that a family member is expected to place the importance of the family over individual needs. Gray (1992) argued that in divorcing families, a sense of familism may not be as strong, and that these mothers and fathers may not forgo their own personal needs for the sake of keeping the family together. For some Mexican-American women, familism may prove to be a buffer against stress, but for others, it may serve as a stressor to the extent that personal needs are not adequately met and psychological adjustment is influenced negatively. Familism, a common characteristic among Hispanics, may prove to be a double-edged sword.

It is also possible that these emergent group differences reflect a measurement problem. Cultural influences on the measures employed have not been systematically considered. Stroup-Benham, Lawrence, and Trevino (1992) examined the factor structure of the Center for Epidemiologic Studies–Depression Scale (CES-D) for single and married Mexican-American and Puerto Rican women and found important group differences. Different numbers of factors emerged for the two groups, as well as incongruities regarding which items loaded on these factors across the groups. Although these authors evaluated a different depression scale, their results raise the possibility that the Beck Depression Inventory, which was used here, and the other assessments of maternal functioning, could have been interpreted and responded to in distinct ways by the Mexican-American single and married women. Thus, higher depression or anxiety, or lower self-esteem scores may not have the same significance for the Mexican-American mothers.

The single, non-Hispanic mothers reported feeling more depressed and anxious than the married, non-Hispanic women, which replicates existing findings (Weinraub & Wolf, 1983). These differences, however, were minimal and never achieved statistical significance. To date, investigators have described maternal adjustment to single parenthood primarily in terms of maladjustment. A recent trend is evident in new research programs, moving away from assumptions about deviant family forms and psychopathology as characteristics of single families and their individual members. By including assessments of competence or positive adaptation, the adjustment of single-parent women and their children may be characterized in terms of resilience, where single-motherhood need not have only negative consequences. In the results reported here, there was plenty of evidence to suggest that single women, both Euro- and Mexican-American, continued to maintain a sense of self-worth comparable to their married counterparts, and they reported having access to equal numbers of personal coping resources.

The present data seem to support further resiliency research on parenting in single-parent female-headed households. That is, parenting in single-parent households may be best characterized in terms of elevated levels of less effective discipline, as well as elevated levels of both warmth and rapport. The single, Mexican-American mothers reported more warmth and rapport and indicated that they used more controlling disciplinary tactics. Though not significantly different, a similar trend was evident for the single, Euro-American mothers, who reported warmer interactions with their children, more monitoring, and more negative controlling or harsher disciplinary practices than did their married counterparts. Thus these mothers may be at more risk for less adequate parenting due to increased stress and reduced support. Single women may, however, be sensitized to the fact that their parenting resources are limited and that on occasion stress may undermine their effectiveness. Recognizing this possibility, they may perceive the need to monitor their children's activities more closely and to engage in more positive interactions. It is important to note that the present data are based on maternal reports and may only reflect these mothers' opinions of how they interact with and discipline (or would like to discipline) their children. Nevertheless, these results raise the possibility that the balance between the use of effective versus ineffective parenting strategies may be more critical for understanding subsequent child outcomes for children in single-parent homes than either variable considered separately.

This study was limited by several methodological issues, not the least of which was the small sample size. Less obvious was the lack of information about length of residence in the United States and/or generational differences in the samples of Mexican-American women that might usefully inform the observed group mean differences and differences in the patterns of correlations. Future investigations of single parenting among different ethnic groups may need to employ these and other variables, enabling investigators to capture richer and more detailed information about respondents' experiences as members of social networks, spouses, parents, and individuals.

These results suggest that the emergent strain perspective for conceptualizing parenting and child adjustment in single parent, mother-headed households may not be appropriate for delineating these processes among Mexican-Americans. Both married and single mothers reported similar levels of externalizing behavioral problems, approximately equal numbers of risk conditions and life events, and similar amounts of support received. Yet the two groups differed in personal adjustment and personal resources, and subtle differences were observed in their reports of parenting. Additional work needs to generate alternative conceptual models for explaining the differences observed within an ethnic group but across family forms, with particular focus on the nature of the marital/spousal relationship and its personal significance.

References

Achenbach, T. M. (1991). *Manual for the Child Behavior Checklist/4-18 and 1991 profile.* Burlington, VT: University of Vermont Department of Psychiatry.

Amato, P. R. (1987). Family processes in intact, one-parent, and stepparent families: The child's point of view. *Journal of Marriage and the Family, 49,* 327–337.

Amato, P. R. (1993). Children's adjustment to divorce: Theories, hypotheses, and empirical support. *Journal of Marriage and the Family, 55,* 23–38.

Bank, L., Forgatch, M. S., Patterson, G. R., & Fetrow, R. A. (1993). Parenting practices of single mothers: Mediators of negative contextual factors. *Journal of Marriage and the Family, 55,* 371–384.

Beck, A. T. (1967). *Depression: Clinical, experimental, and theoretical aspects.* New York: Harper & Row.

Blechman, E. A. (1982). Are children with one parent at psychological risk? A methodological review. *Journal of Marriage and the Family, 44,* 179–195.

Colletta, N. D. (1978). Divorced mothers at two income levels: Stress, support, and childrearing practices. *Dissertation Abstracts International, 38,* 6114.

Colletta, N. D. (1983). At risk for depression: A study of young mothers. *Journal of Marriage and the Family, 54,* 104–117.

Compas, B. E., & Williams, R. A. (1990). Stress, coping, and adjustment in mothers and young adolescents in single- and two-parent families. *American Journal of Community Psychology, 18,* 525–545.

Conger, R. D., Elder, G. H., Jr., Lorenz, F. O., Simons, R. L., & Whitbeck, L. B. (1992). A family process model of economic hardship and influences on adjustment of early adolescent boys. *Child Development, 63,* 526–541.

Costello, C. G., & Comrey, A. L. (1967). Scale for measuring depression and anxiety. *The Journal of Psychology, 66,* 303–313.

Department of Health and Human Services. (1991). Low-Income Poverty Guideline. Supt. of Documents, Congressional Sales Office, U.S. G.P.O. Serial no. 101-24.

Dornbusch, S., Carlsmith, J. M., Bushwall, S. J., Ritter, P. L., Leiderman, H., Hastorf, A. H., & Gross, R. T. (1985). Single parents, extended households, and the control of adolescents. *Child Development, 56,* 326–341.

Eyberg, S. M., Boggs, S. R., & Rodriguez, C. M. (1992). Relationships between maternal parenting stress and child disruptive behavior. *Child & Family Behavior Therapy, 14,* 1–9.

Furstenberg, F. F., Jr., & Nord, C. W. (1987). Parenting apart: Patterns of childrearing after marital disruption. *Journal of Marriage and the Family, 47,* 893–904.

Garmezy, N., & Rutter, M. (Eds.). (1983). *Stress, coping, & development in children.* New York: McGraw-Hill.

Gray, K. D. (1992). Fathers' participation in child custody arrangements among Hispanic, non-Hispanic White, and intermarried families. *Journal of Comparative Family Studies, 23,* 55–68.

Hammer, A. L., & Marting, M. S. (1987). *Coping resources inventory-Form D.* Palo Alto, CA: Consulting Psychologists Press.

Hazzard, A., Christensen, A., & Margolin, G. (1983). Children's perceptions of parental behaviors. *Journal of Abnormal Child Psychology, 2,* 49–60.

Hetherington, E. M. (1988). Parents, children, and siblings six years after divorce. In R. Hinde & J. Stevenson-Hinde (Eds.), *Relationships within families* (pp. 311–331). Cambridge: Cambridge University Press.

Hetherington, E. M., & Clingempeel, W. G., Anderson, E.R., Deal, J.E., Hagan, M.S., Hollier, E.A. & Linder, M.S. (Eds.). (1992). Coping with marital transitions. *Monographs of the Society for Research in Child Development, 57* (2–3, Serial No. 227).

Lahey, B. B., Conger, R. D., Atkenson, B. M., & Treifer, F. A. (1984). Parenting behavior and emotional status of physically abusive mothers. *Journal of Consulting and Clinical Psychology, 52,* 1062–1072.

Laosa, L. M. (1988). Ethnicity and single parenting in the United States. In E. M. Hetherington & J. D. Arasteh (Eds.), *Impact of divorce, single parenting, and stepparenting on children* (pp. 23–49). Hillsdale, NJ: Lawrence Erlbaum.

Longfellow, C., Zelkowitz, P., & Sanders, E. (1982). The quality of mother-child relationships. In D. Belle (Ed.), *Lives in stress: Women and depression* (pp. 163–176). Beverly Hills, CA: Sage.

Marin, G., Sabogal, F., Marin, B. V., Otero-Sabogal, R., & Perez-Stable, E. J. (1987). Development of a short acculturation scale for Hispanics. *Hispanic Journal of Behavioral Sciences, 9,* 183–205.

McLanahan, S. S. (1983). Family structure and stress: A longitudinal comparison of two-parent and female-headed families. *Journal of Marriage and the Family, 45,* 347–357.

McLanahan, S. S., & Booth, K. (1989). Mother-only families: Problems, prospects, and politics. *Journal of Marriage and the Family, 51,* 557–580.

McLanahan, S. S., Wedemeyer, N., & Adelberg, N. (1981). Network structure, social support, and psychological well-being in the single-parent family. *Journal of Marriage and the Family, 43,* 601–612.

McLoyd, V. C. (1990). The impact of economic hardship on Black families and children: Psychological distress, parenting, and socioemotional development. *Child Development, 61,* 311–346.

Messer, B., & Harter, S. (1987). *The self-perception scale for adults,* Unpublished manuscript, University of Denver, CO.

Norbeck, J. S., Lindsey, A. M., & Carrieri, V. L. (1981). The development of an instrument to measure social support. *Nursing Research, 30,* 264–269.

Norbeck, J. S., Lindsey, A. M., & Carrieri, V. L. (1982). Further development of the Norbeck Social Support Questionnaire normative data and validity testing. *Nursing Research, 32,* 4–9.

Olson, D. H., McCubbin, H. I., Barnes, H., Larsen, A., Muxen, M., & Wilson, L. (1982). Family inventories: Inventories used in a national survey of families across the life cycle. (Available from Family Social Science, 290 McNeal Hall, University of Minnesota, St. Paul, MN, 55108).

Olson, S. L., & Banyard, V. (1993). "Stop the world so I can get off for awhile": Sources of daily stress in the lives of low-income single mothers of young children. *Family Relations, 42*, 50–56.

Patterson, G. (1983). Stress: A change agent for family process. In N. Garmezy & M. Rutter (Eds.), *Stress, coping, and development in children* (pp. 235–264). Baltimore, MD: Johns Hopkins University.

Seifer, R., Sameroff, A. J., Baldwin, C. P., & Baldwin, A. (1992). Child and family factors that ameliorate risk between 4 and 13 years of age. *Journal of the American Academy of Child and Adolescent Psychiatry, 31*, 893–903.

Shinn, M. (1978). Father absence and children's cognitive development. *Psychological Bulletin, 85*, 295–394.

Simons, R. L., Beaman, J., Conger, R. D., & Chao, W. (1993). Stress, support, and antisocial behavior trait as determinants of emotional well-being and parenting practices among single mothers. *Journal of Marriage and the Family, 55*, 385–398.

Stroup-Benham, C. A., Lawrence, R. H., & Trevino, F. M. (1992). CES-D factor structure among Mexican-American and Puerto Rican women from single- and couple-headed households. *Hispanic Journal of Behavioral Sciences, 14*, 310–326.

U.S. Bureau of the Census. (1992). Statistical Abstract of the United States: 1992 (112th edition). Washington, DC.

Vega, W. A., Hough, R., & Romero, A. (1983). Family life patterns of Mexican Americans. In G. J. Powell (Ed.), *The psychosocial development of minority children*. New York: Brunner/Mazel.

Wagner, R. M. (1987). Changes in the friend network during the first year of single parenthood for Mexican-American and Anglo women. *Journal of Divorce, 11*, 89–109.

Weinraub, M., & Wolf, B. M. (1983). Effects of stress and social supports on mother-child interactions in single- and two-parent families. *Child Development, 54*, 1297–1311.

Weitzman, L. J. (1985). *The divorce revolution: The unexpected social and economic consequences for women and children in America*. New York: Free Press.

Wilkinson, D. (1987). Ethnicity. In S. Steinmetz & M. B. Sussman (Eds.), *Handbook of marriage and the family* (pp. 345–405). New York: Plenum.

Zill, N. (1988). Behavior, achievement, and health problems among children in stepfamilies: Findings from a national survey of child health. In E. M. Hetherington & J. D. Arasteh (Eds.), *Impact of divorce, single parenting, and stepparenting on children* (pp. 325–368). Hillsdale, NJ: Lawrence Erlbaum Associates.

Chapter 18

Coping With Racism and Discrimination

The Experience of Young Latino Adolescents[1]

Katherine Fennelly, Patricia Mulkeen, and Carina Giusti

Latino youth in the United States face a severe educational disadvantage. As young adults, Latinos are three times more likely to have dropped out of high school before graduating than White or African-American students. In 1992, 40% of Latinos ages 25 to 29 did not have high school diplomas, compared to 13% of Whites and 14% of African-Americans in that age group (U.S. Department of Commerce, 1993).

Explanations for the higher dropout rates and lower school achievement of minority students have been varied. Studies conducted in Latino communities have identified pervasive racism and discrimination as contributing factors to the academic disadvantage of Latino youth (Greenberg, Burgoon, Burgoon, & Korzenny, 1983; Korzenny & Schiff, 1987). Other researchers have suggested that cultural differences in learning styles and interaction patterns influence students' achievement in the classroom. In a study of low-income Black students in Washington, DC, Fordham and Ogbu (1986) found that school, peer pressure, and the fear of being accused of abandoning one's social identity were cited as the major reasons that many Black students refused to study, shunned standard English, and avoided what they perceived to be "White" interests (e.g., the symphony, opera, and the humanities). Some students were ambivalent toward academic success because they defined it as a "White prerogative" and did not want to typify White behavior. Similarly, Ogbu (1981) suggests that a minority student who behaves in ways that lead to achievement in the academic setting may be perceived as "betraying" his or her minority group identity and thus jeopardizing acceptance within that group without any guarantees of being accepted by the majority group. Many educational institutions have actually contributed to the perception that academic success is "for Whites only" through tracking, ability grouping, and programs that appear to minority students to be discriminatory.

Ogbu (1981, 1987) and Bernal, Saenz, and Knight (1991) have described other ways in which minority student responses to discrimination can either hinder or support school achievement. Ogbu (1987) describes patterns of adaptation that can help students to overcome the cultural barriers they face, as well as patterns that can hinder their progress by leading to the adoption of a social identity that is in opposition to majority group values and behaviors. Ogbu's framework suggests that societal forces and classroom events produce lower academic performance and higher rates of school-leaving among "involuntary immigrant" youth: Involuntary immigrants are defined by Ogbu as those "people who were *originally brought into United States society involuntarily* through slavery, conquest, or colonization" (Ogbu, 1987, p. 321, italics in original). The societal forces that he describes include a "job ceiling" for minorities, and unequal access to quality education. In his research in a California community he found that "although there is a correlation between education and jobs in the Black community, it is not as strong as the correlation in the White community because of a job ceiling" (Ogbu, 1981, p. 17). As a result, Black residents did not believe that they lived in a community of equal opportunity. "They point out that racial and ethnic discriminations have traditionally prevented them from obtaining more desirable jobs, higher wages, and promotions on the job on the basis of education and ability, and from buying or renting homes in better parts of the city" (Ogbu, 1981, p. 21). This view leads to an ambivalence about education, which is communicated to Black youth. On the one hand, Black parents (like White parents) tend to agree that education is important to get ahead; on the other hand "they also teach their children verbally and through their own life experiences of unemployment, underemployment, and other discriminations, as well as through gossip about similar experiences among relatives, neighbors and friends—*through the actual texture of life*—that, even if they do well in school, they may not do so as adults in the wider society" (Ogbu, 1981, p. 21, italics in original).

In an examination of the relative economic status of Puerto Ricans, Mexicans, and Cubans, Tienda (1989) found that Puerto Ricans were concentrated at the bottom of the labor queue in jobs that provide very low incomes and which disappear quickly in the face of economic downturns. Education alone did not explain the differences in rate of economic decline among these Latino sub-groupings; Mexican-Americans and Puerto Ricans had similar levels of education, yet Puerto Ricans fared worse in the job market. Tienda examined several contributing factors, including regional differences in the types of jobs available and concentrations of Mexican-Americans and Puerto Ricans.

Tienda's research provides a bridge connecting Ogbu's findings for African-Americans and similar labor market problems faced by Puerto Ricans, in particular. Unstable employment and chronic detachment from the labor market may lead to dissonance between verbal messages received by Puerto Rican adolescents regarding the importance of education and evidence available from the experiences of relatives and neighbors.

Another determinant of school failure among Latino youth may be overt discrimination. Despite widespread attention to this phenomenon and its negative impacts upon African-American children and adolescents, very few studies have examined the experiences of Latino youth. This is a serious omission, because Latinos may be the victims of discrimination for multiple reasons. These can include skin color, English language proficiency, and poverty. In addition to the dearth of studies on discrimination faced by Latino youth, there are few studies of youth of any race/ethnicity which examine discrimination from the point of view of the *victim* (Korzenny & Schiff, 1987). The present study addresses both of these needs by questioning Latino youth and their parents about racism and discrimination.

Methods

The purpose of this exploratory study was to gather the perspectives of Latino adolescents and parents regarding the challenges and rewards facing young Latinos living in a small Pennsylvania city with a very rapidly growing Hispanic population. This was done by means of focus group discussions with Puerto Rican adolescents and mothers. Participants were identified through contacts with local agencies serving Latino adolescents. Separate focus groups were conducted for parents and adolescents. In all, five focus groups yielded information for this study, including three groups of adolescent girls ($n=5$, $n=8$, $n=10$; ages 10-15) and two groups of mothers of adolescents ($n=5$, $n=15$).

Focus Groups

Focus groups are small groups of people selected to meet and discuss questions posed by a moderator. Participants are usually selected to be similar to each other with regard to sex, race, age, and socioeconomic status so that they will feel comfortable openly discussing the topics. The moderator begins by asking a general question, and then follows the flow of the discussion, asking for clarification when necessary. As the discussion progresses, the moderator asks further questions to keep the group on a particular topic of interest to the researchers. This method is an excellent way to learn about the issues that are important to a group of people without imposing preconceived notions (Templeton, 1987; Krueger, 1989).

Selection of Subjects

Participants were selected from a middle school with the largest proportion of Latino students, two after-school programs for Hispanic youth, and a community club in a local housing project with predominantly Latino residents. Originally, adolescent boys and girls as well as mothers and fathers were recruited to participate in the study. Efforts to recruit fathers were unsuccessful. The community contacts involved in this study were unable to confirm a meeting with fathers. A Puerto Rican male moderator (fluent in both Spanish and English) conducted two focus groups with adolescent boys, but due to the boys' reluctance to talk in depth, as well as their tendency to agree with anything the moderator mentioned, these data were not included in the final analysis.

Discussions were held in Spanish and/or English, depending upon the choice of participants at the time of the focus groups. The mothers' focus groups were moderated by one of two native Spanish-speaking women; one group was conducted in Spanish and the other was conducted in English. The groups with adolescents were conducted primarily in English, with some Spanish words or phrases being used in the discussion. The adolescent groups were moderated by two women (one, a native Spanish speaker, and the other, an American of Puerto Rican heritage with a knowledge of Spanish). In all groups, the primary language to be used was determined by consensus of the group members, yet in all but one of the groups, participants used both Spanish and English. Moderators followed the lead of the participants in determining the language to be used, watching and checking for comprehension by posing questions in both languages.

The moderators posed questions designed to foster discussion. Some questions were very general (e.g., "What is life like for a teenager in this community?"), while others explored adolescents' activities (e.g., "What do kids usually do when they are not at school?"), as well as their relationships with peers and adults. Specific questions on prejudice and discrimination were introduced late in the discussion if these topics had not emerged spontaneously (e.g., "Do teachers treat Hispanic students differently than White students?" "Do Hispanic and Black teenagers hang out together?" "What about Hispanic and White teenagers?"). All of the focus group conversations were tape-recorded and transcribed for later analysis. The Spanish was translated by a native speaker and verified by the native speakers who conducted the focus groups.

Conceptual Framework

The data presented in this chapter relate to the experiences and perceptions of Puerto Rican adolescents and parents concerning schools and academic achievement. Our analysis is organized around a framework suggested by Ogbu (1981, 1987). Specifically, the analysis of the focus group data centered on comments by respondents that confirmed or belied perceptions of the following:

1. A perceived job ceiling for minorities, or the general perception that a good education does not necessarily lead to success;
2. Unequal access to quality education;
3. Lowered expectations for the academic performance of Latino youth on the part of teachers and administrators;
4. Cultural differences or communication styles that impede the educational achievement of minority youth.

In addition, comments regarding two characteristics of immigrant youth that may impede school achievement were examined:

5. English proficiency;
6. Frequent moves/family relocation.

Findings

Although the group discussions began with general questions about life in the local community, responses of the adolescents and mothers most often related to experiences and perceptions of schooling. Given the amount of time most adolescents spend in school and the importance of education for a young person's future, it is not surprising that a great deal of discussion was generated around this topic. Discussions with mothers and youth revealed concerns echoing each of the perceptions described by Ogbu among Black families.

Job Ceiling for Minorities

Several Latino parents and girls made comments suggesting that, because of discrimination, a good education does not necessarily translate into success for Latinos. As one mother commented, "we are constantly being stopped by lack of money, lack of a certain type of education; some people just don't let you in because you are a minority. We aren't going to get ahead as far as this goes."

An adolescent described her growing conviction that vocational training might be more worthwhile than college prep:

> I know like a lot of friends of mine might have gone to college and they are sitting at home with no work because there's hardly any work outside. But the ones who went to Vo-tech are already working. Why are you spending your money to go to college when in the future you don't know, but maybe you won't have a job.

Others described pervasive racism and the belief that many Americans don't want Puerto Ricans to get ahead. One mother commented *"Ellos quieren echar el americano 'pa' lante' y derrotar al hispano"* ["they want to pull the American through and defeat the Hispanic"]. Another added: "We are starting to speak better English than most Americans. But we still aren't having a ranch home. We are still not having what we want; we still don't have a bank account."

Several women felt that Latino students study hard, but that they are held down by racism:

> My kids are smart, they are honors students and I am drilling that into them because they don't have a chance.

> They don't have a chance because they are a minority.
> They have a half a chance because they are serious about
> their education. But they can only get so far.

Another mother remarked that Hispanic people must put forth more effort than non-Hispanic Americans, due to the language barrier, but they still do not have as many opportunities as Whites. She commented: "We got to learn more because English is not our language. We got to study more, we got to listen more. Still even though we do that there's someone who won't let us go far." Some of the girls echoed their parents' sentiments: "We try to be all we can be...We try... We try but not always come that way. There is always someone in the way."

Unequal Access to Quality Education

Although many of the mothers and adolescents described their perceptions of pervasive racism and unfair treatment of Latinos in the schools, few described general dissatisfaction with access to quality education. One woman who did said, "There's no excuse for the education that they have had for us. We don't like it. They give you whatever to pacify you to keep you happy." Another woman added:

> Blacks and Hispanics are climbing up the ladder, but there's
> a White person at the top pushing us down. They com-
> plain that we are on welfare ... but they don't provide us
> with education.

The problems with school personnel described by mothers and adolescents suggest that unequal access to a high-quality education is a concern for Latino students and their parents. Both adolescents' perceptions of differential treatment by teachers, as well as mothers' perceptions of poor communication regarding their children's progress, interfere with students' education as well as parents' ability to be involved in their children's education. Perceptions of differential treatment have led parents and adolescents to believe that the education provided to Latino students is not as good as that provided to White students.

While most mothers discussed problems related to their children's education, not all mothers had a negative opinion of the educational opportunities available to their children in the United States. One mother expressed a more positive view of educational opportunities in the U.S.:

> *La educación aquí es más profunda porque aquí si los*
> *muchachos verdaderamente cogen el interés, tu sabes, es*
> *más profunda y estos maestros que son racistas, los dejo en*
> *paz porque aquí hay unas ofertas de estudio fabulosas que*
> *no hay en Puerto Rico; pero entonces todas esas otras cosas*
> *matan las cosas buenas que hay aquí.*

> [Education here is more in depth because it is more inten-
> sive... here if the kids really show interest, you know, it is
> more in depth. If (some) are racists, leave them in peace.
> Because here there are some fabulous opportunities to study
> which we don't have in Puerto Rico. But then all those
> other things kill the good things here.]

Lowered Expectations for Latino Youth

Educational expectations for self are strongly influenced by the expectations of teachers and administrators, parents, and peers.

Perceived Expectations of Teachers and Administrators. Adolescents described the differences they perceive in treatment by Latino and White teachers. Girls viewed Latino teachers as more patient. As one girl described it:

> ... There are American teachers who don't have patience
> with us, and explain everything one time and the second
> time if you don't understand they won't speak to us ... they
> are like 'if you don't understand, that's too bad!' But the
> Puerto Rican teacher... she bends over and explains every-
> thing to them, and she makes sure that they understand.
> She always says 'very good, very good.'

The discussion turned to what teachers know about students in terms of their ability and desire to learn. "They think the White people, all they want to do is earn money, get in school. We want to learn too, but they don't know that." The rest of the group agreed. Adolescents saw these attitudes as related to stereotypes of Puerto Ricans, Blacks, and Whites. One adolescent said:

> ...They think that Puerto Ricans and Blacks are fighters
> and, you know, gangs and gangsters and stuff like that.
> They don't think we are serious or anything. They think
> White people, you know, want to stay in school, will be
> lawyers and all that. That's what they think of us.

Parental Expectations. One of the mothers interviewed suggested that American youth go further than Latino children because of differences in parental aspirations for their children:

> American people from the time they have a baby, they are planning their college and everything for the future. At the same time, we are holding our babies saying baby talk, we are saying 'sweet heart you are going to be a softball player.' But they teach them from young to be a lawyer and all that. We do not.

The theme of parental expectations emerged in the adolescent groups as well. One adolescent explained:

> My dad, dropped out ...he wants me go to school, I don't know... He wants the best for me. When we have a problem at school or something and I don't want to go any more he says, 'for me it was different; you have to go.'

Peer Expectations. Girls also experienced peer pressure not to do homework. Several agreed with one girl's comment that:

> My friend told me 'I'm not gonna do the homework,' so I said 'Oh well me neither.' The next day she shows her homework to the teacher and I didn't do it. And you are the one who fail.

Given school performance problems and ambivalence about academic achievement, for many of the students, whether or not to stay in high school was a more salient issue than future college plans. It was acknowledged that many adolescents drop out of school; some of the reasons given for dropping out were: "they can't stand it any more because of the pressure"; "because of the teacher"; and "because they get pregnant." However, some girls perceived college as an important opportunity. One girl mentioned, "If you go to college that will allow you to have a better life."

Overt discrimination from White classmates produces a different sort of peer expectation. All of the Puerto Rican girls interviewed had heard other youths tell them to go home; go back to Puerto Rico. This was confusing to many of the girls, several of whom had never been to Puerto Rico. One noted "I'm not even pure Puerto Rican and they tell me to go back. Go back where?"

From the data it is clear that both mothers and daughters were concerned that their teachers' lower expectations for Latino youth stemmed from a view that Puerto Rican students were incapable of doing well in school. One girl commented: "They put us down; they talk to us like we're not gonna make it." Several others added that teachers equate difficulty with English with a lack of intelligence. One girl indicated, "They put you in the back of the class, and let's say for example, Maria is in the back and ... they say something to you, they ask you what does it mean. They think you are stupid." In general, the girls perceived their White teachers as people who do not believe that Puerto Ricans can succeed.

The powerful influence of a teacher who does believe in a student was recognized by mothers. Such a teacher can help a student to believe in herself, as described by one mother whose daughter turned around her difficulty in school with the help of a school counselor and a teacher:

> *Ella habló con el conselor y ella misma pues se creó una confianza en la escuela que la empezaron a ayudar y...ahora en la vocacional es la sobresaliente.*

> [She talked to the counselor herself, then she started to feel confident in school and they started to help her. ...(Now) in the vocational school she is the outstanding student.]

Discipline. Both the adolescents and the mothers discussed concerns regarding discipline at school. The girls and the parents both perceived that teachers punish and suspend Latino students more often than White students. Adolescents' descriptions of the reasons for punishment showed that they feel they are punished for small offenses, including speaking Spanish. Several of the mothers perceived that White teachers punish students differently based on their ethnicity. One mother mentioned her son's experience in a school cafeteria:

> *Porque si los latinos estaban hablando en la cafetería donde no podían, entonces les daban a escribir 600 veces 'no hablar en la cafetería, no hablar en la cafetería,' y al blanco no le hicieron eso y el blanco era él que estaba hablando.*

> [If the Latino kids were talking in the cafeteria, where they were not supposed to, they made them write '...Don't talk in the cafeteria' 600 times. ...They didn't do that with the White kids and they were the ones talking.]

The theme of differential discipline was raised by several mothers as well.

Outside of the school setting, there are other sources of stereotypes of Latino youth and families. Both girls and mothers perceived stereotypes in the media, especially in newspaper reports of crime. One mother explained:

> In the newspapers if a Hispanic gets arrested, it is in the paper faster than if it is a White. You never see anything positive that would motivate our kids. Because if you see negative stuff every day then you are going to think negative stuff.

When asked if any of the negative reports in the media were accurate, answers illustrated the range of positive and negative behaviors in the Hispanic community, "some Hispanics, some Puerto Ricans they sell drugs and mess it up for other people" and "there are some Puerto Ricans that they want to be a doctor and get their money like White people." Another commented:

> I think that here, the discrimination is always against the Hispanics and the Blacks. You see, If you go to a store they will say that those (Blacks and Hispanics) are the ones who come to steal. They are the good for nothings. If they see that you are light-complected, but have a Hispanic accent, they say, 'this one came to steal, we have to watch him, follow him closely.'

One young woman described her hope that she would be able to overcome negative stereotypes of Latinos:

> All the things that have happened here have in part motivated me to try to demonstrate to people who say that we are nothing, that I can be somebody. That I can study and move ahead towards a good job and demonstrate that things are not as they think. That the Hispanics are good for many things, we are not trash. I know what people said and that motivates me to continue studying so I can teach them that it is not what they think.

Cultural Differences in Communication Styles and Educational Achievement

Ogbu (1987) suggests that "the relationship between minorities and White Americans who control the public schools is often characterized by conflict and distrust. Many minority parents are skeptical that the schools can educate their children as well as they educate White children." In this study, despite avowed beliefs that education is important for later success, the Latino parents' and children's experiences with the schools led to skepticism.

In particular, the Latino mothers described communication problems with teachers and school administrators. Some women felt they did not get complete information from teachers about their children's performance in school. One woman described the following experience:

> I went down there and asked the teacher how my daughter was doing academic wise. They told me, 'she is doing fine, she is doing wonderful' every time I went down. How come at the end of the year she got all F's on her report card?

Another mother described a similar experience, adding her concern about racial discrimination:

> I'm worried about what they do in the classroom as a parent that's my concern. O.K. I don't know why she told me this—she told me in a teacher's conference —'she is doing well,' but in spelling come to find out it's a D. Don't tell me that's not racist; there is something wrong there. My daughter is not dumb—that's why she is here.

Parental concern over teachers' reports that children were doing well, although they were actually failing, was echoed by several of the women interviewed.

Several mothers were also frustrated about not being able to get extra help for their children when it was needed. Apparently, communication between the schools and parents could be improved by communicating to parents the challenges of being a teacher in an urban multi-cultural school. Only one mother acknowledged how difficult it is for one teacher to meet the needs of every student when class sizes are large. She said, "As far as the teacher knowing if those children absorbed it or not, with a large quantity of children that's really hard. And that's nobody's fault I think."

English Proficiency

Two factors that can interfere with Hispanic adolescents' ability to obtain an education are the difficulty of learning a second language and the difficulty of adjusting to frequent moves. Bernal and colleagues (1991) cite studies showing that students with an English language background demonstrate higher achievement and school completion rates than students for whom English is a foreign language.

An adolescent in the study commented that "most people in my class are White and speak English very well; they don't know how difficult it is. You feel like you are behind them. You feel like...You fell from a big person to a little person."

Another girl described punishment for speaking Spanish in class: "Each time you spoke Spanish in class you had to pay a quarter." Several girls agreed that they had to speak in English all the time, and if they wanted to tell something to a friend in Spanish, teachers would think that they said something bad. One girl mentioned:

> They don't want you to break the rule. They want you to speak English in the classroom. And if you don't, like write a note or something in Spanish, Ah! You are saying something bad. And they take you downstairs and make you say what you wrote. Even if you write something good, they gonna make it bad and when they showed it to one counselor she said Oh! She didn't write something bad. Some people or some teachers try to get you in trouble.

Some girls were not sure whether knowing two languages was an advantage or a disadvantage. One said, "It is positive and negative. I mean, I don't know ... it's both." Some mothers expressed concern that their children were not fitting in with peers because they were not fluent in English. The mothers were concerned that these adolescents were being mistreated by their peers.

Frequent Moves

A study by Rumberger, cited by Bernal et al. (1991), showed that Hispanic adolescents had more academic problems and were much more likely to drop out of school if they had recently lived outside the United States than if they were long-term U.S. residents.

In discussing moves between New York, Puerto Rico, and Pennsylvania, the girls had varied opinions regarding the effect of moving on their school performance. As one girl described the difficulty of changing schools:

> At school...Oh, My God! If you are in one place and then in another because you moved, whatever you learned is soon forgotten. And things that you should have learned you didn't....Whatever you knew, you forgot.

Another girl felt that moving had been beneficial to her:

> ... the last time I moved was two years ago. But instead of
> affecting me for the worse, it affected me for the better. I
> was sort of tired of the same teachers and the same rou-
> tine for five years. I didn't care. That is, I wanted to be
> somebody but I got bored. I was getting lower grades. But
> when I came here, even though I don't really know the
> language well, my grades went up.

Discussion

Few researchers have examined perceptions of prejudice and discrimination from the perspective of Hispanic teenagers. In the
absence of empirical studies on which to formulate hypotheses,
this study sought to collect descriptive, qualitative data to inform
subsequent larger scale studies of the academic achievement of
Latino youth.

The focus group methodology employed is particularly well
suited to an investigation of sensitive topics such as racism. The
interviews summarized in this chapter reflect the perceptions of
participants in five focus groups with Puerto Rican adolescents
and mothers in a small city in Pennsylvania. Without observing
interactions between school personnel, parents, and students, the
authors cannot report on actual events; however, we were struck
by the almost universally shared perceptions of pervasive racism
and discrimination. While the participants may not be representative of all Latinos in the community, it is significant that their
perceptions of unfair treatment surfaced spontaneously among respondents in five different groups discussing such general topics as
school, friendships, and activities for adolescents.

The views of the Puerto Rican women interviewed generally
support Ogbu's assertion that limited economic opportunities for
educated minority adults may produce cynicism concerning the
value of schooling which is then communicated to young people.
While access to quality education was not specifically mentioned in
terms of facilities or funds, mothers and adolescent girls expressed
frustration with aspects of the school experience that interfere with
learning. Mothers were particularly frustrated by poor communication with teachers, which limited their involvement in their
children's education. Girls tended to focus more on disciplinary
issues, including ways in which they felt Latino students were
singled out or punished more harshly than non-Latino students.

The effect of these perceptions is that Latino parents and students do not believe that they are receiving educational opportunities available to White students.

Some comments by mothers and adolescents did describe more positive interactions with teachers and fellow community members. The example given earlier of the teacher who helped a girl enroll in vocational school is one such interaction. A few comments by mothers also acknowledged that some people in the community do not discriminate against Latinos. One mother described an incident in which a White person helped her up from a fall; the group agreed that not all White people are racist, yet the majority of the conversation centered around problems with those who are racist.

Bernal et al. (1991) suggest that, faced with negative stereotypes of their culture, Mexican youth may either devalue and internalize feelings of inadequacy or reinterpret the reasons for their low status. In addition, they may repudiate institutions and values associated with Anglo culture. This is similar to Fordham and Ogbu's (1986) findings that high-achieving Black students tended to reject their home and peer cultures. The study presented here revealed some peer pressure to do poorly in school. Both the girls and the mothers expressed belief in the value of education, nevertheless, this belief is continually tested by pervasive discrimination against Latinos.

Response to discrimination is important in that it may serve as a mediating factor in the influence of discrimination on students' success (Ogbu, 1981). Students' responses to discrimination took two forms: Some young women appeared to reject majority culture pressures to do well in school, and were influenced by the peer pressure to do poorly in school; other young women reacted to discrimination with a desire to "prove them wrong" by succeeding in school and work:

> All the things that have happened here have in part motivated me to try to demonstrate to people who say that we are nothing, that I can be somebody. That I can study and move ahead towards a good job and demonstrate that things are not as they think. That the Hispanics are good for many things, we are not trash. I know what people said and that motivates me to continue studying so I can teach them that it is not what they think.

This response to discrimination is described by Ogbu (1981) as a mediating factor in the influence of discrimination on students' success.

Bernal et al. (1991) suggest that interventions that are contextually appropriate and that communicate positive images of ethnic group membership and academic achievement can improve the academic performance of minority youth. In the community under study such efforts must begin with the employment of Hispanic teachers. Only 4% of the teachers in the community involved in this study are Hispanic, compared to 40% of the students. Some of the students interviewed had a Hispanic teacher in the bilingual program. The perception seemed to be that "Puerto Rican teachers treat us in a better way." One girl commented that:

> American teachers don't have patience with us, they explain everything one time and the second time if you don't understand, that's too bad! But the Puerto Rican teacher...she bends over and explains everything to them, and she makes sure that they understand. She always says 'very good, very good.'

Efforts to improve the school experience of Latino youth should include hiring of Latino teachers and training of school staff in working with Limited English Proficiency (LEP) students. Other important changes would address the need for improved communication between teachers and Latino parents, as well as the incorporation of positive role models for Latino students. These measures would help to promote success in school and work while demonstrating respect and appreciation of Latino culture.

Note

1. This research was supported by a grant from the Carnegie Corporation of New York.

References

Bernal, M. E., Saenz, D. S., & Knight, G. P. (1991). Ethnic identity and adaptation of Mexican American youth in school settings. *Hispanic Journal of Behavioral Sciences*, *13*(2), 135-154.

Fordham, S., & Ogbu, J. U. (1986). Black students' school success: Coping with "the burden of 'acting white.'" *The Urban Review*, *18*, 176-206.

Greenberg, B.S., Burgoon, M., Burgoon, J. K., & Korzenny, F. (1983). *Mexican Americans and the mass media.* Norwood, NJ: Ablex Publishing Corporation.

Korzenny, F., & Schiff, E. (1987). Hispanic perceptions of communication discrimination. *Hispanic Journal of Behavioral Sciences*, *9*(1), 33-48.

Krueger, R. A. (1989). *Focus groups: A practical guide for applied research.* Newbury Park, CA: Sage.

Ogbu, J. U. (1981). School ethnography: A multilevel approach. *Anthropology and Education Quarterly*, *12*, 3-29.

Ogbu, J.U. (1987). Variability in minority school performance: A problem in search of an explanation. *Anthropology and Education Quarterly*, *18*, 312-334.

Templeton, J. F. (1987). *Focus groups: A guide for marketing and advertising professionals.* Chicago: Probus.

Tienda, M. (1989). Puerto Ricans and the underclass debate. *The Annals of the American Academy of Political and Social Science*, *501*, 105-119.

U.S. Department of Commerce (Bureau of the Census). (1993). *School Enrollment—Social and Economic Characteristics of Students: October, 1992.* Current Population Reports, Population Characteristics, Series P20-474. Washington, DC: U.S. Government Printing Office.

Chapter 19

The Relationship of Sources of Support and Service Needs

Resilience Patterns in Low-Income Latino/Hispanic Families[1]

Stephanie K. San Miguel, Gale M. Morrison,[2] and Teresa Weissglass[3]

Parents who are without substantial income or steady employment often find themselves and their children in need of numerous services from an increasingly complex bureaucracy of social, medical, and mental health agencies. Kirst (1991) describes a "spaghetti" of programs in California: thirty-five separate state agencies that administered 160 distinct state programs that address the needs of children. Although numerous, the existing services for children in California have been described in terms such as low intensity, discontinuous, fragmented, and inequitable (Kirst, 1991). Mothers and fathers list numerous barriers, including high prices and inaccessible locations, that prevent access to services. Meanwhile, teachers readily cite and request assistance for problems such as students' poor physical health and mental health concerns that interfere with classroom learning (Morrison et al., 1993). Clearly, while services may be available to families with young children, the ability of agencies to make coordinated, effective services accessible to low socioeconomic families is extremely limited. Given the high need for formal support provision to needy families and the reality of fragmented, uncoordinated service provision, the focus for improved service provision centers on how to coordinate the work of agencies on behalf of families and how to fit service provision to specific needs and characteristics of families. The assumption behind the need to coordinate services is that this coordination will more effectively deliver formal social support to families. Similarly, behind a motivation to fit services to needs and characteristics of families is the enhancement of existing sources of informal social support. Informal and formal social support combine to reduce vulnerability and promote resiliency in families. This study will examine the nature of the resiliency fostered by informal and formal sources of support. Additionally, the effectiveness of specific combinations of these sources of support is likely to vary with the ethnic or cultural backgrounds of the families, a notion that will be further explored in this study.

The role of social support as an important coping strategy and mediator of stress has been well-documented (Pearson, 1986; Whittaker, 1986). In families, social support networks have the potential to provide the support and resources necessary to fulfill family needs and attain family goals (Dunst, Trivette, & Deal, 1988), thus "maintaining families and promoting the growth and development of children and youth at risk" (Maluccio, 1989, p. 276). A family's social support system may be seen as a resiliency factor for children and families. Resiliency or protective factors are those factors that "modify, ameliorate or alter a person's response to some environmental hazard that predisposes to a maladaptive outcome" (Rutter, 1985, p. 800). Support from families and significant others is considered a resiliency factor for children; therefore, the extent to which social support for a family modifies or ameliorates its response to adverse circumstances would be considered a resiliency factor for the family unit.

One family characteristic that is likely to interact with the formal support provided by agencies is the existence of informal support systems (Golding & Wells, 1990). Families are social units that are interdependent with other social units and networks (Dunst, Trivette, & Deal, 1988). A plethora of terms and definitions describe the intra-group assistance and cooperation inherent in human association among families, among peers, in neighborhoods and communities (Pearson, 1985). For instance, the term "social support" refers to the resources—the potentially useful information and things—provided to individuals, families, or other social units in response to the need for aid and assistance (Cohen & Syme, 1985; Dunst, Trivette, & Deal, 1988). In turn, "personal social networks" consist of the persons or institutions with which a family and its members have direct or indirect contact and from which the family derives support (Dunst & Trivette, 1990). These support networks may be informal or formal. Informal support networks include individuals and social groups that are available to provide support on a daily basis in response to either normative or nonnormative life events. Kin, friends, neighbors, ministers, churches, and social clubs all serve as informal support networks. In contrast, formal support networks are the professionals and agencies that are formally organized, on an a priori basis, to provide help to persons seeking needed resources (Mitchell & Trickett, 1980). Thus, physicians, social workers, therapists, and health departments fall into the category of formal support networks.

While the benefits of social support for families have been supported in the literature, the specific relationship between the availability of sources of social support and the extent of need for formal services has not been extensively documented. Undoubtedly, the relationship between social networks and the use of professional services is multi-faceted (Golding & Wells, 1990). Among other things, effectively functioning social networks may diminish the need for professional help, catalyze the use of professional services, or affect when and where services are sought (Gourash, 1978).

A limited number of studies have specifically examined social support and support systems from cross-cultural perspectives (Pearson, 1985). In one study, Golding and Wells (1990) surveyed 1,149 non-Hispanic Whites and 1,244 Mexican Americans regarding social resources and use of professional mental health services. The association of social resources with help seeking was similar for Mexican Americans and non-Hispanic Whites. More specifically, being unmarried and lacking support from one's spouse, work associates, friends, and relatives was associated with the use of formal service providers. In other words, when consistent, caring relationships were missing from an individual's social network, the individual was likely to seek support from formal mental health care providers regardless of the composition and size of that social network. The results of this study supported the hypothesis that social support reduces the need for formal services by providing an alternative source of help.

Nonformal or natural support systems are powerful in many minority groups (Sue & Sue, 1990). For instance, among Latino/Hispanic families, sources of support include all the formally recognized entities that are generally available in Latino/Hispanic communities. Needs for crisis intervention, for emotional support for interpersonal problems, and for information and referral are all addressed by the following natural support systems: extended family, folk healers, religious institutions, and merchants' and social clubs (Delgado & Humm-Delgado, 1982). Thus, the role of family, friends, community self-help programs, and other sources of informal assistance to ethnic minority families merits further investigation.

The authors of this chapter had the opportunity to examine the relationship between sources of support and the social service needs of low-income, predominantly Latino/Hispanic families with young, school-aged children. This study was part of a larger needs assessment that was conducted with the assistance of a State of California Healthy Start Planning Grant. Healthy Start was established in California by State Senator Robert Presley's Senate Bill 620 to fund school-linked education, health, and social services to low-income children, youth, and families at or through schools. An underlying rationale of Healthy Start is that children's problems are often interconnected. Thus, one way to improve the conditions of children's lives is to provide comprehensive, integrated, and intensive services for the child and his or her family.

Beyond documenting the service needs of low-income families with school-aged children, the data include critical demographic information and ratings on the sources of support that were available to parents. Information about the characteristics of families and their sources of social support were used to distinguish between families with different profiles of needs.

Method

Participants

A sample of 185 parents of elementary school students participated in the study. The participants were parents of children enrolled in five elementary schools wherein close to 50% or more of the enrolled pupils were from families who received Aid to Families with Dependent Children program benefits, had limited English proficiency, or were eligible to receive free or reduced-priced meals. Table 1 presents information on participants' home language, ethnicity, marital status, and number of children. Notably, percentages do not add up to 100% in instances where data were not provided by participants.

Table 1
Demographics Information Percents
for Clusters and Total Sample

		Cluster				
Variable	Total Sample	#1	#2	#3	#4	#5
		Percent in Each Category				
Home Language						
English	8.60	6.10	3.00	29.20	16.70	0.00
Spanish	83.20	86.40	97.00	62.50	62.50	92.10
English & Spanish	3.80	3.00	0.00	8.30	12.50	0.00
Ethnicity						
African-American	1.00	0.00	0.00	8.30	0.00	0.00
American Indian	1.00	0.00	0.00	4.20	4.20	0.00
Caucasian	5.90	6.10	0.00	20.80	8.30	0.00
Latino(a)	87.00	89.40	97.00	66.70	79.20	92.00
Marital Status						
Married	56.80	57.60	63.60	50.30	62.50	50.00
Single-Parent	38.40	37.90	36.40	50.00	25.00	42.20
Number of Children						
One or Two	43.76	24.30	39.40	70.80	50.00	34.30
Three or More	52.96	71.20	60.70	29.20	45.90	57.80

Procedures

As part of a collaborative effort by the needs assessment evaluation team and the community, eleven community representatives were asked to conduct interviews with parents of children who attended the participating elementary schools. As a way of identifying the needs and concerns among families from different socioeconomic levels and ethnic backgrounds, some of the interviews were conducted in the homes of the respondents, at social service agencies (e.g., Food Bank and Catholic Charities) and other various community locations (e.g., elementary school campuses, laundromats, and churches). Since some parents had difficulty with reading or writing English or Spanish, some of the interview protocols were read to the parents and their responses filled in by the interviewers.

The initial portion of the interview consisted of demographic information. The second portion focused on ascertaining the extent to which families needed specific types of assistance. In the third portion of the interview, the respondents identified and rated helpful sources of support.

Instrumentation

The social service questionnaire consisted of 20 items representing a wide range of services that families might need (see Appendix). Respondents were asked to rate the extent to which they needed each resource or service (0 = No Need, 1 = Low Need, 2 = Medium Need, and 3 = High Need). The social service questionnaire was created by members of the needs assessment evaluation team in collaboration with local social service professionals who worked extensively with low socioeconomic status ethnic minority families. A pool of potential items was generated through a brainstorming process. Then, the preliminary list of items was evaluated in terms of likely need of families in this community for each particular service. Finally, the list of potential items was edited to reduce overlap and increase clarity for parent respondents. Items primarily included existing services that had the potential to become school-linked with the aid of Healthy Start funding. The Family Support Scale (Dunst, Trivette, & Deal, 1988) asked respondents to indicate the degree to which 18 different sources of support were helpful (0 = Not Available, 1 = Not at all helpful to 5 = Extremely helpful). Dunst and colleagues (1988) reported an alpha reliability of .77.

The Family Support Scale (Dunst, Trivette, & Deal, 1988) is an 18-item self-report measure that assesses the extent to which different sources of support are helpful to families raising a young child. Items are rated on a five-point scale ranging from 1=Not at all helpful to 5=Extremely helpful. Dunst and colleagues (1988) reported an alpha reliability of .77. A principal components factor analysis performed by Dunst et al. using varimax rotation yielded a six-factor solution: informal kinship scale items, social organization items, formal kinship scale items, immediate family items, specialized professional services items, and generic professional services items. In addition, criterion validity of the scale has been determined with respect to the relationships between the total scale score (i.e., the sum of the 18 items), subscale scores, and outcomes in a number of studies examining the effect of social support on parent health and well-being, family integrity, parental perceptions of child functioning, and styles of parent child interaction (Dunst, Trivette, & Deal, 1988).

Results

Items on the Needs Survey were grouped into four factors based on information from a principal components analysis using a varimax rotation (Systat, 1989). A principal component analysis is a method of mathematically grouping items into groupings with other similar items. The determination of four item groupings (variables) was determined through examination of eigenvalues and analysis for substantive meaning. The four factors consisted of Basic Living Needs, Medical Needs, Mental Health Needs, and Cultural Negotiation Needs (see Appendix for factor groupings). These data on social service needs were submitted to a K-means cluster analysis (Systat, 1989), which resulted in five groups of parents based on their profile of need for basic living services, medical services, mental health services, and cultural negotiation services. (See Table 1 for descriptive demographic data of each cluster, Table 2 for the means and standard deviation of each cluster, and Figure 1 for resulting need profiles of these clusters.)

Table 2
Service Need and Social Support Means and Standard Deviations for Clusters

		Cluster				
		#1	#2	#3	#4	#5
Services						
Basic Living Services	M	2.45	1.65	0.88	1.98	1.90
	SD	0.34	0.51	0.65	0.44	0.45
Medical Services	M	2.44	1.97	0.38	2.30	1.12
	SD	0.38	0.59	0.46	0.39	0.51
Mental Health Services	M	2.37	0.59	0.97	1.53	1.97
	SD	0.58	0.46	0.64	0.64	0.59
Cultural Negotiation Services	M	2.49	1.49	0.49	0.42	2.10
	SD	0.43	0.66	0.57	0.45	0.48
Support						
Agency Support	M	0.85	1.09	1.13	1.39	0.53
	SD	1.26	0.86	1.14	0.94	0.90
Church Support	M	1.13	2.23	0.71	1.35	1.71
	SD	1.56	1.56	0.96	1.34	1.64
Relative Support	M	2.05	3.52	2.65	2.52	3.00
	SD	1.88	1.72	1.90	1.83	1.66
Parent Support	M	1.76	2.42	2.58	3.30	2.57
	SD	1.99	2.39	2.24	2.12	2.15

Cluster analysis is a multivariate statistical method designed to reduce or summarize data by identifying and classifying people, objects, or variables into categories or subgroups. Within each cluster the entities are homogeneous, while between clusters, there is considerable heterogeneity (Hair, Anderson, & Tatham, 1987;

Figure 1
Social Service Needs of Family Clusters

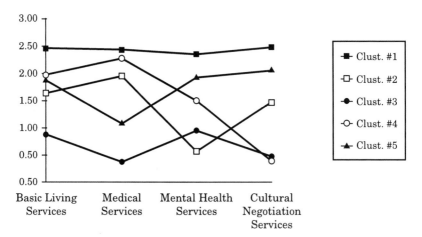

Heppner, Kivlighan, & Wampold, 1992). In contrast to principal components analysis (used to group items), the cluster analysis technique facilitates the grouping of subjects into groups that have similarity to other subjects on the selected variables (variables here being the four social service variables). In the K-means cluster analysis, the investigator chooses the number of clusters for the analysis. Cluster solutions were examined for 4, 5, and 6 clusters. The 5-cluster solution was chosen because it revealed the most substantively meaningful patterns on the four variables in question. As with principal component analysis, item and subject grouping are only as good as the meaning that the investigators attach and explain.

The external validity of the 5 clusters was reinforced by performing analyses of variance between the cluster groups on the Family Support Scale items. Differences between the clusters were found between the following support items: parents, relatives/kin, church members/priest, and professional agencies. These differences will be described below on a cluster-by-cluster basis. A graphic comparison of the standardized support scores for each cluster is found in Figure 2.

Cluster 1 ($n=66$), which was characterized by highest need across all types of services, reported the lowest level of helpfulness

Figure 2
Perceptions of Social Support of Family Clusters

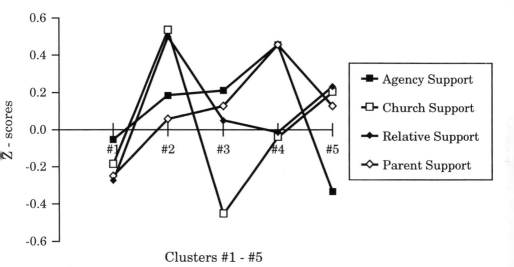

Clusters #1 - #5

in support from their own parents [significantly lower than Cluster 4, F (4, 172) = 2.48, p < .05; Tukey's post hoc test p < .027] and their relatives [significantly lower than Cluster 2, F (4, 168) = 3.88, p = .005; Tukey's post hoc test p < .002]. They also reported a low level of helpfulness from church [significantly lower than Cluster 2, F (4, 167) = 4.62, p = .001; Tukey's post hoc test p < .007]. Cluster 1 was predominantly Latino/Hispanic, spoke Spanish at home, and had the highest number of families with three or more children.

In contrast, Cluster 2 (n=33), which was characterized by lowest need for mental health services, reported the highest level of helpful support from their relatives and church. While this group was also predominantly Latino/Hispanic and Spanish-speaking, they had a greater number of two-parent families and had fewer children than Cluster 1 families.

Cluster 3 (n=24) was characterized by lower need for services than the other clusters. This group had the highest number of families who spoke English at home, the highest number of single-parent families, and the lowest representation in the category of families with three or more children. This cluster also had the only African-American families and half of the American Indian families in the sample. In terms of the support items, Cluster 3 perceived lower support from churches than Cluster 2 (Tukey's post hoc test $p < .002$). Cluster 4 ($n=24$) was characterized by low need for cultural negotiation services. This group perceived professional agencies as significantly more helpful [F (4, 166) = 2.75, p = .03; Tukey's post hoc test $p<.023$] than Cluster 5. It had the highest perception of parents as helpful resources. This group had the second highest percentage of families speaking English at home and the second lowest representation from Latino/Hispanic families. Cluster 4 had a high number of married couples, and predominantly the families in this cluster had one or two children.

Cluster 5 ($n=38$) was characterized by low need for medical services in contrast to high need for mental health and cultural negotiation services. This group saw the lowest amount of support from agencies, had the highest number of Spanish-speaking families, and had the lowest number of married couples. More than 50% of these families had three or more children.

Discussion

Families who are without substantial income often find themselves in search of a variety of services that will fit their and their young children's specific needs for formal services. While exploring the needs of parents in low-income families, five natural groupings or clusters of parents who were similar in their needs for basic living services, medical services, mental health services, and cultural negotiation services were identified. The five groups of parents could also be distinguished on the basis of the support they received from their own parents, relatives or kin, church members or priests, and professional agencies.

Considered together, parents' profiles of needed professional services and perceived social support suggest that needs for formal support are related to perceptions of informal support. For example, parents in Cluster 1 not only expressed the highest need across all types of services, but also reported the lowest level of support from their own parents and their relatives. They also reported a low level of helpful support from church. In contrast, parents in Cluster 2 expressed the lowest need for mental health services and the highest level of helpful support from their relatives and church. This finding is similar to the results of the study by Golding and Wells (1990) in which Mexican Americans and non-Hispanic Whites were likely to seek formal mental health care services when consistent, caring relationships were missing from their social network. Thus, it is likely that high informal support could act as a resiliency factor that enables families to adapt to the challenges posed by low socioeconomic status.

However, an examination of the patterns of support throughout the clusters reveals that informal support may work differently for families from varied ethnic/cultural backgrounds. For example, while the church served as a significant source of support for the exclusively Latino/Hispanic families in Cluster 2, church support was very low for the more diverse families in Cluster 3 which contained the largest percentages of White families and the only African-American and Native American families in the sample. For these families, who had low need for most services, organized religion may not be as major a factor, and therefore not a critical support, in their everyday lives as it is for the Latino/Hispanic families in this community.

Cluster 4 presents an interesting combination of high informal (parents) and high formal (agencies) support. This group of families had a lower need for cultural negotiation services. Perhaps through parental support, they were able to access agency support; that is, parents may have played a role in helping their access to services thereby playing that cultural negotiation role. The dynamic of this possible mediation role needs further exploration in future research.

In addition to informal support, other factors varied from one group of parents to another and might have affected families' needs for services. The ability to speak English might play an important role in determining a family's need for services. In the case of Cluster 3, parents indicated a lower need for all types of services than other clusters. There were more families in this group that spoke English at home than in any other. In turn, Cluster 4 was characterized by low need for cultural negotiation services while Cluster 5 had the second highest needs for these services. Notably, Cluster 4 had the second highest percentage of families speaking English at home while Cluster 5 had the highest number of Spanish-speaking parents. We surmise that unfamiliarity with English may impede access to some services and create a need for other services, while the ability to speak English may catalyze access to services and reduce reported need for services. Thus, the issue of language reminds us that even resilient families may not seek out professional sources of help when it is difficult or unpleasant to do so. Undoubtedly, not only lack of Spanish-speaking staff, but other situational factors such as lack of insurance, expensive care, and lengthy waits at publicly funded clinics may lead to underutilization of formal services (Marin & Marin, 1982).

Demographic characteristics such as number of children and marital status also varied from one cluster of parents to another. Cluster 1, which reported highest need across all types of services, had the highest number of families with three or more children. In contrast, Cluster 3, which reported lower need for services than other clusters, had the smallest number of families with three or more children. It stands to reason that larger families tend to have a greater and more general need for services. The impact of marital status upon need for services was unclear. As in previous studies (e.g., Fox, 1984; Leaf et al.,1985) that indicated that unmarried people were more likely to use mental health services than the married, the families in Cluster 2 had the lowest need for mental health services and the greatest number of two-parent families. Cluster 3, however, was not only characterized by the lower need for services than other clusters, but also consisted of the highest number of single-parent families. Clearly, the relationship between families' demographic characteristics, perceived sources of informal support, and reported needs for formal services is complex.

While the above described patterns of need, support, and demographic characteristics of families suggest relationships between these variables, readers should be reminded that the design of this study and the use of cluster analysis is exploratory in nature. The patterns and relationships described above should be taken as suggestions for future research and exploration. There are always limitations, as well, in attempting to describe patterns for subjects who have been grouped according to broad designations such as socioeconomic class, race, or cultural background. For example, while the term "Hispanic" designates people with familial roots in Latin America or Spain, there are many groups of Hispanics, each with characteristics all its own (Marin & Marin, 1982). Further, there are many other relevant within-group differences, for example, acculturation, that might explain the patterns that we have described in this study.

Given these caveats, the varied patterns of need for services, perceptions of sources of support, and demographic characteristics described in this study underline the need to individualize our view of families and the way that professionals proceed to assist them in providing services to meet the needs of their children. Dunst, Trivette, and Deal (1988) suggest that, as a rule, professionals should never use or create a professional resource or service to meet a family's needs if a comparable resource can be provided by the family's informal network. Dunst and colleagues (1988) assert that formal support "does not replace or supplant informal support networks but rather strengthens them through mobilization of linkages that permits needs to be met" (p. 83). Dunst and Trivette (1990) provide some helpful questions to answer for assessment and intervention purposes: (a) What are the family's needs? (b) What resources are required to meet those needs? (c) Who and what are the major existing sources of support for accessing resources for meeting needs? and (d) Who and what are potential but currently untapped sources of support that can be accessed for meeting needs? (pp. 336-337).

As professionals begin to look more closely at the characteristics of families and match service provisions to the needs and strengths of families, service provision is likely to become more family-centered or family-focused. Family-focused or family-centered service provision represents a significant shift from traditional practices of applying general intervention techniques across all families, without consideration of specific needs and strengths (Simeonsson & Bailey, 1990). Family-focused approaches are based on the belief in "second-order" effects; that is, the family-unit is used as the focus of intervention so that positive effects may be seen in the growth and development of the children of that family. Thus, resiliency is developed in children by enhancing the likelihood that they experience positive and nurturing family environments. In other words, resiliency is developed in families through the provision of an appropriate combination of formal and informal support thereby enhancing the resiliency of the children of those family units as well. Social support to families increases the probability that children will have two critical resiliency factors, the presence of positive and nurturing adults with whom to bond and minimalization of family discord and disruption (Garmezy, 1993).

A final observation about this study suggests that families are overwhelmed, not only with the many needs of their members, but by the massive bureaucracy of the social service system. Additionally, their own barriers of language and unfamiliarity with the "culture" of the social service system serve only to exacerbate their needs and feelings of frustration. These multiple barriers underscore the importance of providing services in a coordinated manner. Services need to be accessible and user friendly. Maluccio (1989) concluded that to be effective, "social support intervention in most cases must be part of a comprehensive set of services to families; that is, it should combine hard and soft services, formal and informal helping, counseling with concrete aid, and social skills training with social network building" (p. 276). Research on the relationship between social support and need for social services may inform the design and delivery of comprehensive services in the schools. Our findings have implications for the importance, when planning and delivering school-linked services, of assessing families' sources of social support and the relationship of this support to their need for and ability to access social services. Indeed, the challenge for professionals is to encourage the use of natural support systems and, concomitantly, to strive to improve professional support services.

Notes

1.   Support for this study was provided by the Santa Barbara School Districts Healthy Start Initiative: Integrated Service Delivery Program. Planning Grant No. 308 was provided by the California Department of Education.

2.   Stephanie San Miguel is an advanced graduate student in the Counseling/Clinical/School Psychology Program in the Graduate School of Education at the University of California, Santa Barbara. Gale Morrison is an Associate Professor in that program.

3.   Teresa Weissglass is Coordinator of the Healthy Start Implementation Program in the Santa Barbara School Districts in Santa Barbara, California.

Appendix

Social Services Questionnaire

Basic Living Services
   Help with finding housing/Homelessness
   Help with AFDC/Medi-Cal/Food Stamps
   Help to learn about Santa Barbara social services
   Legal aid
   Employment information
   Job training
   Transportation help and information
   Child care programs
Medical Services
   Medical services for children and adults
   Dental care
   Vision or hearing exams
   Immunizations
Mental Health Services
   Child and family counseling
   Classes about parenting and discipline
   Alcohol and drug problems information
   Youth activities
Cultural Negotiation Services
   Learning to read and write
   Learning English
   Immigration and citizenship information

References

Cohen, S., & Syme, S. L. (1985). *Social support and health*. Orlando: Academic Press.

Delgado, M., & Humm-Delgado, D. (1982). Natural support systems: Source of strength in Hispanic communities. *Social Work, 27*(1), 83-89.

Dunst, C. J., & Trivette, C. M. (1990). Assessment of social support in early intervention programs. In S. M. Meisels & J. P. Shonkoff (Eds.), *Handbook of early childhood intervention*. Cambridge: Cambridge University Press.

Dunst, C. J., Trivette, C. M., & Deal, A. G. (1988). *Enabling and empowering families: Principles and guidelines for practice*. Cambridge, MA: Brookline Books.

Fox, J. W. (1984). Sex, marital status, and age as social selection factors in recent psychiatric treatment. *Journal of Health and Social Behavior, 25*, 394-405.

Garmezy, N. (1993). Children in poverty: Resilience despite risk. *Psychiatry, 56*, 127-136.

Golding, J. M., & Wells, K. B. (1990). Social support and use of mental health services by Mexican-Americans and non-Hispanic Whites. *Basic and Applied Social Psychology, 11*, 443-458

Gourash, N. (1978). Help-seeking: A review of the literature. *American Journal of Community Psychology, 6*, 413-423.

Hair, J. F., Jr., Anderson, R. W., & Tatham, R. L. (1987). *Multivariate data analysis: With readings* (2nd ed.). New York: Macmillan.

Heppner, P. P., Kivlighan, D. M., & Wampold, B. E. (1992). *Research design in counseling*. Pacific Grove, CA: Brooks/Cole.

Kirst, M. W. (1991, April). Integrating children's services. *EdSource*, 1-8.

Leaf, P. J., Livingston, M. M., Tischler, G. L., Weissman, M. M., Holzer, C. E., & Myers, J. K. (1985). Contact with health professionals for the treatment of mental or emotional problems. *Medical Care, 23*, 1322-1337.

Maluccio, A. N. (1989). Research perspectives on social support systems for families and children. *Journal of Applied Social Sciences, 13*, 269-292.

Marin, G., & Marin, B. V. (1982) Methodological fallacies when studying Hispanics. *Applied Social Psychology Annual, 3*, 99-117.

Mitchell, R. E., & Trickett, E. J. (1980). Task force report: Social networks as mediators of social support: An analysis of the effects and determinants of social networks. *Community Mental Health Journal, 16*, 27-44.

Morrison, G. M., San Miguel, S., Sandowicz, M., Bimbela, A., Medina, H., & Mendoza, J. (1993). *Santa Barbara Healthy Start needs assessment: Report from the UCSB Evaluation Team*. Santa Barbara: University of California, Graduate School of Education.

Pearson, J. E. (1986). The definition and measurement of social support. *Journal of Counseling and Development, 64*, 390-395.

Pearson, R. E. (1985). The recognition and use of natural support systems in cross-cultural counseling. In P. Pederson (Ed.), *Handbook of cross-cultural counseling* (pp. 299-306). Westport, CT: Greenwood Press.

Rutter, M. (1985). Resilience in the face of adversity. *British Journal of Psychiatry, 147,* 598-611.

Simeonsson, R. J., & Bailey, D. B. (1990). Family dimensions in early intervention. In S.J. Meisels & J.B. Shonkoff (Eds.), *Handbook of early childhood intervention* (pp. 428-444). Cambridge: Cambridge University Press.

Sue, D. W., & Sue, D. (1990). *Counseling the culturally different: Theory and practice.* New York: John Wiley.

Systat. (1989). *Statistics.* Evanston, IL: Systat.

Whittaker, J. K. (1986). Formal and informal helping in child welfare services: Implications for management and practice. *Child Welfare, 65,* 17-25.

Chapter 20

Continuity of Caregiving in Mexican-American and African-American Homeless Families[1]

Julia C. Torquati and Wendy C. Gamble

Families with children comprise 38% of all homeless in the United States and are the fastest growing segment of the homeless population (U.S. Conference of Mayors, 1990). Additionally, approximately half of all homeless women are ethnic minorities (DeAngelis, 1994). Although homelessness has been a problem throughout history, many factors at all levels of the social system have contributed to recent increases in both poverty and homelessness. Declines in real earnings, increases in housing costs, changes in the low-income housing ratio, and the transfer of the financial burden from the federal to the state level are the most obvious macrosystemic trends contributing to the "new homeless" (Edelman & Mihaly, 1989; McChesney, 1990). Less obvious are the exosystemic trends, such as the mobility of families, which make it difficult to maintain ties to family, friends, and supportive institutions such as church and school. These trends have been especially difficult for families in poverty. Microsystemic trends such as "the breakdown of the family" and "lack of traditional values" have become popular, yet simplistic, explanations for the ills of society, including homelessness. The nature of microsystemic (family) dynamics and their role in precipitating and maintaining homelessness, as well as contributing to or preventing self-sufficiency, are perhaps the least well understood.

Background

Disentangling the complexity of homelessness requires investigation of factors at all ecological levels. The purpose of the present chapter was to examine the psychosocial context of homeless families with children. Two distinct aspects of the psychosocial context were considered. First, the link between relationship disruption during the primary caregiver's childhood and disrupted relationships in adulthood with adult partners (i.e., boyfriends or spouses) and with their children was investigated. Specifically, the relationship between experience of physical abuse, sexual abuse, or parental divorce during childhood was examined as a predictor of physical abuse, sexual abuse, divorce, and harsh caregiving during adulthood. Potential mediators of continuity between relationship disruption during childhood and adulthood were also examined. Second, the role of current relationships with a partner or spouse as a contributor to housing problems was investigated. Finally, relationships will be discussed as affordances for development and resiliency.

Why Relationships?

Homelessness as a *societal* problem is not caused by problematic relationships (Shinn, Knickman, & Weitzman, 1991). Shinn and colleagues have hypothesized that while relationships influence vulnerability to homelessness for individuals and families, the primary causes of homelessness are structural (i.e., poverty, lack of affordable housing). There is considerable evidence to support the hypothesis that the poor have become poorer during the past fifteen years. Between 1979 and 1983, more than 1.7 million families with children fell below the poverty line (U.S. Bureau of the Census, 1989). While the income of poor families plummeted, rents increased faster among low-income households compared to middle-income households (100% vs. 20%) between 1974 and 1983 (National Association of Home Builders, 1986, in Edelman & Mihaly, 1989). As securing self-sustaining employment and affordable housing becomes more difficult, disruptive social experiences play a crucial role in precipitating and maintaining housing problems.

There are several mechanisms by which early relationships may influence relationships during adulthood, as well as self-sufficiency. Conceptual and empirical accounts of continuity in relationship disruptions from childhood to adulthood will be briefly summarized from three areas to facilitate description of direct and indirect influences of relationship disruption during childhood on relationship experiences during adulthood: 1) physical and sexual abuse, 2) divorce, and 3) attachment theory. Conceptualizations of parenting and empirical evidence illustrating the types of parenting that appear to facilitate optimal child development will be described in order to illuminate potential links between disrupted relationships in childhood and adulthood. The conceptualization of continuity in caregiving to be employed in the present chapter will then be described.

History of Sexual and Physical Victimization

Homeless women report childhood physical and sexual abuse more frequently than domiciled poor women or urban African-American women (Bassuk & Rosenberg, 1988; D'Ercole & Struening, 1990; Knickman & Weitzman, 1989). In a comparison of shelter residents and women living in subsidized housing, Bassuk and Rosenberg (1988) reported that 42% of a shelter sample reported childhood sexual abuse and 41% reported adult physical assault, compared to 5% and 20% of housed mothers, respectively.

Long-term consequences of childhood physical and sexual abuse for women has been well documented. Sexual abuse during childhood have been associated with anxiety and depression during adulthood (Yama, Tovey, & Fogas, 1993). D'Ercole and Struening (1990) also reported significant correlations between histories of victimization and depressive symptoms in a sample of homeless women. Sexual abuse during childhood may influence emotions, self-perceptions, interpersonal relationships, physical health and safety, emotional distress, depression, chronic anxiety, and tension in adulthood (Browne, 1993; Browne & Finkelhor, 1986). Likewise, women with histories of child sexual abuse are more likely to abuse drugs and alcohol during adulthood (Downs, Miller, & Gondoli, 1987; Miller, Downs, Gondoli, & Keil, 1987). Qualities of personal relationships may be disrupted as a result of childhood victimization, manifested as general mistrust, difficulty creating support networks, and difficulty in parenting their own children (Browne, 1993; Browne & Finkelhor, 1985). Symptoms of Post-traumatic Stress Disorder (PTSD) are also common for women with histories of victimization (Browne, 1987). Victimization and abusive parenting may also co-occur, as Straus (1983) concluded that mothers who were physically abused by spouses reported the highest rate of abusing their own children.

Physical abuse during childhood has been associated with difficulties in parenting during adulthood (e.g., Egeland, Jacobvitz, & Papatola, 1987; Steinmetz, 1987; Straus, Gelles, & Steinmetz, 1980). For example, Kaufman and Zigler (1987) estimated the rate of intergenerational transmission of abuse to be five times the rate of abuse in the general population. In a prospective study of a high risk sample, Egeland et al. (1987) found that employing a narrow definition of abuse, 34% of mothers who themselves were victims of child abuse were abusing their own children by the time the children were four years old; only 3% of mothers who recalled sensitive parenting were abusing their own children. Using a broad definition of abuse, 70% of mothers with a history of abuse and 43% of mothers without such a history were abusing their own children. Zeanah and Zeanah (1989) suggest that themes of internal working models mediate intergenerational transmission of abuse, specifically themes of rejection, role-reversal, and fear.

Divorce
Evidence of long-term influences of experiencing parental divorce during childhood is mixed, suggesting considerable variability in adaptation to divorce. Keith and Finlay (1988) reported that children of divorce married earlier, had less stable marriages, and lower educational attainment. Compared to women from nondivorced families, women from divorced families report less trust in men, as well as an increased likelihood to marry and give birth during their teens, to become mothers before they are married, and to divorce their own husbands (McLanahan & Bumpass, 1988; Southworth & Schwartz, 1987). Wallerstein and Blakeslee (1989) reported that two thirds of women from divorced families were anxious and feared betrayal in intimate relationships. Growing up with parental discord may have even greater impact on children's intimate relationships in adulthood, however; in a comparison of adults from divorced and from intact-unhappy homes, adults from intact-unhappy homes had less stable marriages, less marital interaction, less commitment to the marriage, and more disagreements (Booth & Edwards, 1989).

Continuity of Attachment
Attachment theory suggests that early relationship disruptions may increase the probability of relationship disruption for at least two reasons: 1) continuity in relationships is hypothesized to be a function of mental models of self, relationship, other, and the social

world in general (Main, Kaplan, & Cassidy, 1985), and a history of relationship disruptions is likely to result in maladaptive models of the self (i.e., as unworthy or inefficacious), relationships (i.e., as difficult and unpredictable), and the social world in general (i.e., as untrustworthy and/or hostile); and 2) internal working models function to regulate emotion in relationships, and insecure models are more likely to be associated with anxiety and depression than secure models, interfering with adaptive social functioning. Research demonstrating the intergenerational transmission of attachment (e.g., Grossman, Fremmer-Bombik, Rudolph, & Grossman, 1988) and the enduring developmental effects of early relationships (Rutter, 1988) suggests that women who experienced relationship disruptions as children are also more likely to experience disruptions in their relationships with their own children and with adults. This is not to suggest a simple isomorphism between childhood relationship experiences and childrearing styles as a mechanistic phenomena; rather, dynamic internal working models of relationships are the hypothesized mode of continuity (Van Ijzendoorn, 1992).

This hypothesis is supported by investigations of current parental internal working models (assessed by the Adult Attachment Interview) and observations of parent-infant patterns of attachment behavior. Main, Kaplan, and Cassidy (1985) compared infant attachment classification during the second year of life and maternal and paternal attachment classification when the child was six years old; the correlations between infant attachment and maternal and paternal attachment classification were .62 and .37, respectively. Similarly, Fonagy, Steele, and Steele (1991) reported that maternal representations of attachment evaluated prenatally predicted infant-mother attachment patterns 75% of the time; mothers classified as autonomous were likely to have infants classified as secure, while mothers classified as dismissing or preoccupied were likely to have infants classified as insecure. Crowell and Feldman (1991) found that secure mothers were more responsive and affectionate, prepared their children well for separation, and sought physical proximity with their children upon reunion. Conversely, dismissing and preoccupied mothers did not prepare children as well, and were physically distant from their children upon reunion. Bretherton (1990) emphasized that parental behavior is the "output" of *current* internal working models and that a parent with an autonomous model may be better able to facilitate a child's adaptive learning about other relationships, and provide informative and helpful information about specific relationships.

Parenting

Parenting has been conceptualized as a "buffered system" (Belsky, 1984), comprised of: 1) parental personal psychological resources (i.e., mental health, maturity) and ontogeny; 2) child characteristics; and 3) contextual sources of stress and support. The concept of "buffering" implies an interaction in which a *resource*, such as social support, functions as a protective factor in predicting adaptation under high levels of stress, but not at low levels of stress. In other words, the slope of social support in predicting parenting varies as a function of stress level. Applied to the framework of parenting as a buffered system, if deficits exist in any of the three components they may be buffered by the other two components of the system. Belsky (1984; Belsky, Robins, & Gamble, 1984) hypothesized that the components of the system are hierarchically arranged, such that *parental personal resources and developmental history* are the most influential determinants of parenting. This hypothesis is based on the premise that psychological resources exert both direct and indirect influences on parenting, for example, the ability of the parent to establish supportive relationships with spouse, friends, neighbors, and other network members, which provide emotional, informational, and instrumental support for parenting.

Adaptive parenting includes dimensions of: 1) warmth and acceptance; and 2) firm but democratic control, characterized by "demandingness" or developmentally appropriate expectations. Baumrind (1971, 1973) developed a useful typology of parenting styles based on these dimensions. "Authoritative" parents are warm, provide firm control and developmentally appropriate expectations, set clear standards and enforce them consistently, and encourage the child's autonomy. "Authoritarian" parents exert much control over their children, but are less warm and responsive. "Permissive" parents are tolerant and accepting, but make few demands for developmentally appropriate behavior and allow self-regulation of behavior on the part of the child instead of communicating expectations and setting clear limits that are consistently enforced.

These dimensions of parenting have been identified as adaptive because of their observed relations to child outcomes generally recognized as positive. For example, Baumrind (1971, 1973) found that children of authoritarian and permissive parents were low in social and cognitive competence, while children of authoritative parents were high in social and cognitive competence. During adolescence, Dornbusch, Ritter, Leiderman, Roberts, and Fraleigh

(1987) reported that authoritarian and permissive parenting styles were inversely associated with grades, while authoritative parenting predicted higher grades.

As a personal resource, mental health of primary caregivers may be particularly important, since almost half of homeless mothers score above the clinical cutoff for depression (Edelman & Mihaly, 1989; Molnar, Rath, & Klein, 1990) and parental depression has been identified as a risk factor for children's adjustment (e.g., Billings & Moos, 1983; Gelfand & Teti, 1990). Mental illness may impair a caregiver's responsivity and ability to attend to children's needs, and children of mentally ill parents evidence higher rates of disorder than comparison children (e.g., Billings & Moos, 1983; Weintraub, Neale, & Leibert, 1975; Weintraub, Prinz, & Neale, 1978).

Continuities in Caregiving

The adult responsible for the care of a child is referred to in the present chapter as the "primary caregiver," and the act of caring for the child as "caregiving." This terminology emphasizes the *process* involved in caring for a child, rather than simply identifying the person fulfilling the role. The "buffered system" of parenting (Belsky, 1984; Belsky et al., 1984) identifies the characteristics of the primary caregiver, such as developmental history and personality, as the most important determinant of parenting. Relationship disruptions will be examined as predictors of caregiving, and potential mediators between relationship disruptions in childhood and adulthood will be explicated.

Research reviewed on physical and sexual victimization, divorce, and attachment suggests potential mediating pathways between relationship disruptions during childhood and adulthood. Examination of discrete events during childhood as risk factors (e.g., abuse, divorce) is not to suggest that these events function in a mechanistic fashion. Rather, consistent with the perspective of developmental contextualism (e.g., Lerner & Tubman, 1991), individuals are conceptualized as actively contributing to their own development. Based on the research reviewed above, three potential paths between relationship disruptions during childhood and adulthood will be described (Figure 1). First, literature reviewed on victimization, divorce, and attachment suggests that relationship disruptions potentiate difficulties with emotion regulation. Experiencing physical abuse during childhood may increase the likelihood of depression and anxiety during adulthood, which in

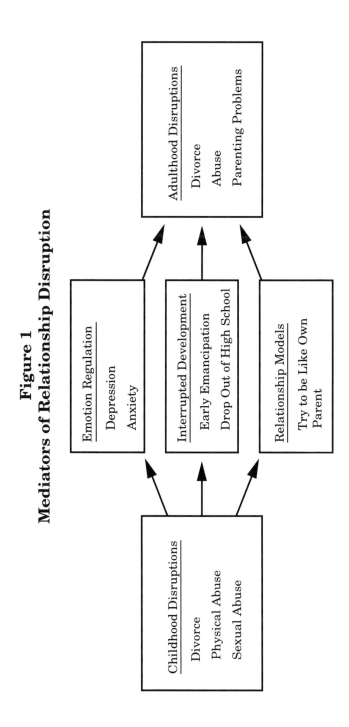

Figure 1
Mediators of Relationship Disruption

turn may increase the probability of revictimization. Depression and anxiety may contribute to vulnerability by inhibiting the development of supportive social relationships, thus increasing loneliness and isolation. Depression and anxiety may also impede development of skills necessary for self-sufficiency, making it difficult to attend vocational or job training, for example; lack of resources necessary for self-sufficiency and difficulty with emotion regulation represent vulnerabilities for victimization. Accordingly, it was hypothesized that relationship disruptions during childhood and adulthood would be positively correlated with depression and anxiety.

Second, childhood relationship disruptions may constrain the achievement of normal developmental milestones, such as graduating from high school. Two indices of interrupted development will be examined in the present paper: 1) dropping out of school; and 2) early emancipation, defined as leaving home prior to 18. Although leaving home early may be considered an adaptive response to a negative or abusive situation, both of these indices serve as markers of incomplete preparation for adulthood, and potentially failure to develop skills necessary to function as an adequate provider, also a vulnerability for victimization. It was hypothesized that dropping out of high school and early emancipation would be positively correlated with relationship disruptions during childhood and during adulthood.

Finally, relationship disruptions during childhood may contribute to the development of maladaptive internal working models of self, relationship, other, and the social world in general. Primary caregivers with traumatic relationship histories may construct models of the self as vulnerable, unlovable, and inefficacious, and of the social world as hostile and untrustworthy. This type of model contributes to continuity in relational style, as the caregiver behaves in such a way as to replicate relational patterns. Zeanah and Zeanah (1989) have suggested that themes of internal working models (for example, rejection, role-reversal, and fear) may underlie continuity of maladaptive caregiving. Difficulties with emotion regulation, interrupted development, and maladaptive models of relationships may make it very difficult to develop mature, warm, supportive relationships with other adults and with children. Difficulties in relationships represent additional vulnerabilities for families at risk for housing problems as a result of structural factors (i.e., poverty, lack of affordable housing). Thus, it was hypothesized that relationship disruptions during childhood would be inversely related to attempts to emulate one's own parents; similarly, it was hypothesized that attempts to emulate one's own parents would be inversely associated with negative parenting, and positively associated with positive parenting. In other words, parents who are dissatisfied with the way their own parents cared for them are hypothesized to have the most difficulty in caring for their own children.

Method

For the purpose of this study, a homeless family was defined as one whose primary nighttime residence is in a publicly or privately operated shelter designed to provide temporary living accommodations (i.e., shelters, transitional housing). This definition is consistent with Wright's (1989) criteria defining homelessness as lacking "regular and customary access to a conventional dwelling unit" and lacking the resources to do otherwise (Wright, 1989, pp. 19-20). Forty-two families comprised of primary caregiver(s) and a target child between the ages 6 and 12 receiving services from five agencies providing housing assistance in Tucson were invited to participate. No families meeting the age and housing criteria who were invited refused to participate. If two children were between the ages of 6 and 12, the investigator alternated between choosing the older and the younger child to be the target child. Data were not included on four occasions because: 1) one child was a month less than 5 years old; 2) one child was older than 12 years; and 3) a six-year-old and a seven-year-old were unable to complete the entire questionnaire packet due to cognitive difficulties resulting from carbon monoxide poisoning.

Ethnicity. Nineteen percent ($n=7$) of the children were Caucasian, 16% ($n=6$) African American, 19% ($n=13$) Mexican American, 16% ($n=6$) Mexican, and 13.5% ($n=5$) Central American (Guatemalan or Salvadoran). Accordingly, 54% ($n=20$) of the children were bilingual. Participating children ranged in age from 6 to 12 (mean=9.2; SD=1.7), and from kindergarten to seventh grade (mean=4th grade; SD=1.8). Slightly more males ($n=21$; 55.3%) than females ($n=17$; 44.7%) comprised the sample of children.

Family Size and Structure. Twenty-two percent of the mothers ($n=8$) were single (never married), 32.4% ($n=12$) were married, 24.3% ($n=9$) were separated, and 21.6% were divorced ($n=8$). Thirty-five percent ($n=13$) of mothers reported being the single head of the household. Fifty-four percent ($n=20$) of the mothers were married or living with their partner. Four families (10.8%) included more than two adults, usually extended family. The number of children living with participating families ranged from one to six (mean=2.8). The mean birth order of target children was 1.6 (SD=.8).

Almost a quarter of the participating families (24.3%, $n=9$) also reported that they had additional children who were not living with them. The reasons for their children living elsewhere reflected three general themes. First, families receiving any type of public assistance or living in transitional housing must comply with very strict regulations regarding the number of children allowed to share a bedroom, and boys and girls are not allowed to share a bedroom at any age. For this reason, primary caregivers had to sometimes decide which children would stay with them, and which child(ren) would live with relatives. Second, some primary caregivers expressed a desire to keep their children out of the environment in which they lived, which they perceived as dangerous and stressful. Two mothers indicated that they felt it was easier to keep their younger children "under their wing," but they were concerned about the safety of their older children and allowed them to live with other relatives. Finally, some primary caregivers did not have physical custody of their children.

Education of Primary Caregivers. Approximately half of both the mothers (48.6%, $n=18$) and the fathers (51.3%, $n=19$) completed high school or earned their GED. Almost 30% (29.7%, $n=11$) of the participating mothers had dropped out of school by the eighth grade. Eight percent of mothers ($n=3$) had attended vocational or trade school, and 10.8% ($n=4$) had attended some college. Similarly, 16.2% ($n=6$) of fathers dropped out of school by the eighth grade, 29.7% ($n=11$) completed some high school, 29.7% graduated from high school or earned their GED, 2.7% ($n=1$) attended vocational or trade school, 8.1% ($n=3$) attended some college, and 10.8% ($n=4$) graduated from college. None of the fathers with college degrees were living with their children.

Employment Status and Income. Nineteen percent ($n=7$) of mothers identified themselves as homemakers; 16.2% ($n=6$) were employed part time, 24.3% ($n=9$) were employed full time, 8% ($n=3$) were students attending vocational or trade school, and 32.4% ($n=12$) were unemployed. Forty-three percent ($n=16$) reported an annual income of $5000 or less, 40.5% ($n=15$) earned $5000-$10,000 during the past year, and 13.5% ($n=5$) earned $10,000-$15,000 during the past year. One family reported an income between $15,000 and $20,000 for the past year. An estimate of the income per family member per year was computed by assigning each family the highest possible value for their income range (i.e., a family in the $10,000-$15,000 range would be assigned a value of $15,000), and then dividing by the number of individuals per family. The resulting values ranged from $625 to $5000 annual per capita income, with a mean of $1938 and standard deviation of $1111, should be considered a liberal estimate of the per capita income of each family member, since each family was assigned the maximum value in their income range.

Procedures

Several methods of contacting families and inviting them to participate were employed. A caseworker at one agency contacted clients and set up appointments. One agency provided a list of all clients with children in the target age range to the investigator, who then knocked on doors of the family apartments, described the purpose and procedures of the study, and set up appointments with the families. Two agencies allowed the investigator to attend weekly client meetings, describe the study, and recruit participants.

Data collection from each family was completed at one point in time. Primary caregiver interviews took approximately two hours, and child interviews took approximately one hour. Teams of two trained research assistants collected data from one family together (one collecting child data, one collecting data from the primary caregiver). English-speaking primary caregivers were interviewed by a graduate student or by a trained graduate or undergraduate research assistant; Spanish-speaking primary caregivers (38% of the sample) were interviewed by a bilingual Mexican-American research assistant. Spanish-speaking children (13% of the sample) were interviewed by the bilingual Hispanic research assistant or by the graduate student. Trained graduate and undergraduate research assistants interviewed English-speaking children. The purpose and procedures of the study, as well as the rights of the participants to confidentiality and to withdraw, were described to participants, who then signed consent (adult) and assent (child) forms. Thereafter, primary caregiver and child data were collected in separate, private rooms. Children were allowed to work at their own pace, taking short breaks as needed. Children were provided with snacks and were allowed to choose stickers as incentives after each set of questionnaires. At the conclusion of the interview, children were allowed to choose a pencil case with a ruler, eraser, and pencil sharpener. All directions, items, and response choices were read to both adults and children. The interviewers marked responses on the questionnaire forms for both adults and children. Primary caregivers were compensated $35 (cash) for their participation.

Thirty-six (95%) of the primary caregivers interviewed were the biological mothers of the children. Mothers were interviewed because: 1) most of the primary caretakers were biological mothers, so interviewing biological mothers would minimize the possibility of systematic variation as a function of *who* was reporting; 2) fewer families included *biological* fathers ($n = 12$; 32%); 3) in families with a biological father or stepfather, the child had experienced the most continuity in the relationship with the mother, so it was assumed that the mother should be more accurate in reporting. One father and one stepfather were interviewed because the mother was unavailable.

Measures

Relationship and Developmental Disruptions. As part of a larger demographic questionnaire, primary caregivers were asked several questions about their housing and relationship history, including marital status, divorce of their own parents, educational attainment, age at which they first lived on their own, absent family members, and incidence of physical and sexual abuse during childhood and during adulthood.

Representation of Caregiving Relationships. Primary caregivers' representations of caregiving relationships were evaluated by the question: "How much do you try to be like your own parent(s) (or person identified as primary caregiver) in the way you raise your own child(ren)?" Followed by the probes: "Are there things you try to do the same?" and "Are there things you try to do differently?" Over half (60%) of primary caregivers indicated that they do not try to be like their own parents at all, and identified specific things they try to do differently. *All* of the ways primary caregivers tried to be different than their own parents included *more positive* and *less negative* caregiving. Caregivers indicated that they try to spend more time with their children, give them more affection than they received, yell at and hit their children less, and talk to them and listen to them more. Many caregivers indicated that in spite of their efforts, to their disappointment they sometimes treated their own children as they had been treated. Primary caregivers' descriptions of their experiences with their own caregivers and their attempts to emulate or modify their caregiving were coded dichotomously. Caregivers who identified ways they try to be like their own parents or who presented a "balanced" picture of their caregiving (i.e., some things the same and some things different, but generally positive representation of own parents) were coded as trying to be like their own parents, while caregivers who stated that they definitely did *not* try to be like their own parents and who could not identify even one way they try to emulate their caregiving were coded as not trying to be like their own parents.

Depression. The Beck Depression Inventory (BDI) (Beck, 1967) is a 21-item scale with a four-point response format evaluating the presence and severity of affective, cognitive, motivational, and psychomotor symptoms of depression. The short form, including 13 items, was used in the present investigation (Cronbach's alpha coefficient=.93). The mean depression score was 6.2 (SD=7.7); 19% scored higher than the clinical cutoff of 13.

Anxiety. The State-Trait Anxiety Inventory (Speilberger, 1983) is a 40-item self-report measure of state and trait anxiety. Participants rated items on a four-point response scale ranging from 1 (least anxious) to 4 (most anxious). Items were summed to provide indices of state and trait anxiety (Cronbach's alpha coefficient=.88). For this study, only the 20-item *State* subscale was used. The mean anxiety score for caregivers was 40.1 (SD=10.7). According to Speilberger's norms, 15 primary caregivers (43%) scored higher than one standard deviation above the mean; six primary caregivers (17%) scored higher than one standard deviation above the mean for the sample, indicating that the mean for the sample was also high.

Caregiving. Qualities of the relationship with the primary caregiver were assessed using three measures. The Parent-Child Relationship Inventory (Hetherington et al., 1992) assessed rapport between parents and children, including, for example: 1) the emotional tone of the relationship (i.e., closeness, expression of affection, responsiveness of the parent); 2) quality of communication; and 3) time spent together *alone.* This measure is comprised of 18 items with a five-point response scale, and includes a parent and child version (Cronbach's alpha coefficient=.85). The Parent Perception Inventory (PPI) (Hazzard, Christensen, & Margolin, 1983) is comprised of two behavioral scales, with nine items each: 1) positive parenting behaviors including positive reinforcement, comfort, communication, and non-verbal affection; and 2) negative parenting behaviors including criticism, physical punishment, and command directives. Each item was rated on a five-point scale ranging from "never" (for children, accompanied by an empty thermometer) to "a lot" (accompanied by a full thermometer); responses in between are accompanied by thermometers with increasing increments. Subscale scores were derived by summing responses for the nine items (children's version reliabilities: positive caregiving Cronbach's alpha coefficient=.88; negative caregiving Cronbach's alpha coefficient=.80). The parent version includes items that parallel the children's version, with the addition of two items evaluating discipline, for a total of twenty items, comprising two subscales with ten items each (positive caregiving Cronbach's alpha coefficient=.85; negative caregiving Cronbach's alpha coefficient=.67).

Ten items were also adapted from previous research evaluating parental monitoring and involvement (i.e., Patterson & Dishion, 1985; Patterson & Stouthamer-Loeber, 1984). Parents rated how frequently they discuss with their child plans for the coming day and what the child actually did during the day, how often the child has a specific time to be in at night, how many of the child's friends the parent knows, and where the child spends his/her time after school, evenings, and weekends. Two items were eliminated because they had no variability (all caregivers indicated that their children were at home with them on weekends; all caregivers indicated that it was "very important" for them to know what their children were doing outside the home). The remaining 8 items were summed to derive a composite score, and the reliability was not adequate (Cronbach's alpha coefficient=.24). Upon closer examination of item frequencies, it became apparent that even items with variance greater than zero were highly skewed; the majority of caregivers gave the response indicating the highest level of monitoring or supervision, and one or two caregivers gave an intermediate response. It is not likely that this was a result of social desirability; caregivers often responded with descriptions of their concern for and vigilance of their children, because they were aware of the potentially dangerous and unstable context in which they live. Most of the parents indicated that their children were with them during all times other than school hours; many children did not have friends outside of school, because they had just moved, or because they were isolated at the shelter. At the emergency shelters, caregivers indicated that they were concerned about the type of people receiving shelter (i.e., their neighbors).

For both conceptual reasons and for ease of analysis, it was determined a priori that the parenting scales would be combined if they demonstrated adequate reliability and intercorrelations, which they did. Positive parenting items from the PPI, and PCR, for both primary caregivers and children, and monitoring items for primary caregivers, were combined into a single aggregate scale, with good reliability (Cronbach's alpha coefficient=.88). Similarly, caregivers' and children's negative PPI scores were standardized and averaged into a single score (Cronbach's alpha coefficient=.80).

Results

Results will be presented in four sections. First, frequencies of relationship and developmental disruptions will be presented. Second, comparisons of developmental and relationship disruptions by ethnic group will be reported. Third, Spearman (nonparametric) correlations between childhood and adulthood relationship disruptions and hypothesized mediators will be presented. Finally, caregivers' descriptions of their relationship difficulties will be summarized.

Table 1
Frequency of Developmental Disruptions
Reported by Primary Caregivers

Type of Disruption	Percent Reporting
Physical Abuse - Childhood	38%
Sexual Abuse - Childhood	24%
Parents Divorced	37%
Early Emancipation	39%
Physical Abuse - Adulthood	35%
Sexual Abuse - Adulthood	14%
Absent Family Members	24%
Ran Away Before 18	37%
Divorced or Separated	46%

Relationship and Developmental Disruptions

Frequencies of each type of disruption are summarized in Table 1. The proportion of caregivers reporting physical and sexual abuse during childhood and adulthood is comparable to proportions reported in other high risk samples. Almost one fourth (24%) of primary caregivers reported they had been sexually abused as children; over one third (38%) had been physically abused as children. Over one third of the caregivers (35%) reported they had been physically abused as adults, and 14% indicated they had been sexually molested as adults. The perpetrators of caregivers' adult sexual molestation included husbands, boyfriends, friends, strangers, police officers, and prison officials (in El Salvador). Over one third (37%) of the primary caregivers reported their own parents had divorced, while 46% reported that they themselves were divorced or separated. One fourth (24%) of primary caregivers reported that they had other family members not living with them. Primary caregivers reported a wide range of ages at which they left home to live on their own (9-29); more than one-third (39%) left home to live on their own prior to age 18. However, both the mean (17.6) and median (17.5) age at which primary caregivers reported leaving home were younger than 18 years of age; over one-third (37%) had been living on their own since age 15 or younger. Similarly, over one-third (37%) reported that they had run away from home prior to age 18. Although primary caregivers reported a wide age range at first marriage (16-28, for those who had been married), the mean age at first marriage was 20.1 years; one-fifth (21.6%) were married by the time they were 18 years old.

Comparison of Disruptions by Ethnicity

The frequency of physical and sexual abuse during childhood and during adulthood, parental divorce and own divorce, early emancipation, absent family members, and running away reported by Hispanic, African-American, and Caucasian primary caregivers were compared using chi square analyses. None of the comparisons reached significance, so the ethnic groups were combined for the remaining analyses.

Spearman Correlations Between Disruptions and Mediators

Continuities in relationship disruption were examined via four sets of correlational analyses. First, Spearman correlations between physical and sexual victimization during childhood and adulthood are presented in Table 2. Two patterns are evident: 1) physical and sexual abuse tend to co-occur, as childhood physical and sexual abuse are correlated .23 ($p < .05$) and adulthood physical and sexual abuse are correlated .55 ($p < .01$); and 2) there is specificity in prediction of abuse over time, as physical abuse during childhood significantly predicts physical (but not sexual) abuse during adulthood, and sexual abuse during childhood significantly predicts sexual (but not physical) abuse during adulthood.

Table 2
Spearman Correlations Between Physical and Sexual
Victimization During Childhood and Adulthood

	Childhood Physical Abuse	Childhood Sexual Abuse	Adulthood Physical Abuse
Childhood Sexual Abuse	.23*		
Adulthood Physical Abuse	.34*	−.06	
Adulthood Sexual Abuse	.11	.25*	.55***

* = p<.05; ** = p<.01; *** = p<.001

The second set of correlational analyses examined the Spearman correlations between childhood and adulthood disruptions and emotion regulation (depression and anxiety) (Table 3). Robust correlations were obtained between depression and both childhood physical abuse (.70, $p < .001$) and adulthood physical abuse (.57, $p < .001$). Physical abuse during adulthood also was significantly associated with anxiety. None of the other relationship disruptions significantly predicted anxiety or depression.

Table 3
Spearman Correlations Between Relationship
Disruptions and Emotion Regulation

	Depression	Anxiety
Parents Divorced	.14	.13
Childhood Physical Abuse	.70***	.18
Childhood Sexual Abuse	.04	−.02
Divorce	−.06	−.05
Adulthood Physical Abuse	.57***	.24*
Adulthood Sexual Abuse	.12	.20

*=p<.05; **=p<.01; ***=p<.001

Correlations between relationship disruptions and disrupted development, operationalized as early emancipation and dropping out of school, are summarized in Table 4. Childhood physical and sexual abuse both significantly predict early emancipation, but

Table 4
Spearman Correlations Between Interrupted
Development and Relationship Disruptions

	Early Emancipation	Dropped Out
Childhood Sexual Abuse	.27*	.01
Childhood Physical Abuse	.40***	.11
Parents Divorced	.09	.41***
Negative Caregiving	−.24*	.34**
Positive Caregiving	−.11	.00
Adulthood Sexual Abuse	.03	−.25*
Adulthood Physical Abuse	.05	−.10
Divorce	−.20	.42**

*=p<.05;   **=p<.01;   ***=p<.001

they do not predict dropping out of school; conversely, parental divorce significantly predicted dropping out of school but it did not predict early emancipation. Positive caregiving was unrelated to early emancipation or dropping out of school. Dropping out was positively associated with negative caregiving; early emancipation was inversely associated with negative caregiving. Dropping out of school was positively associated with divorce during adulthood.

Spearman correlations between caregivers' attempts to emulate their parents and relationship disruptions during childhood and adulthood are presented in Table 5. Contrary to hypotheses, childhood sexual abuse was unrelated to attempts to emulate one's parents; childhood physical abuse was marginally ($p=.06$) and inversely related. As hypothesized, physical and sexual abuse during adulthood was inversely associated with caregivers' attempts

Table 5
Spearman Correlations Between Caregivers' Attempts to
Emulate their Parents and Relationship Disruptions

	Try to Be Like Own Parents
Childhood Physical Abuse	−.20
Childhood Sexual Abuse	−.02
Parents Divorced	−.03
Adulthood Physical Abuse	−.31*
Adulthood Sexual Abuse	−.26*
Divorced	.17
Positive Caregiving (own children)	−.14
Negative Caregiving (own children)	−.04

to be like their own parents. None of the other disruptions were significantly associated with attempts to emulate parents.

Continuity of Relationship Disruptions, Caregiving, and Housing Problems

Relationship disruptions described by primary caregivers often precipitated and/or maintained housing problems. Caregivers also described ways in which relationship disruptions and housing problems made the task of caregiving more difficult. Brief descriptions of the way in which relationship disruptions precipitated or maintained housing problems will be presented, followed by a summary of caregivers' descriptions of difficulties in caregiving as a result of relationship disruptions and housing problems. Finally, difficulties maintaining relationships as a result of housing problems will be described.

Relationship Disruptions as Precipitators of Housing Problems

Nine caregivers (22%) indicated that separation or divorce precipitated their housing problems. Two of the caregivers were fleeing domestic violence and had obtained restraining orders against their husbands. Both had moved in with their parents after leaving their husbands, and both subsequently left their parents' homes because of conflicts with their own parents; one woman's mother chased her with a knife and threatened to kill her. The other woman's father was an alcoholic who drank himself into a stupor every evening while the mother screamed at her and her children. Interestingly, both caregivers remarked that as children and as adults they felt they were scapegoats; while their siblings' conduct was not questioned or judged, they were interrogated, criticized, and abused. Four caregivers terminated their relationships with their husbands or partners because of drinking or substance abuse. One caregiver was not aware that her husband was using cocaine and not paying rent until they were evicted.

One caregiver left her home in another state because she had been ordered by the court to allow her ex-husband visitation of her six-year-old daughter, whom he had sexually molested. She had recently married a man whom she had known for four months, and was certain he would do "anything" for her and her children; unfortunately, her partnership with him also proved to be a vulnerability to housing problems as well, as the family was dismissed from the program because he refused to attend vocational school (although she did attend). One caregiver explained that her five-year-old son had been abducted for a year (when he was four years old) by his father, who was living with her sister. When she learned of their whereabouts she convinced the father to allow her to visit the child. She obtained physical custody of the child and left. Without other resources, she had applied for AFDC and food stamps, and she expressed concern that the father, who had no legal parental rights to the child, would discover their whereabouts.

One caregiver described her predicament succinctly: "I think a big part of my problem is that I keep ending up with jerks." She remarked that she would think that a man was nice, become involved with him, and then find out that he drank too much, did not like her children, or caused other problems in the family. She had just come from another state with her boyfriend and her three children; along the way, her boyfriend had been jailed for driving without a license and she had spent the rest of their money bailing him out. She said that she was not sure if they were going to stay together, because the kids "got on his nerves."

Relationship Disruptions and Maintenance of Housing Problems

Substance abuse emerged as a problem for at least two caregivers who were still living with their husbands. Both were working, and trying to save money, while their husbands would spend the money on alcohol. One would hide the money she saved, and her husband would take it and disappear for several days. Tragically, her first husband disappeared in Guatemala, and she moved to the U.S. with her children. She continued working and saving for a home, but felt an obligation to family members from Guatemala, and would support them as they emigrated to the U.S., making it difficult to save money for herself and her children. Yet another woman's husband undermined her attempts to save money for a security deposit on an apartment. They had arrived in Tucson from Oregon, and she had found full-time employment as a nursing assistant. However, her husband complained that the house was never cleaned and dinner was not on the table when he got home, so she quit her good job and worked part time in the evenings for minimum wage. She was not cashing her paychecks in order to save money, while he would spend all of his paychecks going out and drinking. He had screamed at her one evening the week before the interview, because she had bought shoes for the children to wear to school, and he did not have enough cash to buy two six packs of beer. Another woman was living with a man who spent 100 days in jail every year for not paying child support to his other children; refusal to pay child support made it difficult for him to find gainful employment, since his social security number would inform the IRS of his whereabouts.

Extended family provided limited support for primary caregivers and their children. In some cases, extended family was avoided because of issues of substance abuse, or physical or sexual abuse. Since only about one third of the families in the present study were from Tucson, two-thirds of the sample had no extended family nearby. There even seemed to be some evidence of intergenerational continuity in housing problems, as one caregiver indicated that her mother-in-law repeatedly rented very expensive houses with pools and simply lived there until she was evicted, never paying rent. She then would sleep in a park or in her car, or stay with relatives or friends.

Housing Problems and Disrupted Caregiving

Disruptions in caregiving described by caregivers included physical separations from children, difficulties caring under stressful circumstances, and difficulty providing for children's social, emotional, and educational needs. Four caregivers indicated that they had been separated from their own children for varying lengths of time as a result of housing problems. In all cases, caregivers left children with relatives until their housing situation stabilized. Often older children were left with relatives and younger children stayed with caregivers, as one mother described that it was easier to keep the younger child "under her wing," and she was concerned that the older child would get in trouble or be in danger as a result of living in shelter or transitional housing. Although difficult, separation appeared to be an adaptive choice.

Several caregivers indicated that worries about housing problems made them irritable with their children. One mother was so depressed about her inability to find an affordable apartment that she was unable to prepare dinner for her children one evening; another woman staying at the shelter came over and fed the children. Living in a shelter or motel makes it very difficult to maintain continuity in children's social relationships, as they often had to change schools and were unable to participate in extracurricular activities. Several caregivers also had difficulty enrolling their children in school, because they had recently moved and did not have the children's medical records or birth certificate. Children often missed school while their caregivers made arrangements to provide the necessary information. One nine-year-old boy had not attended school for a year because he was too afraid to leave his mother; his father had beaten her repeatedly.

Housing Problems and Difficulty Establishing and Maintaining Relationships

Two-thirds of the present sample had recently moved to Tucson and had no friends or extended family nearby. In some cases, caregivers remarked that the extended family had its own problems, and they did not want to be a burden; two caregivers stated that they had not told their families that they were living in a shelter.

Primary caregivers expressed great interest in establishing relationships with other families, but wariness about doing so. At one shelter, families often expressed concern about the kind of people who might be staying there, and uncertainty about whether they should allow their children to play with the other children at the shelter. Two women at the shelter referred to each other (during their separate interviews) as "the blonde." Eventually, they began to interact with and trust each other more. Two caregivers living in the same complex described a tenant who was intoxicated most of the time, and had detonated an M-80 outside the door; the tenant was the person responsible for his four-year-old son while his wife worked. Caregivers were concerned about this and similar situations in which other children were left unattended frequently, and preferred to keep their children indoors, or only go out or to the park if they were personally supervising them. Caregivers who were in transitional housing in one apartment complex indicated that there was gang activity, so they kept their children indoors most of the time. Caregivers adapted to repeated negative social experiences by being very vigilant about associating with other people; unfortunately, that vigilance also represented an obstacle to developing truly supportive social networks.

Discussion

The purpose of the present chapter was to examine the continuities between relationship disruption during primary caregiver's childhood and disrupted relationships in adulthood with adult partners and with their children, as well as potential mediators of continuity between relationship disruption during childhood and adulthood. Participating families demonstrated diverse strengths in the face of adversity. Although caregivers described difficulties with caregiving, their love and concern for their children emerged as a sustaining resource. Consistent with Rutter's (1988) conceptualization of resilience as dynamic, rather than a characteristic of person or context, the present chapter conceptualized the individual as actively contributing to their development; as such, primary caregivers demonstrated resilience in their ability to utilize affordances for development in their environments, including, for example, social relationships, resources for health and education, and even critical stressor events in their lives as opportunities for reflection and organization.

When asked if there were other family members not living in the household, one stepfather volunteered that he had an infant who had been abused and murdered several years before by the child's mother's boyfriend. He indicated that he had been physically abused by his own stepfather, and both he and his brother used drugs heavily. He realized that he could have prevented his child's tragic death if he had been sober and responsible, and decided to make significant changes in his life. He had been with his current partner for over two years, and both of them were attending vocational school. He described his desire to be a good parent, to be warm and to be the kind of person his children would feel they could come to for anything. He said that he emphasized the importance of school to the children, and helped them with their homework. His stepdaughter's independent description of his caregiving was consistent with his own, and she also reported that she earned good grades and wanted to be a lawyer when she grew up. This caregiver was able to use a tragedy as an organizing experience, actively shaping his own developmental trajectory. This represents one of the important strengths and sources of resilience of minority families in this study.

The frequency of relationship disruptions reported by primary caregivers in the present investigation are similar to those reported by other high-risk samples. Physical abuse was the strongest predictor of depression and anxiety, and physical and sexual abuse during adulthood were the only disruptions that predicted attempts to emulate parents. Physical and sexual abuse tended to co-occur both in childhood and adulthood, and there was considerable continuity between abuse during childhood and adulthood. Further, the continuity was specific; physical abuse during childhood was correlated with physical (but not sexual) abuse during adulthood, while sexual abuse during childhood was correlated with sexual (but not physical) abuse during adulthood.

Emotion regulation, interrupted development, and relationship models were examined as potential mediators of relationship disruption during childhood and adulthood. Although present data suggest the possibility that depression may strongly mediate the relationship between physical abuse during childhood and adulthood, *both* childhood and adulthood abuse preceded measurement of depression and represents a limitation to this study. On the other hand, it is assumed that caregivers were able to accurately report their educational level and age at emancipation. Having parents who had divorced was robustly correlated dropping out of high school; dropping out significantly predicted negative caregiving (of own children), and divorcing one's own spouse. Contrary to hypotheses, dropping out of school was inversely correlated to adulthood sexual abuse. Consistent with hypotheses, early emancipation significantly predicted childhood physical and sexual abuse; contrary to hypotheses, early emancipation was inversely correlated with negative caregiving. It may be that some caregivers who experienced negative caregiving as children actively attempted to provide more positive care to their own children, and their own accounts of their caregiving support this hypothesis. When asked to describe how they try to be similar to and different from their parents in the way they raise their own children, *all* responses were either more positive (i.e., talk more, listen more, spend more time with) or less negative (i.e., yell less, hit less). Interestingly, attempts to emulate own parents was inversely associated with adult physical and sexual abuse, and unrelated to any of the other disruptions.

Probably the single greatest source of resilience of the primary caregivers in this study was their desire to be good parents for their children. A poignant example of this desire is evident in the account of a primary caregiver who had divorced an abusive husband and whose nine-year-old son had experienced serious emotional problems during the previous two years; he had not attended school for a year because he would not leave her side, expressed great fear most of the time, and the week before the interview had put a rope around his neck and threatened to kill himself. In spite of the problems with her son, she emphasized that she felt "rich," because she was blessed with her children, which were the primary source of her happiness. This theme was resonant with the majority of primary caregivers in the sample. For many of the primary caregivers, their happiness was equivalent to their children's happiness. They made great efforts to do what they could with what they had in order to make their children happy.

The role of current relationships with a partner or spouse as a contributor to housing problems was also described. According to the descriptions provided by primary caregivers, presence of a partner represented a vulnerability in some cases, as substance use and/or domestic violence precipitated or maintained housing problems. Although financial instability and lack of affordable housing are primary causes of housing crises, recognizing the diverse needs and obstacles faced by families with children is essential to understanding and addressing housing problems. In many cases spouses and partners offered little emotional, practical, or economic support to primary caregivers and children, and often represented *additional* emotional and economic stressors.

The relationship disruptions examined in the present chapter, with the exception of positive and negative caregiving, are extreme examples of relationship experiences. For example, physical and sexual victimization at any age is traumatic; future research should examine finer gradations of relationship disruptions, including, for example, more extensive evaluation of relationship models, and more detailed accounts of relationship satisfaction with partners and others.

Note

1. The research is partially based on the first author's dissertation supervised by the second author and submitted to the Gradate College of the University of Arizona, in partial fulfillment of the requirements of the Ph.D. The authors gratefully acknowledge the cooperation of participating families and agencies.

References

Bassuk, E.L., & Rosenberg, L. (1988). Why does family homelessness occur? A case-control study. *American Journal of Public Health, 78,* 783-788.

Baumrind, D. (1971). Current patterns of parental authority. *Developmental Psychology Monograph, 4,* 1-103.

Baumrind, D. (1973). The development of instrumental competence through socialization. In A. Pick (Ed.), *Minnesota symposium on child psychology* (Vol. 7). Minneapolis: University of Minnesota Press.

Beck, A.T. (1967). *Depression: Clinical, experimental, and theoretical aspects.* New York: Harper & Row.

Belsky, J. (1984). The determinants of parenting: A process model. *Child Development, 55,* 83-96.

Belsky, J., Robins, E., & Gamble, W. (1984). The determinants of parental competence. In M. Lewis (Ed.), *Beyond the dyad* (pp. 251-279). New York: Plenum.

Billings, A., & Moos, R. (1983). Comparisons of children of depressed and nondepressed parents: A social-environmental perspective. *Journal of Abnormal Child Psychology, 11*(4), 463-486.

Booth, A., & Edwards, J.N. (1989). Transmission of marital and family quality over the generations: The effect of parental divorce and unhappiness. *Journal of Divorce, 13,* 41-58.

Bretherton, I. (1990). Communication patterns, internal working models, and the intergenerational transmission of attachment relationships. *Infant Mental Health Journal, 11*(3), 237-252.

Browne, A. (1987). *When battered women kill.* New York: Macmillan/ Free Press.

Browne, A. (1993). Family violence and homelessness: The relevance of trauma histories in the lives of homeless women. *American Journal of Orthopsychiatry, 63*(3), 370-384.

Browne, A., & Finkelhor, D. (1986). The impact of child sexual abuse: A review of the research. *Psychological Bulletin, 99,* 66-77.

Crowell, J.A., & Feldman, S.S. (1991). Mothers' working models of attachment relationships and mother and child behavior during separation and reunion. *Developmental Psychology, 27*(4), 597-605.

DeAngelis, T. (1994). Homeless families: Stark reality of the 90s. *The American Psychological Association Monitor, 25*(5), 1.

D'Ercole, A., & Struening, E. (1990). Victimization among homeless women: Implications for service delivery. *Journal of Community Psychology, 18,* 141-152.

Dornbusch, S.M., Ritter, P.L., Leiderman, P.H., Roberts, D.F., & Fraleigh, M.J. (1987). The relation of parenting style to adolescent school performance. *Child Development, 58,* 1244-1257.

Downs, W.R., Miller, B.A., & Gondoli, D.M. (1987). Childhood experiences of parental physical violence for alcoholic women as compared with a randomly selected household sample of women. *Violence and Victims, 2,* 225-240.

Egeland, B., Jacobvitz, D., & Papatola, K. (1987). Intergenerational continuity of abuse. In R.J. Gelles & J.B. Lancaster (Eds.), *Child abuse and neglect: Biosocial dimensions* (pp. 255-276). New York: Aldine de Gruyter.

Edelman, M.W., & Mihaly, L. (1989). Homeless families and the housing crisis in the United States. *Children and Youth Services Review, 11,* 99-108.

Finkelhor, D., & Browne, A. (1985). The traumatic impact of child sexual abuse: A conceptualization. *American Journal of Orthopsychiatry, 55,* 530-541.

Fonagy, P., Steele, H., & Steele, M. (1991). Maternal representations of attachment during pregnancy predict the organization of infant-mother attachment at one year of age. *Child Development, 62*(5), 891-905.

Gelfand, D.M., & Teti, D.M. (1990). The effects of maternal depression on children. *Clinical Psychology Review*, *10*, 329-353.

Gottman, J.M., & Fainsilber-Katz, L.F. (1989). Effects of marital discord on young children's peer interaction and health. *Developmental Psychology*, *25*, 373-381.

Grossman, K., Fremmer-Bombik, E., Rudolph, J., & Grossman, K. (1988). Maternal attachment representations as related to patterns of infant-mother attachment and maternal care during the first year. In R.A. Hinde & J. Stevenson-Hinde (Eds.), *Relationships within families: Mutual influences*. London: Oxford University Press.

Hart, C.H., Ladd, G.W., & Burleson, B.R. (1990). Children's expectations of the outcomes of social strategies: Relations with sociometric status and maternal disciplinary styles. *Child Development*, *61*, 127-137.

Hazzard, A., Christensen, A., & Margolin, G. (1983). Children's perceptions of parental behaviors. *Journal of Abnormal Child Psychology*, *2*, 49-60.

Hetherington, M.E., Clingempeel, G., Anderson, E.R., Deal, J.E., Hagan, M.S., Hollier, E.A., & Linder, M.S. (1992). Coping with marital transition: A family systems perspective. *Monographs of the Society for Research in Child Development*, *57*(2-3).

Kaufman, J., & Zigler, E. (1987). Do abused children become abusive parents? *American Journal of Orthopsychiatry*, *57*, 186-192.

Keith, V.M., & Finlay, B. (1988). The impact of parental divorce on children's educational attainment, marital timing, and likelihood of divorce. *Journal of Marriage and the Family, 50*, 797-809.

Knickman, J.R., & Weitzman, B.C. (1989). *A study of homeless families in New York City: Risk assessment models and strategies for prevention* (Final report: Volume 1). New York: Human Resources Administration, Health Research Program, New York University.

Lerner, R.M., & Tubman, J.G. (1991). Developmental contextualism and the study of early adolescent development. In R. Cohen & A.W. Siegel (Eds.), *Context and development* (pp. 183-210). Hillsdale, NJ: Lawrence Erlbaum.

Main, M., Kaplan, N., & Cassidy, J. (1985). Security in infancy, childhood, and adulthood: A move to the level of representation. In I. Bretherton & E. Waters (Eds.), Growing points of attachment theory and research. *Monographs of the Society for Research in Child Development, 50* (1-2, Serial no. 209).

McChesney, K.Y. (1990). Family homelessness: A systemic problem. *Journal of Social Issues*, *46*(4), 191-205.

McLanahan, S., & Bumpass, L. (1988). Intergenerational consequences of family disruption. *American Journal of Sociology*, *94*, 130-152.

Miller, B.A., Downs, W.R., Gondoli, D.M., & Keil, A. (1987). The role of childhood sexual assault in the development of alcoholism in women. *Violence and Victims*, *2*, 157-172.

Molnar, J., Rath, W.R., & Klein, T.P. (1990). Constantly compromised: The impact of homelessness on children. *Journal of Social Issues*, *46*(4), 109-124.

Patterson, G.R., & Dishion, T.J. (1985). Contributions of families and peers to delinquency. *Criminology*, *23*, 63-79.

Patterson, G.R., & Stouthamer-Loeber, M. (1984). The correlation of family management practices and delinquency. *Child Development*, *55*, 1299-1307.

Putallaz, M., & Heflin, A.H. (1990). Parent-child interaction. In S.R. Asher & J. Coie (Eds.), *Peer rejection in childhood* (pp. 189-216). New York: Cambridge University Press.

Rutter, M. (1988). Functions and consequences of relationships: Some psychopathological considerations. In R.A. Hinde & J. Stevenson-Hinde (Eds.), *Relationships within families: Mutual influences*. London: Oxford University Press.

Shinn, M., Knickman, J., & Weitzman, B. (1991). Social relationships and vulnerability to becoming homeless among poor families. *American Psychologist*, *46*(11), 1180-1187.

Southworth, S., & Schwartz, J.C. (1987). Post-divorce contact, relationship with father, and heterosexual trust in female college students. *American Journal of Orthopsychiatry*, *57*, 371-382.

Speilberger, C.D.(1983). *Manual for the "State-Trait Anxiety Inventory (Form Y)."* Palo Alto, CA: Consulting Psychologists Press, Inc.

Steinmetz, S.K. (1987). Family violence. In M.B. Sussman & S.K. Steinmetz (Eds.), *Handbook of marriage and the family* (pp. 725-765). New York: Plenum Press.

Straus, M. (1983). Ordinary violence, child abuse, and wife beating: What do they have in common? In D. Finkelhor, R. Gelles, G. Hotaling, & M. Straus (Eds.), *The dark side of families: Current family violence research*. Beverly Hills, CA: Sage.

Straus, M.A., Gelles, R.J., & Steinmetz, S.K. (1980). *Behind closed doors: Violence in the American family*. Beverly Hills, CA: Sage.

U.S. Bureau of the Census. (1989). *Poverty in the United States: 1987* (Current Population Reports, Series P-60, No. 163). Washington, DC: U.S. Government Printing Office.

U.S. Conference of Mayors. (1990). *Status report on hunger and homelessness in America's cities: 1989*. Washington, DC: Author.

Wallerstein, J.S., & Blakeslee, S. (1989). *Second chances: Men, women, and children a decade after divorce*. New York: Ticknor & Fields.

Weintraub, S., Neale, J.M., & Liebert, D.E. (1975). Teacher ratings of children vulnerable to psychopathology. *American Journal of Orthopsychiatry*, *45*, 839-845.

Weintraub, S., Prinz, R.J., & Neale, J.M. (1978). Peer evaluations of the competence of children vulnerable to psychopathology. *Journal of Abnormal Child Psychology*, *6*, 461-473.

Wright, J.D. (1989). *Address unknown: The homeless in America*. New York: Aldine de Gruyter.

Van Ijzendoorn, M.H. (1992). Intergenerational transmission of parenting: A review of studies in nonclinical populations. *Developmental Review*, *12*(1), 76-99.

Yama, M.F., Tovey, S.L., & Fogas, B.S. (1993). Childhood family environment and sexual abuse as predictors of anxiety and depression in adult women. *American Journal of Orthopsychiatry*, *63*(1), 136-141.

Zeanah, C.H., & Zeanah, P.D. (1989). Intergenerational transmission of maltreatment: Insights from attachment theory and research. *Psychiatry*, *52*(2), 177-196.

Chapter 21

Ethnicity, Culture, and Resiliency in Caregivers of a Seriously Mentally Ill Family Member

Pilar A. Parra and Peter Guarnaccia

In the last decades, families have been confronted with a new challenge—the care of seriously mentally ill family members. In the majority of cases, women carry the responsibility of caring for the ill family member. Among these families, minority families have a double burden, that of the stigma attached to mental illness and that of marginalization as members of racial and ethnic minority groups. This chapter focuses on these families who, with limited resources, are able to find ways to confront and resolve problems that arise in the care of a seriously mentally ill relative.

From Hospital Care to Home Care

The process of a drastic reduction of patients in public mental health hospitals since the late 1950s is known as deinstitutionalization (Mechanic & Rochefort, 1990). This process is the result of several interrelated forces, such as the availability of new medication, changes in the legal rights of patients, the movement towards community treatment, and the decision to cut the budgets for state psychiatric hospitals. Although it was expected that the mentally ill patients would be able to be reincorporated into the communities, reintegration was often unsuccessful. Communities were not ready to provide the needed services to maintain the chronically mentally ill at minimum levels of functionality. Progress in services and supports in the communities has been slow and has deteriorated since the late 1970s and throughout the 1980s (Johnson, 1990). Availability of housing in the major cities turned out to be one of the main problems in the discharge of patients from the hospital (Baxter & Hopper, 1984). The changing age structure in the population, as a result of the "baby-boom" generation, intensified the problems of deinstitutionalization, as there were more patients who needed more housing and services (Mechanic, 1989). One consequence was that mentally ill people were discharged to the streets, nursing homes, various community living arrangements, and family homes. One of the most visible results of the deinstitutionalization process in the last three decades is the visibility of mentally ill homeless people. Studies show that approximately 20 to 30% of homeless adults have a history of psychiatric hospitalization (Caton, 1990; Belcher, 1990; Bean, Stefl, & Howe, 1987). A second consequence of deinstitutionalization has been family problems. Currently, it is estimated that between 35 and 65% of patients discharged from psychiatric hospitals return to live with their families (Goldman, 1982; Lefley, 1987a). Families of the chronically mentally ill find themselves with most of the burden but few community services, little support, and a lack of practical advice from health care professionals or hospital and clinic staff members on how to handle their ill member. Thus the care of the severely mentally ill has moved from the hospitals to the home, and at home, women take a major role in the care of the patient (Cook, 1988). Although not all seriously mentally ill persons discharged from psychiatric hospitals would live with a family member, few other housing arrangements are available for them. Families still play an important role providing various forms of care and support to their ill family member living in a community residence, a rented room, or their own apartment (Grosser & Vine, 1991).

This chapter builds on literature that focuses on the strengths, coping strategies, and resilience of families caring for the chronically mentally ill (Cook, 1988; Hatfield & Lefley, 1987; Rutter, 1987; O'Leary, 1992). This study examines the resilience of minority families, and the strategies they employ to meet the personal and health care needs of a seriously mentally ill person. Because of the traditional division of labor, women are usually perceived as responsible for the nurturing of an ill child, and they are most likely to remain at home to care for ill family members (Cohler & Grunebaum, 1981). In particular, this chapter examines the strategies and mechanisms women use to cope, adapt, resolve, attenuate, or negotiate the problems that arise when they care for their mentally ill relative.

The unpredictability of mental illness creates the need for various types of support in the care of a seriously mentally ill relative. At times, the ill person can lead almost a normal life. The person is able, at differing levels of efficiency, to take care of his/her immediate needs (e.g., grooming, helping with chores, using public transportation, etc). At other times, the same person can be transformed, where s/he will refuse to take her/his medicine, to go to appointments, to bathe, or to eat, and s/he may exhibit disruptive and/or aggressive behavior to self or others. In some cases, caregivers report confinement to their homes because the ill family member cannot be left alone. Psychiatric conditions are often chronic, and the possibility of cure and recovery is limited. Family members caring for a seriously mentally ill patient face a long-term responsibility that eventually will affect them physically and/or emotionally (Lefley, 1989; Goldman, 1982). Families from all social classes and ethnic backgrounds face similar dilemmas when they have to provide for a family member with a mental illness. The main concerns reported by families are the future care of the ill family member when parents or other family members no longer can help, the lack of adequate housing for mentally ill patients, and the limitations of the few mental health services offered by the communities (Lefley, 1987b; Guarnaccia, Parra, Deschamps, Milstein, & Arguiles, 1992; Horwitz, 1993). Families have also reported concerns about the lack of respite care services (Zirul, Lieberman, & Rapp, 1989).

Resilience

What are the circumstances under which some caregivers and their families can do so much with so little, and continue to do more? What makes some members within a family more resilient to adversity and gives them strength to face the everyday problems related to the responsibilities of caregiving?

Resilience is defined as the ability to confront and resolve problems and the capacity to utilize personal or social resources to enhance limited possibilities (Rutter, 1987; Cochran, 1992; O'Leary, 1992). However, resilience does not ensure that all stressors will be resolved; people can be resilient in some circumstances and vulnerable in others. Factors identified with resilience include: (1) personal characteristics; (2) affectionate ties within the family, including a strong network support system of family and friends; and (3) the active search for external support systems, such as churches and other services (e.g., mental health services) (O'Leary,

1992). These factors generate self-esteem and self-efficacy and sustain and reinforce resilience.

Families negotiate risk situations through the utilization of personal or societal resources. The presence of support networks has proven to be very beneficial. The social support provided by these networks of family and friends has positive effects on the health and well-being of the patient and the caregiver (Cohen & Syme, 1985). Relationships with kin, friends, and acquaintances form an interactive network exchange of goods, affection, and various types of support important for individuals and families. For example, studies have shown that these networks help families survive in times of harsh economic conditions (Stack, 1974; Elder, 1985). Other studies have indicated that the social support provided through networks reduces psychological distress (Gore, 1981; Hirsch, 1981). The role of networks is especially important among immigrants. The migration experience is a stressful experience, and affects each family member differently. The migrant typically enters society at the lower levels of the social strata, and his/her primary group relationships are altered (i.e., separation of part or the total family). The acculturation process (acquisition of language and the predominant values and behaviors of the host society) is also a source of distress (Rogler, Gurak, & Cooney, 1987). A third of the U.S. Latino population was born outside of the United States (U.S. Bureau of the Census, 1990) and consequently they face problems related to migration and acculturation.

Description of the Study and the Data

This analysis is based on the study of the role of the main caregiver and other family members in caring for a mentally ill family member. It consists of 74 in-depth interviews with the identified main caregiver. The main caregiver was the person who spent the most time with the ill member, who was most informed of his/her medical needs, and who took a more active role in providing for the needs of the mentally ill person. The families were identified through family groups and client populations of public community mental health centers and state psychiatric hospitals in New Jersey. The questions were directed to the main caregiver, but information on other family members was included as well. The objective of the study was to determine how the family responded to and coped with one member's illness. The interview followed a questionnaire with two sections, the first one consisting of a series of open-ended questions. Respondents were asked to tell the story of the illness of their family member: "what made you think that something was wrong with your family member," "what did you think the problem was first," and a narrative of the first and last hospitalization. The interviews were tape recorded and transcribed. This first section provided the basis for the qualitative analysis. The second part of the interview followed a structured questionnaire and covered the family's overall experience with the mental health care system, conception of the illness, social support systems, and burdens experienced as a result of having a seriously mentally ill family member. Finally, a sociodemographic section was included. The tables and the chart in this chapter are based on the quantifiable data from the interviews. The interview lasted approximately one to one and a half hours. Families were of Latino and African-American ethnicity. Women were the identified main caregiver in 64 (84%) of the cases.

Because of the difficulties in gathering a random sample of families with a seriously mentally ill family member, the sample is an opportunistic one. Caution needs to be taken when generalizing from this sample to larger groups. However, the study's intent was to highlight the strengths of families, particularly the tactics women caregivers employ when dealing with the complexities of caring for a mentally ill family member, the value they place to keep them at home, and the sense of the family responsibility toward their ill family member.

Family Characteristics

Of the 74 families, 45 (68%) were Latino families and 29 (39%) were African-American. Two-thirds of the Latino families were Puerto Rican, the remaining came from the Caribbean or Central or South American countries.

Many of the primary caregivers were parents—42% in the Latino families and 76% in the African-American families. Women played a predominant role as main caregivers. Everyday care was in the hands of a woman relative more than 80% of the time, including mothers (52%), sisters (11%), daughters (11%), and wives or other relatives (9%). The remainder were fathers (2 cases), brothers (3 cases), and husbands (5 cases). The average age of the caregiver was 48 for the Latinos and 54 for African-Americans, while the average age of the ill member was 40 and 34, respectively.

Sociodemographic information about the sample is presented in Table 1. Household income was calculated by aggregating all sources of earnings for the previous year, including social security

Table 1
Social Characteristics of Main Caregiver

	Ethnicity	
Social Characteristics	Latino (*n* = 45) %	African American (*n* = 29) %
Age		
(Mean)	48	54
39 years or less	33	11
40–59 years	38	58
60 years +	29	31
Gender		
Female	80	90
Male	20	10
Relationship of caregiver to ill member		
Parents	42	76
Daughter/son	20	3
Spouse	22	0
Sibling	13	21
Education		
Elementary or less	46	7
Some high school	27	14
High school diploma +	27	79
Family income		
$9,999 or less	41	18
$10–19,999	37	18
$20–29,999	18	14
$30–39,999	2	18
$40,000 +	2	32
Household composition		
Dual parent/extended head	67	38
Female head	33	62

income and welfare benefits. Latino families experienced considerable economic disadvantage. Forty-one percent reported a family income of less than $10,000, and 37% reported earnings between $10,000 and $20,000, even though the majority had at least one employed family member. Half of the Latino caregivers had only attended elementary school or less, which probably curtailed their possibilities for better paying jobs. Almost one-fifth of the African-

American families reported earnings of less than $10,000 and half reported a family income of $30,000 or more. The African-American caregivers were better educated; 79% had a high school diploma or more. Economic conditions were also closely related to the marital status of the women. The sample reflects the increasing number of women who are heads of households. Among the Latino households, one-third were headed by a woman, and two-thirds were headed by two parents. For the African-American households, 62% reported a female head of household. A high proportion of Latino (78%) and African-American caregivers (59%) reported their ill family member lived with them. Twenty-two percent of Latinos and 41% of the African-American ill family members were living alone or in a residential program. Among respondents who did not have their family member living with them, they reported daily or weekly contact and various forms of assistance, care and support.

Latino families maintained strong ties to their language and culture. Although the families had lived in the U.S. an average of 22 years, 80% reported that all their close friends were Latinos, and the preferred language was Spanish (84%). The majority of the Latino caregivers were born outside the United States. Latino and African-American caregivers reported the presence of members of their extended families and other networks such as friends and religious groups. Some families maintained close contact with the staff of their mental health systems. In general, both groups reported almost exclusive use of public mental health services.

Both Latino families and African-American families had limited economic resources, and the income support that the ill member received was often a significant help in allowing families to continue to care for their family member. These social security programs, including medical insurance and income support, are vital to maintaining minority and low-income individuals in care and in the community.

The main concern of the aging parents was who would take care of their mentally ill son or daughter. In the absence of spouse or children, siblings are possible caregivers. However, the majority of parents did not expect nor want to give the responsibility for care of the ill person to their other children. Horwitz (1993) found that siblings may assume some responsibility, but seldom as much as their parents. At a national level, the National Alliance for the Mentally Ill (NAMI) has raised this issue to promote policies that would deal with this impending problem.

Fostering Resiliency

Next, the conditions that enhance resilience in women caregivers will be examined. Since more than four-fifths of the main caregivers surveyed were women, this chapter focuses on their experiences. The cultural construction in the interpretation of mental illness allows them to hope for a cure and exonerates them from the notion of "blame" for the illness of their ill family member. Families were viewed at one point in the history of mental illness as the cause of that illness, and they were blamed by medical staff for their over-involvement with their mentally ill family member. Families thus faced not only the stigma of mental illness, but the blame for the illness itself. However, in this sample, African-Americans blamed the illness on the hardship of their lives and traumatic events like death or abandonment by the father. Latino families blamed external factors and events or an intrinsic weakness of the ill person that did not allow him/her to deal with the stresses of life.

Women caregivers found strength in the ways their cultural heritage defined caregiving, where it is not perceived necessarily as a burden, but is "what one does for the family and for the ill." This help is carried out with considerable support from other family members, friends, and church members. The women learned to have some control over the illness while living and caring for their family member. They learned how to use mental health services and to recognize the importance of medicine in the treatment, and in the case of some Latino families, they relied on alternative cures for the mental illness as well.

Conception of Mental Illness

Families were asked to describe the kind of problem they thought their family member had. The responses to this question were recoded into four categories: a "medical" problem (chemical imbalance, mental failure); an "emotional" or nervous problem, with the use of the idiom *nervios* among Latinos; a "personality" problem, which included personality descriptors like selfish or aggressive; or a "social" problem, referring mainly to problems in relationships. In this sample, the majority of Latinos did not reflect upon the illness within a medical model but as a problem of the emotions and of *nervios*. *Nervios* is a Spanish idiom that describes physical distress, emotional disturbance, and social dislocation (Guarnaccia & Farias, 1988). The concept of *nervios* helps to avoid the label of *locura,* or enduring madness, and helps to reduce the enduring stigma of having a "crazy" person within the family. This approach to the understanding of mental illness allows the family to avoid the fact of the chronic condition of their schizophrenic or psychotic family member. For Latinos, mental illness is viewed as a continuum that ranges from "being nervous," and "suffering from nerves," to having a "mental failure," and "craziness" (Guarnaccia et al., 1992). This model allows for hope of improvement and avoids the medical interpretation that a severe mental illness like schizophrenia will never be cured. Hope of improvement is also reinforced by religious beliefs that with "God's will" a cure is possible. These notions help them to cope with the long-term care of the family member. The notion of mental illness as a continuum of stages is also present among the African Americans. Feeling hopeful is an important attitude that reinforces resilience (Bar & Cochran, 1992).

This interpretation is reflected in the strong hope for the cure of their family member expressed by 67% of the Latinos questioned. Latino respondents, when describing the illness, crises, and hospitalizations of their family member, consistently utilized the category of *nervios*. When asked for their conception of the mental illness, 40% categorized it as an emotional problem. One respondent offered the following description of her 28-year-old son:

> *Los doctores dicen que es bipolar ...pero yo diría que mi hijo lo que es un nervioso más en la vida, una persona enferma de los nervios. Uno completamente loco, lo primero que pierde es la memoria, no sabe quien es la madre, el padre, la hermana ...y mi hijo no está así.* [The doctors said he is bipolar, but I would say that what happens to my son is [he] is another nervous one in life, a person sick of his nerves. One that is completely crazy, the first thing he loses is the memory, he would not know who is the mother, the father, the sister ...and my son is not like that].

Cultural heritage also shaped the African-Americans' responses to the mental illness and treatment of their relatives. Furthermore, resilience emerges from their strong religious tradition as well as their long struggle against racism. African-American women talked about discrimination or unequal quality of the health services received by their family members and themselves. A mother with a schizophrenic son commented on her attempt to participate in a family support group:

I have been to family groups, when you go to this group sessions they let one person dominate the whole session. I couldn't see when I could tell them my problems. I told the psychiatrist—this is a waste of my time, you let one person dominate for the whole two hour session. I just stop going. It seemed that they just listened to the white people. I don't mean to sound prejudiced but they didn't want to hear what the black person had to put into the conversation. They must thought we were ignorant, but I am not nearly ignorant, I have read everything I can get my hands on about his problem.

African-American caregivers were more demanding and critical of the services received. Another mother commented on her long struggle for services:

If you have a [sick] child, I don't care how much money you make. I think he was entitled to get into the program.

For two-thirds of the African-Americans, the conception of illness was clearly defined by a medical model, with diagnostic labels for their ill member, such as schizophrenic, bipolar disorder, depression, etc. For African-Americans, the interpretation of the problem as emotional referred mainly to the constant state of nervousness and anxiety of their family member. One-fifth of the African-American caregivers described the problem as one of selfishness or aggressiveness. The hope for cure was present in 60% of African-American families. Their religious beliefs sustained their hope of cure.

For Latino and African-American families, a cure was not necessarily interpreted as one of full recovery, but a cure to the extent that the ill member would be able to function with a certain amount of independence in their everyday life. In the words of a Latina mother with two adult sons and a daughter diagnosed with schizophrenia:

No es que van a volver a nacer sanitos [con el tratamiento] pero ellos pueden curarse, pero no totalmente ... eso es lo que yo le pido a Dios. [It is not that they will be reborn healthy—with the treatment—they can get cured, but not totally. I pray to God for that.]

Minority families strongly expressed their choice to have their ill member living with them. When families living with the ill person were asked if they would like to have him or her live apart, more than half of the Latino and 48% of the African-American caregivers rejected the idea. In some cases, this was the result of economic conditions and/or the limited availability of convenient housing for the mentally ill. However, women caregivers expressed the idea that given the circumstances, their ill family member was better off with them, and they preferred taking direct care of their family member. They also expressed the sentiment that they were the ones that knew and understood him/her better, and they expressed their belief that an ill family member should be taken care of within the family. Among Latino and African-American families, there exists a sense of responsibility and pride in having their ill family member with them (Guarnaccia et al., 1992). A daughter living with her mother reported:

> *Hace 13 años me la traje de Puerto Rico, mis hermanos no la atendían. Siempre estaba sucia. Yo siempre he ayudado a mi mamá en las buenas y en las malas.* [Thirteen years ago I brought her from Puerto Rico ... my brothers were not taking good care of her, she always was dirty. I always have helped my mother in the good and in the bad.]

A wife with her husband and three children living together commented:

> *A mi me llaman del Welfare y me quieren mandar a trabajar, pero yo no lo puedo dejar solo porque la unica persona que lo puede comprender soy yo, y como lo voy a dejar solo, que él se me vaya a andar, se me pierda.* [The welfare call me and—they—want me to go to work, but I can't leave him alone because I am the only one that can understand him, and how I am going to leave him alone, what if he goes wandering, gets lost.]

An African-American mother living with her 37-year-old son said:

> I try to give him a place to live and I try to keep him clean and let him go to places and do things like everybody else. I don't leave him here in the house by himself unless I am only running out for a few minutes.

Support System

Women taking care of a seriously mentally ill relative developed strategies to deal with the uncertainty of the mental illness. They learned to recognize when a crisis was approaching their family member and how to activate their network of support to seek advice, discuss their needs, and decide what to do. Thus, resilient caregivers were actively making attempts to gain control over their lives.

Caregivers were asked about different types and sources of support. The questions ranged from support at times of crisis to everyday tasks such as rides to the clinic for an appointment and child care while attending the ill family member. They were also asked about sources of support to talk about concerns and when in need of advice (see Table 2).

Table 2
Caregivers' Social Support and Expectations of Cure

	Ethnicity	
Support	**Latino** (*n* = 45) %	**African American** (*n* = 29) %
Size of Network		
One	7	7
Two	14	28
Three	20	3
Four +	59	62
Sources of Support for Advice		
Family	38	45
Medical	27	17
Religious	2	7
Nobody	22	10
Other	11	21
Sources of Support for Concerns		
Family	58	59
Medical	2	3
Religious	9	3
Nobody	16	3
Other	16	31
Expectations of Cure	67	60

Several Latino women reported strong support from their extended families. However, if the extended family breaks down or is geographically separated, then they develop alternatives for support, such as neighbors and friends, church, and health professionals. Approximately 60% of the Latino and African-American families reported four or more persons in their immediate support network. When in need of advice, the family remains the most important source of support (38% and 45%, respectively), followed by medical personnel. Those who reported fewer support networks relied heavily on their religious beliefs for solace.

Religion played an important role for the caregiver and their families. Although caregivers did not report religious leaders as a main source when in need of advice or to talk about their concerns, 40% of African-American and one-third of Latino caregivers said they had received help from a religious leader at different times during the long struggle with the illness of their relative. Women reported attending church meetings and prayer gatherings where their ill member could participate.

An African-American mother commented on her faith in the healing of her daughter:

> My kids were brought up in church. They have faith, enough faith to carry them through. I think this is what pulled her through....When I talked to her, I said this to her—fight it, be strong and fight it....I left my Bible open to scripture. The next morning after the doctors told me that she was very sick, they said—We don't know what happened, but she took a turn for the better.

Latinos have been more open in seeking help from alternative sources such as spiritists, who employ a combination of religious and folk healing beliefs and practices to deal with mental or other illnesses that are believed to have a spiritual explanation. Among their rituals is the cleaning of the person afflicted by the wrong spirits. The ritual of cleaning includes prayers while the person is brushed throughout his/her body with flowers or fresh greenery (Garrison, 1982; Hohmann et al., 1990). One mother commented on the help received by an spiritist healer:

> *El va cada unos meses y ella lo limpia, y el viene contento y satisfecho....y con su medicamento, porque no lo voy a negar eso lo ayuda.* [He goes every few months, she gives him a cleaning, and he comes back happy and content ... and with his medicine, because I am not going to deny, it does help].

Everyday Care

One characteristic of resilient caregivers, and of women in particular, is that they do not perceive the caring for their ill family member as a burden. Extensive research has been done to highlight the negative aspects of caregiving (Platt, 1985; George & Gwyther, 1986), but little attention has been given to the positive aspects of it, where families, and women in particular, place a value in providing care (Guarnaccia et al., 1992).

When caregivers were asked what they did for their ill family member, they seldom mentioned the diverse tasks they performed. A more detailed questioning revealed however, that a whole set of chores, such as cooking and cleaning, was done on a daily basis. However, these chores were not necessarily perceived as a burden by the caregiver but as what you do for your family. One woman commented on the work she did for her 67-year-old sister:

> *Estando yo aquí en la casa, yo siempre soy la que cocino, yo le lavo a ella cuando voy a lavar la ropa de todo mundo y después limpio la casa, y le limpio su cuarto, lo normal que uno hace en casa.* [When I am here at home I am the one who always cook, I make her laundry when I do the laundry of everybody, then I clean the house and clean also her room, just the normal that one does at home.]

An African-American mother considered that she did not do much in the care of her son besides giving him company, but later on she added: "He has a nice apartment and I go and clean it."

In our sample, Latino women performed more responsibilities than African-American families, with the exception of the administration of money of the ill member. Both Latino and African-American caregivers perceived themselves as the main emotional and social support of the ill member (see Figure 1).

Caregivers also recognized themselves as the ones who best knew the ill person's inclinations, preferences, and limitations. They recognized themselves as the ones that knew how to deal with the everyday challenges that the care of their ill member poses. A mother narrated the care of her son diagnosed with schizophrenia fifteen years ago:

> *... y cuando no quería tomar su medicina, las hacía polvo y la hechaba en un paquetito y las guardaba. Yo se las daba en natillas, dulce de arroz, le hechaba el medicamento y la batía bien, y así se la dí por años.* [... and when he did not want to take his medicine, I blended the pills to dust and kept them in little bags. I used to give him the medicine in desserts, 'sweet creams,' 'rice pudding.' I gave him the medicine like that for years.]

Figure 1
Female Caregiver's Responsibilities
in Caring for Ill Member

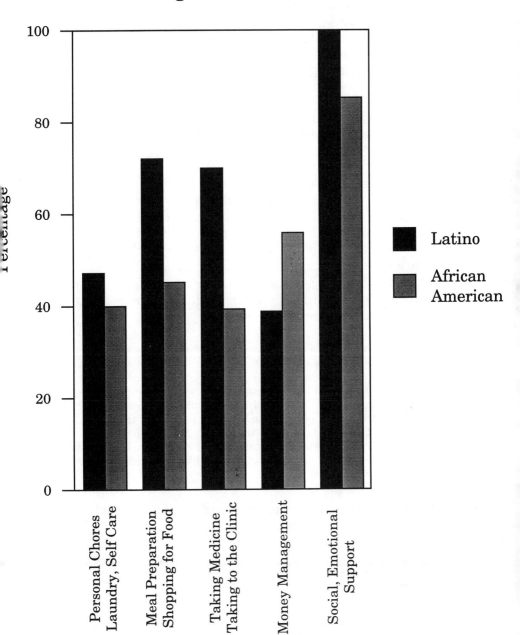

Caregivers recognized the symptoms when a crisis approached their ill family member and initiated some action to deal with the impending crisis. After a series of hospitalizations, they knew how to approach mental health services and find ways to access available community services. They learned how the system works, and they became more aware of their rights. They became assertive in dealing with their ill member when s/he became dangerous to others or her/himself. An African-American mother reported her decision during a crisis with her son:

> The only way I could get help for him was the day he broke down the back door, we pressed charges against him. The only way I could get help for him was by getting him incarcerated.

Finally, resiliency was also revealed in the way the caregivers looked upon their ill member and themselves. Caregivers focused on strengths rather than weaknesses, reinforcing self-esteem. The caregivers expressed clearly what would benefit their family member. When the family member was feeling well they tried to encourage skills at home, such as laundry, cooking, and taking care of their own grooming. They would have liked to see them working a part-time job, seeking self-reliance for their ill family member. A mother of a 25-year-old son commented:

> ... si cada estado hiciera unas factorías para los enfermos, que los pusieran a trabajar, que aprendieran, que hicieran cosas que no los agoten ... y pagarles un chequecito de 15 o 20 dólares, estarían entretenidos y se considerarían hombres porque trabajan. [... if each state would build factories for the mentally ill people, and put them to work, they could learn, they could do things that would not exhaust them ... and pay them a small check of 15 or 20 dollars ... they would entertain themselves, and feel like men because they worked.]

An African-American mother expressed a similar thought on the need of jobs for the mentally ill:

> I think he should be trained for a job. It should be more opportunities for the mentally handicapped, they are honest, dependable, hard workers.

The caregivers tried to find activities where the person could interact with others and have some social life. For most families, there were few alternatives, so this was a very difficult task. Nevertheless, they encouraged group therapies, welcomed the informal gatherings that some mental health centers offered, and they took their ill family member to church-related activities. An African-American taking care of her brother commented:

> I take him out, I take him places, I try to pull him out of the house and get him to go to the movies, or to go to a ride.

A woman from Puerto Rico, with limited economic resources, explained:

> *Cuando él se pone nervioso, le digo—ponte el coat, vamos a caminar para las tiendas—no ha comprar nada, a mirar ... también lo llevo de visita a casa de una amiga mía.* [When he gets nervous, I say to him—put on your coat, lets go for a walk to the stores—not to buy anything just to look ... I take him also to visit to my friend's house.]

Conclusion

The care of a chronically mentally ill family member requires a long-term commitment, and caregivers and their families are struggling to meet the needs of their sick parents, daughters, sons, or spouses. Even though many families face economic hardship, and in many cases discrimination because of their minority status, the study found traits and conditions under which families foster resilience in the effort to provide care. This study shows that women and their families recognize that their strength and resilient traits come from the ties they have with their immediate and extended families, as well as with other members of their social networks. Cultural and ethnic traditions and beliefs help them to cope with mental illness. Religious beliefs reinforce their feelings of hope. In some cases, the recurrent utilization of mental health services helps families to better use the system and improve communication with staff. Nevertheless, the care of a seriously mentally ill family member also has negative impacts in the family. Some caregivers reported the negative impact the long-term care of their mentally ill relative has on their health and that of some other family members. They expressed their desire to have more day programs with vocational, job training, and social activities that would give their ill family members a sense of worth and boost their self-esteem, and at the same time give the caregivers and their families some respite from the everyday care of their ill relative.

To the extent that mental health providers take into account these characteristics to further resiliency among minority families, the continuity of care for the mentally ill persons in their families' home could be maintained with great benefit to those suffering with a serious mental illness.

References

Bar, D., & Cochran, M. (1992). Understanding and supporting empowerment: Redefining the professional role. *Empowerment and Family Support, II,* 1–8. Ithaca, NY: College of Human Ecology, Cornell University.

Baxter, E., & Hopper, K. (1984). Trouble on the streets: The mentally disabled homeless poor. In J. A. Talbott (Ed.), *The chronic mental patient: Five years later.* Orlando, FL: Grune & Stratton.

Belcher, J. R. (1990). On becoming homeless: A study of chronically mentally ill persons. *Journal of Community Psychology, 17,* 173–185.

Bean, G. J., Stefl, M. E., & Howe, S. R. (1987). Mental health and homelessness: Issues and findings. *Social Work. Journal of the National Association of Social Workers, 32,* 411-416.

Caton, C. L. (1990). Solutions to the homeless problem. In C. L. Caton (Ed.), *Homeless in America.* New York: Oxford University Press.

Cochran, M. (1992). Parent empowerment: Developing a conceptual framework. *Family Science Review, 5,* 81-92.

Cohen, S., & Syme, L. (1985). Issues in the study and application of social support. In S. Cohen & L. Syme (Eds.), *Social support and health.* Orlando, FL: Academic Press, Inc.

Cohler, B., & Grunebaum, H. (1981). *Mothers, grandmothers, and daughters.* New York: Wiley.

Cook, J. A. (1988). Who "mothers" the chronically mentally ill? *Family Relations 37,* 42–49.

Elder, G. H. (1985). Linking family hardship to children's lives. *Child Development, 56,* 361–375.

Garrison, V. (1982). Folk healing systems as elements in the community. In U. Rueveni, R. Speck, & J. Speck (Eds.), *Therapeutic intervention: Healing strategies for human systems.* New York: Human Services Press.

George, L. K., & Gwyther L. (1986). Caregiver well–being: A multidimentional examination of family caregivers of demented adults. *Gerontologist, 26,* 253–259.

Goldman, H. (1982). Mental illness and family burden: A public health perspective. *Hospital and Community Psychiatry, 33,* 557–560.

Gore, S. (1981). Stress buffering functions of social support: An appraisal and clarification of research models. In B. S. Dohrenwend & B. P. Dohrenwend (Eds.), *Stressful life events and their contexts.* New York: Prodist.

Grosser, R., & Vine, P. (1991). Families as advocates for the mentally ill: A survey of characteristics and needs. *American Journal of Orthopsychiatry, 61,* 282-290.

Guarnaccia, P., & Farias, P. (1988). The social meaning of *nervios*: A case study of a Central American woman. *Social Science and Medicine, 26,* 1223–1231.

Guarnaccia, P., Parra, P., Deschamps, A., Milstein, G., & Arguiles, N. (1992). Si Dios quiere: Hispanic families' experiences of caring for a seriously mentally ill family member. *Culture, Medicine, and Psychiatry, 16,* 187–215.

Hatfield, A. B., & Lefley, H. P. (1987). *Families of the mentally ill.* New York: Guilford Press.

Hirsch, B. J. (1981). Social network and the coping process: Creating personal communities. In B. H. Gottlieb (Ed.), *Social networks and social support.* Beverly Hills, CA: Sage.

Hohmann, A., Richeport, M., Marriott, B., Canino, G., Rubio–Stipec, M., & Bird, H. (1990). Spiritism in Puerto Rico. Results of an island–wide community study. *British Journal of Psychiatry, 156,* 328–335.

Horwitz, A. (1993). Siblings as caregivers for the seriously mentally ill. *The Milbank Quarterly, 71,* 323–339.

Johnson, A. B. (1990). *Out of bedlam: The truth about deinstitutionalization.* New York: Basic Books.

Lefley, H. P. (1987a). The family's response to mental illnes in a relative. In A. B. Hatfield & H. P. Lefley (Eds.), *Families of the mentally ill* (pp. 3–29). New York: Guilford Press.

Lefley, H. P. (1987b). Aging parents as caregivers of mentally ill adult children: An emerging social problem. *Hospital and Community Psychiatry, 38,* 1063–1070.

Lefley, H. P. (1989). Family burden and family stigma in major mental illness. *American Psychologist, 44,* 556-560.

Mechanic, D. (1989). *Mental health and social policy* (3rd ed.). Englewood Cliffs, NJ: Prentice–Hall.

Mechanic, D., & Rochefort, D. A. (1990). Deinstitutionalization: An appraisal of reform. *Annual Review of Sociology, 16,* 301–327.

O'Leary, V. E. (1992, January). *Resilience in women.* Paper presented at the Spring Foundation Conference, Stanford University, Palo Alto.

Platt, S. (1985). Measuring the burden of psychiatric illness on the family. *Psychological Medicine, 15,* 383–391.

Rogler, L. H., Gurak, D. T., & Cooney, R. S. (1987). The migration experience and mental health: Formulations relevant to Hispanic and other immigrants. In M. Gavira & J. D. Arana (Eds.), *Health and behavior: Research agenda for Hispanics.* Chicago: University of Illinois at Chicago.

Rutter, M. (1987). Psychosocial resilience and protective mechanisms. *American Journal of Orthopsychiatry, 57,* 316–331.

Stack, C. (1974). *All our kin: Strategies for survival in a Black community.* New York: Harper & Row.

U.S. Bureau of the Census. (1990). *General population characteristics.* Washington, DC: U.S. Department of Commerce.

Zirul, D. W., Lieberman, A., & Rapp, C. (1989). Respite care for the chronically mentally ill: Focus for the 1990s. *Community Mental Health Journal, 25,* 173–184.

Index

A

acculturation 200–202, 434
adolescent mothers 183–198
  peer support of 185, 190, 194–195
  support of male partner to 184–185, 190–192, 194–196
African American 401–429
alcohol and substance abuse 200–217, 295, 298, 301, 307
alcoholism 295–324
Asian 225–242, 243–263, 265–274
assessment instruments
  Adult Attachment Interview 405
  Beck Depression Inventory (BDI) 350, 361, 414
  Center for Epidemiologic Studies–Depression Scale 361
  Child Behavior Checklist 300, 352
  Community Support Index 121
  Coping Resources Inventory–Form D 351
  Costello-Comrey Depression and Anxiety Scales (CCD) 351
  Diagnostic Interview Schedule (DIS) 300
  Family Coherence Index 120–121
  Family Crisis Oriented Personal Evaluation Scales 120
  Family Inventory of Life Events and Changes (FILE) 349
  Family Pressures Index 120
  Family Problem Solving Communication Index 120
  Family Support Scale 390, 392
  General Life Events Schedule for Children (GLESC) 300
  Hawaiian F-COPES 120
  High School and Beyond Survey (HSB) 51–52
  National Survey of Families and Households 74, 79
  Norbeck Social Support Questionnaire 188–189, 349–350
  Parent Perception Inventory 351–352, 414–416
  Parent-Child Relationship Inventory 414–416
  Parenting Practices Scale 352
  State-Trait Anxiety Inventory 414
  Suinn-Lew Asian Self Identity Acculturation Scale 267
  Sydney Attribution Scale (SAS) 267
  Taylor Manifest Anxiety Scales 351
attachment theory 403–405, 407–409
autism 163–166, 168–171, 173–176

C

caregiving 402–429, 431–450
child care 253, 254, 257, 285–286, 289, 292
child-rearing practices 172–176
crisis 4–5, 8, 10–18, 20, 22–26, 32
cultural affinity 204, 207–208, 211, 216
cultural identity 126–127, 200, 202, 211–216
cultural socialization 256–257

About the Editors

Hamilton I. McCubbin is Dean of the School of Human Ecology; Professor of Ch and Family Studies and Social Work; and Director of the Center for Excellence Family Studies, the Institute for the Study of Resiliency in Families, and t Family Stress, Coping and Health Project at the University of Wisconsin—Madis He holds academic degrees from the University of Wisconsin–Madison (BS, MS, Ph He undertook postdoctoral studies at Yale University, University of Minnesota, a Stanford University. He has authored, edited, and coedited 18 books and mainta scholarly research on families over the life cycle and families under stress, w particular emphasis on family postcrisis responses and resiliency.

Elizabeth A. Thompson is Research Associate and Postdoctoral Scholar at t Center for Excellence in Family Studies and the Institute for the Study of Resilier in Families at the University of Wisconsin—Madison. She holds academic degrees fr St. Olaf College (BA) and the University of Wisconsin—Madison (MA, PhD). She is t author or coeditor of six books and maintains scholarly research in the advancem of qualitative methods with families faced with stigmatized hardships and adversiti

Anne I. Thompson is Assistant Dean at the School of Human Ecology and Associ Director of the Center for Excellence in Family Studies, the Institute for the Study Resiliency in Families, and the Family Stress, Coping and Health Project, Univers of Wisconsin—Madison. She holds academic degrees from the University of Wisconsin Madison (BS, MS, PhD) and undertook postdoctoral studies at Bryn Mawr Colle She is the author, editor, and coeditor of eight books and maintains scholarly resea on families, the workplace, and health.

Julie E. Fromer is Editor at the Center for Excellence in Family Studies and t Institute for the Study of Resiliency in Families at the University of Wisconsi Madison. She holds academic degrees (BA) from Dartmouth College, New Hampsh and (MA, PhD dissertator) from the University of Wisconsin—Madison.